NO MEMORY FOR PAIN an autobiography

Director-General of Medical Services, Australian Army.

F. Kingsley Norris

NO MEMORY FOR PAIN

an autobiography

Heinemann
Melbourne

William Heinemann Australia Pty. Ltd.
Melbourne
© F. Kingsley Norris 1970
First published 1970
National Library of Australia Card Service Number
and International Standard Book Number 0 85561 007 7
Registered at the G.P.O. Melbourne for transmission
by post as a book.
Printed at The Griffin Press, Marion Road, Netley, South Australia
Designed by Vane Lindesay

To Dorothy, Pat and Margaret:
Seldom have so many had to put up with so much.

Contents

	List of Illustrations	ix
	Foreword by Sir Robert Menzies	xi
	Prologue	xiii
1	Childhood	1
2	Schooldays and Holidays	9
3	Medicine at Melbourne University	34
4	War in the Middle East	49
5	Return to Study	68
6	Private Practice	76
7	Between the Wars	90
8	World War II Begins	102
9	The Syrian Campaign	115
10	Travels through the Middle East	131
11	New Guinea, 1942	142
12	Kokoda	160
13	Recuperation and Disease	187
14	Post-War Appointments	203
15	Through America	218
16	D.G.M.S.	228

17	Japanese Impressions	239
18	World Tour	250
19	War In Korea, I	267
20	Army Medicine	278
21	War In Korea, II	288
22	Retirement	302
23	Civil Defence and Good Neighbour Councils	308
24	Migration and Higher Education	319
25	London Revisited and British Universities	328
26	Europe and European Universities	339
27	England Again	360
28	Miscellany	374
29	Random Thoughts	380
	Epilogue	383
	Index	

List of Illustrations

Frontispiece

Between pages 58 and 59

The family home at Lilydale

Our 'Army'

The family home at Bendigo

The Norris family, Romsey, 1896

First stage appearance, 1907

Christmas Day, 1914

Between pages 138 and 139

Gregan McMahon as Moriarty

Grandfather

My father

Maj.-Gen. Allen, Gen. Wavell, Lieut.-Gen. Sir John Lavarack

Lieut.-Gen. Morshead, Gen. Douglas MacArthur

Maj.-Gen. George Vasey

Between pages 234 and 235

The Golden Stairs, New Guinea, 1942

The Kokoda Trail, New Guinea, 1942

Crossing the Kimusi River, New Guinea, 1942
Shaggy Ridge, New Guinea, 1942
Forward operating unit at Soputa

Between pages 314 and 315
Dorothy was a sister at the Children's Hospital
Maj.-Gen. F. E. Hume
North Korean prisoners
USMC Helicopter in action
Coleg Harlech, Harlech
School of Army Health, Healesville
Farewell party. Author taking the march past

Foreword

My old friend, 'Dum' Norris, has set down in this book a fascinating narrative which embraces, in the record of one man's life, a vivid picture of medical history both civil and military, and verbal vignettes of famous doctors and celebrated Australian soldiers.

Books of history are of several species, all quite different.

Some contain the story of the relationship between nations, their recurrent problems and occasional bitter conflicts. For the historian such books, if they are not to be bogged down in too much detail, must be seen and stated broadly.

Some, with which as students we became familiar, deal with the names and personalities and lives and deeds of monarchs and governments. These frequently suffer from failure to pay sufficient attention to the history of the ordinary people whose quality after all will determine the quality of the nation. But I may compendiously describe this kind of history as political.

Some, giving prime weight to these considerations, concern themselves with social and human developments over the centuries. They serve the great purpose of reminding us of the continuity of human experience and deliver us from the grievous error of thinking and behaving as if we were a generation which needed no instruction from the past and owed no duty to the future. This has been for years a favourite theme of mine. I attribute the steadfastness and sanity of the British people to their inborn sense of continuity; a sense which delivers them from extremes of passion or despair.

Some are economic histories which grow more complex as their source materials become more detailed and far-ranging. The statistician has come into his own; and since Adam Smith there has been such an expansion of economic knowledge and of sometimes conflicting expertise that economic history has become a subject all of its own; not so readable perhaps as the 'drum and trumpet' history which we knew once, but of great importance if the history of mankind is to be properly comprehended.

I cannot help feeling a deep sympathy for the political historian of the future if he designs to write a political history of our time. After the event, and after perhaps a considerable time lapse, what will be his source materials? The newspapers, who not uncommonly deal in black and white, will perhaps throw very little light on the individual characters which will, after all, provide the subtleties of history. If he reads the speeches of statesmen and politicians, how will he know whether the words and ideas of those who spoke or read them were their own or the result of the labours of others? He will, I frequently think, have great difficulty in seeing the leading characters of our period 'in the round'. And yet they will need to be seen and understood in the round if history is to reveal the truth.

This is where books like this one by 'Dum' Norris and other books of personal memoirs become most important. Their importance will be all the greater if such books represent clear and honest and, if possible, whimsical observation and are recorded in clear and simple English. This is particularly true when, as in this book, we become acquainted not only with individuals of great significance, but also with the types of people who make up a society. I have learned many things in the perusal of this book, and have been reminded of many things which I had forgotten. In short, I feel better informed and, as a result of reading the book, more appreciative than ever of the great quality and character of the writer and more conscious of many aspects of our varied history as seen through the eyes of one man of the most astonishingly versatile experience.

R. G. MENZIES

Melbourne, May 1970

Prologue

During the wars and whenever I have been abroad, each night I recorded my experiences and impressions of the day. When later I consolidated these for the family, they asked, 'What about the earlier years?'

By a merciful gift of providence, we have no memory for pain. We can remember an experience only as unpleasant but we cannot recall the actuality of a hurt or a hardship. Fortunately we can retain a vivid memory of happy events and quietly chortle over them years after their advent, and sing and whistle melodies of long ago.

Beau Nash lived during the reigns of seven British monarchs—I have lived during the reigns of six. If you live long enough and are lucky, you have a deal of fun. Before this fun faded I set out to record my earlier years and found that I had not become like the unfortunate who consulted his psychiatrist:

'I keep forgetting things, where I am, what I have come for, where I put things, what day of the week it is.' 'How long has this been going on?' asked his psychiatrist. Then after a long pause, 'How long has *what* been going on?'

I have one regret: that I can no longer walk far and fast as I enjoyed until a year or so ago. I suppose after clambering among the Owen Stanley Ranges in New Guinea during my fiftieth year, I could not expect to escape some insult to my weight-bearing joints. One should forget one's regrets, most experiences if accepted are to the good and after all many unfortunate fellows have lost their legs.

Only when my wife had patiently transcribed my hieroglyphics and corrected my spelling could Miss Frances Moloney type this material and I am deeply grateful to them both.

I passed these five-hundred-odd pages among a few of my contempories who had shared some of these experiences and it was generously suggested that these should be published. I pointed out that a deal of my meanderings were of personal interest only. However, with the guidance of Mr David Kendall of William Heinemann Ltd., I winnowed the grain from the chaff and, to paraphrase Colonel Calverley:

> 'I took of these elements all that was fusible,
> Melted them down in pipkin or crucible,
> Set them to simmer and took off the scum,
> Here is this book—the residuum.'

Chapter 1 Childhood

Unlike those of a kitten, the eyes of a child are open at birth, but for some time each eye receives a separate visual impression until these two mosaics fuse into what we know as sight. The recording of this comes a year or so later, when suddenly to a young child, as if a curtain had been lifted, comes an indelibly registered series of isolated adventures.

To me, two are perfectly clear: a narrow bridge across a stream in bright sunshine and on the far side a lady holding an armful of flowers; snow—a snowman on some steps in the dull grey of a winter's evening, twinkling lights and from somewhere the scent of apples. These vignettes are clearly painted on my mind with no association as to sequence, time or place. The sunshine was probably at Lilydale, where I was born, the snow picture almost certainly at Romsey in the foothills of Mount Macedon, where my father practised medicine in the nineties.

My first clear recollection of my father was seeing him being carried in and laid on a couch. I can still see his pale face and damp, dark hair; in some way I was frightened by his silence. He was an inveterate reader and even when riding on his rounds always carried a book in his pocket. It seems on that day he was reading while his horse was taking him down a quiet country lane. In his absorption he failed to notice an overhanging bough and was swept from the saddle, to be found some time later with a mild concussion and a broken jaw.

From Romsey we moved to Bendigo in the late nineties and slowly, as the mists cleared, a film strip of places and faces began soon to be followed by a never-ending moving picture.

Bendigo at that time was reclining in the shadow of the Golden Age, during which some hundreds of millions of pounds worth of gold had been won in the space of a few years. Some mines were still working and the dull thud of the stamps as they crushed the quartz passed almost unnoticed. In the heart of the city the wheels spun at the poppet head of the famous Red White and Blue, while the engines puffed and pounded above the shaft nearly a mile deep. As with all gold activities, the Chinese—still with their pigtails—were seen everywhere: merchants, market-gardeners and pedlars with large wicker baskets of fish and vegetables suspended from a yoke across their shoulders. The Easter Fair for the local charities was, and still is, the annual occasion for Chinese pageantry. Besides the fireworks and crackers, the highlight was a great green dragon weaving along the crowded streets, its huge ferocious head turning this way and that, followed by a long glittering body writhing along on its hundreds of human legs.

Many of those who were to play a prominent role in our national history had grown up in Bendigo. Sir John Quick, a one-time miner, had assisted in the framing of our Federal Constitution and was later a Minister in the first Federal Parliament. He lived in White Hills near James McColl, one of Victoria's first Senators. The Castles sisters, Amy and Dolly, were famous in the Australian musical world and abroad. To the youngsters of Bendigo, the millionaire Lansell family gave a fabulous Christmas party at Fortuna.

Bendigo was certainly a place. Those were the days when ladies called and visiting cards indicated their 'day':

          MRS MILLER-BROWN
          The Arbour,
          Wattle Tree Road   3rd Thursday

On that day an unpredictable number of ladies would call upon Mrs Miller-Brown and be admitted by a maid in stiff-tailed, white cap, a neatly starched white apron and cuffs over a long, black dress, disclosing only her buttoned boots. A silver tray would receive the cards—one for the visitor and two smaller ones for her husband. The tray with these ritual records would remain on the narrow buhl walnut table in the hall. Then in the drawing at that time was probably in his early thirties. His one pride was horses, his favourite a smart chestnut filly, Mona, particularly attractive in a dark green gig. Sometimes at the end of the day we would see our mother, the gentlest of souls, leading a weeping William firmly into the stables, then bolting the two doors. This seemed wrong and when eventually I asked Mother why, she turned a pained face and said, 'William has been drinking again' and I received the impression that our idol had plumbed the depths of hellish iniquity. There certainly was a strange smell about William at the end of the day. I rather liked it but gradually began to associate this smell with sin. No one ever thought of calling William Billy or Bill. He was never aggressive and my heart bled for him whenever Mother had to lead him firmly into the stables, his blue eyes shining mistily through his tears, his nose becoming moist and more red and his drooping moustache more and more wet and despondent.

Many of our days were spent in the stables around the horses in the stalls below or among the bags and bales of fodder in the loft above. I remember for the first time seeing mice running among the stalls and was thrilled to see what I thought must be little horses. One day, playing in the loft, I found a half empty bottle that smelt of William. In triumph I took this to Mother: she gave me the impression that I was handling a four-second Mills bomb with the pin out and I was tremendously impressed by her bravery when she seized it and hurried behind the stables. As she did not appear for some time, I thought that dreadful bottle had destroyed her, but all was well and soon a weeping William was safely under lock and key again.

William was wonderfully good to us; everybody knew him and waved as he passed. He was a great favourite with the Chinese, many of whom were Father's patients. There was one special merchant, Kim Kook, who kept a shop in the Chinese quarter. Whenever we drove that way, William would pull up, 'Hop down, boys' as he handed us down from the buggy and, after an interval in the incense-laden dark shop, we would clamber up again laden with Kim Kook's crackers, bung bungs, jube jubes and bananas, all gratis. It was this that probably fired my first ambition to have a banana barrow on a city kerb but this soon faded, to be replaced by a yearning to be a fireman. One of the most thrilling room over tea (Chinese or Indian), with the thinnest of thin bread and butter, hot scones and madeira cake, began the gossip of the afternoon.

In our domestic circle, besides Father and Mother, my older brother and myself, were included two characters—Aunt Sarah and William. Aunt Sarah was our great-aunt—I gather our paternal grandmother's sister—but there was something vague about the genesis of Sarah Bone; when, where or if Mr Bone graced o disgraced this world we never knew. Neither Aunt Sarah nor any body else ever spoke of him, but Aunt Sarah certainly wore a old-fashioned wedding ring, a broad, gold band like a fetter. Sh was a member of our family circle as far back as I can remembe

Aunt Sarah was tall and thin with thin mousy hair, which sh combed firmly back into a tiny bun, but a few thin wisps alwa managed to escape. Out of doors Aunt Sarah crowned her he with a kind of straw decker surrounded by a band of black velv She always wore long dark clothes and around her long lean ne was a fence of boned lace. With this frustration above and sweeping dress below, nothing of Aunt Sarah was visible exc her thin face above her angular jaw and her thin, blue-vei hands beyond her tight-fitting sleeves. We presumed she undress at bedtime but we just could never think of Aunt Sa dissociated from her clothes.

She had two great interests—her indigestion and her tene lace. She was always pernickety about her food, picking at it a sated hen, and she would sit primly hour after hour wor away with her cotton round a series of pins embedded in a cha covered cork. I never remember Aunt Sarah going on a holid leaving us for even a day until many years later, still triump over her teneriffe lace, she was finally conquered by her indige and departed this life. I am afraid we were rather unkind to Sarah, who was really very kind to us.

William was our groom, William Rothque, but at first I call him only 'Wor Wor'. William had been a jockey in Li where I was born. After a severe fall my father had patche together and taken William into service to look after the and drive him on his rounds. William was a short, grizzly-Irishman with a bowed back, a limp and an attractive moustache designed for sucking. To me he always seemed room over tea (Chinese or Indian), with the thinnest of thin bread and butter, hot scones and madeira cake, began the gossip of the afternoon.

In our domestic circle, besides Father and Mother, my older brother and myself, were included two characters—Aunt Sarah and William. Aunt Sarah was our great-aunt—I gather our paternal grandmother's sister—but there was something vague about the genesis of Sarah Bone; when, where or if Mr Bone graced or disgraced this world we never knew. Neither Aunt Sarah nor anybody else ever spoke of him, but Aunt Sarah certainly wore an old-fashioned wedding ring, a broad, gold band like a fetter. She was a member of our family circle as far back as I can remember!

Aunt Sarah was tall and thin with thin mousy hair, which she combed firmly back into a tiny bun, but a few thin wisps always managed to escape. Out of doors Aunt Sarah crowned her head with a kind of straw decker surrounded by a band of black velvet. She always wore long dark clothes and around her long lean neck was a fence of boned lace. With this frustration above and her sweeping dress below, nothing of Aunt Sarah was visible except her thin face above her angular jaw and her thin, blue-veined hands beyond her tight-fitting sleeves. We presumed she did undress at bedtime but we just could never think of Aunt Sarah dissociated from her clothes.

She had two great interests—her indigestion and her teneriffe lace. She was always pernickety about her food, picking at it like a sated hen, and she would sit primly hour after hour working away with her cotton round a series of pins embedded in a chamois covered cork. I never remember Aunt Sarah going on a holiday or leaving us for even a day until many years later, still triumphing over her teneriffe lace, she was finally conquered by her indigestion and departed this life. I am afraid we were rather unkind to Aunt Sarah, who was really very kind to us.

William was our groom, William Rothque, but at first I could call him only 'Wor Wor'. William had been a jockey in Lilydale where I was born. After a severe fall my father had patched him together and taken William into service to look after the horses and drive him on his rounds. William was a short, grizzly-haired Irishman with a bowed back, a limp and an attractively wet moustache designed for sucking. To me he always seemed old but at that time was probably in his early thirties. His one pride was horses, his favourite a smart chestnut filly, Mona, particularly attractive in a dark green gig. Sometimes at the end of the day we would see our mother, the gentlest of souls, leading a weeping William firmly into the stables, then bolting the two doors. This seemed wrong and when eventually I asked Mother why, she turned a pained face and said, 'William has been drinking again' and I received the impression that our idol had plumbed the depths of hellish iniquity. There certainly was a strange smell about William at the end of the day. I rather liked it but gradually began to associate this smell with sin. No one ever thought of calling William Billy or Bill. He was never aggressive and my heart bled for him whenever Mother had to lead him firmly into the stables, his blue eyes shining mistily through his tears, his nose becoming moist and more red and his drooping moustache more and more wet and despondent.

Many of our days were spent in the stables around the horses in the stalls below or among the bags and bales of fodder in the loft above. I remember for the first time seeing mice running among the stalls and was thrilled to see what I thought must be little horses. One day, playing in the loft, I found a half empty bottle that smelt of William. In triumph I took this to Mother: she gave me the impression that I was handling a four-second Mills bomb with the pin out and I was tremendously impressed by her bravery when she seized it and hurried behind the stables. As she did not appear for some time, I thought that dreadful bottle had destroyed her, but all was well and soon a weeping William was safely under lock and key again.

William was wonderfully good to us; everybody knew him and waved as he passed. He was a great favourite with the Chinese, many of whom were Father's patients. There was one special merchant, Kim Kook, who kept a shop in the Chinese quarter. Whenever we drove that way, William would pull up, 'Hop down, boys' as he handed us down from the buggy and, after an interval in the incense-laden dark shop, we would clamber up again laden with Kim Kook's crackers, bung bungs, jube jubes and bananas, all gratis. It was this that probably fired my first ambition to have a banana barrow on a city kerb but this soon faded, to be replaced by a yearning to be a fireman. One of the most thrilling birthday presents I have ever received was a fireman's small brass helmet, a red tunic and a belt complete with a small and fortunately blunt tomahawk.

One day in this wonderful outfit I was standing hand-in-hand with William at the front gate when down the street came a fire cart. William hailed the driver, who was probably returning from the mundane duty of checking the fire alarms, and, to my breathtaking delight, I was handed up to the front seat and allowed to hold the slack of the reins as we quietly ambled around the block. But to me I was driving the galloping horses with thundering hooves and flared nostrils just in time to extinguish the greatest fire ever. That night, exhausted after my splendid exhibition, I insisted on sleeping in my uniform with my helmet beside me in case of another emergency!

On another day, William took my brother and myself into the show grounds across the road from our house. Buffalo Bill was the star attraction. In the centre of the arena was a large black rectangle erected vertically on poles. Scattered over the board in small recesses were oval white objects which William explained were eggs. To a crescendo of rolling drums, Buffalo Bill galloped out on to the arena, up reared his great piebald horse as he swept his sombrero from his head and bowed, I was convinced, to *me*. Then with the fringes of his leather jerkin flapping, he burst into a mad gallop towards the board, up went his rifle, crack—and down ran a little yellow stream from an egg. Reining his horse on to its haunches, he suddenly wheeled, thundered back and—crack, crack, crack—until no eggs remained intact and the board was streaked with yellow. Whether this was achieved by aim or artifice I never knew but did not question the deadliness of bearded Buffalo Bill.

About this time my brother and I found a solution to one of our problems. As with many others, neither my brother Jack nor I approved of our Christian names. One evening we crept down to the horse troughs and, each in turn sprinkling water on the other's head, solemnly declared, 'I christen you Bill' and ever afterwards we called each other Bill. My new name stuck to me and my mother always called me Billy, but my brother Jack was called Bill only by me. From this confusion arose the idea among people that there were three Norris boys: Jack, Frank and Billy, and there must have been something odd—not quite right—about Billy, as no one remembered having seen him.

This was the age of magic and as a special treat one Saturday afternoon we were allowed to go hand-in-hand with William to see Dante at the City Hall. Spellbound, we watched a lady sawn in half and then re-appear in one piece; rabbits, flowers and handkerchiefs appeared from empty cylinders; cards and lighted cigarettes were snatched from the air and finally, when Dante, handcuffed, roped in a bag and locked in a chest in front of us, suddenly appeared walking down the aisle, I was speechless.

Some time later when I heard that Dante had been accidentally shot dead while hunting, it just did not seem possible and I was very sad.

About this time some misguided folk decided to arrange a youth concert in aid of the Ministering Children's League and I was asked to join the cast. I had no singing voice and I had no idea what this League was nor what wonderful work it was doing, but we raised a few pounds singing 'Soldiers of the Queen', 'Dolly Grey' and 'The Absent-minded Beggar'. That was not the end of it, however. For many years up to and including the time when I was practising in Collins Street, I received, as I suppose every other surviving performer did, *Sea Breezes,* the annual report of the Ministering Children's League. To the delight of my family and probably the postman, mine was always addressed 'Master Frank Norris'.

For some time I had been learning the elements of reading and writing under the care of a governess, another of Father's patients; my parents were always caring for lame dogs. At the ripe age of six, I entered the most junior class of the State School in the park alongside the forbidding gaol. I remember little of this experience except two indelible incidents: a member of our class being violently sick beside me and a visit to our room one morning by the bearded headmaster, who applied the strap to some offending youngster in front of us all. I hated this school.

Just before the turn of the century the Boer War began in South Africa. It is impossible for those who have experienced only world wars to appreciate the tremendous interest throughout Australia during this confused campaign. This was before Federation and the A.I.F. was not born until fifteen years later in World

War I. Each State sent its own contingent such as the Victorian Mounted Rifles, the New South Wales Lancers, the Queensland Bushmen, to be merged into the British Army in the field. Many Bendigonians, including doctors, had enlisted and how we hated Cronje De Wet, Smuts and Botha, and how blind we were to the British blunders in the early battles. Donald Macdonald's despatches were discussed in every home and hotel bar. The great sieges of Mafeking and Ladysmith were the main topics, and cigarette cards and lapel buttons of their defenders, Baden-Powell and White, were worth dozens of others in a swap.

All youngsters had armies of lead soldiers—the favourites were the kilted Scotties—but we boys had to have a *real* army. We enlisted the little son of a local clergyman and another friend of ours, who insisted on bringing his sister into the force. At that time we had no idea of the role of camp followers, so we made her a nurse. As these two were McCallums, we decided on kilts as the basis of our uniform, although Father was of Northern Ireland stock and Mother's people came from Wales. Above our kilts all semblance of uniformity was missing; for example, I wore an old fez. We had our cannon: a stovepipe mounted on the axle and the wheels of a discarded perambulator. Galloping our ordnance into the front line, we would light some of Kim Kook's bung bungs, hastily toss them down the muzzle and gloat over the havoc among the enemy. We had casualties (a few real ones from the bung bungs) but usually they were simulated by the parson's little son. He was lighter and younger than we were and did what he was told!

But life was not just all playtime and we were encouraged to do odd jobs about the house. Father was keen on the do-it-yourself idea. When we wanted a kennel for our dog, he said he would show us how to build one. In his methodical way, Father carefully drew a plan and ordered the timber, which was stacked on the large back verandah against a rainy day when we would all get on with the job. Except for one door, this verandah was enclosed in walls of lattice, providing shade. Came a wet weekend and, while we passed the timber, the tools and the nails, under Father's industry the kennel took shape and soon was finished. Then came the catastrophe—the kennel was too large to go out through the verandah door. Although I never heard Father swear then or since, we discreetly withdrew. Overnight a more suitable plan was drawn and next day a more satisfactory kennel was erected and taken in triumph down near the stables. Whether it was because of this or for some other reason, shortly afterwards we moved to a larger house in another area. Over the hill nearby were groups of those melancholy heaps of grey slag that always mark a mining site. Not long after we had settled into our new home there was a memorable bonfire and on a pitch dark night I was taken out on to the verandah as the post office clock struck twelve harsh notes, bands played and fireworks lit the sky, as the new century was born with Queen Victoria still on the throne.

Five months later I was taken from my bed to see another huge bonfire on the vacant ground outside the gaol. All kinds of wild noises and cheering were abroad. It was Mafeking Night—the town had been relieved.

Early in the new century we all moved to Melbourne. As we waited for the train that was to take us to our new adventure, the train from Melbourne drew into the station. Down from one carriage stepped a strange figure in a wide-brimmed black hat and a fur-collared overcoat, to be greeted by a group of V.I.P.s. After a few minutes Father took us up to be introduced to this unforgettable man, a small but keen, pale rather aesthetic face, reddish hair and a sandy tuft on his chin. His greeting was with a firm but delicate hand—it was Jan Paderewski, who was on a concert tour of the city.

Chapter 2 Schooldays and Holidays

The occasion of our leaving Bendigo was the realization of my father's vision. After an outstanding medical course at the University of Melbourne, during which he had gained all the available exhibitions, Father married and entered general practice in Coalville, a little mining town in Gippsland. Even at that time he realized the importance of preventive medicine and public health, and, carefully husbanding his savings for post-graduate study, after gaining his M.D. he sailed as Ship's Surgeon to London soon after I was born. Such had been his constant study that he received the Diploma in Public Health at the London School in the minimum period. When he returned there was no demand for such a qualification and he continued in general practice.

At that time public health in Victoria, the Cinderella of public services, was administered by Dr Gresswell, an importee from the United Kingdom, as no one in Victoria had the necessary qualifications for the position. With the turn of the century, after more than one outbreak of smallpox, a mild epidemic of bubonic plague in Sydney and the high annual summer incidence of typhoid fever, it was realized that public health demanded more serious consideration and Father was appointed as deputy to Dr Gresswell. The department was administered from a few rooms in the grim railway buildings in Spencer Street, where the depressing 'public works brown' that was universal on government public buildings surrounded the inhabitants. Within a few years the Health Department moved to the present ornate building in Queen Street, the cost of which had so exceeded the estimate that the contractor was driven to suicide.

Leaving Bendigo meant the end of our close and warm association with William, as we no longer kept horses. He married and entered service as a groom in Lilydale, the scene of his old jockey days. Later he took a wayside hotel, which failed, and then set himself up as a hansom cab driver and finally as a horse doctor in the country. Many years later there was a ring from Mount Royal Old Men's Home and there I found William, very old, very lonely and very tearful. It was a privilege that in William's few remaining months it was possible to repay something of his wonderful forbearance and unending kindness of so many years before.

At first we lived at St Ives in Domain Road, South Yarra, a solid, sombre old building, one of the few to survive in South Yarra, and where the Church of England Girls' Grammar School was first established. Soon we moved to a villa in Acland Street. There were few gadgets in the homes in those days. Lighting, with few exceptions, was by gas mantle on an open jet, hot water came from a cistern attached to the stove or in the bathroom from a Douglas gas bath heater or one stoked with chips of wood. There were no refrigerators; with a pair of long tongs the iceman would place a block of ice into the ice chest and the food was stacked in the shelves below. Ice-cream was made by turning and turning a container of custard, packed around in a wooden pail with ice and salt. There were no tins of boot polish; cakes of 'blacking' were mixed with water into a paste, which was brushed on. There were no stainless knives—these were polished with a brown powder on a knifeboard about eighteen inches long or on a hand turned machine. The telephone was a cumbersome contraption fastened to the wall. Maids were paid ten and twelve shillings a week, a cook general a few shillings more. A boy's haircut cost threepence, an adult's sixpence.

Tradesmen rang each morning for the orders, which they delivered later in the day. Chinamen drove fruit and vegetable carts to the back gate and at Christmas time 'John' always presented Mother with a colourful jar of delicious preserved ginger in syrup. There was, of course, no radio or television but the biograph was flickering, with many interruptions, the early black and white silent movies on the screen on Saturdays. To ride outside on the dummy of the cable tram at a steady twelve miles per hour was an unending delight, especially when the gripman threw the cable and called out, 'Hold fast round the curve'. There were no official tram stops—passengers hailed the car or alighted where they chose. The conductor marked your fare with a punch with a pleasant bell-like ring, on long coloured strips pinned to the front of his tunic. There were no sections; children paid a penny, adults twopence or threepence according to the route. There were horse trams: one from Royal Parade to the Zoo; one from Victoria Bridge to Kew Cemetery (one night this was stuck up by armed bandits); one from Hawthorn Bridge via Power Street and Riversdale Road to Auburn Road; and one from Sandringham station to Beaumaris. Actually the first electric tram in the Southern Hemisphere ran from Whitehorse Road to the old wooden tower at Doncaster, a private venture started in the eighties which soon went into liquidation. While motor-cars were always an object of interest, carriages, Broughams and Victorias with crested doors were seen in the city streets every day, driven by liveried coachmen and with footmen in cockaded, shiny black silk hats, and they created no comment.

Down the lanes drove pedlars crying, 'rabbie, rabbie, rabbio' and selling rabbits at ninepence a pair, skinned and cleaned. There were 'clo props' men with forked saplings on their carts, and each week the "bottle-O, bottle-O' man wheeled his little truck around. This was well before the days of so-called modern music and discotheques, but every Thursday evening a German band of four brasses would delight us with their melodies and be happy with sixpence.

Sometimes a Neapolitan organ-grinder with his musical box on a pedestal would grind away his sentimental tunes while his little monkey, in a red velvet feathered bonnet and tunic, would snatch his wide-brimmed black hat, jump down from his shoulder to the permitted length of the chain and solicit our custom.

Behind our first house in Acland Street was a tradesmen's lane leading in from Domain Road. Twice each week the fruit and vegetable 'John' would drive along and tie his horse to a post. While he went in with his basket to the various houses that backed on to the lane, the temptation of the fruit-laden cart was too much for my brother and for me. While one would keep 'yow', the other would grab some fruit. One day John caught us and came in to Mother, very cross. She challenged us with thieving and we confessed. 'All right,' said Mother, 'I want each of you boys to write down exactly what you have taken and pay John back from your pocket-money' (sixpence a week). Many years later Mother showed me a rather grubby school exercise sheet, which for some reason she had treasured. In a childish hand it read:

> FRANK
> 3 apples
> 2 bananas
> 7 cherries (I think)
> 2 apricots

Years later I was to realize how lucky I had been to get off so lightly, when I had to give medical evidence at a Children's Court. In the case before mine, a little boy of nine was charged with offensive behaviour 'in that he wilfully and with intent kicked a missile, to wit a muddy football, over a fence and besmirched the washing on a neighbour's clothes-line'. Apparently the small boy had been rather a nuisance in the district and he pleaded guilty but said he did not do it on purpose. The austere, bearded man on the bench, who had long forgotten his own boyhood, glared at the criminal: 'You begin by kicking a football on to other people's property and ruining their washing, then you throw stones and break windows, next you hit someone in the eye and blind them or perhaps kill them and you go on until you end on the gallows.' The boy was sobbing, his mother was sobbing and I was deeply moved by this appalling picture of what lay ahead of a little boy who had kicked his football over the fence from his wretched little backyard in Richmond.

Living in Acland Street, we were within a few minutes walk of the Melbourne Church of England Grammar School. At first my brother and I attended Wadhurst, the preparatory school. The Headmaster was an Irishman, Pat Wilson, tall, thin on top and with a scanty, sad walrus moustache. I started in the First Form, conducted by a school mistress, Miss Carney, and I well remember my first day. Soon after the work began, another new boy came in late, caught his foot in the blind cord and fell over. For the rest of the morning until he was sent home he blubbered his heart out. Years later, Sos Wertheim was to represent Australia in the Davis Cup Team.

In those days there were no houses, there was no school uniform or even a school tie, and one member of the senior school football team sported a moustache. In the Prep, Norfolk jackets, blouses and sailor suits were the order of the day. On one of the Wadhurst walls is a photograph of the school personnel, which I well remember being taken. Towering above the boys in the back row stands Pat Wilson, on each side of him two of the other four members of his staff. Among the hundred and twenty boys, some with long curls down to their shoulders, are many of Australia's leading citizens in embryo.

School punishments were either 'lines'—fifty or a hundred lines to be written from a selected book after school, 'Saturday'—when for one or two hours a boy had to sit in a schoolroom on Saturday morning, or 'the cuts'; during my school career I was awarded all three.

In the big school each master had his cane but in the Prep only Pat Wilson laid it on. Each afternoon at the end of school we all assembled in two large classrooms thrown into one. Pat would read any announcements and then call up the boys who had been reported to him during the day. Before all of us these wretched victims had to hold out their hands and take it. There were two regular recipients who, by cunningly crouching low before the swish, made Pat bend down so far that his stroke lost most of its venom. One of these boys, Willie Guilfoyle, won high distinction in World War I, where he lost an eye, and in World War II was in charge of one section of the balloon barrage over London; finally he was accidentally burnt to death by an exploding primus stove. This boy was the son of the Curator of the Botanic Gardens and one of our closest friends. Many of our weekends were spent playing in these glorious gardens, to which we had a key, and in the summer evenings could enter after the gates had been shut. Sometimes on Saturdays the three of us would go down to Albert Park Lake, rowing and catching yabbies. On one particular fine Saturday, when we called to pick up Willie on the way to the lake, we found him about to wheel his father around the gardens on a tour of inspection. Mr Guilfoyle suffered from gout and when the exacerbations were upon him it was the custom to swathe the throbbing foot in a mass of cotton wool and bandages and mount him into a wheelchair with an extension as a footrest. Charming and genial at most times, he became most irascible when in pain.

On that day, with Mr Guilfoyle armed with his thick fiddleback blackwood walking-stick to point out certain features or to whack Willie's legs when he slacked on the job as pusher, we wandered round the many paths, up and down the slopes around the lake. This was far less exciting than rowing at Albert Park and Willie stood it all, including the whacks, until we were nearly back to our starting point and making a fair pace along the path below Government House and above the lawn that slopes sharply down to the lake. The combination of a series of whacks, the disappointment of a frustrated Saturday afternoon and the lure of the lake shimmering below was too much for Willie. Something snapped within him and he turned the chair from the path on to the lawn and gave it a shove. The old man, suddenly aware of his changed direction and his acceleration, called loudly to Willie, whacking the empty air behind him, but Willie and we had remained at an ever-increasing interval, watching the awful career of the chair and its burden gathering speed. At the edge of the lake the chair paused momentarily, but obeying Newton's law, the old man did not, so accurate had been Willie's aim the splash was splendid. We ran for our lives, my brother and I to our home, Willie, I learned later, to his fowlhouse. There, by crouching beyond the various hen roosts and other obstructions until long after dark, he was, temporarily at least, immune from whacks. Neither my brother nor I ventured outside our gate during the rest of that weekend and we were terrified whenever the doorbell or the telephone rang. We did not dare visit Willie's home for many weeks but later, when we did call, all seemed forgiven and we resumed friendly family relations.

After a year or so at Wadhurst I apparently became rather cranky and difficult. Fortunately this was before the days of those behaviour specialists who arrogantly assume the monopoly of common sense. I was taken to that wise physician, Dr Richard Stawell, who advised that I should be turned out to grass for a while. I soon became rather bored with pottering round at home, catching, chloroforming and mounting butterflies that fluttered

Schooldays and Holidays

about our garden, and arrangements were made for me to go as a weekly boarder at a small private school in Portarlington.

Each Monday morning at ten o'clock I would board the *Edina* at Queen's Wharf on the Yarra and by midday step off at the Portarlington Pier and carry my bag to the school on the hill. It was a funny little school. There were two other boarders: two girls older than myself. It was conducted by two middle-aged spinsters and presided over by their father, whose only activity as far as I could see was to fiddle with his long white beard and whiskers and to milk the family cow in the intervals.

I vividly remember the glorious melon jam and clotted cream.

There were a dozen or so boys and girls from about the area and the only thing I remember learning was to rule my homework at the top and down the margin of each exercise sheet neatly in red ink. For the first few days of each week I was miserably homesick, then for the remaining three days I emerged from this gloom, cheered by the thought of my journey home under the personal care of one of the sailors who always smelt strongly of William at his worst.

I did not realize at the time that each week I was sailing with history on the *Edina*. Laid down on the Clyde in 1853, this iron ship with her clipper bow was first named *Edinburgh* and traded between Leith and Hamburg. In addition to her single screw, she was fitted with three sail-bearing masts with yards at the fore. When the Crimean War began, the Admiralty took over the vessel as H.M.S. *Edina* and embarked troops and horses for the Black Sea. From Scutari, *Edina* sailed to Balaclava and various ports in the area; almost certainly Florence Nightingale was among her passengers.

After the Crimea, *Edina* was sold for the Australian trade and under sail, with her engines idle, she arrived in Hobson's Bay early in 1863 and was bought by Mr Stephen Henty. Her engines were again brought into action and she entered the Melbourne, Warrnambool, Port Fairy and Portland run. On her second voyage she encountered the first of her many adventures in Australian waters. While anchored in Lady Bay at Warrnambool, the scene of many disasters, she was driven on shore by a gale, which pounded and dumped her on the sand. Within three days, however, she was afloat again and heading for Melbourne. Next she entered the New Zealand trade during the gold rush to the Southern Island but after a year or so Mr Henty sold her for £9500 and she was off again on the Western District trade. On one of her return trips she struck a portion of the reefs at Port Phillip heads but she sailed on with water rising in the hold and berthed safely at Queen's Wharf. Later the same year she ran aground off Point Gellibrand but was undamaged.

She was then bought by Captain Howard Smith for the Queensland coast and soon she was up to her tricks again, bumping into a paddle ship off Maryborough. As reported by Dickson Gregory, 'the only damage done was the wrecking of a bathroom . . .', when the occupant had only just time to emerge from the bath as *Edina* poked her nose in, then quickly withdrew like a lady.

Back again in Melbourne after another face-lift, she settled to her long and final daily route, the Melbourne-Geelong run via Portarlington—saloon, two shillings single, three shillings return: steerage, one shilling and one-and-six. On this run she really did cause trouble, the Gellibrand area seemed to have a fatal fascination for her. Here she collided with the Tasmania-bound *Manawatu* and sank her, fortunately with no loss of life, then grounded on her old site near Williamstown. Next year she rammed and sank the *Excelsior*, one of her rivals on the Geelong run, fortunately again with no fatalities. For some years she behaved herself but it was too good to last. Again she grounded on her favourite shoal and finally in 1931 rammed and sank the tug *Hovell* at the mouth of the Yarra.

When Wesley College won the Head of the River on the Barwon in 1933, the *Edina* and her captain returning to Melbourne were a mass of purple and gold. She was crowded with triumphant Wesley boys, hooting the siren till she berthed.

Unlike most old ladies of the Victorian age, she had no sense of protocol. When His Royal Highness, the Duke of Gloucester, in H.M.S. *Sussex*, sailed into Port Phillip in 1934, the old *Edina* broke all the rules, steamed through the lines of the official escort and passed the first signal welcome to the Duke. After all, she had escorted the then Duke of Edinburgh up the Bay more than sixty years before—why should she be left out this time?

By 1958, however, her course was run. Having sailed more than a million miles and carried an even greater number of passengers, after surviving four groundings and five collisions in which she sank three of her opponents, this grand old lady, the world's oldest screw steamer, this 'Peter Pan of the seas' unconquered and unbowed, surrendered to the wreckers. Such was the saga of the ship that, for a few months, I boarded every Monday morning and Friday afternoon.

After two terms at this school, I returned to Wadhurst and after a year entered the Big School. Even here, there was no school uniform. Pleated Norfolk jackets, often with 'apple catchers' —bloomers with cuffed stockings like those of the golfers of the day—were the rule, with a dark navy-blue suit for formal occasions: a suit tailored at Buckleys cost about three guineas. Straw hats with a white embroidered mitre on a dark blue hatband were as common as ill-fitting blue caps with the same white mitre in front. Prefects wore the school crest on their hatbands and caps, the sixth form and first teams a gold wire mitre, probationers and second teams a silver wire mitre. Shoes were sissy; black boots costing about sixteen shillings were the order of the day. There were no blazers except for the first teams: white-edged for rowing, blue for football, plain for cricket and athletics. The under-age members of the athletics team wore a white blazer with a dark blue mitre on the pocket. I wore my first long trousers on the occasion of the church service to mark the Jubilee of the School in 1908.

The Public School Sports were held in May and the boat-race, alternately on the Barwon and the Yarra, was in October. Football was played on the League grounds: ours was the M.C.G., Wesley had St Kilda, Xavier South Melbourne, Scotch the Old East Melbourne ground, and the Geelong schools played at Kardinia Park. At half-time, from behind the goals, the boys of each contesting school crossed straight across the ground. The shortest distance between two fixed points is a straight line and the inevitable happened. The most memorable clash was in 1905. The Grammar boys leapt the picket fence led by the biggest boy in the school holding aloft a Grammar flag on a stout pole. This boy is now a knight and a highly respected citizen. The Wesley boys with their flag came across from the opposite goal. Somewhere about the centre it happened. One minute two reasonably orderly marching groups of boys—suddenly a mêlée. The object of the exercise was to keep the flag flying and snatch the opponents' caps. For half an hour the battle raged while the umpires and the teams looked on, impotent, from the stand. Slowly the fight fizzled out and the game was on. Within a few days extravagant letters appeared in the press deploring 'this exhibition of hooliganism'.

After a similar but milder episode in East Melbourne when we played Scotch, the matter was taken in hand by the Headmasters and, while the boys were allowed to change goals at half-time each school had to march around the boundary in a clockwise direction; thus conflict was avoided and decorum was restored. In contrast to this behaviour was the relative sedateness of the thousands and thousands of people—men and women, boys and girls—who attended one of the great social events of the year: the Public School Boat Race on the Yarra. The cheering and shouting, the cries for the winning crews from the boat house, the ducking of the winning cox were all clean, healthy fun, no throwing of flour bombs or other missiles, no paint scrawled on property—these came later.

Apparently no academic teaching qualifications were required of the masters in the Big School. As a consequence they were a very mixed bag and no old boy of the school was among the staff. The Headmaster, George Blanch, an Oxford M.A., was always known as Gus; anyone with an Oxford accent was called Gus after Augustus of the comic papers. Gus Blanch was a charming man, however, and a good teacher. There was an ex-British Army officer, Gascoyne, who conducted his classes on parade. Another oddity was 'Tag' Curtis, whose cane never left his hand during a lesson, to be administered several times during each period, with or without cause, just to keep his hand in. Little P. A. Robin, always known as 'Par', was an excellent English and History teacher and in spite of his diminutive size always maintained discipline. 'Boo' Baker had few qualities beyond ability to run the dramatic club and write sickly, sentimental sketches as curtain-raisers for the annual school play. At the conclusion of these there would be loud cries of 'author, author', and 'Boo' would step shyly from the wings with his grey hair, blue eyes, black moustache and green waistcoat, to acknowledge the rousing applause. 'Whiskers' Beard was another Englishman, said to be a wrangler and mathematician of some note. Through his abundant whiskers he would roll out formula after formula.

'Ally' Wilson was a character. His prominent nose supplied his nickname from the Ally Sloper of the comics. Ally frightened Latin into me. When everyone was seated, he would stroll into his classroom, wander over to the window and stare out over the playing-field. Suddenly he would wheel and march back to his desk shouting 'Ho ho' with accent and rising cadence on the second 'Ho', pick up a couple of books, fling these at the class, who were expected to wake up, catch them and return them to him. Then on went the lesson and a jolly good one, too. He never missed an inattentive boy, even if his back was turned while he was writing on the board. He would suddenly turn round and shout 'Ho ho, little so-and-so, your bottom is in jeopardy!' and so it was if you did not pull your socks up. The reality of the danger was in inverse ratio to your prowess at cricket or football. Ally was the Sports Master and universally popular. We were studying the Gallic wars at that time and had come to the conflict between Caesar and Dumnorix, the Aeduan. Suddenly he roared at me, 'Come out here, little Dumnorix', and the name has stuck to me ever since. As Sir James Darling once said, 'A school nickname endureth for ever.'

'Spuddo' Giles was another Englishman, a great favourite and a good English teacher in spite of the potato in his mouth. You could always smell Spuddo, as he invariably wore a Harris tweed coat from which the lovely smell of the peat never departed. Spuddo's one love was his yacht—a series of 'Utekas'. During the holidays and weekends he would invite a group of boys to man his craft on cruises round the Bay or over to Tasmania, where, after he eventually retired, he lived on his latest yacht. There was an enduring affection for Spuddo.

'Foxy' Walker was a wonderful teacher of any subject, especially French and Chemistry. His sharp alertness earned him his nickname but there was no guile or cunning in Foxy's make-up. He had a great understanding of boys and there was deep sorrow when he was knocked down by a bicycle and killed.

'Burr' Blackwood was among the greats, English and the Classics being his subjects. He had two oddities: the interpolation of a series of 'burr burrs' while he was talking and a strange use of 'f' instead of 'p'. He translated one Latin passage as 'Ulysses bored Folyphemus's eye with a fole'. Burr was a great trout fisherman (he wrote a book on this), and he had the reputation of having introduced the running drop kick into Victorian football.

'Boz' Thompson, who always began his lesson with 'Boys, boys'—which sounded to us like 'Boz, boz'—taught Maths and English to Seniors. He was remarkably astute at detecting cribbing and in our class we had an arch cribber. Each lesson was devoted to a duel between this boy and Boz. Sometimes the boy would get away with it, at others Boz would win. Then Boz would call the boy out, unlock his cupboard slowly as if in pain, produce his thin cane, and lay it on. The victim later became ordained and a pillar of the church. Charlie Brown was robust and could roar like a bull and did so, but he could teach Physics and everyone liked Charlie Brown. There were others, of course, but these were the characters that endured quite clearly over the years.

At that time there were stables near where the Memorial Gates now stand and about forty boys from Toorak and Malvern rode their ponies to school. Next to the stables was the tuck shop, presided over by Mrs Stowe, who always kept a stick handy. If too many boys stretched their hands across the counter, she would pick this up and, with a series of raps, run along the hands as if playing the scales on a xylophone. Next door was the carpenter's shop, where little Mr Sloggett taught cabinet work and dropped all his aitches. To complete this area was Jack Graham's boxing class in the old pavilion. Jack was said to have been no mean prize fighter before becoming a lion tamer. His close-cropped grizzly hair, his twisted and flattened nose set on his rugged and scarred face, were certainly not in the usual academic picture. If the weather-vane of Father Time at Lords were shorn of his wings and he stepped down, there stood 'Old Mac', the groundsman. No one knew his full name, he was always just 'Old Mac'. Tall, lean, with a long thin beard, he always prepared his wickets with graceful sweeps of his scythe, whetting the blade with a hiss and a kiss of a stone slung from his waist, then rolled the pitch with a leather-shod horse and roller.

My brother was nearly three years older than I and in his company at school I picked up odd words, many of which neither he nor his companions really understood and which certainly were quite above my head. One evening at dinner, during which I had difficulty in keeping still because of an odd itch, my father turned said, 'Will you stop wriggling, what is the matter with you?'

'I think I have syphilis,' I said.

There was a tremendous silence, my gentle mother gasped 'Oh' and Father, to say the least of it, taken aback, rose from the head of the table and said, 'Go to your room *at once*!!' Those were the days of parental discipline, when parents were not afraid of their children. Off I went, closely followed by Father.

'What do you mean by saying that? What have you been doing?'

'Nothing, Father—look', and I peeled off my coat and shirt and pulled up my singlet. 'It's terribly itchy.'

'What on earth have you been eating? You have hives.'

And family decorum and decency were restored. It was left to time and calomel to relieve my distress and teach me a lesson not to use words I did not understand. When I was comfortable again my wise parent explained to me the unconscious enormity of my iniquity.

On Saturday mornings I rode the family bicycle a couple of miles over to the Continuation School, now the site of the Royal Australasian College of Surgeons. About twenty of us attended a sloyd class, learned the elements of carpentry and gained a knowledge of timbers, many of which were imported—oak, beech, walnut, ash and cedar—and at that time there was a plentiful supply of beautiful Tasmanian blackwood. We were all about ten or twelve years old and many of those Saturday morning friendships have endured—Frank Tate, Ron Stott and Billy Kent-Hughes.

On my way home I always stopped at Hearnes famous sausage shop in Flinders Street opposite the Cathedral for two pounds of 'mixed', our regular Saturday supper, until one morning while riding across Princes Bridge I found a string of sausages trailing from my bike on to the road; that evening we had scrambled eggs.

Every few years a wagonette loaded with luggage would draw up at our gate and down would step Father and his father. Grandfather had originally come to Australia in the late sixties and when he retired had served for some years as a tea blender with

Robert Harper & Co. I can just remember once seeing Grandmother, a slight little figure propped up in bed in Kew. After she died Grandfather went back to England but after a year or so came out again and stayed with us until he again felt the call of home. This to and fro movement continued until he died. He always travelled around the Cape on one of the White Star ships, the *Medic* or the *Runic*, troopers in the Boer War and later in World War I. They were one class ships and the fare from London to Melbourne was from £21. Grandfather was of moderate height, beautifully bald with a tidily trimmed white beard and moustache, and was always neatly dressed.

On his last visit in 1907 I was taking in his early morning tea but received no answer to my knock. When I entered I found him peacefully dead in his bed. This was my first experience of death and I have always remembered Father saying as he looked down at that quiet, pallid face, 'He made it all possible for us.'

The only unpleasant memories of those days were my visits to the dentist at the top of Collins Street. I can still see him clearly and whenever I smell anyone eating musk jubes I can still smell him. He always wore a long black frock-coat with shiny lapels, had small cunning eyes and a wax-pointed moustache. His main instrument of torture was a foot-treadled drill but he also had a horrid little fine wire corkscrew tool with which he used to extract our devitalized nerves. He would hold this up and gloat over it before inserting the thing down the canal of the tooth. Such was my terror of this painless procedure that once I actually fainted before he began.

This was quite different from Father's attention to my first teeth when they had served their purpose. He would say, 'Come along now, I will have it out before you can say "Jack Robinson".' Then as the forceps tightened on what was left of the tooth, I started on Jack Robinson but the forceps in my mouth so cramped my articulation that when later I claimed I had said it before Father held the tooth aloft, he always said he had not heard it. Anyway, even without any anaesthetic, I felt very little pain and the threepence in the glass next morning was worth it.

Besides the carriages in Melbourne streets, wagonettes were plentiful and the clop clop of the horses in the rubber-tyred hansom cabs was a familiar sound. For a time our old groom,

William, drove one and occasionally would call round to our house in South Yarra, drive us along Alexandra Avenue, round the Domain and home again. William, who was always sober when he drove us, would lift up the small trap-door in front of his high perch on the roof of the cab and chat about old times. The glass doors in front of the two passengers were closed and opened by a lever worked by the driver on top to avoid any attempt to escape without paying the fare. On a good road a ride in a hansom cab was a comfortable and a cosy privacy.

About this time I had my first ride in a motor-car. Father had established a tuberculosis sanatorium among the shapely red gums in the pleasant fields at Greenvale on the lee of the granite studded hills just north of Broadmeadows. Sometimes my brother and I would visit this lovely quiet spot and on these memorable occasions a car would call at our home. It was one of the first Oldsmobile models, steered by a tiller from the front seat, where Father sat beside the driver while my brother and I clung to the rear seat with our backs to them, looking out over the way we had come. There was only a small windscreen but no hood, and a series of swings had always to be given to the starting handle in front before we moved off at a steady twenty miles per hour when the road was clear. If we returned in the dark the acetylene lamps were lit and we were wrapped around in rugs.

Alfred Deakin, the most eloquent of Australian Prime Ministers, lived in Walsh Street at the top end of our street. The youngest daughter, Vera (now Lady White), was of our age and sometimes on a Saturday my brother or I, with our one family bicycle, would join the Deakin cycling party and ride down to Mordialloc or other nearby places. During the summer we would occasionally all take the Johnston Street cable-tram to Studley Park Bridge, which was the terminus, hire boats and row up to Rudder Grange for a picnic. Inspired by Vera Deakin, we decided to put on a play for some charity.

Vera brought in three of her friends and we contributed two from our school. While we rehearsed, the machines in our homes hummed merrily, making our costumes. I vividly remember my embarrassing get-up as a servant in the seventeenth century: a brown sateen jacket, full brown bloomers with long brown stockings, a stiff, uncomfortable ruff and a floppy Tudor hat that fortunately hid most of my face. Whether we made any impression on the audience I do not know but on the site of our one-night performance at St Chad's in Martin Street, South Yarra, later arose the successful St Martin's (Little) Theatre in what is now St Martin's Lane.

On the opposite side of Acland Street was the estate of the Town Clerk of Melbourne, Edmund Fitzgibbon. His house was set in the centre of a large block of land surrounded by tall cypress trees. This extended the whole length of Acland Street and along Anderson Street and Walsh Street for more than a hundred yards. A statue in his memory stands in St Kilda Road south of Princes Bridge. When he died the estate was subdivided and Father bought portion of the Acland Street frontage opposite our home; Donald McKinnon built on the area extending to Anderson Street and Percy Brett on the area extending to Walsh Street. The great cypress trees had to come down first and I vividly remember the pungent smoke from the burning of these firs. All my spare time was spent across the road with the bricklayers and the carpenters making the doors and window frames from red pine. Mr Guilfoyle kindly planned the layout of our land and soon after the house was built the garden was a joy. From our high attic sleepout we had a splendid view of the unending activities on Hobson's Bay and Port Phillip beyond. Replacing the old Fitzgibbon house had arisen a new Fairlie, built by Mr Purchas, the architect. Sometimes when she was in Melbourne Dame Nellie Melba would live in the top flat of Fairlie and on rare occasions we could hear her glorious voice in full throated ease, thrilling into the night from her balcony.

The holidays in our youth linger vividly in the memory. Mine fall into three separate pictures.

When we first came to Melbourne at the beginning of the century, each year we went down to Point Lonsdale, then a quietly secluded place with few houses. A few days after Christmas, which we always spent at home, there was a flurry of dress baskets—oblong, box-like affairs of thin woven cane, about three feet long, a foot wide and a foot high—into which could be crammed what always seemed to be an unlimited amount of clothes. Then the corresponding cover, like an oblong extinguisher, would be pushed over the filled case and, after it had been sat on to reduce the mass to a reasonable size, was encircled by two leather straps passing through a wooden handle. Whenever you carried this wretchedly awkward thing, it banged you unmercifully about the legs. Suitcases and light travelling gear had not been devised at that time and a journey, long or short, meant either a great cabin trunk, a dress basket, a gladstone bag or a paper parcel.

On the great morning, a little before nine, a wagonette would arrive, Father, Mother, their two boys and the dress baskets would be loaded aboard and off we would jog to Port Melbourne. Sometimes we would somehow struggle with the luggage to the tram stop at the corner of Park Street, push on the luggage, drag it off at Flinders Street and, with the help of a porter at a shilling, get ourselves and our luggage on to the boat train. There were two bay boats—the green *Ozone* and the pale blue *Hygea*; one went down the Bay via Mornington, Sorrento and home via Queenscliff, the other the reverse passage. The ship's siren was always blowing when we pulled in to the wharf. This only added to the excited shambles of the passengers as they scrambled and tripped across the train lines to the gangways, fearful of being left behind. All aboard and at ten o'clock the siren hooted, the gangways were pulled up over the paddle housing, the ropes cast from the bollards to splash into the sea and be hauled in, plash, plash, plash churned the paddles and we were off past the old Cerberus anchored off Williamstown, past the Gellibrand Light and down the Bay.

It always seemed a long sea voyage, made joyful by the string band, and my chief delight was to watch a blue uniformed gentleman with an 'Old Bill' moustache plucking nonchalantly at his harp strings as if he did not care a hoot for the rest of the band, or anybody else for that matter. When the band ran out of puff, one would take off his peaked cap and roam over the deck inviting contributions. This was the time for me to dart down the stairway and watch the engines. There was none of your hidden power shut away under steel gratings and secluded in the bowels of the ship, for these bay boats had no bowels—they drew only a few feet. Amidships under the main deck they proudly displayed the might of two great shining steel arms, relentlessly threshing round and round in that hot oily atmosphere driving the paddles. From side to side wandered the man who tended them; he seemed so puny as he squirted oil from a long-nosed can. Years later, when I read H. G. Wells's gruesome tale *The Lord of the Dynamo,* my mind turned at once to those great panting arms and I could understand Azuma-Ji's worship of his snorting monster.

Punctually at noon we swung slowly alongside the Queenscliff pier. The ship shuddered as the paddles were reversed and the ropes were thrown across the white churning water. The gangways were run out and down we went to find our land legs and the smell of fish, which always seemed to greet us at the Cliff. The dress baskets were piled on the trolleys to be pushed along the narrow railway, past the blue and white lifeboat on to the end of the pier where Cobb & Co.'s two-decker buses were waiting for their passengers. With any luck we would scramble up on top and watch the driver handle his stout horses. Somehow everyone and his luggage became fitted in, then off along the glaring limestone road we trotted, around the park, past the fort, then alongside the railway with Swan Bay beyond. It seemed another long journey before we reached our boarding house at Point Lonsdale less than three miles from where we had left our boat.

Then the fun of unpacking before we dashed in to lunch. We were always made to lie down for an hour after our midday meal but we were always too excited to sleep; this seemed an irksome imposition, but parents possessed an unchallenged authority. Motor-cars presented no hazards and at three o'clock we would dash across the road to the beach where there was always a wealth of interest for youngsters. The sea, of course, has no smell but along the beaches the drying kelp and weed give off a nostalgic memory associated with the seaside.

Each morning after breakfast we would hurry over to the beach, rather embarrassed by the bright red sailor collars Mother always insisted on our wearing, either on our blouses or, if in our trunks, over our bare backs. She said this was the only way she could keep her eye on us. If the tide was in we swam, dog-paddled or floated in the safety of the shelving shallows. When the tide fell, we would sail our boats or paddle over the slippery weed-clad rocks with their fascinating pools where tiny fish, always eluding our grasping hands, darted to and fro over the mother-of-pearl shells glistening with all the colours of the rainbow.

By day great steamers, with all their promise of adventure, would pass in and out through the Heads. Occasionally a full-rigged ship would glide gracefully by in the wake of a little tug and at night the rows of twinkling cabin lights spelt romance.

On other days, if the tide permitted, we would wander round the rocks to the Point. On the little jetty there was always a short, bald-headed man patiently fishing, but I never saw him catch anything. This was Mr Vasey, the father of Major-General George Vasey, who entered my life many years later. We would clamber up the wooden steps to the signal station and on rare occasions up the spiral staircase to the lighthouse platform, but I have never had a head for heights and soon clambered down again, frightened by the dreadful attraction to jump over. If the tide was out, we would slip and splash over the flat reef covered with weeds. It was fascinating to watch the ocean rollers leap and roar as they crashed across a rock to sink and swirl back, roaring and sucking in their sullen fury of defeat. Under the cliff was the narrow entrance to the dank darkness of Buckley's cave. Buckley, a convict, had arrived with Collins's settlement at Sorrento in 1803. After a few weeks he escaped and, wandering right round the Bay, arrived in the area on the other side of the Heads; thirty-two years later he walked into Batman's camp at Indented Head. Whether Buckley lived in our cave is doubtful, but we never questioned it.

Easter was the exciting time at the Heads. There seems always to have been a Russian scare and during the seventies of last century strong land defences were established, guarding Port Phillip Bay, the Fort at Queenscliff, another at Nepean across the water, within the Bay—South Channel Fort on an island and Fort Franklin at Portsea. Great guns were installed: some were muzzle loaders, others, like the large disappearing guns at Nepean and those in the concrete emplacements of the Queenscliff Fort, were modern. The brick walls of the fort were loopholed to repel attack from the land.

There was a great to-do every Easter time. The little white military launch *Mars*, under the command of a tall, dark, lugubrious man with the delightful name of Muchmore, began fussing hither and thither. On those rare occasions when I was able to be within earshot of the launch, Muchmore's language and blasphemy were a wonder and a rare joy. Towing a Hong Kong target at a safe distance, the *Mars* would puff out into the Rip and weave the targets to and fro within range of the guns. To us youngsters, steeped in the battles of the Boer War, the great discharges and the splashes of shells seemed the real thing, and when at night the searchlights swung their beams across the narrow entrances there was no doubt about it. How accurate it was no one seemed to know but the targets always remained intact. History relates that the only casualty from all this training over the years happened in the early days of the Russian scare, which seems to have cropped up at fairly regular intervals and apparently was taken very seriously. Queenscliff was instructed to fire across the bows of a Russian ship attempting to escape through the Heads. As the vessel came within the field of fire, she hugged the coast so closely that the selected gun, a muzzle loader, had to be depressed further and further, but apparently the retaining wad, or whatever was used in those days, had not been rammed home sufficiently. As the gun was depressed, the cannon-bell, true to Newton, rolled slowly out, bounded down the cliff and, much to his annoyance, struck the leg of an elderly gentleman who was quietly paddling.

After a few years my father bought some land along what is now known as Maroondah Highway, two miles from Healesville. He built our cottage on the high ground overlooking Graceburn Valley with Mount Riddell beyond. We had no motor-car but at that time there were three trains each day from Melbourne, the thirty-nine miles was a journey of more than two hours with a stop at Lilydale for passengers' refreshments and a drink for the steam-engine. At the Healesville station, a row of wagonettes was always waiting and for one shilling a head we ambled to our cottage.

At that time there were four terms in each school year with holidays at Easter, Midwinter, Michaelmas and the long vacation in the summer, and as well as the holidays we spent many weekends at Healesville. My brother and I each had a horse—mine a black pony mare. I called her Lorna Doone as I was buried in the book at the time. Lorna was a stocky, round-bellied little mare, which probably accounts for the shape of my legs, described so nicely in German as Obeiden. It was always a delight to ride my pony into the village to be shod. Every country village had its smithy with his forge, and shoes were made to order, not off the hook as is usual today. I remembered some of the verses from one of my very early pantomimes. The dame sang or pattered a series of parodies on well-known ballads:

> 'Under the spreading chestnut trees
> The village blacksmith stands and he's
> As strong as glue
> And he owes not a sou.'

There were no spreading chestnut trees in Healesville and the smithy was a rather ramshackle wooden shed, dimly lit until with a few powerful thrusts on the great bellows, the coals in the brick furnace leapt into yellow and blue flames, tossed up their sparks and then subsided into a hot glowing red.

> 'He has his hammer and his rule
> And children coming home from school
> Play larks with the sparks
> And pass rude remarks.'

It was fascinating to watch the smith select a straight strip of iron from the rack, toss it into the glowing coals, stirred into life by the deep breath of the bellows; then, seizing the glowing bar with his long tongs, he would place it across the rounded end of the anvil and, after a few ringing strokes of the hammer, bang the bar into something the shape of a horseshoe. Back into the coals, out again to the anvil for one surface to be grooved for the nails and the holes punched. Then the shoe, held in a spike, was held against the upheld hoof with the unforgettable smell of the hot iron on the horn as a pungent puff of smoke arose from the impact. Back to the furnace, adjustments on the anvil, then with a hiss the shoe was plunged into a tub of cold water. Holding the upturned leg between his knees, covered with a blackened leather apron, the smith would trim the hoof to a tidy fit with a rasp. Then, taking the shoe from the tub and the nails from his mouth, he hammered the shoe home, a final filing of the protruding nails, a swish of black paint on the hoof and the good job was well done.

We climbed every nearby mountain: on the slopes of Mount Munda with the lovely Mathina Falls, on the crest of Mount Juliet where a stone cairn gave a glorious view of the Black Spur and the Dividing Range.

A few miles away was the aboriginal Reserve at Coranderk, a favourite ride of ours and where we learnt to throw a boomerang. Nearby in a little chalet lived Madame Leuba, an old Swiss patient of my father, who would always have tea and cake or, if in season, raspberries and cream for us, and while we rested she would sit down with a small quaint zither and croon some of her old Swiss songs. Myxamatosis was unknown in those days and with our .22 rifles we were always able to keep the rabbits up to Mother. On each side of our property were orchards and I now look back with regret that we were encouraged to shoot the fruit-eating birds with no thought to the loveliness of their plumage or their right to live.

Nothing could have been healthier than the outdoor life we led in all weathers, clambering over the hills and riding along the valleys of that lovely place. This was before the Maroondah Dam was constructed and we had a licence to fish in the various streams controlled by the Board of Works, as they all contributed to the water supply of Melbourne. Blackfish were abundant and on the hot summer days nothing was more delightful than wading up the streams, casting for trout. The one sad memory of this time was the tragic death of a young Melbourne choir boy, Hal Noyes. Their cottage was next to ours, a primus stove exploded, the boy's pyjamas caught on fire and in a few days he was dead. In St Peter's Chapel in Melbourne Grammar there is a beautiful mosaic in his memory.

Under the Constitution, quarantine was the only matter relating to health that was controlled by the Federal Government. When Father was appointed the first Federal Director of this Department in 1908 he sold our Healesville property and built a small cottage nearby, as for some years our holidays were to be spent at the Quarantine Station at Portsea. At that time there was a quiet charm about the Portsea village, which consisted of Goss's Store, a few fishermen's cottages, Cain's limestone hotel, Marlborough House and two or three holiday homes. We stayed in the even quieter Quarantine Station at 'Pykes', an old limestone cottage on the hill. Along the sea-front stood the long, two-storey, barrack-like buildings, those on the high ground for first-class passengers, then came those for the second-class, and down on the flat accommodation for the third-class. These grim limestone blocks had been built in 1857 to protect the colony from the introduction of diseases from overseas.

Along by the grey sandy bush track leading to Point Nepean was an overgrown cemetery where those who had died in isolation, or been drowned from wrecks on the treacherous ocean beach, were buried. Near the short jetty was a squat, solid sandstone memorial to those who had died of yellow fever on the *Ticonderoga*.

When we first went to the Quarantine Station there was a small leper settlement with four isolated patients living their pathetic lives in small wooden huts. When they died, as lepers inevitably did in those days, they were cremated and the huts burnt down.

My brother and I were old enough to take care of ourselves on the sea and we hardly ever let a day pass without rowing out into the South Channel and bringing home fish. Our curved bathing beach at the foot of the cliffs in front of our cottage was a little private gem and the sea within a few yards of the beach shelved into deep water. There were many bush tracks through the low ti-tree and wild currants to the cliffs above the ocean beach. There, lolling back on a cushion bush, we could watch the fascination of the great southern rollers in their many moods as they boomed on to the beach and against the rocks. Then we would climb down and clamber over London Bridge and the reefs around.

One memorable weekend we were taken to Mount Buffalo. This beautiful plateau was about to be developed by the Government as a tourist resort and Father, in his capacity as Chief Health Officer, had to report on the site. Mr Catani, the engineer of the Country Roads Board, went with us. This remarkable little bald-headed, bearded man had come to Australia years before with two other Italians: Baracchi, the astronomer, and Cecchi, the musician. Catani's sons were at school with us, big and little 'Puss' Catani. The first all-weather mountain road to the plateau had just been completed. We trained to Porepunkah from where we drove in a four-horse coach with that famous character, Mick Docherty, who while he drove never stopped talking and entertaining us with his fund of stories. There was no chalet at that time, only tents, and on horseback over the next two days we rode across the plains to the Horn and around all the great named granite rocks.

After years of no academic distinction whatever, it remained for the world of school sport to receive my outstanding achievement. For two years after our school had won the first Combined Sports Cup in 1905, I was a member of the running team and each year we slipped farther down the ladder.

In my final year at school, as all the good players had left, I was appointed Captain of the football team—that year we had one of our worst records.

Pat Aitken, a new master, had introduced lacrosse into the school and a few of us became enthusiastic. To everyone's surprise, the first year we entered the competition we won the Premiership of the lowest grade.

It was in cricket, however, that I was able to achieve a record that has stood and probably always will stand the challenge of time. There was a sudden dearth of boys foolish enough to take up wicket-keeping, and, *faute de mieux*, I was chosen for the first eleven. In my enthusiasm for keeping wickets, I had neglected some of the finer points in batting and had reduced this aspect of the game to a simple routine. When, as eleventh man, I reached the crease, having studied the more mature batsmen such as Hobbs and others, I took block and marked it with a bail, hoping that this gesture would delude the bowlers and others into the idea that I intended to stay in. I then applied my routine. As the bowler retired to his mark, I lowered my eyes to the block and raised the bat to my shoulder; as he delivered the ball I reversed the procedure, raising my eyes and lowering my bat. Three things could happen:

1. If my timing was right and the ball was on the middle stump, I stopped it.
2. If my timing was right but the ball was off the wicket, nothing happened, provided the wicket-keeper held it.
3. If, as usually happened, sooner or later and generally sooner, the ball was straight but my timing was wrong, I was out.

We had a remarkable team that year and with one exception a very strong side. When we played Scotch we closed at 6 for 600 odd—a record at the time—and every member of the team received two replicas of the scoreboard, one printed on dark blue, the other on white silk. Alas, Norris is bracketed with four others: 'did not bat'.

In this manner I established a Public School record of two runs for the season's total.

This was to be improved 100 per cent, however, when we visited Sydney for our annual match against the Grammar School. Sydney batted first and we had them all out on the opening day with half an hour to play. As we went back to the pavilion, our captain said to me, 'You might as well keep the pads on and open the innings.' I realized what a sound captain he was until I heard him saying to one of the usual openers, 'It doesn't matter if he gets out, we have only a few minutes to bat and he may last that long.' And so for the first and only time I opened the batting for the Melbourne Grammar School first eleven. Never before or since have I been within ten wickets of this important role. The opening bowler was one Trumper, a younger brother of the famous Victor, and I can vividly remember his vicious determined face. As he moved back to take his run, I threw my classical routine into action. Once again my timing was astray and so were the ball and the keeper. In my relief at the unusual outcome, I was startled to hear the batsman at the other end yell, 'Come on', as we passed, 'Two in it', and back I tore to my original position as striker.

So surprised was the umpire at seeing me still there, he forgot to signal a bye and when after the next ball I returned to the pavilion I found my name credited with two, thereby raising my annual total to four. After all, one should never dispute an umpire's decision and with this enduring record my Public School cricket career was closed.

Such was the ordinary life of an ordinary day boy at the Melbourne Church of England Grammar School in the first decade of this century. This School has produced three Australian peers and two Australian Prime Ministers: Alfred Deakin, the most eloquent, and Stanley Bruce, probably the most gracious.

Chapter 3 Medicine at Melbourne University

When I entered the University in 1911, there were fewer than 2,000 students. There were no quotas, a matriculated student could enter the faculty of his or her choice, and the failure rate was at least no higher than has been the case since students have been selected solely on their earlier academic record. Many who later would have been excluded by the present policy have proved leaders in their various professions.

My father was a doctor, my brother was in the third year of his medical course, and it did not occur to me to do otherwise. I have never regretted it.

The Melbourne University in 1911 possessed a charm and spaciousness around the grace and dignity of Wilson Hall, but all have passed away. The contemplative open spaces have been crowded with a variety of buildings and after the devastating fire in the 1950s Wilson Hall was replaced with a modern structure. The original tall Stevens stained glass window behind the dais gave way to a large symbolical figure emerging from chaos towards an oddly shaped sun, encouraged in this progress by a ghost-like, emaciated angel; a background rather distracting.

Many of the professors lived in two-storey brick houses set in their gardens near the periphery of the campus and the whole area was enclosed in a stout iron picket fence.

Students took pride in their appearance. The men shaved their faces and the girls did not shave their legs and were attractively feminine, the sexes being easily distinguishable even when clothed. The men wore straw hats with the diagonal blue and black band of the University or the horizontal colours of the three colleges—Trinity, Ormond or Queens (Newman was not built until after

World War I). Gowns were worn by the girls and were compulsory for all students in certain lectures. During lunchtime, if the weather was fine, groups gathered on the lawns around the lake, throwing their scraps to the friendly ducks and swans.

Until it was transferred to the site in Russell Street, the National Museum had been housed in the building which later became the University Union. One specimen survived to my time, the skeleton of a whale, which remained outside under a long galvanized canopy, a pathetic collection of huge jaws, ribs and vertebrae bolted and wired together.

After ten years at a Public School, the move to the University was an abrupt experience. There was no prescribed homework, no Ally Wilson or Foxy Walker to challenge me by name, to spurn or spur my efforts. Provided I answered my name in 75 per cent of my lectures, or arranged for someone else to do this for me, I could do as I liked. Certainly I had to attend my practical work but otherwise I could study or loaf as I chose, and if I failed my year I could keep repeating it until I passed, funds were exhausted, or I tired of the University. There was one evergreen student who had spent ten years slowly arriving into third year. He had been left a reasonable sum for the years of his medical course, why then should he hurry to graduate?

A new experience was to find girls in the classes. They always sat in the front rows of the lecture theatres, entering to the rhythmic stamping of the male students. Women had been admitted to the medical course in 1887 but for some years the University Council had insisted upon 'separate dissecting rooms and hospital instruction and separate lectures in those subjects in which it is inadvisable on grounds of decency that lectures should be attended by both sexes in common'. Fortunately by the time I began my course the Council had seen the light and we were lads and lasses together.

The professors directing my three subjects, biology, chemistry and natural philosophy, were intellectual giants. All three were knighted, Fellows of the Royal Society, charming men and splendid teachers. Baldwin Spencer, the biologist, was a remarkable man and an artist in his own right. While a student at Oxford he had studied under Ruskin. He was a discerning patron of Australian artists and later, when his private collection of more than three hundred items was sold in 1919, it was recorded, 'The sale of the Baldwin Spencer collection may be said to mark the end of the first half century of true Australian art.' The sale was conducted in the pre-war German Club in Alfred Place, which after the war became the Naval & Military Club.

Spencer always seemed to be talking rather than lecturing and it was possible to record in our notebooks all he said, almost word for word. With a chalk in each hand he would turn to the board and with beautifully deft, simple strokes and colours present the reality of his subject.

As first president of the Sports Union, Spencer originated the blue and black colours and inspired their popularity by always wearing a straw hat with this band. He was a keen follower of football and, due to his enthusiasm, the University team entered the League for a few seasons. This gave vocal delight to the crowds who, imagining that every member of a University team was a medical student, hurled anatomical advice and insults whenever our team was playing.

Spencer was a famous anthropologist and frequently visited the centre of Australia and undeveloped areas in other countries, gathering a wealth of aboriginal lore, which is now exhibited in the Baldwin Spencer Collection of the National Museum of Melbourne. There was a rather delightful story told after his return from Patagonia. In the seclusion of his study one evening over port after dinner, he was describing to some of his colleagues the mating habits of the sea birds of that grim region. 'The male birds wade ashore, flap their wings, and give their harsh mating cry.' Spencer had just given a vocal and arm-waving demonstration of this when Lady Spencer knocked and entered. She turned to her husband: 'Were you calling, dear?'

A short course of botany was included under biology and Professor Ewart had lectured in this subject the previous year, but in spite of his undoubted erudition, he just could not control his class. When it became the practice to pelt him with pittosporum berries whenever he turned to the board, he finally gave up the unequal struggle and declined to lecture to medical students. He was followed by Tommy Hall, to the delight of those students who could sing the many verses of a ribald ditty of the day. Tommy was very kindly to students and always commanded their respect. His final lecture as he drew himself up to his full circumference, concluded: 'Gentlemen, there are two Botany questions we can set, one the circulation of nitrogen, the other the nutrition of a green plant; last year we asked about nitrogen. Good luck.' Tommy never let any student down, sure enough our question turned out to be, 'Describe in detail the nutrition of a gum-tree.'

Orme Masson, the chemist, was a delightful lecturer and the prince of demonstrators. His bench experiments always confirmed his predictions in a dramatic manner, to a round of prolonged applause. Masson, the son of a professor of English Literature and an Assistant to the great Ramsay at Bristol, had enhanced a heritage of learning and grace which entranced us all. Seldom did a student attempt any funny business in Masson's lectures, but on one occasion a student did introduce a dog from the back row. When Masson turned from the board and saw the dog, he called it quietly and down it came to him. In the silence of the expectant, wondering class, Masson picked up the animal, saying in his gentle but clear voice: 'You must go out, puppy, only the puppies who pay are allowed to attend my lectures.' And to the stamping applause of the class Masson passed the dog through the door.

I saw little of Tommy Lyle, the natural philosopher. Having obtained Honours in Matriculation Physics, I was exempt from attending Nat. Phil. lectures and had only to do the practical work, so I missed the privilege of listening to this great man from Trinity College, Dublin.

With only two subjects to be passed, my first year was a strange contrast to school life and there were plenty of opportunities for sport and other extramural activities. During the winter months I played with the lacrosse team every Saturday. When the Canadian team visited Australia in 1908, John Latham, a law graduate, was a member of the Australian team and when we played our Saturday club matches at home on the University oval, to the benefit of the team and his own physical fitness, Latham played on the defence wing opposite me. From that time I valued his friendship and advice for more than forty years.

Latham's subsequent career was outstanding. World War I and an active role in the peace conference, a leading practice at the

Victorian bar, a Minister of the Crown in Federal Parliament, and for a brief space Acting Prime Minister, Australian Ambassador in Tokyo, and finally Chief Justice of the High Court of Australia.

Sir John Latham told me of one of his many enduring experiences during World War I. With a group of legal graduates he enlisted in the ranks. One day in camp at Broadmeadows he and his tent mates were fallen in, stood to attention by the Sergeant-Major and lectured on litter. 'Call yerselves eddicated gentlemen, do yer? This morning I was hinspecting the tents and when I came to yours what did I see? *Filth!* Right turn, quick march.' He led them to their tent and again with caustic reference to 'eddicated gentlemen' he pointed to the floor of the tent. *'Filth!'* And there were a couple of dead matches.

Sir John Latham, G.C.M.G., etc., said that for years afterwards whenever he found a dead match, even on a busy city pavement, he had an almost irresistible impulse to stoop and pick it up. Such was the enduring impact of a sergeant-major's censure.

At the University I continued my close school friendship with Len Read, later a judge, and Rob Loosli. We were soon joined with two other medical students, Colin Friend and Bob Lawrence. For threepence at the Melba Theatre in Bourke Street we were frequently entertained by that prince of comedians, Charlie Chaplin, and his silent films spoke for themselves. Many of our holidays were spent together and during our first Easter vacation Bob Lawrence and I walked from Warburton across the Baw Baws to Walhalla. The snow had fallen early that year and laden with our packs we could follow the track only by the poles in the knee-deep snow. From Walhalla we relaxed in the little train that followed the lovely Thompson Valley to Moe.

At that time there was a wealth of interesting and entertaining plays available to amateurs and many of the leading British dramatists were writing for the repertory stage. The introspective, analytical, psychological plays, leaving the audience bewildered and wondring what they were all about, came later. During my school days and University year, I don't think I missed a play on the professional stage, nearly always from the gallery for which we paid a shilling or two shillings at the early door. 'Peanuts or lollies,' cried the boy upstairs. There were the spectacular melodramas produced by Bland Holt at the Theatre Royal in Bourke

Street—now the site of a G. J. Coles store—and later those of William Anderson who built the Kings in Russell Street. These were most elaborately staged, with real horse races, real waterfalls, wrecks at sea and bloody battles. It was the age of musical comedy with first-class voices, charming melodies and delightful dancing, and the Christmas pantomime was splendid entertainment for young and old. The Variety of Rickards, later the Tivoli, was of world standard. At each performance two real or pseudo 'niggers' sat each side of the proscenium and between turns back chatted while they rattled the bones (short portions of beef ribs, held between their fingers).

I filled in much of my spare time with an active interest in the newly formed University dramatic club but at that time there was no Union Theatre. The opening performance was held in the Princess Theatre where, following *Rosencranz and Guildenstern* as a curtain-raiser, Galsworthy's *Silver Box* was presented. Later we played Barrie, Shaw and other contemporary dramatists. We played in the Turnverein, an old German beer hall set in a garden where the Note factory now stands. Under the hall was a skittle alley with the booming rumble of the bowls below a detriment to the drama.

During my first year, Gregan McMahon, a leading character actor, under the J. C. Williamson management, founded the Melbourne Repertory Theatre and he invited me to join his company. It was a grand experience to be associated with such a superb actor and I remained attached to his company through my University years and afterwards. We played in either the Turnverein or the Athenaeum Theatre until our own theatre, The Play House, was built just across Princes Bridge where the A.P.M. building now stands. We covered the field of the repertory plays of that time and during one long vacation toured Tasmania.

McMahon was invited to present an item as a contribution to a charity matinee at His Majesty's Theatre. He selected a scene from Ibsen's *John Gabriel Borkman,* a dialogue between Jack Fowler as Foldal and myself as Borkman. While we waited in the wings for our scene to come on, I watched a lady with a glorious voice and a wild flowing wig as Ophelia in the mad scene from *Hamlet*. It was Dame Nellie Melba, and while she did not notice me, I can honestly say that I have appeared on the same stage as the great Melba.

Early in my 'stew vac', preparing for my first year exams, I had a letter from Gaston Mervale, who at the time was producing a dramatized version of Conan Doyle's *Speckled Band* in the Princess Theatre, asking me to call and see him during an interval. When I knocked at his dressing-room door, the door was opened by a sinister figure in a long black coat and top boots. He was playing Doctor Ryland and the vividly painted scar across his cheek did not improve his face. I had first seen Mervale some years before as Klingsor in *Parsifal* and his cynical, cruel mouth had left an indelible impression. Like many stage villains, however, he was really a charming, kindly man but he revelled in his stage villainy. He was about to venture a silent film of Du Maurier's *Trilby*, in which he gained a remarkable reputation as Svengali on the London stage. He offered me the part of 'Little Billee' at £5 a week during rehearsal and production. This was a poser. I wanted desperately to do it and the money was more than welcome, but I knew that my parents, quite rightly, would object as I was supposed to be working for my exams. I talked it over with my brother, who agreed that if I gave him £3 of my weekly salary, he would undertake to keep my parents in ignorance as to how low I had fallen. I had only two subjects to pass and was fairly well up in these, so I accepted this blackmailing proposition.

Compared with moving picture production, even at that time, Mervale's set-up was a hollow mockery. He had erected a low, shed-like building on some vacant ground on the cliff about Brighton Beach, a little way beyond the station. Each morning I went down by train and with the other members of the cast rehearsed among crude scenery from 10 in the morning till three in the afternoon. To watch Mervale make up as Svengali was a revelation. He fixed the dark hair of his Mephistophelean whiskers with varnish, the usual spirit-gum evidently too subtle for his hard dial. He was an extraordinary artist and I never failed to be awed by the intensity of the scene where he entrances Trilby of the cracked notes into the glorious voice of 'Sweet Alice Benbolt'. It made me squirm.

Then suddenly the whole thing fell to bits. I had a letter saying the production was suspended. Whether my own contribution had wrecked the show or something else happened, I do not know, but that was the end and the film, thank goodness, never saw the light of day. The effect of Miss Gwen Burrows as Trilby, in her negligee, being embraced on the screen by a first year medical student would have been devastating to his future. So ended my movie career. As I passed my first year, however, the fiasco soon faded.

In 1904 Father had succeeded Dr Gresswell as Chairman of the Board of Public Health. Among other advances he had established tuberculosis sanatoria at Greenvale and in country centres, and instituted a Diploma of Public Health at the Melbourne University, which became defunct soon after he left the State service. Probably the most important contribution was his preparation in collaboration with Professor Osborne of the first Pure Food Act in Victoria. To quote from the Health Bulletin issued by the Department in 1967: 'Victoria was the first State in Australia to introduce food legislation with its Pure Food Act of 1905 and, within the next seven years, similar Acts were in operation in all States.

'Of this legislation, the London *Times* wrote in 1914: "Australia was the first of the dominions of the British Empire, and probably the first country in the world, to enact pure food legislation and to establish standards to which manufacturers of food must conform. There was a pure food act of the amplest description in Australia before the bill for the American Act came before Congress. Indeed, at an International Conference held in Paris in 1908, a resolution was passed applauding the work of Victoria in this connexion as the most complete and advanced in the world."'

The only matter relating to health included in the original Federal Constitution was Quarantine and in 1908 Father was appointed the first Director of this new department administered under the Minister for Customs and housed in the Spring Street building now occupied by the Victorian Football League.

In 1911 when Father was appointed Medical Officer to Australia House in London, the name was changed to the Federal Health Department under Dr Cumpston as Director and a Federal Ministry of Health was established. This was quite illegal but as the Department brought down much valuable but invalid legislation, it remained unchallenged until 1945 when, as a contribution to national health, the Federal Government proposed to make all medicine free. The B.M.A. in Australia challenged this in the High Court and with little argument was successful. Only when a later referendum gave this previously assumed authority to the Federal Government did a Federal Ministry of Health become valid but with no authority for any form of civil conscription. This was driving home the final nail into the coffin of nationalized medicine in Australia.

Before my second year began, there was another move for the Norris family when Father was appointed Government Medical Officer attached to the Australian High Commissioner in London. Our house in South Yarra was sold and my brother and I entered Trinity College.

Trinity at that time consisted of only two wings, Clarke's and Bishop's, with the College Oak shading the circular lawn which filled the angle between them. The Dining Hall was where it is now and the Warden lived in the building just beyond, which included the Small Chapel. Unless disturbed by the students at Ormond, the College cows munched and browsed on the bull-paddock where the Chapel now stands.

Dr Leeper, the Warden, was a great classical scholar, 'Bones' to us as a tribute to his tall figure and skin covered frame. Bones had held this position since 1876, first as Principal and later as Warden. His North of Ireland blood had frequently roused him to champion the North in public controversies on any Irish question. With his rectitude, he was a stickler for procedure at University Council meetings and he was among the most fervent of those who had resisted the entry of women to the medical course.

The really important person on the staff was Spiller, the hall porter. A short, stocky Cockney with a watery eye and a drooping wet moustache, Spiller always found everything you lost; if your gown was missing before Hall, Spiller would produce one—probably yours. From the centre of his spider web just inside one door of Lower Clarke's, Spiller would record all late entries, it being a point of honour not to return through a window. His stumpy pipe never left his mouth and during the winter he would sit at his ease in a large comfortable armchair set at an acute angle from the grate and with an accuracy the envy of our full forward spit into the fire.

Spiller lived just across Sydney Road and any student who went over with a message would be astonished at the remarkable collection of furniture and furnishings that crowded his rooms. No wonder every new student had to furnish his study anew; within an hour or so of any student's leaving Trinity, his study was bare!

In Hall we sat four each side of the table with a Senior at the head who had authority to fine any of his diners in cider or in beer. We had to attend at least two chapels each week, otherwise we were fined in coin of the realm. I protested to Bones that this was religiously unreasonable, as anyone who had plenty of money could lie in bed without embarrassment, while those who, like myself, were eking out a miserable allowance, felt financially impelled to attend chapel. Bones did not see it that way and said, 'All right, you won't come to chapel at all', and shortly afterwards when I went to a service he asked me to retire.

College life was wonderfully full and happy. A day student at the University had little contact with other years of his own faculty and even less with students doing other courses. The Union at that time was given over mainly to billiards, snooker and poker and was frequented mainly by the devotees of these diversions. But in college I had the valuable association with students in the various years of all the faculties and the appreciation of a tutor/student relationship unavailable at the University.

I shared my study with my brother for the first year, then with a law student. We paid twopence for our bath, putting the coins in the bath-heater, and two shillings a week for our firewood, which we carried to the open fire in our study. Bicycles were our means of transport across Tin Alley to the University lectures and if our bike was missing, Spiller, for a small consideration, would always find it for us quickly. There were no cars in college but a few students had motor bikes; usually things of threads and patches, they had no self-starters but were mounted by pushing the machine and, when it began to fire, leaping upon it before it gathered speed. We organized a race for these superior people, from the College to Sunbury and back. As far as I remember about twelve started: five failed to reach Sunbury, only two finished back at Trinity, and the others all eventually turned up, by other transport. The winner, Neville Faulkner, years later was to prove a most efficient

Provost-Marshal in the Seventh Division during World War II, having won a Military Medal on Gallipoli as a corporal.

When my second year began, I felt I was on the medical road. We wore white coats, we studied the function of human bodies and dissected them.

It would be difficult to find two men more appropriate to their subjects, physiology and anatomy, or more differing in their personalities than Professor Osborne, the physiologist, and Professor Berry, the anatomist.

When Ossie was coming to Australia there was a question as to whether he would take the chair of English or of Physiology, both within his ambit. To our good fortune he came to our medical school. Tall and rosy, this man from Belfast, an assistant to the brilliant Starling, wove the romantic development of human functions in graceful language. He illuminated his lectures with allusions to Napoleon, Billy the Kid and other famous and infamous figures of history and his essays on scientific and literary subjects are charming and courageous with new light.

Dr James Barrett lectured on the physiology of sight and hearing. Barrett was a Melbourne graduate of the eighties who had gathered all the postgraduate degrees in medicine available at the Melbourne University, a Fellowship of the English Royal College of Surgeons, and had established a large practice in diseases of the eye, ear, nose and throat, areas which at that time were combined as a specialty. In addition, he had a most versatile and deep knowledge of music and other arts, an unbounded energy which bounded into very many fields of community service. The founding of the Bush Nursing Hospitals throughout Victoria was perhaps his most enduring monument. He belonged to that band of medical truants who have contributed far beyond their professional services. Barrett was unpopular among his colleagues, partly because of the publicity given to his many activities and to the numerous presidencies he held, but Barrett was a big man physically and mentally.

Dickie Berry, 'the bone man' from Edinburgh, was a stern, precise personality as befitted his subject, anatomy. His short, lean, alert figure with a dominant, intellectual head, was crowned with close, curly dark hair. When he spoke to a student, with his keen eyes, his mouth set between two deep lines and the sting of his slightly gravelly voice, he commanded the occasion and obliterated any realization of his physical stature; at times he almost resembled one of his emaciated cadavers. Only when as a graduate I joined his staff as a demonstrator and looked after his children did I appreciate the hidden humanity and charm of the man.

Berry took an active part in medical politics of the day and was twice President of the then Victorian Branch of the British Medical Association. He was foremost among those who at long last persuaded Parliament to build a new Melbourne Hospital on the pig market site and to realize his vision of a clinical school alongside the University. Berry was forthright and fell foul of many of his colleagues, and it was inevitable that he and Barrett should clash; he did not hesitate to describe his antagonist in most lurid terms. Sir Albert Coates, who was Berry's senior assistant, relates an attempt by the Chancellor to bring these two together. Berry, said Coates, was prepared to bury the hatchet, but someone remarked that Barrett might prefer to hatchet the Berry.

'Wallie' Fielder lectured and demonstrated to us in histology. Fielder was a clergyman and always appeared in his clerical garb. He was a kindly, trusting soul and whether because of his cloth, his continual smile or his charming personality, students never took advantage of his meekness.

It is a tribute to these great teachers that I passed my third year.

In fourth year we started our clinical studies at the old Melbourne Hospital. Despite the earlier agitation for a new site, the Melbourne Hospital had been re-built on the existing area and completed just before I became a student there. Berry's vision, in spite of Parliamentary consent, had to wait till 1940 for achievement. Originally the honorary medical staff had been elected annually by the public subscribers to the hospital; each year before the Annual Meeting a violent and undignified vote canvassing crusade was pursued by the aspirants for these positions. As a result, the medical staff did not necessarily represent those most suitable for the postings and the hospital and the students suffered accordingly. Later the electoral college principle of these appointments was introduced and fortunately by the time I entered the hospital the early deplorable practice had ceased. With the exception of three or four of those who had been appointed under the old régime and still survived *ex gratia,* the medical, surgical and specialist honoraries were all highly qualified and mostly first-class teachers who practised their profession and entered patients' homes.

One memorable day all the students crowded into the gallery around the operating theatre to attend Mr Charles Ryan's last operating day. As a compliment to the surgeon, each student wore a cornflower in his buttonhole, Charlie's favourite flower. Ryan was a character and students followed him on his rounds with his short, solid, jaunty, self-assured figure striding along the wards.

After three years of his medical course in Melbourne, Ryan graduated in Edinburgh only a few years after Joseph Lister in Glasgow had made his tremendous contribution to surgery. Having taken his degree, Ryan wandered over Europe and enlisted as Military Surgeon in the Turkish army at a salary of £200 a year, paid each month in gold. In his book, *Under the Red Crescent,* Ryan has recorded a day-to-day and almost a shot-to-shot account of the siege of Plevna and the later stages of that campaign which earned for him near death from typhus, the name of Plevna Ryan and the decoration of the Order of Medjidie. With such experiences, Charlie was naturally full of reminiscences with which he would delight his students. Later he was appointed Turkish Consul in Australia and on official occasions was outstanding in his fez and his Consular trappings. During the Gallipoli campaign, as consultant surgeon, he created a sensation when a temporary armistice was declared after the first few weeks of the landing to clear the dead in no man's land. Between the lines Anzacs and Turks left their trenches and for a few hours mingled over the foul area, fraternizing in the strange lull. When a Turkish officer suddenly recognized Ryan's decoration, he rushed up and flung his arms round Charlie and kissed him.

I was seated next to my brother when Charlie entered the theatre, capped, gowned and scrubbed up; he would not wear a mask and I cannot remember if he even wore gloves—he certainly did not at Plevna and probably did not wash his hands in the heat of battle. Waiting for the anaesthetist to give the all clear, Charlie strolled over to the students, with his bare hands pulled a cigar from under his gown, lit it and began another of his delightful bloodthirsty battle stories. When the anaesthetist gave the signal to begin, Charlie threw his cigar into a bucket, turned to the table, was into the abdomen in a twinkle, out with the offending organ in another, and leaving the closing of the wound to his resident, thanked the theatre staff, bowed to the students and strutted out to rousing cheers.

The patient made a rapid and uneventful recovery.

Stethoscope obtruding from the pocket of his white coat and prominent plessor were the mark of a medical student, hoping— and not unsuccessfully—that he would be called 'Doctor' by the patients. At the University, pathology was the major subject in fourth year. There were lectures and examinations in other minor subjects but practically no one ever failed in these and path. was the hurdle.

We were persuaded, rather than lectured, into pathology by Professor Allen. Harry Brooks Allen, after graduating in Arts and Law with first-class honours, then completed a most brilliant medical course, again with first-class honours in every year. He was the first medical graduate to be appointed to the Medical School (in 1880, as a demonstrator in anatomy and two years later as a professor of both anatomy and pathology). His bearded head, coyly set on one side, nodded as his soft cooing voice cajoled and implored pathology into us. He was a tremendous personality, despite his disarming gentleness.

One of the minor subjects was materia medica. We attended lectures at the Pharmacy College and learnt to make up pills, plasters and prescriptions and to identify the various vegetable and other ingredients that entered into dispensing. Fortunately, a series of questionable mnemonics helped us to remember the various preparations and their therapeutic actions. As the conclusion of the course we had to pass an oral and a practical examination, in which few failed, and I was lucky. As the candidate ahead of me came out from the oral he said: 'Now I remember the blasted thing, I just couldn't think; he showed me elaterium —you know, sea cucumber, a purgative.' When I went in, the examiner showed me a little grey disc of something that I had never seen before and have not seen since.

'What is this? And what is its action?' he asked me.

Taking a long shot and hoping for the best, I answered: 'Elaterium, sea cucumber, a purgative.'

'Very good, you are the first candidate who has known this', and he beamed as he handed me a small, heavy glass jar containing a silver-like liquid.

'Mercury,' I said.

'Good again,' said the examiner.

On the Saturday before my exams began, a group of us from Trinity went to the races; it was not an expensive outing. Cable-tram to the station cost twopence, a pot (and it *was* a pot) of beer at Hosies Hotel threepence with a good counter lunch thrown in, a second-class return fare to Caulfield sevenpence, entry to the Flat free, and at the end of the day a twopenny back to Trinity. A jolly good afternoon for 1/2d. We bet in two shillings. The principal race of the day was the Australian Hurdle. During the week the press had referred to a rumpus somewhere in the Balkans, someone in a town with an unpronounceable name had shot an Archduke. Looking down the list of starters I found a black horse called Battleship and, knowing nothing about breeding or form of horses, I thought this an obvious tip and it was—I won.

Next week I sat for my exams and was reasonably satisfied, but was uneasy when I found my name posted among a few who were required for an oral with the Professor. When my turn came, Allen looked quizzically at me and, holding up my paper, said he could not read portions of some of my answers and invited me to explain my hieroglyphics. I was, and still am, a wretched writer.

Years later when I was examining in medical finals, I had the same problem with a paper of one student. Remembering Allen's generous approach to a similar situation, I summoned the student to my rooms and asked him to read the indecipherable passages, giving me his word that he would read only what he had written. He passed as I had done in similar circumstances under Professor Allen.

Once over the fourth year hurdles, it seemed nothing could interrupt my steady progress to finals two years later, and I arranged to spend a carefree vacation with Dr Shields, a country practitioner, at Yea.

But I was wrong. It was August 1914 and I had not realized that one shot at Sarajevo was to change the face of the world.

Chapter 4 War in the Middle East

Every day at Yea the newspapers enlarged their headline news from Europe. Belgium was invaded, and Great Britain issued an ultimatum, to be followed in twenty-four hours by a declaration of war. Europe was on fire and then suddenly Australia was drawn into the blaze, 'to the last man and the last shilling', as announced by Mr Andrew Fisher, the Labor Prime Minister. An expeditionary force was offered, accepted, and the A.I.F. was born.

In 1885 New South Wales had despatched a small colonial contingent to Suakin during the earlier Sudan campaign and each of the six States had sent its own troops to serve with the British Forces in South Africa fifteen years ago. At first these were named according to their State of origin, as mentioned earlier, such as the New South Wales Lancers, the Victorian Mounted Rifles and the Queensland Bushmen; only in the closing stages of the Boer War were Commonwealth troops engaged.

Although Federation had been officially achieved at the turn of the century, national thinking was far from universal before 1914, but was accelerated by the formation of the Australian Imperial Forces.

Recruiting was opened and the doors were crowded. I do not believe that the stirring challenge to right a wrong really meant very much to me or to thousands of others, but what an opportunity, what an adventure if only I could be in time, as according to the papers it might all be over in a few months.

I broke my holiday at Yea and dashed back to Trinity soon before my third term was to begin. There I found a group of fellow students all of the same mind: enlist!

Fortunately I was just twenty-one and my parents, who were

in London, could not say nay or counsel me as to the wisdom of first finishing my course, as many others were doing.

We told the Warden of our decision and trooped down to the Town Hall for a not too strict medical examination. All clear and, on paper anyway, I became a soldier, No. 101, at seven shillings a day (one shilling deferred). My name, my number and my religion were to be stamped on an identity disc, to be worn *at all times* around my neck. Many recruits, on being asked their religion, said, 'What will I put down?' 'Anything you like,' was the advice or, if suggested by a bystander, they recorded one of the various denominations.

Next day we trooped down to Victoria Barracks for our posting. I had no idea what unit to join, but after talking it over with a medical student from Trinity who was applying for the 2nd Field Ambulance, with which he had served in the Militia, I decided to keep with him.

In the Barracks we joined a motley crowd carrying their bare essentials in all sorts and sizes of containers, suitcases, gladstone bags and newspaper parcels. Sergeant-Majors with needle-pointed, waxed moustaches and voluminous voices were shouting instructions in an endeavour to reduce the chaos to some sort of order. From one corner came the command, 'All for the 2nd Field Ambulance, fall in here.' I fell in. 'Attention, left turn, quick march.' In the crowded confusion I became separated from my fellow student and also from my sense of direction—I turned to the right and found myself in another group. Fortunately I recognized three students of my year. Carrying our odd bags and parcels, we marched off in the rain along St Kilda Road, puffed with the cheers of the pedestrians on the footpaths, and then entrained for Broadmeadows.

Only when we were lined up on the platform did I realize that I had joined a Light Horse Unit. I was among friends, however, and one unit was as good as another as far as I knew and I preferred a horse to my feet. It took me twenty years to catch up with the 2nd Field Ambulance when I was appointed to command it between the wars. From Broadmeadows Station we shambled along in the rain for about a mile and turned into the camp.

There was only one short metal road in the area, after which we plodded across the sticky black mud to our lines, sited in the most remote corner of the camp. Our bell tents had been erected and, having sorted out our group of ten, we dumped our gear and sat down, sheltered from the rain at last.

There was a trumpet call which someone recognized as Cookhouse and I picked up my enamel pannikin and eating irons and joined the line. We were marched past a soyer stove bubbling with army stew and buckets of steaming tea, all standing in the rain. With a generous dollop of stew on my plate, two thick slices of bread and jam and a ladle of tea in my pannikin, I had my first and by no means worst army meal, sitting in the mud in our tent.

Of all survivals in the Army, there was nothing to challenge the soyer stove, a large, deep copper bowl resting on a large, upright metal cylinder admitting a fire below. When William Russell, *The Times* correspondent during the Crimean War, sent back his despatches of the crude field conditions of the troops, the Government of the day sent out Alexis Soyer, the famous chef of the Reform Club, to improve the feeding arrangements. To this decision we owe the soyer stove, which still survives in army field cooking equipment. Soyer devised other improvements, including the use of solid methylated spirits as a fuel for individual cooking and a quaint day-time tunic for Officers that could be reversed into a mess jacket.

During that afternoon I received my first issue. We filed into the Quartermaster's marquee and collected our clothing and equipment. A blue dungaree suit, a white linen hat, two pairs of socks, a good pair of army boots, a towel and a cake of soap, a 'housewife' complete with needles and thread, a jack-knife with a hook for removing stones from horses' hoofs, a mess tin, knife, fork and spoon, a water bottle and carrier, three grey army blankets, a kit bag, a palliasse and a ground sheet. Hung around with all this gear and looking like Father Christmas, I retired to my tent to sort it all out. Then back to the Q.M. Store to fill my palliasse with straw, back again to the tent to make and roll up my bedding, then fell in on parade.

Camp routine orders were read, mess orderlies and piquets detailed, and the rest of the day, about an hour of daylight, was my own.

A couple of us wandered around the camp meeting friends here and there, school mates and fellow students, all, in spite of the rain and the mud, cheered with the fun of the day.

After the evening meal of bread and jam and tea, the hurricane lamp allowed us to play poker in our tent, but, richer or poorer, we soon tossed down on our palliasses radiating from the tent-pole, oblivious of the Last Post and Lights Out. During the night we learnt our first lesson, always to loosen the tent guys in the rain.

Reveille called us at six. The brass Cavalry trumpet is more melodious than the Infantry copper bugle and many of the Cavalry calls are beautiful. A shave, a cold shower behind hessian, then P.T.—physical jerks by numbers under the command of the transport Sergeant, a tall, tough, lean Hussar veteran with his ribbons of the Sudan and Boer Wars. The multiple colours of many of the campaign ribbons were determined by the terrain, his Sudan decoration yellow, black, red, yellow, represented the red British troops facing the black dervishes across the desert. The higher the decoration, of course, the fewer the colours. Breakfast, a dollop of porridge splashed with milk, the inevitable two thick slices of bread and jam, and tea. Then roll my bedding, fold my blankets and tidy my kit. The trumpet sounded for parade and elementary drill—Attention—Stand at ease—Stand easy—Stand at ease—Attention—Right turn—Left turn—About turn—Salute—all by numbers. Then quick march. Cavalry drill was much simpler than Infantry drudgery with no Form Fours, as it was then. We fell in in line, then told off by sections of fours, yelling out our numbers—1-2-3-4, 1-2-3-4—and so on, slinging our heads to the left so that our next file would be able to hear above the noise of the horses and the jangling of the harness. Each section would then wheel to the right or the left and we were in column ready to move off.

Many in our unit had enlisted directly from the militia, the N.C.O.'s taking their stripes with them. On the whole they were a good lot and helped those of us who had forgotten most of our Cadet days at school or had never known them. One Sergeant did not like me and I did not care for him. He had been a gardener in the Fitzroy Gardens and rather seemed to resent students on principle. Whenever I answered his question as to what I was doing or where I had been, he always replied, 'Oh, was yer?' So I will call him Sergeant Wasyer. The higher anyone's education, the more menial was the job for which he was detailed by Sergeant Wasyer. 'A fell sergeant and strict in his arrest.'

Drilling and route marching, route marching and drilling, was good exercise but rather dull. Then came the issue of uniform. The famous felt hat, a baggy, pleated tunic like a khaki Norfolk jacket, riding breeches, leggings and spurs, rising sun badges and a greatcoat.

One of our students, Bill Armstrong, was the proud possessor of a motor bike in camp and he often gave the C.O. a pillion ride into the city. Whether because of this or just because he was a jolly decent fellow of fine physique, Bill was promoted to Corporal and helped to soften the blows of Sergeant Wasyer's indignities.

When we had been in camp about ten days our horses arrived, stout army recruits, and we drew our saddlery. It was said that when one recruit heard that the horses were on the way, he went to Bill Earl and said that he had never ridden a horse. 'That's all right,' said Bill, 'I'll find one for you that's never been ridden, then you'll both start off from scratch.' My own equestrian experience had been limited to my fat little pony at Healesville, but fortunately I was able to select a horse short enough to be mounted without the indignity of a box or a tree stump. Another life had entered into mine, that of my horse.

Under the instruction of our old Hussar Sergeant, we picked up the elements of equitation and for the first time I heard the lovieliest of trumpet calls: Stables—'Come to the stable all men that are able and give your poor horses some hay and some corn. . . .'

Probably because there is something missing in my make-up, I have never considered the horse as a noble animal, but rather as a silent companion. Everyone talks to his horse and assumes the animal understands, there is a silent response in his eyes and in the movement of his head. To me the relationship was that of a dumb, reliable, faithful servant. From the advent of my horse, I became aware that besides myself and close to me, I had a living thing to care for, one who was dependent on me and who could be relied upon to serve me in my dependence.

The day began with early morning stables. Grooming with

curry-comb and brush, then leading three haltered horses to water while the stable piquet cleaned the lines, mixed the feed and filled the nosebags. After watering we led the animals back to the horse lines, which consisted of long stout ropes pegged firmly to the ground with heel ropes in the rear. As each horse was hitched to the lines behind a well filled nosebag, the hungry whinnyings ceased after the final notes of the trumpet—'Feed your horses, feed your horses'—and the nosebags were snuggled over their muzzles. Then we could have our breakfast.

Morning parade—'Stand to your horses'—and each man stood to attention on the near side of his horse, holding the reins. Next command, 'Prepare to mount', and each man turned to his horse and, holding the reins and the pummel of the saddle with his left hand, he placed his left foot in the stirrup; 'Mount' and the legs swung over the saddles. 'Sections right', 'Walk march' and off we went through the camp to the road. With a swinging move of his elbow, the C.O. then gave the order 'T rr o tt'. And the exercise began. This went on day after day, every fourth night horse piquet, men and horses growing closer together.

One day a routine order was issued throughout the camp for all Old Melburnians to assemble at 1500 hours in a large marquee near the chateau. When a hundred or so of us had gathered there, we found one of our most notable Old Boys, Alfred Deakin, standing on the platform. With his graceful and sincere eloquence, he inspired us all and then in single file we marched past him; he shook each of us by the hand and presented us with an Old Melburnians badge.

We had been in camp about six weeks when the rumours began. All doubtful information was known as a furphy. The communal latrines for rankers were the great gossip centres, certainty, conjecture and rumours were bandied about from seat to seat: 'Somebody said . . .' 'I heard that . . .' 'It looks as if . . .'. The sanitary cart consisted of a large galvanized tank mounted on two wheels and drawn by a horse, on the side of which, in bold letters, was the name of the maker—FURPHY.

In a few days it was obvious that something was astir and on Saturday, 16 October 1914, a a detachment of our unit marched out and did not return. Next day after church parade we were told to pack and pile our kit-bags and, after a dinner of soup, tough roast mutton and rice pudding, there was a full muster mounted parade. Off down the camp road, left wheel, past the old hotel at the road junction, then right wheel down Sydney Road leading to the city. At Latrobe Street we wheeled to the right and headed for Victoria Docks where our transport *A27 Southern*, a coal-burning tramp of 3,000 tons, was berthed. Most of our stores were already aboard and we found the New South Wales portion of our unit ready to welcome us. We had our horses loaded in their stalls by the end of the afternoon, and with none to wave farewell, we were away as the evening shadows added to our mixed feelings.

That night I was horribly sea-sick. Our old tramp could not be relied upon for more than nine knots, and so we, the first transport to leave Victoria in World War I, had to sail before the others in order to reach the assembly area, King George's Sound at Albany, in time to join the convoy.

As we wallowed westward, the Bight was sullen and ill-tempered and many of us were sick all the way across. Here was a grand opportunity for Sergeant Wasyer, and another medical student and I were detailed in our misery to clean out the officers' baths and toilets twice a day. Only after seven days in the depths did the calm of St George's Sound come to our mercy.

The day we dropped anchor I reported sick and was sent to the isolation block with German measles. Here another patient, a tram conductor from Sydney, and I passed a glorious week with nothing to do, plenty to read and beds to sleep in. At the end of the week we were released ... to duty.

Sunday, 1 November 1914, will be an enduring memory. Slowly in single file the forty-eight transports moved out to the Southern Ocean. It was a gloriously clear sunny morning, the grey of the New Zealand transports contrasting with the black, the green of many of the Australian ships. The convoy carrying 30,000 troops and more than 10,000 horses manoeuvred into three lines—half a mile between lines and half a mile interval between each vessel and the next, our tramp was just in the rear of the flagship *Orvieto* and to us the rear of the convoy was over the horizon.

Our departure had been delayed by the uncertainty of the whereabouts of the German warships. When Von Spee's squadron was located off the South American coast, there still remained the cruiser *Emden*, playing havoc in the Bay of Bengal and sinking ships in the Indian Ocean across our course. Guarding our convoy, 'the greatest effort of sea transportation of troops to a distant seat of war that the world had ever seen', were the R.N. Cruiser *Minotaur*, the R.A.N. Cruisers *Sydney* and *Melbourne* and the Japanese Cruiser *Ibuki*.

Discharged from hospital, I slipped into the daily routine. Our three hundred horses were housed in stout wooden stalls, bolted to the iron decks on each side of the ship in the fresh air above, and in the heavy dimness of the deck below. Each stall was floored with stout oregon planks and each thirteenth stall was vacant. This was not a matter of superstition but to make possible the 'mucking out'. We worked in pairs to clean out twelve stalls twice a day. My opposite number, John Knox, was a hefty, jolly Irishman, who after serving as a policeman in his native land had migrated to Australia and become a gripman on a Melbourne cable-tram. First thing each day we marched off to our respective stalls, fortunately ours was on the top deck in the freshness of the morning. The panels dividing the blank stall from the first horse were taken down and horse number twelve was slapped, shoved and persuaded into the clean stall, number thirteen, and the panels replaced. One of us, generally John, moved into the now vacant dirty stall, and at the word 'go' we upended the floor boards and while he held them out of the way, I got busy with the shovel and broom, sweeping the sloppy, stinking mess into a large basket, up to the rail and over she went into the ocean. Down with the next panels, over with the next horse, up with the boards, in with shovel and broom, into the basket and over again, and so on till our twelve horses had clean stalls. When they had been groomed, watered and fed, we went down to our own breakfast in the mess deck over the propeller.

During the mornings and afternoons we rolled strips of coconut matting over the narrow iron decks, took off most of our clothing, except our underpants and boots, haltered our horses and led them round and round and round for the exercise of both. One night in four we were detailed for horse piquet, quietening those who were restless and dragging up those who had stumbled and caught their legs under the rails. Early in the voyage, we had opened two stalls into one among each group of thirteen horses, hoping that the animals would lie down at night as there was plenty of room in a double stall. But they would not move off their feet. We tried slinging them under their bellies to take the weight off their legs but they kicked and struggled under this restriction, which had to be abandoned. There they stood and shuffled day in and day out, with their legs slowly swelling to twice their normal size, and rubbing their tails until they were bare of any hair. Otherwise they kept their condition and so did we who tended them.

Every few days men would be detailed to descend into the depths of the hold and hoist up supplies for the cooks. In spite of Sergeant Wasyer, this fell to my lot only twice. The second time, we had to drag out a foul smelling cask of something and roll it into the slings for hoisting on deck. As the lid was prised off, all work ceased on top, what had been a foul smell became a horrible pervading stench and I retired to the rail and was sick. Along came the bos'n, and pushing his thick, hairy, tattoed arm through a layer of green slime, he brought up a strange looking thing like a thick piece of wet chamois leather. He opened his jackknife and, cutting off a piece, chewed it for some minutes between his tobacco-stained jagged teeth, and then, in his broad Northern dialect, roared: 'Tripe, and sweet as a f - - - n noot!' Before he could pass this to the cookhouse, half a dozen of the lads rushed in, dragged the cask to the side and heaved it over to the sharks in the Indian Ocean. Decorations have been awarded for less but there was a mighty row and an enquiry about the destruction of Army property. As chemical decomposition and bacterial putrefaction had obviously previously completed the destruction of what was intended as our ration of tripe, no penalties followed beyond a reprimand.

During the day our old tub wallowed along at a steady nine knots in rear of *Orvieto*, but at night in the blackout we generally slipped back and so, as it turned out, set the pace of the convoy.

Day in and day out the same old routine, muck out, water and feed, exercise and horse piquet, with little time to follow the fascination of the flying fish as they broke from the bow wave, but so laden and low in the water was our ship that sometimes one would land gasping on the deck.

Only once was the monotony broken. While I was exercising my horse one morning there was a flurry among our escort— *Melbourne* dashed off ahead, soon to return to the convoy, and

Sydney turned sharply to starboard in a dense cloud of smoke and was soon over the horizon. The other cruisers took post closer to the convoy. Later in the morning John Knox, ahead of me in our procession, stopped and turned to me. 'Did you hear that?' I had heard nothing above the noise of the horses.

'What was it, John?' I asked him.

'Gunfire', and he was right. *Sydney* had engaged the raider *Emden*. Later that day we heard the story. *Sydney* had picked up a radio call from Cocos Island reporting the presence of a strange war vessel. Off went our escort to see what it was all about, and although *Sydney*'s six-inch guns outranged *Emden*, she was hit more than once before the raider was driven on to the reefs, a burning and battered hulk. Possibly our old *Southern*, with her crawl, had so delayed the convoy that a major tragedy had been avoided. Later when Captain von Müeller, *Emden*'s Commander, was shown the chart of our position the night before the action, he said he was fifty-two miles from us that night, and that if he had got up to us he would have run alongside the cruiser on the port bow of the convoy, fired a torpedo and in the confusion got in among the transports. 'I think I would have sunk half of them before your escort came up to me and I would have been sunk in the end—I always expected that.' We knew that von Müeller was somewhere about but there was no radar in those days. With *Emden* destroyed and *Königsberg* stranded on the African coast, the Indian Ocean was at last safe, and lights went up for concerts on the deck at night.

Stoking a coal tramp in the tropics was far from fun and volunteers were called to take shifts in trimming the bunkers, with permission to sleep on the fore-deck between shifts. Our allotted sleeping quarters were hammocks slung from the ceiling of our mess deck, sited aft over the thump and shudder of the propeller below. Anything was better than this and a dozen of us seized the chance to shovel coal from the bunkers over to the firemen. It was hot and dirty work but not nearly as unpleasant as being alongside the boilers, and the relief of lying out on the bow deck in any available breeze was worth it.

Our three days in Colombo were an unpleasant swelter. There was no shore leave and our ship was soon covered in grime from the baskets of coal carried on board by an endless chain of dark

*The family home at Lilydale.
Father in the buggy,
about 1894.*

Our 'Army'.

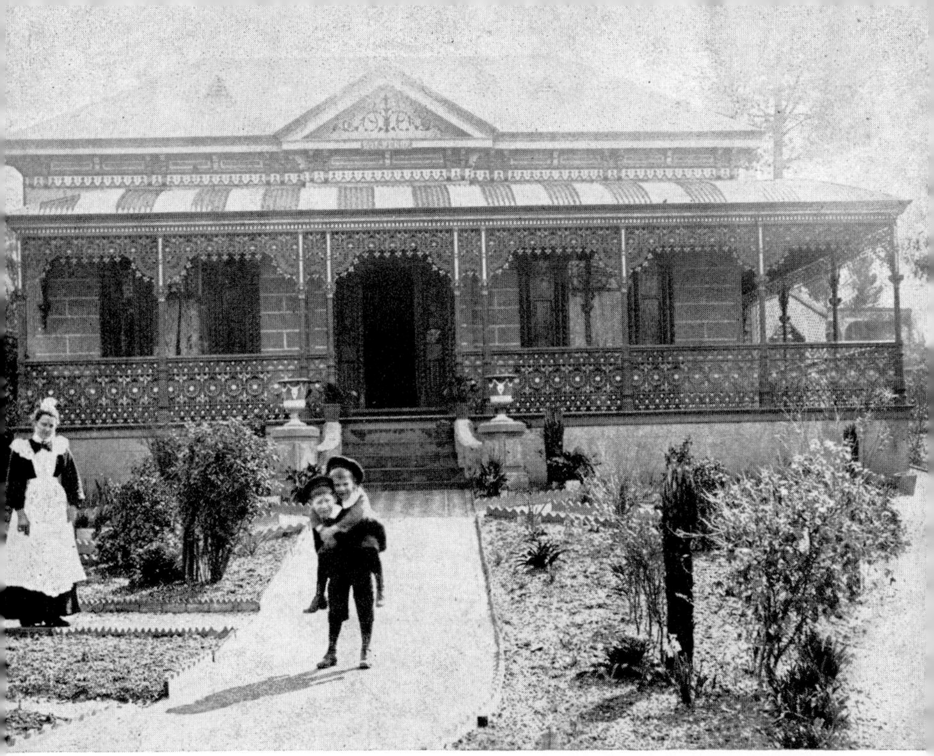

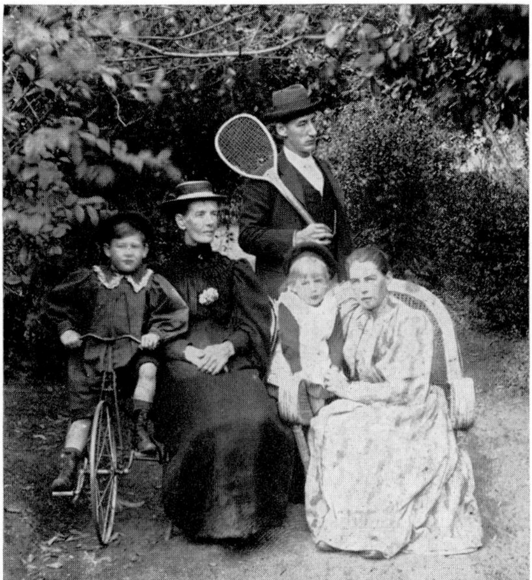

The family home at Bendigo.

The Norris family, Romsey, 1896.
Reading from left to right—Jack, Aunt Sarah,
father, self, mother.

First stage appearance, 1907.
Author centre stage.

*Christmas Day, 1914, at Maadi,
including eight medical students.*

*Christmas morning, 1914, Rt. Hon. George Reid addressing the troops.
(Courtesy: Australian War Museum.)*

men. As we were not allowed to empty our baskets into the harbour, the mounds of manure slowly melted into stinking dark rivulets on the deck. It was a delight to be at sea again, with the relief of heaving our midden overboard. How relative is joy!

Our escort was now joined by the 'Packet of Woodbines', a five-funnelled Russian Cruiser *Askold*, which had survived the Russo-Japanese War ten years before. Across the Arabian Gulf into the Red Sea and round the island of Socotra, famous for its aloes, whose laxative properties we had studied in Mat. Med. only a few months before, but which now seemed back in the dim ages. Suez, then through the Canal, garrisoned with Imperial troops in their trenches, who cheered us on our way, a day's delay in the Bitter Lakes, Port Said with bum-boats—the gully gully men with their mystifying chickens—then finally Alexandria. With the entry of Turkey into the War, the situation in the Middle East had changed and the A.I.F. was to be disembarked in Egypt.

We tied up at night, led our poor horses down the gangway and loaded them on to rail trucks, then off down to Cairo. Dawn was just breaking when we collected our horses and led them slowly out to Maadi, a detached English settlement a few miles into the desert. To the horses the sand was heaven. At last they could roll and move in comfort but the sight and the smell of the camels and the rusty creak of the donkey's bray continued to upset them, and it was many days before their legs were normal and we could ride them again.

Leave was liberal and there was plenty of interest in and around Cairo; we had spent very little money during the voyage and pay books were healthy.

My first visit was by tram to Mena, where I fell a victim to one of the many pleading dragomen, complete with camel. Someone once described the camel as an animal designed by a committee. Crouched on the sand, the camel, a supercilious beast, moves his head slowly from side to side with a contemptuous sneer, chewing his food with a sideways sway of his lower jaw and dribbling a green slime from his sloppy lips. Whatever is repulsive about a camel, there is seldom anything but beauty in the handwoven, beautifully coloured saddle bags, ending in tassels, slung across his back.

The rising of a camel from his crouch is a three stage process:

hind legs up, forelegs half up and then straighten up. The walking gait is not so bad to sit, if you sway with the stately measured tread, but the trot or amble is hades until you get the hang of it. Up I swayed along the curving road that leads to the first pyramid of Cheops. Only when I was right against this huge structure did I appreciate the enormity of its construction, the effort and the cruelty that must have gone into the production and placing of those huge blocks of stone. With Abdul's help I clambered up to the opening leading to the tomb, then guided by him and his flaring 'Magnesium ribbon Sargent McKenzie', down along the narrow passages into the king's chamber, with a stone sarcophagus robbed of its royal mummy and regalia centuries ago.

Then of course I had to climb to the top of the pyramid. It really was not climbing but clambering, shoved and hoisted from behind by Abdul, and the view from the top was worth while. The thin ribbon of green along the Mena Road and the fertile banks of the Nile, with the suddenness of the desert on each side and Cairo shimmering away to the Mokattam Hills beyond. Domes and minarets rising through the haze, with the green of the delta reaching to the horizon.

Beside me were the other two pyramids with their dwarfed daughter pyramids at their feet and just below, in contemplative silence, the Sphinx. There seemed little truth in the fable that Napoleon's cannon had blasted away the nose, but nearby, a little more than a hundred years before, he had driven the Mammelukes to disaster at the Battle of the Pyramids.

Coming down was a nightmare, as I tremble at heights. There I was 480 feet up with the steeply sloping side of the pyramid enticing me to disaster. I surrendered my cowardly body to Abdul, shut my eyes and made it. Such was my relief at feeling firm sand at last beneath my feet, that I suffered Abdul to mount me again on his wretched camel and amble down to the tram terminus. I passed him a handful of piastres, which he seized with poor grace and with what I learnt afterwards was a foul low curse in Arabic.

Cairo itself, both the old and the new city, was an unending entertainment and we always went about in small parties. In those days Cairo radiated from the Mohamet Ali Square, with a fine bronze equestrian statue of this Egyptian patriot set in the gardens. One side was commanded by the Opera House built to celebrate the opening of the Suez Canal and where Verdi's *Aida*, composed for the occasion, was first presented. Across the Gardens were two famous hotels, Shepheard's and the Continental. It was said that if you waited long enough at Shepheard's, you would sooner or later see all the crowned heads and V.I.P.'s in the world.

Only commissioned officers were permitted to enter Shepheard's, but from the pavement below we rankers could watch with envy the waiters with their red jackets, tarbooshes and baggy white pantaloons, as they served drinks around the tables above us.

Along the pavements were small tables and chairs, but no sooner would one sit down and order a drink than an endless stream of fly-specked touts would gather and, before our ordered drinks arrived, press sherbet and gazooza, a rather lovely name for lemonade, upon us. Others brought food, fruit, carpets, 'antikers', chairs, couches, fly whisks, rhinoceros hide whips, jewellery and dirty postcards. 'You likeit feelthy postcards, Sargent McKenzie?' These leering pests were the worst of the lot and the hardest to get rid of, except the baksheesh boys holding out their filthy hands and 'Gibit baksheesh, gibit baksheesh, Sargent McKenzie.' Then along would come a native policeman with his cane, which he would lay about and for a few minutes you would be left alone, and then it would all start again. Only in the seclusion of Groppi, a delightful garden cafe under the spreading Groppi tree, would you be left alone. The mouski, the bazaars of Cairo, were probably the most fascinating in the world. Despite the constant pestering by the big and little itinerant Arabs, we never tired of wandering down the narrow dark alleys. We watched the metal workers beating their silver and copper, the ivory carvers, the carpet weavers and the merchants offering from their narrow stalls all manner of strange goods and materials, some very beautiful, others just shoddy. The prospect of a purchase meant tiny cups of sweet Turkish coffee, cigarettes and then hard bargaining, but however low you beat them down, you realized later that you had paid too much.

If any sick had to be evacuated from our camp, they were loaded into our horse-drawn ambulance wagons and driven to the British hospital in the old Citadel, beside the Mosque of Mahomet Ali, the most imposing and commanding structure in Cairo. Our wagons were postilion driven. The near horse of each pair was saddled as well as harnessed and mounted by a driver with a large metal and leather leg guard on his right leg to defend him from the pole and the other horse, which he controlled with a short-handled whip. On the driver's seat of the vehicle rode the wagon orderly, who was responsible for the brakes. A drive through Cairo, in spite of the smells, was always good fun. The narrow streets were crowded with Arabs, camels, donkeys, goats and fowls, but the native policemen shouted and belted them aside to clear the way. Progress was slow but never monotonous, and when my detail as wagon orderly for the day came along, all went well on our journey into the Citadel.

The fun began on our way back; our route lay through the least reputable street in the disreputable portion of the city—the wazza, the red light area. As we turned into this narrow way, I had a front seat view of a most remarkable sight. From an upstairs balcony came sailing an iron bedstead complete with its streaming mosquito net canopy, like a bride eloping and leaping into the arms of her lover. Crash on to the roadway and then pandemonium. I jammed on the brakes, the driver pulled up his horse and for a few moments we watched while smoke began to curl from the buildings and girls in various dress and undress rushed out, shouting, to join the clamorous, congealing crowd. We had just room to turn and retreat as the shouting and yelling rose to a roar. We turned down another street as the smoke was billowing and fire carts were clanging and cleared out at the trot as the other streets were deserted.

We had witnessed the opening shot of the famous or infamous Battle of the Wazza.

A band of Australian soldiers, according to the New Zealanders (or a band of New Zealand soldiers, according to the Australians), had counter-attacked this brothel area in reparation for their disabilities. We learnt later that the battle went on for hours; as often as the fire hoses were adjusted they were slashed by the troops and it was the end of the day before the fires could be controlled and order restored. After that, the area was out of bounds for all troops, and because of this disturbance Australian troops in World War II encamped near Cairo.

The climate in Cairo over the winter months was ideal. Clear, windless, warm days under the cloudless blue of the sky, then the suddenness of night with its canopy of twinkling stars and a crisp keenness. Later we were to know the intense, dry heat of the summer, sometimes up to 120° in the shade, but it was never humid or heavy.

Christmas Day dawned and to greet us, outside many of our tents, were flowering plants blossoming in the sand. Later that morning the whole camp was paraded before a red-carpeted dais raised on the sand. There among a group of senior officers sat a rotund, paunchy man in a long black frock-coat and shiny black silk hat, all looking somewhat odd in the desert. It was the Hon. Sir George Reid, who had called to give us his blessing. When all were assembled he rose, still wearing his silk hat, and addressed us. Out from this great body came a high, squeaky voice—it was like an elephant giving birth to a field mouse.

Years later, when I read Alfred Deakin's *Federal Story*, I came across the most pungent description of this remarkable man:

'Even caricature has been unable to travesty his extraordinary appearance, his immense, unwieldy, jelly-like stomach, always threatening to break his waistcoat, his little legs apparently bowed under its weight to the verge of endurance, his thick neck rising behind his ears, rounding to his many-folded chin, a heavy German moustache concealing a mouth of considerable size from which there emanated a high-pitched voice rising to a shriek or sinking to a fawning, purring persuasion with a nasal twang.'

Among so many restless troops in those days before amplifiers, it was difficult to hear what he said, but I gathered it was some sort of pep talk, more 'bull' as one man said. As we broke off, each man received a small gilt box bearing the head of H.R.H. Princess Mary, as she then was, with her good wishes. Whatever we thought of George Reid, we did appreciate the Royal gift of chocolate. Extra rations of beer, turkey and plum pudding made the day reasonably cheerful on this, my first Christmas away from home. Later, however, the day was marred when the residents of Maadi came around seeking the plants which had disappeared overnight from their gardens.

On Sundays we rode over to the Helouan prison a few miles further up the Nile. When the prisoners had been locked in their cells, we were treated to a revel in their communal hot showers, very welcome after the morning cold douches in the frost behind hessian.

On New Year's night after returning from my weekly hot shower, I began to feel uneasy in my tummy. We all turned in early as none of our tent were on horse piquet and I soon fell asleep. Once you have adjusted the sand under your palliasse to the various curves of your body, such a bed is delightful after a heavy day. Soon I awoke with a deadly sick feeling and a real stomach ache. Fortunately I was sleeping next to the tent flap and could be sick outside by just rolling over. So constant in our life had become the background of strange and sometimes violent noises from the various animals, horses, donkeys and camels, which noisily regurgitate at ease, that my humble contribution disturbed none of my tent mates.

When mercifully reveille came at dawn, I just could not get up and reported sick. The medical officer on duty heard my story, poked me in the tummy, said I had appendicitis and would stay in my tent for observation. Soon the pain passed and I thoroughly enjoyed my day off duty and being waited upon. By evening I felt fit. A few days later I was sent across to an Australian General Hospital which had been established in Mena House at the foot of the pyramids. There I was examined by Colonel Fred Bird, who had been one of my surgical tutors at the Melbourne Hospital. His was a tall and most distinguished figure with the essence of persuasiveness and grace. 'Yes, my boy,' he said, 'you must have it out, I will arrange a bed for you in the next weekend.' Mr Bird had offered his honorary services to the British Army and had travelled in our convoy with the intention of joining the R.A.M.C. in the United Kingdom. When our division was diverted to Egypt he was attached to an Australian General Hospital as one of the Consultant Surgeons to the Mediterranean Expeditionary Force.

And so at Government expense I was operated upon and for a fortnight was washed and waited upon in a bed tucked away in the corner of the large dining hall in one of Egypt's exclusive hotels. At first the odd meals, including a supper of cocoa and porridge, and the disturbing washing hours were irksome, but after a few days I was comfortable and contented to wallow in the luxury of it all. For a doctor or a nurse to have his or her abdomen opened is an invaluable experience, for, until this happens, it is not possible to appreciate that one uses his abdominal muscles for every movement, including talking and smiling.

Before I was allowed out of bed my brother Jack walked into the hospital. I had no idea that he had enlisted as a medical officer in No. 2 Australian General Hospital, which had just arrived to take over Mena House. 'Hullo, Bill,' he said. 'Hullo, Bill,' I said, to the confusion of those standing by, and the relief of having him near me was wonderful. At his suggestion I transferred as a medical orderly to his unit and, as I was the only medical student in this hospital, which had been raised in New South Wales, the medical officers readily gave me every opportunity to carry on my clinical studies. I was taught to give anaesthetics, a new field to me, and one much less complicated and less efficient than nowadays. We gave an induction with Ethyl Chloride followed by closed or open Ether, or for surgery about the head or neck straight Chloroform, which fortunately has disappeared. My tutor, Major McKenzie, was a master of these various media and I became reasonably proficient. He recorded on paper my experience in anaesthesia and later this was accepted by the Melbourne University as exempting me from any further tuition.

Once a week I visited the Kasr el Aini Hospital in Cairo where the Senior Surgeon, Mr Madden, an Australian, worked on the accidents, wounds and infections that befell the Arabs, not the least serious and common of these being the camel bites on the shoulders of the boys who led them, many of which wounds were infected with tetanus.

Early in 1915 war with the Turks came closer, and in some remarkable way they had managed to drag four great metal pontoons across Sinai to the Suez Canal. One night between Tousoom and Serapeum, a crossing was attempted as a preliminary to an invasion of the delta. The Imperial troops on the Western bank had, however, been alerted and the warships in the Bitter Lakes joined in the battle; the effort failed with a dozen or so Turkish casualties and a retreat.

All training around Cairo became more intense and soon the Infantry camps at Mena and Zeitoun became more and more deserted as the troops moved out and embarked at Alexandria for Lemnos in the Aegean Sea. On Sunday, 25 April, came the news of the landing at Gallipoli and the welding of the Australians and the New Zealanders into the famous Army Corps, A.N.Z.A.C. The casualties were heavy and the Australian General Hospitals in Cairo soon began to fill. Colonel Bird, who had brought four Australian nurses with him, offered himself and his team to the Hospital Ship *Cecilia*, which with the *Gascon* was ferrying casualties between the Dardanelles and Alexandria, a distance of about 700 miles. Colonel Bird asked me if I would join him: I jumped at the chance and with my C.O.'s permission entrained for Alexandria, only to find the ship had not arrived, so I had to hang around for a few days until *Cecilia* tied up and unloaded the casualties. I began to feel uneasy: I had an infected hand and my tummy was awry. When Colonel Bird landed and saw me, 'My boy, you are sick; let me examine you.' I had dysentery, and dysentery is a disease that cannot be concealed for long. 'You can't come like that among all my wounded, my boy, you must go into hospital.' And so for a while it all fell through. As a patient with no battle wounds, I was sent back to Cairo in a hospital train and I felt rather foolish when I was admitted into a bed at the hospital that I had left such a short time before, but which now had moved from Mena House to Ghezirah Palace, alongside the Sporting Club on an island in the Nile.

This of course was in the pre-antibiotic days and the medical treatment of dysentery consisted of frequent draughts of sodium sulphate, fortunately less nauseous than its magnesium twin, epsom salts. Under this now outmoded attention I rapidly recovered and under conservative treatment my hand healed. Soon I was up and about, wearing the familiar blue jacket and trousers of the convalescent.

Across the road from our hospital was an open air variety show, the Abbe de Rose. One night another convalescent and I, without permission, went across. We were just enjoying the side-splitting antics of a tall, thin comedian dressed from neck to toe in skin-tight black when two military police appeared, imposing with their red caps and chain epaulettes. 'Where are your passes?' We had none. 'Come on, fall in outside,' and outside, with other A.W.L., we fell in and off we were marched across the Bulak Bridge, through Cairo, where from the various low haunts other M.P.'s had picked up drunks and debauchees. The motley, swaying, shouting, singing column was headed to the military prison at Abassia, a mile or so along the road to Heliopolis.

With little gentleness we were herded through the gates, which clanged and were locked behind us, then crowded into a large prison compound with a cement floor. There must have been more than fifty of us and we two were probably the only stone cold sober soldiers. We huddled in a corner while the shouting, the singing and the revolting sound of men being violently sick continued till a grating in the door was opened and the nozzle of a fire hose backed by a goodly pressure of water damped the ardour and the anger of us all.

Fortunately the warmth of the night and the crowding of human bodies took the chill off the dousing, but sitting on a concrete floor against a wet wall, in soaking hospital clothing, was one of my most miserable nights in many campaigns. Next morning, after a breakfast of sloppy porridge and lukewarm tea, we were picked up by an escort and transport from the hospital. I was paraded before the C.O., Colonel Martin: 'If you are fit enough to play, you are fit enough to work. Report for duty and you are under open arrest.' Later that afternoon I was detailed as a medical orderly with a batch of patients entraining for Alexandria. This meant another wretched sleepless night, but in the morning I was told that I had to serve on a troop-ship returning to England. This was a wonderful relief and a great surprise, as my father and mother were in London, and my heart was light when we embarked on the troop-ship *Ceramic* en route for the United Kingdom.

Whether there is a statute of limitations concerning military offences I do not know, but I heard nothing more of my crime, which is probably enshrined somewhere in the archives of the first A.I.F.—a recorded gaol-bird.

Chapter 5 Return to Study

There were many convalescent Cockneys on board and it was amusing to hear them talking in their rhyming slang, whole sentences with every substantive replaced by a rhyming word. This strange jargon has been recorded for more than a hundred years and may have developed from the earlier 'cant' of thieves, enabling them to talk secretly in front of other people. For instance, a man might say, 'I'm going round the Johnny Horner (corner) to the rubadubdub (pub) for a few pigs' ears (beers), then I'll grab my weeping willow (pillow) and have a bo peep (sleep).' Sometimes the rhyming phrases were abbreviated, which made it all the more difficult to understand. 'The godfers' for the god forbids (kids), 'my soap and' for my soap and water (daughter), 'the bubbling' for the bubbling brook (cook). Nicknames are of course fairly universal: all Greys are Dolly, Rhodes—Dusty, Clarks—Nobby, Redheads—Blue, and of course Murphys—Spud.

Early one morning we sailed into the Grand Harbour of Malta, an unforgettable memory on that calm, clear morning with the deep blue of the sea up to the towering cream cliffs of Valetta. Here nearly 400 years before had passed the finest hours of the Knights of the Most Venerable Order of St John of Jerusalem. The Grand Master, Jean Valette, with his 8,000 knights and members of the Order, had withstood the Great Siege by Suleimen's 30,000 fanatical Saracens during the burning summer months of 1565. At the final victory only 500 of the Order could stand on their feet. I was sent ashore to collect some medical stores and from the steps of the Cathedral of St John stood before the tomb of Valette, 'Worthy of Eternal Honour'.

We disembarked at Plymouth and after the harshness of the

desert, the softness of the English fields, the hedges and the villages of the Western Counties were like a soothing eyebath. We travelled in a hospital train and were attended by R.A.M.C. orderlies, who checked us all on the nominal roll. The orderlies in our compartment had a broad North Country dialect and seemed rather intimidated and confused by Australian soldiers, one of whom gave his rank as Acting Lance-Private's Batman. This was solemnly entered. 'Bah goom, do they 'ave thim in Australian Army?'

My father and mother were at Paddington Station to meet the train. It was nearly three years since I had seen them and for a few minutes none of us could speak. It was strange to see my father, who was organizing the hospital accommodation in the United Kingdom for the Australian soldiers, in the uniform of a Lieutenant-Colonel.

After a few formalities and when we had handed over our patients, I was given leave. We drove to our flat off Bayswater Road and dumped my gear. In the soft lingering twilight of the summer evening we drove through London. There is always only one first time and probably to every sentient person of British stock the first sight of London is most moving. It certainly was to me, as names and places of which I had read became suddenly real, like the realization of a dream. Down Park Lane, the homes of famous names and wealth facing the solemnity of great trees in Hyde Park, past the Duke of Wellington's house and down Piccadilly with the flower ladies holding out their bunches of violets at the foot of Eros. The Haymarket and round into the heart of the Empire, Trafalgar Square, with the fountains playing at the foot of Nelson's Column. Then past the gay, jaunty figure of Charles I on his charger, gazing eternally down Whitehall towards the window from which he stepped to his execution. Parliament House, Big Ben and the Abbey, down Victoria Street where the Australian Army Office was sited before the A.I.F. establishment at Horseferry Road nearby, around Buckingham Palace, softened in the fading light, up Constitution Hill and under Winged Victory to Hyde Park corner, back to the flat and so to bed, an ineffaceable memory.

A few days around some of the wonders of London, the lunch of steak, lark and kidney pie at Johnson's old Cheshire Cheese in Fleet Street, the Tower and the Galleries and then I had to report for duty.

I was posted as medical orderly to No. 1 Australian Hospital at Harefield Park in Middlesex, the private home of a patriotic Australian, set in acres of beautiful parkland with age-old oaks, elms and chestnuts. There I met up with two other medical students from Melbourne, also orderlies, and on our off-duty time we wandered over the lovely countryside. Across the village green, outside the Park gates, was the 'local', where we generally called, hot and weary, after our wanderings. Our first visit was a near disaster—we decided to have cider. At home in Melbourne cider had been a mild and pleasant drink, and with our thirst we called for a pint and we were served with draught. This was dynamite and fixed us for the rest of the day; after that we always stuck to beer!

Every second weekend I was free to return to our flat in London and together we drove into the Home Counties or walked around London. One of our favourite visits was to a cinema at Marble Arch, where Charlie Chaplin was always a delight. Back in Melbourne I had revelled in Chaplin's early silent black and white artistry, which I could enjoy for 3d. at the little Melba Theatre in Bourke Street. We usually had a little difficulty at the entrance, owing to our respective ranks—my father's crown and star and my arm bare of even one stripe. Officers and other ranks were not supposed to associate in places of amusement in London.

One Sunday we drove to Epping Forest for lunch. As the car stopped an elderly and beautiful lady leaning on a companion's arm walked slowly by. When she had passed Father said: 'That was Ellen Terry.'

One Saturday night there was a zeppelin raid, a mild affair compared with the blitz twenty-five years later, but some damage was done. On the Sunday afternoon we all went out to have a look and came to large hole just off Oxford Street. Leaning over the barricades keeping back the inquisitive crowd, I was just about to take a photo of the crater when a big bobby grabbed my arm. 'Here, Soldier, you must come along with me.' Father and Mother both protested my innocent intent, so he took them along also, and off we went to Bow Street police station. Father explained who he was, who I was and where we lived, and gave the phone number of our flat, which the Sergeant rang, but naturally as we were all out, there was no answer. Evidently I had offended against D.O.R.A.—the Defence of the Realm Act. It was all rather silly, as pictures of the damage had already appeared in the Sunday papers. There it was, however, and I seemed doomed to gaol for the second time. After about three hours of endeavour by my father in hunting around on a Sunday afternoon to verify our bona fides, we were allowed to go on our way, but without my camera. A few days later Scotland Yard rang to say they had developed the film, which had nothing of treachery or treason, and I could have this and the camera if I called for them. How many have had their films developed without charge by Scotland Yard?

Many of the stately homes in England and in Scotland had been thrown open to Australian soldiers. At the Headquarters in Victoria Street my father received a message from one of these in Scotland that an Australian soldier staying with them had become rather cranky and asked that someone be sent up to look after him or bring him back. As there was no one else available, I was detailed for this duty and to give me some semblance of authority I was appointed an Acting Lance-Sergeant, so for the time being I had risen from the lowest of ranks. I set off by the night train to Glasgow, changed on to the Oban line, changed again at Connel Ferry for Barcaldine on the west coast of Scotland, a little wayside station. I was met by a dogcart and a liveried driver, who chatted as we drove off a few miles to the lodge gates leading to a lovely old granite mansion set in a forest of firs. As I entered the great hall and Mr Ogilvie, my host, came forward to greet me, my military boots, not designed for rugs on the floor, literally let me down as my forward movements sent me flat on my back—a dramatic but not impressive entrance. Having had a rather unfortunate experience with one Australian soldier, the butler took me round to the servants' quarters for a cup of tea. While I was enjoying this the daughter of the house came in, sat beside me and chatted away asking questions about this and that in the most friendly way, but as I realized later, summing up this other Australian soldier as apparently an officer had been expected. Seemingly I was not too gauche as I was given a lovely room looking over the fir-covered hillside and invited to join them all at dinner.

While I was making the best of my sloppy uniform and my scanty kit, the other Australian soldier strolled into my room. He was obviously rather odd and started straight away on most intimate information about himself, but he was quite docile and when he heard I was a medical student he seemed to feel his troubles were over. I had a straight talk to him and told him that if he behaved himself and pulled his socks up I had authority for us to stay on a few days before we went back to London.

Our host, complete with kilt and highland evening dress, was piped in to dinner and all went well. My charge behaved perfectly normally and for a few days we drove around the lovely west Scotland countryside for picnics, the heather in bloom and the birds whirring from the stubble as we crossed the fields. One day at the little seaport of Oban, another to Ballachulish and Appin Ferry with its memories of *Kidnapped* and the Red Fox, through the pass of Glencoe with the lowering clouds lingering over the loneliness of this tragic vale and on to Fort William, the brutal area where Cumberland relentlessly pursued and slaughtered the fugitives from Culloden. It was all over too soon and we were back in London again.

There I was told that all medical students had been recalled to Australia to finish their courses and I was to sail in a few weeks on the old White Star liner, *Suevic*.

This ship and her sisters, the *Runic* and the *Medic*, had trooped in the Boer War, but in between the two wars *Suevic* had run on the rocks on the English coast and been abandoned. Later the fore portion had been cut off and left stranded, while the aft section had been towed into dock and fitted with a new bow.

The few remaining days of my leave were crowded with seeing as much of London as I could and buying my first motor bike. I was persuaded into buying for thirty pounds a second-hand J.A.P., which was fitted with a variable gear. Theoretically, by turning a handle, the driving belt was lowered or raised between two revolving discs, thus providing a variable driving ratio. All went well on my only trial run before embarking at Liverpool, then with pride I pushed my machine up the gangway and saw it safely lashed and covered.

Return to Study

So that I could act as dispenser on the ship, I was allowed to retain my (temporary) three stripes and was able to mess with those exalted N.C.O.'s, the Sergeants. We had several hundred Australian patients on board, convalescing from wounds and generally able to look after themselves, but it was a grim journey, with only one port of call between Liverpool and Melbourne around the Cape. At Dakar on the African coast we unloaded our one gun, which all ships carried in the submarine infested area. Then no sight of land for weeks, down to the roaring forties with the westerlies sweeping huge waves, roaring and rolling the ship day after day in the intense cold of that course and breaking many bottles in my dispensary.

Whenever the weather was fine and the ship reasonably steady, the troops would sprawl on the hatchways and over the decks, and we would soon hear the call: 'Housie, housie, who'll have a card? You come in a wheelbarrow and go away in a motor-car. Now lay it down thick and heavy, the more you put down the more you pick up.' And housie housie, now called bingo, would while away the weary hours. The players would buy a card for sixpence and when they were all out the promoter called the numbers as he drew them from a bag: 'legs eleven, clickety click, sixty six, the old cock and hen, number ten, Kelly's eye, number one, dinkey doo, twenty two', etc. until someone who had filled a line called out 'house' or, if all the lines had to be filled, 'full house' and collected his money, leaving a generous rake-off for the promoter. But Melbourne at last and it was good to be home, though it was raining.

I had about fifty pounds in my pay book and fortunately an aunt in South Yarra, where I stayed until I could look around and make arrangements for finishing my course. At that time diphtheria and scarlet fever were endemic and the infectious diseases hospital at Fairfield was always crowded. With so many doctors abroad with the A.I.F., as practically every able-bodied young medical graduate had enlisted, Dr Scholes, the Superintendent, was desperately short of staff. He had approached the Dean of the medical school and been given permission for final year students to help him, and another returned student, 'Treacle' Hurley, and I were appointed to Fairfield. This solved my accommodation and financial problems, as the salary was £3 a week with full keep.

There was, however, still the question of how I could fit in my necessary clinics at the Melbourne Hospital in the mornings and my various lectures in the afternoons, and carry out my duties at Fairfield. I came to an arrangement with Sir Harry Allen, the Dean, that if I attended my clinical mornings at the Hospital, I would be exempt from all lectures. Dr Scholes was agreeable to this, so all was well.

Here my motor bike promised to be of service but I had bought it without proper enquiry and with only one preliminary ride. I had failed to appreciate its temperament, and anyway I was unmechanically minded. Seldom did the wretched machine provide me with a return trip. All would seem well as I started off in the morning. This was still before the self-starting days and I had to run along beside my bike, firmly gripping the handlebars, and when the right explosion occurred I leapt on to the saddle and away I went. This sounds easy but was no mean feat. I soon mastered this part of it and went off full of hope, but seldom was this realized. Often before I arrived at the Hospital something went wrong and the bike stopped. In spite of all I could do I was at the mercy of the nearest garage and I finished the journey on foot or on the tram, depending on where the mishap took place. I knew and was known by all of the garages between Fairfield and the Hospital. The next day I would go in by public transport, pick up my now functioning bike on the way back and ride to Fairfield in temporary triumph. This uncertainty and expense were beyond me and I sold the wretched thing for £5.

My year at Fairfield was most valuable. Dr Scholes was a wonderful teacher and from him I learnt practically all there was to know about the common infectious diseases, as we were able to study their day to day course. We learnt many things about these diseases that are not recorded in text books. Diphtheria is a disease that affects the muscles of the heart and we soon realized that one of the ominous symptoms was the patient's calling for fizzy drinks—whether this was due to some sinking feeling or not, we always sent for the parents. I doubt whether a medical student today ever sees a case of clinical diphtheria or could handle that terrifying suffocating type and could relieve the distress by intubation.

So splendid was our clinical teaching in the hospital wards at the Melbourne and with our time for reading at Fairfield, we did not seem to suffer from the absence of any lectures, and when finals came and there were questions on scarlet fever in the medical paper, I found them less trouble than I had expected.

A few weeks later, as a doctor, I was appointed Resident Medical Officer at the Melbourne Hospital with a salary of £50 a year. Until a few years before, the residents were not paid but were allowed to pool the fees from certificates, attendances at court and other small perks, these amounting to about £60 a year for each resident. Then the Board of Management became magnanimous and decided that the residents should be paid £50 a year, but with a proviso that all outside fees must be returned to the Hospital.

Chapter 6   Private Practice

The Melbourne Hospital in Lonsdale Street had been built originally in 1846 and over the years expanded as the demands increased, until at the turn of the century it covered the area now taken over by the Queen Victoria Hospital. Then began the battle of the sites as more accommodation and more facilities were needed. The Pig Market site opposite the University in Parkville was proposed and debated but the diehards clung to the old site and won the day. With all the inconvenience of building the new hospital while it continued to function, the new slowly replaced the old. Only a small group of buildings on the Russell Street frontage remained, a pathology block and two wards for septic and refractory patients, 21 and 22. The new hospital had just been completed when I became a resident in 1918.

Within little more than twenty years the rebuilt hospital proved unsatisfactory and inadequate. At long last the Pig Market site, which had been granted some years before, was accepted and 'the Vision Splendid', as the architects postered it, began to rise. Soon after the outbreak of World War II this was completed, just in time to be taken over by the American Forces as No. 4 American General Hospital to accommodate the casualties from Guadalcanal and from the American camps around Melbourne.

The life of a resident medical officer in 1918 was vastly different from that of an R.M.O. nowadays at the Royal Melbourne Hospital, Parkville. It was, of course, a different age. None of the residents were married; indeed, a married—even an engaged—medical student or Resident was a museum piece. The resident staff consisted of a Medical Superintendent, a medical and a surgical Registrar and twelve junior residents. So sound and general was undergraduate medical training at that time that many medical students successfully entered general practice on graduation, but most sought a year's residency at a general hospital before doing so.

The Royal Australian Colleges had not been established and the relatively few graduates who intended to specialize studied for the Melbourne University post-graduate degrees in Medicine or Surgery, or both. Only after World War I was there a steady flow to the United Kingdom seeking postgraduate qualifications abroad, and during my residency only one Melbourne Hospital honorary surgeon possessed his English Fellowship. Besides the Melbourne Hospital, the Alfred and St Vincent's accepted students for their clinical studies and for years the Alfred Hospital had maintained the tradition founded by O'Hara and Hamilton Russell of appointing honorary surgeons only from among those with their English Fellowship.

The practice of medicine and surgery was simpler and more limited than is the case today, and less demanding. There was less specialization and there were fewer special departments. Modern diagnostic and laboratory investigations were relatively in their infancy compared with those now available and which have contributed so greatly to advances in medicine, but not necessarily to the development of the faculties of those who apply these findings to the welfare of their patients. With the exception of quinine for malaria and the arsenicals for syphilis, antibiotics were not available and medical therapy had advanced little, if at all, over the last fifty or a hundred years. Doctors wrote prescriptions based on a knowledge of their ingredients, their action and their dosage. The age of high-pressure salesmanship, with their proprietary medicines, had not dawned, nor was the mail cluttered with samples and expensive literature concerning 'Our latest ethical products'. (What happened to their unethical products I never found out.) But undoubtedly, in spite of all the modern commercial ballyhoo and waste paper, the advances in medical therapeutics and the benefits to the patients have been little short of miraculous.

So valuable was the training of a junior R.M.O. that these positions were keenly sought and gratefully accepted at £1 a week. We had one half day off duty each week and one weekend in three, from Saturday midday till Sunday night. On our days off we left the wards or the theatre only when our duties were completed, sometimes quite late in the day; we expected and accepted this.

It fell to my lot to be associated with one of the two remaining honorary physicians who had been appointed under the old system of subscribers' votes. Johnny Nihil, M.D. Durham, was a dear fellow, but he seldom seemed to notice students and I had ample opportunity to develop any teaching ability I may have had. On one of those rare days when Johnny decided to clinic to students, he selected a patient with kidney disease. After much waffling, he crystallized his approach to the subject: 'Gentlemen, Great Britain is fighting for her very existence at this moment in Europe. I have told you about a red kidney and about a pale white kidney and I regret, for patriotic reasons, there is not a blue kidney, then we could have waved the good old red, white and blue. Ha. Ha. Ha.' He then moved on to the next case and, forgetting about the students, he turned to the Sister: 'Let us have a look at the feet and legs, please Sister', then to the patient: 'take a breath in and out as if sighing' and after a few moments of contemplative application of his monaural wooden stethoscope, he returned this to his pocket, thanked the Sister and walked out.

Johnny was always bright and cheerful and to be present at a ward conference between Johnny and another honorary was the week's brightest moment. One of our patients developed a rash and Johnny summoned Jockey Noyes, the skin specialist, in consultation. Jockey had suffered a head injury while hunting in his younger days, and while it had in no way impaired his mobility, it had accelerated and somewhat confused his mental processes and speech mechanism, until without finishing a sentence he would hurry on to the middle of the next one. As Johnny Nihil always talked at the same time, little light was thrown upon the problem, but everyone seemed happy and satisfied and each consultant politely thanked the other, both at the same time, for his advice and help.

Johnny Nihil was an exception; most of the Honoraries were first-class clinical teachers and engaged in active practice. Some had been general practitioners before taking higher degrees and specializing in medicine or surgery, and it was thanks to my honoraries in the absence of any lectures, that I had been able to pass my finals. J. F. Wilkinson, a contemporary of my father, was outstanding in his practical approach to a patient. 'Wilkie' had commenced practice at Bright, in the rugged north east of Victoria, where he had pioneered the Buffalo Plateau long before there was any road up the mountain. In a busy general practice, he had studied for and obtained his M.D., then came to Melbourne and was appointed an honorary out-patient physician to the Melbourne Hospital and a demonstrator in biochemistry at the Melbourne University. He was a sound general physician, with a keen interest in diabetes and other metabolic diseases. Wilkie was rather short, wore whiskers and a neat beard, and his blue eyes twinkled in quiet amusement whenever a student made a gaffe.

Gracious and gentle Dickie Stawell, another contemporary of my father, always had a large student following. He was particularly interested in neurology and was masterly in training his students to observe and examine the patient with the faculties 'God has given you'. He was intolerant of a student who could not express himself in precise English. I well remember the day when he asked me to examine a patient. 'Shall I do a Babinski, sir?' I said. He looked at me with a sad expression and in his quiet, pained voice, he replied: 'Do a Babinski? Do a Babinski? What I presume you mean, sir, is will you elicit Babinski's phenomenon.'

Sydney Sewell also leaned to neurology and was a master teacher of all clinical investigations and their significance. He could be bitingly sarcastic, cooing like a dove with his silky voice, then bang, exposing the student's stupidity, but inviting no resentment as next minute he would praise and smile.

On the surgical side I was associated for a short time with Mr Fred Bird, who had been so good to me in the Middle East during the war. Always immaculate and debonair, he would bow to the Sister and greet his resident with a handshake and a smile as if this meeting was all he needed to complete his day's happiness. While he was operating, he would frequently refer to the resident assisting him: 'I think I should do this, don't you, Doctor?' as if referring to a colleague. Z. Zwar was a wonderfully sound general surgeon, not spectacular but always gentle, and a stickler for intelligent assistance from his resident and the theatre staff. He always came in for his emergencies and, demanding the highest standard for after-care for his patients, achieved excellent results.

When I look back and realize that very few blood transfusions were ever given, that antibiotics were unknown and that clean interval surgery nearly always healed by first intention, I can appreciate what master surgeons these men were and how meticulously clean and careful was their technique and how sound their judgement.

A month with Frank Andrew in the ear, nose and throat wards was exacting. After finishing the out-patients at the end of the afternoon, he would commence operating in the theatre about 6 o'clock. Meals meant nothing to him but he required the assistance of his hungry residents sometimes till after ten at night. His keenness and energy seemed inexhaustible. A month with a gynaecologist, Reggie Morrison, was a relaxation after my tour with Frank Andrew. Reggie, the perfect gentleman, was never hurried in his ward or in the theatre, but meticulous in his quiet attention to every detail and to decency.

My training under these men, together with two months in casualty and frequent calls for anaesthetics, made an excellent year of general training. We were expected to carry out most of our laboratory examinations and surgeons were generous in passing to us, under their help and supervision, many of the straightforward operations.

With this experience, many of the residents entered general practice with confidence. Those who wished to specialize applied for a second year resident appointment as Registrars, or for one or other of the special hospitals. I had always been fond of children and during the last few years of my course I had decided to practise my profession in paediatrics; fortunately, at the end of my year at the Melbourne Hospital, I was appointed as a resident at the Children's Hospital.

This hospital had been established on the walled home site of Sir Redmond Barry in Pelham Street, Carlton, and at the time consisted of two double-storeyed wards, one medical and one surgical. The residents' quarters were upstairs in the administration block, which also included Matron's flat. There was a busy outpatient department, a nursing home, a pathology block and a small isolation ward. In all, between two and three hundred beds and cots were available in the wards and on their large balconies. To care for these were six in-patient honoraries, an honorary out-patient staff and four residents, which included the Senior Medical Officer or Superintendent. When I joined the resident staff, Dr Vera Scantlebury, who later contributed so splendidly to the welfare of infants, was the Medical Superintendent, the other two residents were women—Dr Annie Bennett and Dr Bertha Donaldson.

Of the honoraries, two—Rowden White and Stewart Ferguson —were exclusively physicians, Willie Wood a surgeon and Hobill Cole, Alan Mackay and Jeffreys Wood were surgeons and physicians. That dynamic person, Harry Douglas Stephens, was here, there and everywhere, although his official appointment was out-patient surgeon. Presiding over the laboratory was that doyen of pathologists and master of the bon mot, Reggie Webster. Occasionally, as from another world, would be seen an odd figure wandering round the hospital. This was Peter Bennie, bespectacled, bearded, and in a long black frock-coat, who had at one time been an honorary surgeon and pioneered many variations of the Thomas splint.

Hobill Cole, Stewart Ferguson, Harry Stephens and Jeffreys Wood were the only medical men in Victoria devoting their attention exclusively to children, and they all had very large practices as consultants and as private practitioners. Based on their extensive experiences, they were all excellent teachers.

Infant mortality until early in the century was a persistently distressing figure, mainly due to the dangers of artificial feeding. With the development of the science of nutrition, the pendulum began to swing and by the twenties the position had considerably improved. Fortunately those who taught at the Children's Hospital brought their sound common sense to bear on the scientific advancements and were not enmeshed in the minutiae of mathematical detail and decimals. These emerged in a later era when the pendulum swung into the phase of fussing about normal function, to the detriment of the child, the tiresome distress of the mother, and the baby was hardly considered as a human individual but merely as a graph or a statistic.

To attempt to adjust a child to a line or a graph based on statistics may bring about untold harm. Lord Horder expressed this so well: 'I have never, like some folk, regarded the way of health as a sort of tightrope along which we make a slow, intrepidating progress, the least bias to this or that side not immediately corrected or corrected too slowly, and we plunge headlong into an abyss. . . . The man who talks to you about the secrets of good health is either a crank or has something to sell. There is no mystery about health, it is not masonic.'

Later, as so often happens, commerce and salesmanship hopped on the bandwagon of science, peddling all kinds of expensive and unnecessary foods, many of which frustrated the development of digestion in the infant and defied the necessity for teeth. Even breast-feeding was subject to the mastery of mathematics, being repeatedly interrupted for reference to the scales. After all, as the advertisement says, 'Mother knows best.'

Possibly this commercialized answer to a simple problem and this fussing about normal function have been factors in the appearance of certain odd nervous and social problems of young children in those families which have been bent or broken before intense salesmanship, the impact of the attractively advertised tin or carton and the lure of expensive and often inaccurate baby scales.

There was always a variety of interest in the wards and in the out-patients, but the exciting days were the 'bloody Wednesdays'— the tonsils and adenoid sessions in the out-patient department. Hordes of unsuspecting children and their mothers were gathered in a large room awaiting the attention of the specialist. When he arrived, there began a scene reminiscent of the grim days of the commune. Presiding over the shambles was Sister Thomas, a squat, middle-aged figure always sniffling. She would enter the room, pick up the first victim, and direct the mother to the post-operative room, around the walls of which stood low, padded benches. These were the days of the guillotine under ethyl chloride, and within a few minutes a bloody bundle, wrapped in a gory sheet, was placed beside the anxious, waiting parent, who was ordered by Sister Thom to 'keep an eye on him, Mother, he's all right'. Rapidly the waiting-room thinned out as the other room became crowded with crying children and weeping mothers, but by the afternoon all was clear, taxis and other conveyances had removed the victims. It was really surprising that any post-operative worries were very exceptional and only once do I remember a difficult situation.

By some error a small boy requiring another operation had arrived among the tonsil victims and, when a vacancy occurred in the mass procedure of the afternoon surgery, he was picked up by Sister Thom and cast upon the operating table. As usual, another bleeding bundle was soon carried out to the mother, who seemed nonplussed at the blood about the head of her little son. Before Sister had disappeared on her way for the next victim, she was challenged, 'Do they always bleed like this, Sister, when they're circumcised?' 'He's all right, I tell you,' said Thom and waddled back to the theatre, where she explained the mishap to the surgeon, a man of deft technique and infinite resource. Shedding his gory gown, he went out to the bewildered mother and explained that, 'under the anaesthetic his breathing was bad. We had to clear his airway and he's now all right. Later on we will be able to circumcise him in safety.' Her gratitude was very moving.

Some years later a somewhat similar mishap occurred at the Melbourne Hospital when a Chinese interpreter had his tonsils removed before he could explain that he had come to the Hospital only to assist a fellow countryman who could not speak English. In the excitement of the occasion the interpreter had lapsed into his native tongue, which no one could understand.

When I was a resident, patients with bone and joint tubercle filled many of the surgical beds, as the Orthopaedic Hospital at Frankston was not built until some years later. These children with distorted hips and spines were long-stay patients.

At the end of the year, Dr Scantlebury went overseas and the other residents entered general practice. I was invited to stay on as Medical Superintendent at £250 a year, and together with the new residents, one lady and three men, made up a very happy family. As the honorary surgeons were generous to me with their surgery, this year proved excellent training for my practice and I began to study for my M.D. At the end of my year, Dr Hobill Cole invited me to become his assistant in his large private practice. For years it had been the policy of this generous gentleman to take under his wing and into his home young men who intended to devote their careers to children. Harry Stephens, Walter Summons and Reggie Webster had preceded me. This was a wonderful opportunity, which I gratefully accepted, and I moved into the Cole ménage at the corner of Elgin and Rathdowne

Streets, Carlton, a most interesting home. Dr Cole possessed a valuable collection of Australiana, and also had collected books published in England during the sixties of the last century, beautifully illustrated with woodcuts by Sandys, Birket-Foster, Tenniel and others.

In 1919, as an aftermath of the war, a pandemic of virulent influenza was raging, with all doctors taxed to the limit irrespective of any specialty, and the Exhibition Building converted into an emergency hospital. Within a few hours of my arrival at Dr Cole's home, I was called to a house in North Carlton. I hopped on a cable-tram, which at that time passed our door, found the address in North Carlton and was led into a small, dark back room almost filled by a female huddled in bed. When the light was switched on, I found a stout, cyanosed and gasping young woman, obviously very ill with influenzal pneumonia. This was before the days of antibiotics, so I ordered the then recognized treatment for my patient and gave a grave outlook to the anxious parents.

No sooner had I returned than the phone rang and an agitated male voice asked me, 'How is Miss Austral?' I said I knew no one of that name. 'But I have been told that you have just attended to her.'

'I'm sorry,' I said, 'there is some mistake. I have just visited Miss Florence Fawaz.'

'Don't you know who she is?' he almost shouted. 'Your patient is Florence Austral, one of the greatest dramatic sopranos, and she is to give a concert in the Melbourne Town Hall tomorrow night before she leaves for abroad.'

'I'm afraid she won't be singing in any earthly Town Hall tomorrow night,' I replied. 'She is really desperately ill.'

'Oh God, what will I do? What will I do?'

As far as I could hear this rhetorical question was unanswered and he hung up. Florence Austral did not sing in the Melbourne Town Hall next night, but as a great Wagnerian artist she sang and gave delight in the opera houses of the Old World for many years afterwards.

Dr Cole had a considerable practice among the many Chinese families living in Little Bourke Street and I was often called to attend their children. The atmosphere of their dark houses was impregnated with the mingling scent from bananas, dried food and fish, smoked pork, ginger, onions, lichee nuts and incense—all contributing their quota to a strong and not unpleasant memory. The children were delightful patients and the smiling parents always most grateful and generous. Only with difficulty could I escape without some titbit pressed into my hand or secreted in my bag. I made many friends among these people, who worshipped Frank Hobill Cole.

In Lister House I had my introduction to consultant practice. Dr Cole's ethical standards, his kindliness towards his patients and his meticulous guarding of the patients' confidence in their general practitioners who sought his opinion and guidance, were inspiring examples to me. In his considerable surgical practice I either gave the anaesthetic or, if the patient's own doctor was not available, assisted him. There could have been no more impressive experience for a young man to start practice than such an association with his senior, rightly held in the highest regard and respect by his colleagues and beloved by his patients.

One evening I was called by Dickie Berry, my old anatomy professor, to see one of his children. Few, if any, of us students had known Dickie as anything but a humourless anatomist among cadavers and an anthropologist among skulls; it never occurred to us that he was a family man. But from the first moment I entered his home in the University Grounds, his profile changed and his human and humorous character was apparent. Fortunately, as usually happens with sick youngsters, the girl did well and we became close friends, a relationship that survived occasional duels at bridge between our two families. I was appointed one of his four demonstrators in anatomy at £50 a year and with the study essential in any teaching I began really to know my subject and realized for the first time how fortunate I had been to pass my anatomy examination with my limited knowledge at that time.

About this time I became engaged to Dorothy, a sister at the Children's Hospital. Although the conditions were vastly different from those of today, nursing positions were eagerly sought at this hospital. For the first year of her training, a probationer nurse paid a ten guinea premium and received no salary, during the second year she received five shillings a week, and 7/6 during her third and final year. The nurses were on duty seventy-two hours each week, with one day off duty from 6 p.m. one evening to 10 p.m. the following night. At her final examination Dorothy was awarded the Madge Kelly Prize, the highest award for a nurse in Victoria. Some years later our daughter Pat, a nurse at the Royal Melbourne Hospital, won the same prize.

It was during this period that I achieved obstetrical fame. During a holiday crossing to Tasmania, Bass Strait was at its worst, the old *Loogana* was pitching and rolling and I was horribly sick. In the throes of my misery, sleepless and helpless in my bunk, there was a knock on my cabin door at some hour beyond my regard for time. A stewardess entered and asked if I was a doctor. 'Yes,' I murmured, 'but I am beyond medical aid.' 'There is a lady very ill down in the steerage, will you please come?' I went and followed her down the swaying passage smelling of food and rubber, pausing every now and then to demonstrate that I also was very ill. In a stuffy cabin I was able to control my heaving stomach long enough to diagnose the obvious condition—a well advanced labour—then rush out to the corridor for further relief, but my stomach had been emptied long since. When I was able to return, all was over—lying in the bed was a strange object, a deflated, pale blue balloon, something I had never seen delivered during my student days. The stewardess looked at me for guidance, I looked at her for an explanation, then a wriggling solved the problem: a baby born within a caul. This was a most fortuitous circumstance, according to the old wives' tale that a baby born with a caul will never be drowned (was not David Copperfield born with this immunity?). A pair of nail scissors from a table nearby soon produced a crying baby from his envelopment and all went well with the mother and her little son, but not so with my poor sore stomach.

Certainly I had delivered babies during my course, but as this was the only woman I have confined (if you can call it that) since graduation, I can justly claim as a doctor a record of 100 per cent of mothers and babies alive and well, all babies boys, no anaesthetics, no complications. How we can lie with statistics! Somewhere in this world, if he is still alive, is an aged gentleman, bearing one of my names as a grateful compliment from a deluded mother who, when discussing her confinement with others, was proud of the skill and honorary attention of a leading obstetrician.

After I had been with Dr Cole for two years, Dorothy and I

were married. As rooms in Collins Street were beyond our means, I decided to establish a children's practice in one of the suburbs. We rented an unfurnished house in Burke Road near the Camberwell Junction for £3 a week, spent all but £67 of our savings on furniture and surgery equipment and ventured beyond the safeties of the past.

Naturally, for some time the development of a children's practice in a suburb surrounded by general practitioners was slow, but Dr Cole had encouraged others to help me and fortunately I was able to obtain some insurance examinations at the then fee of one guinea. We had no car and I travelled on foot, by tram and train, and at times, when it was absolutely necessary, by taxi.

I had been appointed as surgical clinical assistant to Rupert Downes at the Children's Hospital. As the clinic on Monday and Thursday mornings commenced at 9 a.m., this meant leaving home about 8 a.m., an excellent discipline in starting the day's work early. Gradually the practice developed and I was able to share rooms at No. 12 Collins Street with Dr Stewart Cowan, an old school and Trinity friend, and when the Alfred Hospital established a Children's Department, an honorary appointment to this service was a milestone.

One of the most heartening compliments a medical man can receive is a request from a colleague for his attention. Whenever my colleagues, however senior to me, paid me this compliment, I never experienced any intrusion of their own ideas, but they always most kindly and loyally carried out my advice.

Someone once said that it is a good idea to have an urchin at the edge of a crowd telling you that your crown is not quite straight. One morning when I arrived early in my rooms before the attendant, the bell rang. I answered the door to an elderly lady, who said: 'Are you the doctor?'

'Yes,' I replied. And she began then and there in the doorway to reel off many of her female ailments. 'Excuse me,' I interrupted her, 'you should consult another doctor. I look after children.'

'That's all right,' she said. 'I suppose you must make a start somewhere!'

After a few years, with the aid of the bank, we were able to move to a larger property on top of the Burke Road hill, where there was plenty of room for our two daughters and their friends to play. On Saturdays we had our tennis parties with Colin Macdonald, Gerry Ashton, Bert Coates, Heaton Clark, Theo Frank and Geoff Pennington and other good friends who have since passed on. Generally on Sunday mornings, with Frank Tate, Ron Stott and Colin Macdonald, we were on the first tee at Metropolitan Golf Course by 9 o'clock.

I had moved my rooms to 32 Collins Street. One morning there came a little patient holding the hand of a heavily built man. I seemed to recognize him but could not place him till I remembered that I had seen him as 'Doc Rowe' doing some remarkable conjuring at a smoke night. After I had given my attention to the patient, I asked the man to tell me something of his conjuring tricks and by arrangement we began my education in the art of deception. Many of the conjuring tricks performed on the stage use elaborate equipment but Doc Rowe was wonderful with his sleight of hand. Soon I was fairly proficient in the basic manipulations associated with card-sharping, swallowing ten razor blades then producing them strung on a long thread, tearing paper to shreds and restoring it *in situ*, multiplying billiard balls, producing cigarettes from the air and then causing them to vanish, the evergreen trick with metal rings that join themselves in the air and then become separated, and many other wonders that were really very simple.

Doc Rowe explained that the quickness of hand need never deceive the eye if you knew when and where to look, but the art of sleight of hand is to distract the eye at the critical moment by patter, by gesture, by an extraneous movement elsewhere, or by a noise such as firing a pistol. He told me of Chung Ling Soo, one of the really great conjurors. As a youth this man, with the name of a Scot, had the ambition to be a conjuror but his patter was pathetic and commanded no one's attention, so he hit on the brilliant idea of not saying a word, but appearing in a distracting costume. I remembered seeing Chung Ling Soo on the Tivoli stage; he entered slowly and silently, dressed in long, flamboyant, flowing Chinese robes, he paused near the front of the stage, slowly turned right round to show that he was alone and bowed low to the audience. As he stepped aside, there were two little Chinese children. It looked a miracle but then I learned that, in spite of his apparent bulk in the robes, he was really a slight man and that these children had clung to a belt around his waist as he walked slowly on to the stage. When he bowed low, they simply stood down. Each Chinese child moved silently to a side of the stage and when the man himself was about to bring about a coup, the children would make some movements and, such was the arresting brilliance of their robes, that the attention of the audience was immediately distracted, at least momentarily, which was all he needed, and the deception was achieved.

For years I had a good deal of fun with a number of simple illusions, but as I had learnt to false deal, false shuffle and deal four aces, I have declined ever since to play poker and have remained faithful to bridge according to Culbertson. When the paper reported a mishap when doing the swallowed razor blade trick, my apprehensive wife successfully implored me never to do it again.

Chapter 7 Between the Wars

Colonel Rupert Downes, with whom I was associated at the Children's Hospital, was D.D.M.S., the Senior Army Medical Officer in Victoria. His military career began as a trumpeter in Sir Rupert Clarke's private artillery, 'The Rupertswood Battery'. In World War I Downes was the youngest Lieutenant-Colonel and held high medical commands during the Palestine Campaign. For some time after the war ended it was difficult to persuade medical men to serve with the voluntary Citizen Military Forces (had we not just won the war that was to end all wars?). Many of those who had served with the A.I.F. felt that they had done their bit—others who had not experienced that privilege could not see any point in 'playing round with soldiers', but to me after my brief experience in the ranks, where I had learnt to be led, the opportunity to be a commissioned officer was irresistible and in 1923 I joined the Army Medical Corps as a provisional Captain in a Cavalry Field Ambulance. Oddly enough, during all my military service, I have never received a parchment or paper notifying me that I held the Sovereign's commission. There were only two other officers on strength in my unit, Lieutenant-Colonel Teddy White, the Commanding Officer, and Major Eric Gutteridge as his second in command. I was the one junior officer and my seniors naturally looked to me to get on with the job and fortunately we had a first-class warrant officer, who had all the answers and taught me what I should know and do.

The cavalry units were enlisted from the country areas, most of the men bringing their own horses to camp; practically all the officers had served in Palestine during the war and the annual camps were an unending delight of good comradeship. After the day's strenuous exercises, the good hearty fun and games of a cavalry mess at night, with the old campaigning songs shouted to the roof, were something always to remember.

During the year we attended night parades every fortnight, went on weekend bivouacs and conducted tactical exercises without troops. We fought all over the Mornington and Bellarine peninsulas, we defended Melbourne from the Dividing Ranges and from the foothills of Mount Macedon, and had a strenuous but thoroughly enjoyable time. Although our exercises were based on the lessons of World War I, so fundamental had been the principles that later when we were challenged in the desert, in the mountains and in the jungle, we realized how sound had been our training under the direction of Rupert Downes.

After a couple of years, having passed the examination for Major, I was appointed to command the Cavalry Divisional Hygiene Section, probably the smallest command in the Army: one officer (myself), seven N.C.O.'s (all specialists) and thirteen other ranks. We were responsible for supervision and instruction in the Divisional Hygiene facilities and although to some I was known as Dan, Dan the Sanitary Man, our yellow armbands gave us some standing. We learnt and taught how to improvise the disposal of wet and dry garbage, including the menacing horse manure, to improvise incinerators and latrines, to build grease-traps, to destroy mosquitoes and flies and to render filthy water safe to drink. It was all rather interesting.

In 1927 it fell to the lot of my unit to attend the official opening of Federal Parliament House in Canberra. H.R.H. the Duke of York, later King George VI, accompanied by his Duchess, now the charming Queen Mother, performed this ceremony, as his father had done at the Proclamation of the Australian Commonwealth in 1901.

My unit was detailed to supervise the emergency conservancy arrangements for the many thousands of visitors who were expected to camp in the area during the week of the celebrations. Such, however, is the power of the press, which throughout Australia reiterated 'the primitive and inadequate accommodation available', that instead of the 60,000 to 70,000 expected, barely 6,000 visitors attended and our task was simple. We were housed in tents about the grounds of the Telopea Park School and the only hardship was the grim impact of the cold shower as we shivered behind hessian screens early on those May mornings.

There were two memorable occasions during that week. The brilliant crisp sunshine of an early morning glowing on the white starkness of the Houses of Parliament, the steps crowded with ambassadorial and service colour, the dignity of the Guard and the bandsmen, while Dame Nellie Melba from the top step led the singing of the National Anthem.

The military review next day had its moments. Rehearsals had been conducted, during which the magnificent black charger for the Duke had been ridden on to the parade ground with no sign of uneasiness, while bands blared, troops marched past with glittering fixed bayonets and the guns fired their salutes.

On the afternoon of the ceremony, however, when the troops were all drawn up, as the Duke with his escort rode to the saluting base, at the first note of the National Anthem suddenly the black horse reared almost erect. There was a gasp, a hush, then a rush to save the frail rider, and Colonel Farr, in charge of the parade, put his arm around the Duke and helped him to the ground. Farr then mounted H.R.H. on his own horse and all went well, but it had been an anxious moment.

There were other activities available for medical men who had the time and the inclination to share in them. We had our medicos' cricket team, a team of keen if not very expert cricketers. On Wednesday afternoons we played matches with the various Club elevens and some of the public schools. From behind the wickets I had known many slow bowlers, but among our medicos we had the slowest of slow bowlers in Dave Roseby, with his gentle movement to the wicket and his dilatory and deceptive high trajectory ball. So reluctant seemed the ball to reach the other end that the batsmen, unaccustomed to this tempo, became exasperated and impatient of its arrival, and hastening to meet it, were often stumped, or, tired of waiting, made a mishit. Dave always collected a bagful of wickets, in which I, as 'keeper, was privileged to share.

The Melbourne Medical Society was active at this time. Visits with our wives were made to various industries and other places of interest about Melbourne and the nearby country. Some years before, Dr Springthorpe had organized a medical hare and hounds pack in this Society. After covering a few miles of the countryside, the pack gathered at the Old England Hotel at Heidelberg to recover that which they had lost en route, before sitting down to a good dinner. But after a few years of this jollity the pack disbanded.

We paid an annual subscription of one guinea but as the expenses of our activities were practically nil and as there were always a number of members who could not attend the annual dinner of the Society held at the Windsor Hotel, this was provided and excellently provisioned from our subscriptions. In 1935 Dr Mark Gardner was our president, and representatives of the legal profession our guests. Mark gave a most entertaining address on medicine and the law and concluded with a suggestion that a medico-legal society be formed next year, along the lines of similar societies in the United Kingdom. This was the genesis of a society which, with alternate medical and legal presidents and an honorary secretary from each of the professions, is still very active.

The first address before this Society was delivered by Professor Wood Jones, who had succeeded Berry in the Chair of Anatomy. Freddie Wood Jones was a most remarkable man, and, without a note, could hold an audience enthralled on a diverse range of topics. On this occasion he chose the subject of hanging, its history, its technique and some of its notorious victims. He concluded by recommending a submental knot based on his anatomical mastery as being the most certain and humane method. Questions were invited and, as usual at any medical meeting, one of the oldest members, Dr Ostemeyer, who because of his deafness always sat on the aisle in the front row, violently criticized Wood Jones for his comments on the Resurrectionists, Burke and Hare of Edinburgh and their association with Dr Knox. As with practically every argument or bout in which he took part, however, Freddie Wood Jones was declared the winner.

Membership of the Branch Council of the British Medical Association provided an interesting insight into the administrative and medico-political problems of a professional association. Perhaps the most interesting personality on the Council was our honorary treasurer, 'Mollie'. Dr Mollison was the Government Pathologist and as such appeared, as did his English counterpart, Spilsbury, in all the famous and infamous murder trials. His benign, round and ruddy cherub face, crowned with fluffy white hair, gave an authority to his evidence based on years of experience. The sight of Mollie, with a great waterproof apron, thick red rubber gloves and gumboots, quietly conducting a most unpleasant post-mortem examination, while softly murmuring his progressive findings to the recorder, was something to remember. I heard Mollie present his fiftieth unbroken annual financial statement to the Council. He always spoke so softly in his gentle voice that few beyond those close to him heard his words, but no one ever asked a question. Such was Mollie.

The ability to chair a meeting efficiently is not given to many medical men, but in John Newman-Morris and later in Cecil Colville, we had ideal chairmen, and only once did I hear one of them challenged. There was a long agenda and as there was a quorum present, John Newman-Morris opened the meeting a few minutes before 8 o'clock. Apologies were received and the minutes had just been read and confirmed when the clock struck the hour. Dr Kenny, a stickler for procedure, who had been present all the time, rose to a point of order and informed the Chairman that, as 8 o'clock was the official time of the meeting, all previous business was out of order and insisted that the meeting begin again. Of course he was quite right, as the Chairman conceded.

The British Medical Association in Australia was a powerful organization—more than 90 per cent of registered medical practitioners were members of this voluntary body. A registered medical practitioner may legally practise whether he is a member of his professional association or not, but the almost universal voluntary acceptance of membership provides its solidarity. Only while such solidarity is sustained is it possible to resist successfully any intrusion into the essential doctor-patient relationhip by a government or any other powerful body. Where such intrusion has been permitted, the standard of medical practice and the welfare of the patient and the practitioner have suffered.

There was and still is the popular gibe encouraged by Bernard Shaw's *Doctor's Dilemma* of a great trade union, but a professional association differs fundamentally from a trade union, which I understand is concerned solely with the welfare of its members. The British Medical Association—or, as it has now become, the Australian Medical Association—not only safeguards the interests of its members but also demands a standard of behaviour and service in relation to the community.

Another interesting opportunity that came my way was membership of the Medical Board, a Statutory Body responsible for the standard of medical practice in the State and for the registration of those persons fulfilling the requirements of the Medical Act of Victoria, a Sovereign State in this respect as in minor details these Acts vary in each State. Only with such registration can a person legally claim to be a medical practitioner, sue for fees or prescribe certain scheduled drugs. After due enquiry, the Medical Board has the power to deregister any person found guilty before it of infamous conduct in a professional respect as specified in the Act. Later, after World War II, the flood of migrants into Australia bore on its waves many applicants for registration who came from foreign medical schools but not coming within the requirements of our Medical Act, and attacks were made on the Medical Board for not exercising discretionary powers, which of course it did not possess.

In the mid-thirties I was invited by the A.B.C. to give a weekly broadcast to schools on health and hygiene; these were to be of fifteen minutes at noon on Mondays throughout each school term. This was an interesting commission but required a deal of preparation, as each script had to be typewritten and submitted for approval two weeks before the broadcast. Personally I find it more difficult to give a fifteen-minute talk than to speak for half an hour or more.

My session came on just after the midday weather reports and I arrived in the studio before these were concluded. On one eventful day the commentator's mind was wandering a little and I heard him give the rain as 'Sale 120 inches, Maffra 130 inches, Bairnsdale 90 inches.' Just then the control reminded him that these should be points and, turning his head only slightly aside, his 'Lord, I'm flooding the bloody place' must have gone out over the air.

How humiliating it can be to watch others listen to a record of your voice and occasionally I would record my school talks and visit a school to watch the youngsters' reactions. At the beginning all would sit up with their exercise books and pencils poised, when the talk began they made notes, but after a few minutes one or two would obviously lose interest and begin to tease those next to them who seemed to be following what was said. At the end of the session I was never quite sure how much of my talk had really gone across to them, but I enjoyed those broadcasts, which ceased only with World War II.

In 1928 I was invited to become a member of the Melbourne Beef Steak Club. During the 1770s a Club of this name had been established in London, and ours was founded in 1886 when a small group of congenial companions gathered together once a month for food and fellowship. We have no clubrooms and when I joined we dined in a private room at the Grand (now the Windsor) Hotel, later at the Oriental Hotel and finally at University House. Each member in turn is Master at the dinner which comprises soup, two large selected sirloins of beef, cheese and coffee with wines and brandy. Before the dinner begins, the Master is installed with traditional ritual:

FORM FOR INSTALLATION OF THE MASTER
at the
OPENING OF EACH MONTHLY DINNER

'The Sauce to Meat is Ceremony.' *Macbeth.*

Before the Steaks are served the Brethren take their seats at the table, the Master, Past-Master, and Recorder, stand at the head of the table, thus:

Right   Centre   Left
PAST-MASTER   MASTER   RECORDER

(*The Past-Master wears the Collar of Office.*)

RECORDER (*Raps on Table. The Brethren rise.*)

    Now hearken well unto your trusty Lord,
    Who erstwhile ruled the Beefsteak's festive board!

PAST-MASTER:

    My office past—here stands my chosen heir,
    To him I yield the honours of the Chair.

RECORDER (*to Master*):

    Stand thou prepared this honoured part to play?

MASTER:

    Right well, i'faith—and shall all forms obey!

RECORDER:

    What say the Brothers? Speak with conjoint voice.

OMNES:
> Content we are and do applaud the choice.

PAST-MASTER (*to Master*):
> Thee do I clothe with symbol of thy pow'r,
> *(Invests him with Collar.)*
> To rule our feast, and guide the mirthful hour,
> To reign our Beefsteak King, and lead the way
> For Fancy's frolic and for Reason's play.
> *(Here all sit except the Master.)*

MASTER:
> Assembled Steaks! Accept a Brother's thanks,
> For this, your last promotion from the ranks,
> Be my poor part to rule your feast tonight,
> And haply shine in your reflected light,
> To ope the scene where all may bear a part,
> And watch the kindly play of heart with heart;
> To find occasion in some neighbouring eye
> For mirthful challenge, and for gay reply.
> To give some sense—to folly too—her share,
> In this, our feast of philosophic fare;
> To hold the watch—in need the time to call—
> When Brothers struggle for a friendly fall,
> Or try each other's skill—but with no show
> Of hurtful malice—or unkindly blow.
> To please, my aim! Be it your dearest wish,
> With mirth and cheer to season every dish,
> Let each tonight give Fancy free'st vein,
> And at her touch become a boy again,
> So all may say, 'Now, surely Love is here,
> To bless our Brotherhood of Beef and Cheer!'

Someone once said that the human brain is a remarkable organ which commences to function soon after we are born and ceases to function when we get to our feet to speak. No matter how many times a Master has previously taken the Chair, he almost invariably becomes tied up and confused in his rendering of the couplets which he is expected to recite from memory, and he is frequently interrupted by promptings and corrections from other members who have not to face the ordeal. At one memorable dinner the Master (Dr Frank Tate) silenced all assistance. Frank, among many other interests, is a master photographer and had produced a coloured talkie of a ventriloquist's doll reciting his piece word-perfectly while sitting on his knee. Some Masters attempt surreptitiously to read the ritual, but as the paper is soon snatched away, they flounder worse than ever.

After dinner we used to have the club song, a dreadful, dreary dirge, and Wood Jones said this was why he resigned from the Club—he couldn't take it. Then, to soften the blow, Skeats, a tenor, would treat us to some Gilbert and Sullivan, but for some years now all musical harmony has disappeared.

When the long table has been cleared and the chairs arranged, the Master gives his talk, the subject of which is never announced until he is on his feet, travel, history, philosophy, humour, sport, and the more controversial the better, as each member is expected to contribute to the discussion that follows. Among our herd of twenty-five are a Supreme Court Judge, a vice-chancellor, a head-master of a public school, three doctors, engineers, business and industry executives.

The Annual Dinner in July is highlighted by the financial statement rendered in verse by Hugh Brain, and similarly audited by Joe Sutcliffe, and, unlike many professional financial statements, ours are always perfectly clear. I commend these to accountants and auditors.

The records of each dinner have been preserved and each member in turn is Recorder for one dinner. At the 493rd dinner in September, it came to my turn to record the Master's address when Sir James Barrett presented an account of his service during World War I.

> James Barrett heard the Tocsin ring
> He didn't shout he didn't sing
> But shone his buttons—belt as well
> Gargled his throat for a battle yell
> and Marched up to Kiarra's poop
> No worthier Anzac in the troop.
> His crowns shone bright—his spurs agleam
> The toute ensemble just a dream

Until ptomaine smote Barrett's bingy
The food was poor—the ice was stingy.

He marched into the land of Pharaohs
Surrounded by a band of heroes
He conjured hospitals from naught
Bricks from the sands of the desert he wrought.
Measles, sore eyes, woes of Venus
He treated kindly not as heinous
Crimes of men, with lights of blue
And sound advice—blue ointment too.
Hotels de luxe complete with staff
And palmwood beds not by a half
Sufficed—So skating rinks and Luna Park
And Atliers—all bore the mark
Of the Barrett Birdwood combination
(Birdie had called him in consultation).

The wounded came with scarce a warning
He emptied trains from eve to dawning
So well had everything been planned
Was scarce a hitch—it went off grand
He packed them here—he packed them there
James Barrett packed them everywhere,
With comfort bountiful in measure
Their food their linen and their leisure
The efficiency of it all was such
Success rewarded the Master's touch
Australia safe with such foundation
Britain demanded this importation
The British army needed weeding
Barrett the man to do the leading
He bored and boarded men by day
Classified and winnowed hay
From grain, and built divisions
Palestine hung on his decisions.

Square pegs from out round holes he drew
Lead swingers—misfits—Barrett knew
The stuff to give them and he spoke
The word that shattered all the hoke-
us pokus of the backline men
He sent them back to fight again.
James Barrett felt without reservation
His greatest work was manhood preservation.

There were many other deeds to note
But in the semi-darkness wrote
This Scribe as Barrett verified his word
With magic slides and all we heard
We saw recorded on the screen
(Good healthy stuff—nothing obscene)
Figures and men a kaleidoscope
Of twin ideals and so I hope
I have his pardon for the gaps
That in this rambling records are perhaps
The outcome of it all, you know
We won the war (books tell us so).

With these various activities and a growing consultative practice, my time was reasonably full, but by the middle thirties there was a growing uneasiness in world affairs and a stirring among the armed services. After twelve years with the Cavalry Division, I was posted to command the 2nd Field Ambulance, the infantry unit I had missed as a private in 1914 when I mistook a left for a right turn, but after twenty years I caught up with it. After all, if you wait long enough, what you seek generally turns up at last. This brought me into the field of infantry training and tactics, but I found the exercises fairly straightforward. Each year senior medical officers throughout Australia attended staff exercises in strategic areas about the eastern coast. The steel and coal activities north of Sydney were considered a high priority and over the ground and waterways round and about Newcastle we planned on papers with great success. Before these exercises began we were given certain top secret basic assumptions in the event of war:

1. Singapore could not be invaded from the land and would persist as a naval bulwark against invasion from the north.
2. Beyond this we could expect little assistance from the United Kingdom in the early stages.
3. We could expect no assistance from the U.S.A.

Such was the General Staff appreciation at that time.

Early in 1939 I was asked by the G.O.C. of the Infantry Division, with which I was serving at the time, if I would take over the command of a C.M.F. battalion. A medical man serving in a combatant unit was nothing new. On Gallipoli Alfred Derham, a young medical graduate, was a combatant officer in the Fifth Battalion, and was one of the first to win the Military Cross. The two senior officers of the Australian Contingent to London on the occasion of the Coronation of King George VI were medical practitioners; the commander, Dr Frank Lind, was later to command a brigade of the 8th Division in World War II. I would gladly have accepted the posting had it come my way but advanced war plans were rapidly being developed, and as the vials of wrath were filling, I was transferred back to the Cavalry Division with a Staff appointment. When the gathering clouds burst at the end of the year, the phoney phase of World War II began.

Chapter 8 World War II Begins

As soon as recruiting was opened I offered my services to the D.G.M.S., General Downes, but he asked me if I would chair a committee for the control of medical equipment so that the services and the essential civilian needs would be assured. Although I would have preferred to be with the troops, I was persuaded of the job's importance and we began to survey the service and civilian requirements for essential medical equipment. Surprises emerged at once as to how dependent we were on the importation of even such simple things as ampules and clinical thermometers. It was an interesting survey but I was delighted when within a few weeks I was offered the command of the 2/1 Casualty Clearing Station and handed over to Sir Alan Newton and Paddy Moran.

When the war began towards the end of 1939, in Australia there was at first a reluctance to realize our responsibilities, a wait-and-see attitude contrasting with the rush to the depots in 1914.

Perhaps the strange early tempo of the war in France contributed to this. I do know that when I took over my command attached to the 6th Division and began recruiting, I had more applications from medical officers over forty years of age than from those in their twenties and thirties. It was the same when I enlisted other ranks—thirty-nine was the upper age limit for privates and I was inundated with applications from 'thirty-nine' privates reluctantly admitting their service during World War I.

A Casualty Clearing Station is a small, compact medical unit on the lines of communication in rear of the Divisional Field Ambulances and eventually I was able to form a wonderful team —I still believe the best and happiest medical unit in the 2nd A.I.F.

As my second in command I had Newfort White, who had had

a long regimental experience with the Infantry; there were three Fellows of the Royal College of Surgeons—Bob Officer, Orme Smith and Bowie Somerset; my radiologist was Reg Crisp, my dentist Arthur Prytz; and my quartermaster Alf Raine. In charge of my eight splendid nurses was 'Han', later Matron Hannah of the Alfred Hospital, Melbourne. My Officers' Mess was completed by two first-class padres, Fairlie Forrest, who was later wounded and captured in Crete, and Padre Benn, always known as Bowyang. Could any C.O. ask for more? My N.C.O.'s were a tough lot, many with experience of World War I, and my men, after a little judicious and quite irregular weeding, made a wonderfully happy command.

In a small unit there are necessarily a number of postings for men with some special training even in menial tasks. I asked each man his occupation and most of the special postings were easy to fill. One posting in the manning chart, the unit sanitary detail, remained unfilled until a slight, sandy-haired Scot presented.

When I asked him his occupation he said in his broad Glasgow brogue: 'I 'eaded 'em at 'Orsham, Sir.'

'You what?' I asked him again.

'You know, Sir, I 'eaded 'em at 'Orsham,' and picking up an empty petrol tin, which served as my waste paper basket, he heaved it on to his head as if it were heavy and walked towards the door. This action rather than his words recalled a familiar sight in Bendigo years before that city was blessed with sewerage. Jock got the job, to his great delight, and to my never-failing satisfaction and the respect of the Unit.

When at last my Unit was assembled, I realized that I had all the elements of a tempest, with a Raine, a Snow and a Blizzard. In the rear of a divisional area and not in direct contact with the enemy, medical officers attached to units along the lines of communication sometimes consider they are doctors rather than soldiers. In an army, however, every individual, even a specialist, must be basically trained as a soldier and has to conform to what at times appear to be irksome routine procedures at variance with civilian custom. By and large, military organization and method, evolved slowly over centuries of trial and error, prove remarkably efficient and could be applied to civilian activities. More than once in New Guinea, cooks had to toss aside their aprons and take up their rifles in defence of their area. At Red Beach in Finschhafen, 'Skipper' Dorney and his medical personnel fought back a Japanese attack on their dressing station.

In order that those of my officers and men who were new to the army should realize this, I arranged that, rather than be bogged down in purely medical duties at Puckapunyal, the unit would be moved to the old Liverpool camp in New South Wales for a period of general training unhampered by attending to any sick.

This camp site, established in World War I, was in bad condition and had been condemned, the huts were dilapidated and the conveniences inconvenient. This was all to the good in the training, however, and everyone, officers and other ranks, learnt to make the best of a bad situation such as they would meet later. Australians may be poor planners but they are generally remarkably good improvisors and I have never seen Australian soldiers fail to improve their conditions, however foul they found them, whether in the desert, among the mountains, the snow of Syria or in the jungle.

It soon became known in the township of Liverpool that an A.I.F. Medical Unit was in the area. I received a very kindly letter from the lady who directed the local Welfare Service asking if the members of her committee could visit 'our hospital', bringing comforts for the patients. In times of war such a service is of great value, not only to the sick soldiers but also to the civilians who, denied the privilege of serving in the active forces, rightly feel that they are doing their bit. But we had no hospital and no patients. After consultation with my officers, I decided to establish both on Sunday afternoons and I wrote saying we would welcome this kindly service.

We improvised a hospital ward, more appealing perhaps in its crudeness, and each Sunday a dozen 'patients' were detailed, complete with charts, a few bandages and suitable accessories. After midday dinner, these details were pyjama'd, placed in their beds and properly briefed ready to receive. Along came the kindly ladies with all varieties of comforts for the sick, who tried, more or less successfully, to look and speak 'sickly'. After we had given the ladies tea and seen them out of the lines with appreciation and hopes for further visits, the 'patients' were regimentally dressed once again and the various comforts enjoyed by the men at their evening meal. I believe we were never found out and a good time was had by both parties. If any of those generous ladies happen to read this, I hope they will forgive me.

After some weeks of this basic training, the unit was moved back to Puckapunyal. The second A.I.F. division was being formed soon after we returned and I was appointed A.D.M.S. on the staff of Major-General Lavarack commanding the 7th Division.

I had many misgivings about leaving my C.C.S It was such a happy command and I knew would give splendid service in action, as later it proved. In the 6th Division boxing competition my men had won five out of the seven contests, which reflects the staunchness of this small unit. There were compensations, however, in serving on the staff of my new Divisional Commander, Major-General Lavarack, himself an outstanding regular soldier. He had received his first commission in the pre-Duntroon days, entering the regular Army through the Garrison Artillery responsible for manning the various coastal defences around Australia. J. D. L., as we called him, was a man of singular charm, of wide reading and knowledge, but with quick flashes of anger at unpredictable times. The A.D.M.S. of a Division was the last of the really thrilling posts in the Army and, as Senior Medical Officer on the Divisional Staff, I commanded three Field Ambulances and had access to the whole divisional area, including the front line troops. I was responsible for advising the Divisional Commander regarding the general health of his troops, which ultimately is his responsibility, and preparing plans for the A.Q.'s responsibility, the care and evacuation of casualties. The medical service comes under the Adjutant-General's branch and was considered to have no association with operations, the responsibility of the G. Branch. Our dyed-in-the-good-book G.I. rather looked upon me as an interloper when I approached him as to the overall picture of any operation, and as the Senior A. Officer, a regular, believed that no civilian soldier, whatever his training, could know about military history or army staff methods, I went my own merry way and we generally managed to find most of the answers.

My first intimate contact with high ranking staff officers was bewildering, and while their disciplines and physical courage were usually an inspiring example, their general knowledge of the world around us was often limited. They were all, with very few exceptions, pleasant social companions away from a rigid military atmosphere, and I owe many of my most valued friendships to my association with these officers. Just as a civilian soldier, who had not lived a circumscribed life, was at first bewildered by his regular comrades, so must they have been bewildered by his independence of thought and action.

Our Divisional Headquarters assembled in the wooden huts about the Victoria Barracks in Melbourne, but our troops were training in all the States in the Commonwealth. During the month before we embarked overseas, I came to know personally all my officers and many of their N.C.O.'s and men and to appreciate how jolly lucky I was.

When the warning came that our transports were assembling, I had to select my batman. Not all armies have batmen on establishment, but for any officer to be relieved of the daily drudgery of cleaning, washing, ironing and the many other essential domestic duties, is a definite contribution to his efficiency. Furthermore, batman is a posting eagerly sought by many private soldiers; apart from the perks they feel rather superior, although they are not exempt from drill and weapon training. They proved their value in defence many times in the jungle.

I asked for half a dozen willing lads from the Caulfield depot to be paraded before me. They turned up—a mixed bag varying in age, physique and in intelligence. I interviewed them each in turn and was not impressed until a pint-sized little chap of uncertain age came in. He was untidy in an ill-fitting uniform, with rather furtive little eyes and the features of a fox. He gave what was meant to be a salute, stood at what he assumed was attention and looked me over in silence. I told him to 'stand easy' but as his 'attention' was as relaxed as any stance could be, he made no movement; any further degree of ease would have been to sit or lie down.

I began to question him. 'What did you do before you enlisted?'
A laconic 'Jockey' squeezed through the corners of his tight lips.
'Were you any good?'
'Rode a winner in a cuppla steeplechases.'
'Did you ever pull a horse?'
'A few times.'

'Were you ever rubbed out?'
'Twice.'
'Ever been injured?'
'A cuppla broken collarbones.'

All this time he was obviously trying to sum me up and waiting for the next question. 'Why did you enlist?'

'I thought I would give it a go.'

After a few more general questions I dismissed him. 'I don't mind givin' you a go,' he said over his shoulder as he strolled out. I interviewed the others and then decided to give the jockey boy 'a go'. There was something about him that appealed to me and 'Bernie' (that is near enough to his Christian name) became my batman.

I gave him a straight warning about pulling himself together in his appearance and general behaviour and he seemed impressed with his appointment as he threw what he took to be a salute and strolled out. He did give me a go—a very fair go—and looked after me wonderfully well. I never heard him swear or found him drunk, I never heard him laugh and he practically never smiled, but when he did it seemed to hurt him.

He did everything I asked of him and more, but he always gave me the feeling that he, a senior, was conferring a great favour upon me, his junior. He often told me what to do rather as an order than advice. My clothes were always clean and well cared for and from some source he was always able to replace lost buttons or badges, socks or handkerchiefs, he made my bed neatly, comfortably, and he always had my hut or tent tidy.

But in spite of all my urging, Bernie never looked a tailor's dummy and he did not seem to appreciate that he was in the army or what it meant to be a soldier. He had no respect for any other officer, whatever his rank, but he had a dog-like devotion to his duties for me. He seemed to be happy, or at least not unhappy, nothing appeared to disturb or worry him, and the other batmen seemed to be rather in awe of Bernie.

He failed or seemed to fail to recognize the rank of any other officer. On the transport, when for the first time he found himself standing beside our Divisional Commander, he was intrigued by the badges of rank on the General's shoulders. 'Where do you get them?' he said to the General in his colourless conversational voice, thinking the crossed swords and batons would look well on my uniform. General Lavarack looked down on him with his dark scowl. 'Who are you?' he asked. 'I'm Bernie, Colonel Norris's batman', and later that day I was asked to 'do something about that extraordinary batman of yours'. When I told the General who this extraordinary batman was and something of his career as a jockey, J. D. L., recalling that Bernie had once ridden a winner he had backed, relaxed and the two of them became almost friends. I'm sure that in this relationship Bernie had no feeling of inferiority.

Alas, alack, Bernie was not to father and mother me for very long. Soon after we arrived in the Middle East, all batmen were required to undergo a rifle drill and range practice. Bernie's rifle, almost as big and as heavy as himself, lay painfully on the lumpy union of his fractured collarbones, and every shot he fired—heaven only knows where—nearly knocked him over and bruised his shoulders, so very reluctantly Bernie and I had to part and he was returned to Australia.

A few years after the war my wife came to me and said, 'There is an odd looking little man at the door, he wants to see you. He says his name is Bernie, but I don't like the look of him.' No one ever did like the look of Bernie but I brought him in. 'I've got my eye on a cuppla good yearlings if you'd like 'em,' he said, as usual out of the corner of his mouth. I explained to him that I was really not interested in horse-racing, let alone buying yearlings. 'You'd get 'em cheap,' he said persuasively. Eventually I convinced him there was nothing doing and after a long, silent pause, giving me time to change my mind, he went away sadly shaking his head and leaving me with the impression that perhaps I was making the mistake of my life. I never have seen Bernie since the day that I let him down.

Some people are reluctant to have anyone alongside them in a position to carry out their duties, but I believe that it is a sound rule that if anyone or anything is essential, there should be at least two always available. Not only should this apply to personnel but to such things as glasses, dentures, diaries, watches, pens and pencils. I was extremely fortunate that Stanley Williams, a cheerful, imperturbable colleague, was able to fill the position of my deputy.

Stanley was the good friend of everyone and a most reliable comrade to have beside me. I never had any qualms about wandering away from Divisional Headquarters while Stanley was with me. All through the war I was blessed with loyal and efficient, companionable deputies. Munro Alexander followed Stanley Williams, then Keith Jones and Andy Fraser, none of them fortunately yes-men. I could not possibly have carried on without their kindly help and advice. I did not spare them and they never failed me, bless them all. I was very fortunate with my clerks. Jack Syder, my Senior, was a man of the highest principles and a tower of strength and an inspiration to all with whom he came in contact.

Our Divisional Commander, who did not possess a sparkling sense of humour, could not at first make Stanley Williams out. Every member of the army had to be immunized against those diseases that had decimated armies in the past. Only during this century have the number of battle casualties even approached those of disease. The responsibility for these injections fell to my deputy, and when General Lavarack came in for his issue he found Stanley Williams sharpening a needle on the sole of his boot. 'What on earth are you doing?' growled J. D. L. 'Sir, I always like to have a sharp needle for Generals, it doesn't hurt so much.' Of course, the actual syringe and needle to be used had been sterilized and were waiting in a bowl of spirit. With all due aseptic care the General had his stabs. Later that day he sent for me. 'Who is this odd fellow Williams you have got? He was actually sharpening the needle on his dirty boot.' I explained that this was only Stanley's little joke and that all precautions were observed on these occasions. 'If anything happens to me you're both finished in my Division.' Nothing did happen and, as was inevitable, J. D. L. and Stanley Williams became jolly good friends.

After a few months training, the Division embarked on the second convoy of the three great ships—*Queen Mary*, *Mauretania* and *Aquitania*. This last vessel had been a troopship during the Gallipoli Campaign and was saved from the scrap-heap only by the outbreak of World War II. These ships had been taken directly off the trans-Atlantic run and their stores still contained the good things of the table.

As Senior Medical Officer on our ship, the *Mauretania*, I was provided with a sumptuous suite—bedroom, bathroom and a very comfortable lounge—and it was certainly travelling under conditions that I would never have been able to afford in a private capacity. The troops were quartered in the cabins and very few had ever experienced such luxurious accommodations. Fears were voiced as to what vandalism the rough soldiery would bring to bear but this was, however, another example of the rule that, surround people with decent things and they will generally be respected, for there was practically no destruction or defacement in these crowded and beautifully furnished ships. We paused at Fremantle to embark our Western Australian troops and then sailed for Bombay, which was as far as these ships were routed. Beyond this point into areas accessible to enemy air power was considered too hazardous for these ships.

The troops were encamped around Bombay and in the hills about Deolali while the onward transports were assembling; Divisional Headquarters was accommodated in the Taj Mahal Hotel overlooking the Gateway of India, built for the arrival of King Edward VII to the Durbar.

It was my first acquaintance with this city, a medley of great riches and dire poverty among the smells of India and disgraced at that time with the degradation of Grant Road, the red-light district, which in the interest of the health of the troops I visited one night, protected by the Commissioner of Police, and immediately advised the G.O.C. to place out of bounds to all troops. A bearer had been provided for each of the senior officers and I had the experience of the remarkably efficient and unobtrusive service of these men. Any little or great need was generally anticipated and immediately attended to. A tailor would be summoned in the morning and returned with the garment in the same day—clothes were immaculately cared for, even if my badges were at times arranged in an odd sequence. Whenever I came out from my room in the hotel, there was my bearer squatting outside my door. Stanley and I visited our troops stationed in the hills, accompanied by my bearer always quietly anticipating our comforts and needs so that the journeys were delightful.

General Lavarack flew on to the area in the Middle East where our Division was to assemble, but within a few days after he arrived in Palestine, he developed dysentery. This was bad luck for him but a blessing for the Division, as henceforth I had only to suggest to him any measures to prevent the prevalent bowel disorders (the 'Gippy' tummy) when he would immediately issue blistering orders and enforce them; it was too easy.

With visits to the troops in the hills, wandering down the fascinating bazaars and relaxing at the Yacht Club, our days in Bombay passed very pleasantly. The Division re-embarked on a fleet of smaller ships—ours was *The President Dumé*, a French ship with many of the qualities of the smaller ships of France. I shared a flamboyant suite with our G.I., Colonel John Chapman, a D.S.O. of World War I, and a dear fellow with all the charm and emotion of his Irish stock. When we crossed the line, John, well fortified, made a regal and commanding Neptune until the dignity of his court was dispersed when one of the victims dragged John into the pool, to the delight of the troops and obviously of John himself. He could play well and perhaps his masterpiece was the long routine of 'Colonel Spophski', which he followed perfectly in word and action and would soon bring all members of the mess into this delightful fun.

Slowly in convoy we moved along the canal to Ismailia, where Brigadier 'Ginger' Burston, Senior Medical Officer of the 2nd A.I.F., together with Major 'Weary' Dunlop, came on board to put me in the medical picture. After lunch we entrained for a weary journey across the waste of Sinai, relieved only by the occasional village or oasis, then on through the cold night across the border beyond El Arish into Palestine and Gaza with our final halt at Deir Suneid in the early hours of the morning. A fostering unit had a hot meal waiting for us, our tents were standing and our beds made, and so in spite of the howling of the jackals I slept through what remained of the night.

Our Division was dispersed for some miles along the rail and road running north from Gaza. General Blamey and his corps headquarters were sited in this ancient town, the scene of Samson's rise and fall. Bordering the roads and fields round Gaza, the stout cactus hedges still stood where twice in World War I they had defied Murray's Cavalry, and on the rising ground of Ali Muntah to the east could be seen the Turkish trenches that had commanded the area until outflanked by the capture of Beersheba by what was probably the last cavalry charge in warfare. To the west the town petered out along the road that led down to a delightful beach, gay during the weekends with hundreds of browned soldiers bathing in the blue of the Mediterranean, brightened by the costumes of the nurses from the General Hospital on Gaza Ridge.

Our Divisional Headquarters was tented on a gently sloping hill overlooking what had once been the fertile fields of Philista, but which over the centuries had been sterilized and buried under dunes of drifting sands. Nearby was the typical Arab village of Deir Suneid, a collection of mud huts separated by unpaved muddy lanes down which ran all the village drainage. Along the alleyways at all hours of the day moved black-robed women with faces hidden by their yashmaks, except for their dark eyes. The grace of these women and young girls was remarkable as they moved balancing their water jars or other burdens on their heads, often with no steadying hand. The communal village well was a busy rendezvous. Dirty bare-footed youngsters, unmindful of the flies clustering on their faces, in their eyes or on their running noses, played—of all games—tipcat or hopscotch among the wandering geese, dark brown goats and fat tailed sheep, with the padding camels swaying by under their great loads of burseen and the inevitable fat Arab ambling astride the rump of a weary little donkey.

Donkeys, of course, are among the V.I.P.'s of the Middle East and for their diminutive frame and spindle shanks must be the most remarkable amongst the beasts of burden. Bearing great fat lazy Arabs or heavy sacks of corn, they jog along, turned this way or that not by a rein but by a belt on the side of the head with a donkey stick. They seldom complain but who could blame them if at times they fling up their heels or dig in their feet, refusing to move until their master lights a small fire beneath their narrow bellies. A story was around the mess that a soldier, protesting to a fat Arab riding on his donkey with feet dangling just clear of the ground, while his wife, with a large burden balanced on her head and obviously far advanced in adding to the five filthy urchins, dragged her weary feet at the rear of the cavalcade. 'You lazy brute—why doesn't your wife ride?' 'She no got donkey,' seemed sufficient explanation from the Arab.

The rocky, undulating countryside was splendid for hard training after the softening of the voyage. It was the dry season and apart from the occasional air raid warnings, which came to nothing beyond the few sprained ankles as men ducked in the dark into the slit trenches, there were no interruptions.

I soon realized that something was missing from the countryside. Around some of the Arab villages in the south there are a few olive groves and oranges about Jaffa and Tel Aviv, but the hillsides were bare except for rocks and the pink oleanders blushing among the white stones of the dry Waddis. Driving from Gaza to Beersheba, about thirty odd miles, I always looked for the one lone tree standing like a sentinel on some rising ground, and I remember another in a bend of the road before the village of Beit Jirja. We were told that the Turks had imposed a tax on trees and it was cheaper to cut them down than pay tribute; certainly the firewood for our cookhouses was very expensive. Since World War II, however, Ezekiel's prophecy has come true: 'This land that was desolate is become like a garden of Eden'; not quite like a garden of Eden, but hillsides of greenery with tamarisks and sombre pines.

After a few weeks I was given permission to visit the 6th Division in Egypt. I travelled by train through Cairo and Alexandria and on to the Western Desert as the first campaign in this area was about to begin. All was very hush-hush, there was only a mild sand-storm at the time but it was impossible to realize that there were thousands of troops in the area, so well were they camouflaged and dug in. I spent a couple of days with my old friend, Clive Disher, A.D.M.S. of the 6th Division, and even in the discomforts of the place, Clive, as always, made me feel comfortably at home with his warm welcome, but I had to push back to Palestine as the attack on Sidi Barrani was about to begin. On my way back I spent a few hours with my old unit, 2/1 C.C.S. in what remained of the Egyptian barracks at Mersa Matruh.

In many parts of Palestine drivers of our Staff cars always had a loaded rifle beside them. One day I was driving down the one wide street of Beersheba. It was the day of the camel market and the town was crowded with wandering Arabs of all ages, donkeys, camels, goats and sheep. In spite of our crawling progress, a sheep got under our front wheels and began to bleat loudly.

We stopped, but before I could get out to see if any damage had been done, from a nearby butcher's stall rushed a wild looking bearded Arab brandishing a large knife. I said to Hatherly, my driver, 'Don't move but take off your safety catch,' and I drew my pistol. The Arab dashed through the crowd right up to the car, then disappeared underneath, the bleat suddenly ceased and I waited in the jitters to see what was to happen. After a few minutes the butcher sprang up, bloody and unbowed, holding the slaughtered carcase in his arms, still dripping from the great gash in the neck. The Arab was laughing with glee as he dashed back to his stall and hung the slaughtered animal from the hook among the flies that swarmed over the horrible dark looking meat exposed to the dust and dirt of the road. Slowly we moved on and all was well.

Chapter 9 The Syrian Campaign

The task of our Division was to move to Mersa Matruh in the desert and develop the defences of the perimeter as a backstop to the forces farther west, and apart from occasional harmless visits from enemy aircraft, we were left alone to get on with the job. Our Divisional Headquarters slept in a few of the remaining stone houses and by day carried on with the inevitable paper down in a vast deep concrete command post. Our first medical task was to establish a large underground dressing station on a spit running out to the sea, and with the ever willing help of the engineers, we constructed what was wanted. The way of the engineers was not always smooth. I remember one occasion when engineer stores were urgently required and a signal was sent to the G.I., who administers the R.E. Service, but this officer returned the signal as it had not been properly abbreviated according to the good book. In one history of the Crimea Campaign nearly a hundred years before, it is recorded that an officer whose command was heavily pressed by the Russians sent an urgent request for reinforcements and ammunition, and received instead a message: 'All communications to this department must be written on foolscap with a two inch margin.'

Having completed our underground dressing station, we fortunately did not have to use it, as soon after it was finished we had our next move back to Palestine for the Syrian Campaign. Rommel in his rush to the delta no doubt blessed us as he swept through Matruh to his disaster at Alamein.

Matruh was administered by a regular British town Major, an elderly, very regular soldier and a delightful English gentleman, but hardly with us in the year 1941, and fearful of Australians. I had sent for an additional medical unit, but had some difficulty in siting them in the already dangerously crowded area. Eventually I decided on a small grove of date palms and went along to the town Major to seek his agreement.

'Old boy,' he said in a pained voice, 'they're not Australians, are they?'

'Yes,' I replied. 'What is wrong with Australians?'

'Old boy, they're such thieves, such thieves.'

'Nonsense, old boy,' I said, 'they're no worse than any other troops.'

'Oh yes they are, old boy. I had a yacht with an engine here and when the first lot moved in my engine had disappeared in a few days and by the end of the week I could not find my yacht.'

'How do you know the Australians took them?' I asked him. 'What about the Wogs?'

'I know, old boy, I know' and then in a hushed voice: 'This morning something dreadful happened.' Good heavens, I thought, probably his watch or his wallet had gone now. 'Something dreadful, they have taken my closet.'

Certainly a wooden privy in an area almost devoid of timber was a proud possession, but anyone who had the effrontery to flaunt such a convenience before troops in that woodless area was asking for trouble. I consoled the old boy by promising to provide him with a more mod. con., which in some way we were able to do, and grudgingly he gave his consent to my selected site. Later that day when I saw an easily recognized portion of his little house about to be consumed in one of our unit cookhouse fires, I asked no questions.

Firewood was always a problem in the Middle East, especially in the desert. A satisfactory means of lighting a small fire for cooking was to fill an empty perforated petrol tin about one-third with dry sand, then pour in and mix a pint of petrol. This burned with a blue flame for quite a while, long enough to boil water or fry sausages, and when the flame died down a gentle kick on the tin would rejuvenate it.

Two gallons of water per man each day sounds all one would want, but when this has to be used for all purposes including drinking, cooking and washing, it does not go very far; however, with a large sponge, I managed. There was a sense of cleanliness in the desert, and often later in the jungle I heard members of the 6th and 9th Divisions, who had served longer and more strenuously, sigh, 'Oh, for a nice, clean stretch of desert!'

One of my ingenious medical officers came across a small spring in his area and with his masterly scrounging of bits and pieces he rigged up a hot shower for his men. Captain Ronald Humphries, always known as Humph, was one of those masters of improvisation and was said to have written the annual Sydney University Revue, painted the scenery and played the principal part—and from what I knew of him I could quite believe it. One of his inventions was a modification of the Thomas splint for a casualty evacuated on a donkey, and many ingenious ideas for equipment in the jungle. He had several escapes during action but was finally killed by a falling tree in the North of New Guinea.

We rather enjoyed our period in the desert and were all healthy. Night did not come gently: it fell suddenly, bringing down the cold that quenched the heat of the day. With the coming of the dawn, there was a clear crispness in the air and a feeling of goodness to be alive as the whisps of mist faded before the intensity of the light.

Fortunately the extensive mine fields around and within the perimeter were clearly marked in daylight, but I was apprehensive when walking about at night and we had the almost inevitable casualty. It was said that the original Egyptian designer of the field had gone up with a master plan in his pocket when he inadvertently trod on one of his own mines. The whole field had to be plotted again and we considerably extended the perimeter and laid hundreds of additional mines.

I generally found time to visit most of the units in the area every few days and the cheerfulness and good heart of the Australian were a wonderful tonic to a dugout Colonel. On one of my visits to a field regiment I missed one of the senior officers and was told that he was sick in his quarters. I went along to see him and found a broken man. The rare appearance of an enemy plane, none of which did any real damage, and the challenge of the new environment of the desert had been too much for him, and as he did not improve over the next few days, I went to the Divisional Commander. I explained that the man was sick and that he should be evacuated to Alexandria at once as he was unfitted for front line service. I had a deal of difficulty in persuading J. D. L. that this was sound advice and I pointed out that no one could adequately assess his reaction to any circumstance till this had been experienced. Even with the aid of psychologists or not, nobody knows his reaction to being shot at till this actually happens and everyone has a limit of endurance. In some this is long delayed, in others it is reached sooner, but with many people it is possible to prolong their endurance by proper training in robustness, which Lord Wavell placed high in the essential qualities of a soldier.

Unfortunately, over the years, much time and money has been devoted to the elimination not only of drudgery but also of physical and mental effort. War is responsible for a gross exaggeration of the trials and challenges of civilian life. If we have been brought up to evade these, when as inevitably happens we are faced with responsibility, decision and danger, we must try to escape in some way. It was a melancholy experience to be told that in one large military hospital, not in Australia, the majority of inmates had suffered no physical wounds. It is not a stigma that an individual cannot face a certain situation—it is unfortunate and should be recognized as such. Sometimes this temporary disability on service can be adjusted without evacuation by simple medical care and sound common sense, rather than a disturbing and destructive analytical probing couched in pseudo-scientific jargon. To hold an officer in a forward area after he has demonstrated his inability to overcome his unfortunate reaction to the challenge is extremely hazardous, for he may do far more damage to troops under his command than the enemy may bring about. When evacuated to a rear medical unit, apparent recovery often follows in a short time and herein lies danger as it did in this case. When we returned to Palestine and were preparing to invade Syria, General Lavarack sent for me saying that this officer wanted to join his unit and J. D. L. couldn't see why not. However, again I was able to persuade him that this would be dangerous and I have never seen the officer since. Quite possibly he is a most successful man in civilian life, where endurance may not be so much in demand, but soldiering on active service, in spite of his professional training, was not his line of country.

The Syrian Campaign

No sooner had the defences of this lovely Mersa or anchorage of Matruh been reasonably assured than our Division was recalled to Palestine. This was just another incident in the up and down yo-yo campaign in the Western Desert, which began at the end of 1940 with the first lap of the Benghazi handicap and, after seesawing up and down the desert, ended with Alexander's triumph at Tunisia in 1943. During this interval the Nile Delta and the oil-fields in the Middle East had remained tender spots, but unaware of the menace of Rommel from the west, attention had been directed to Greece.

After the fall of France, the Allies watched and waited, while the Vichy French developed their defences over the Syrian Mandate. When on their way to Iraq the Nazi airmen were accommodated by the French on the Ryak airfield, the situation became intolerable and it was resolved to invade Syria, forestalling Axis control and the threat from the north of a pincer prong on the Canal.

Our Division streamed eastward back to Cairo, crossed the Canal at Ismailia and into the weary waste of Sinai again, where we bivouacked by the roadside during a bitter night. At dawn we moved on into Palestine to concentrate among the old Roman olive groves in the north between Acre on the coast and Safad high in the eastern hills, with our Divisional Headquarters sited in a monastery at Nazareth overlooking the fertile plain shimmering in the blue haze of the summer heat.

We were to advance across the border along two good roads, the coastal road at the foot of the cliffs north of Haifa and the inland road crossing the border at Metulla. We had a casualty clearing station at Haifa and another in a monastery at Nazareth, and for some days after the border had been crossed we were able to have most of our casualties rapidly back to these medical units. The essence of good casualty attention is a matter of time, not distance, and within two or three hours of the men being wounded in the first clashes, the casualties were safe in comfortable beds, cared for by highly trained surgeons and physicians, and smiled upon by charming nurses. Under these conditions I was able to retain the main portions of my field ambulances on wheels prepared to move forward as the advance proceeded after the initial resistance had been overcome.

One of our problems in that area was malaria and this was the Division's first encounter with the disease that had decimated armies over the centuries. When Sennacherib and his Assyrians 'came down like a wolf on the fold', marching his troops through the highly infested Jordan Valley and then climbed up into the cold of the Judaean Hills, chronicles record, 'the Lord sent an angel which cut off all the mighty men of valour and the leader and captains in the camp of the King of Assyria'. More than 2,000 years later, when Allenby's troops rose up from their camp in the Jordan Valley for his lightning thrust towards Aleppo, which resulted in victory over the Turks in 1918, he achieved his object just in time. Within a few weeks his Army was crippled with malaria. In spite of this melancholy history and the fact that some millions of deaths from malaria were still occurring each year, it was difficult to persuade certain high ranking staff officers of the seriousness of this situation, and only when I reported our first death from malaria was it generally realized that a man could die from 'fever' quite quickly.

There was some uncertainty as to the reaction of the Vichy French; this was the first occasion in which the Allies had actually fought against our former friends. In the optimistic but fallacious hope that we would meet only token resistance, loud speakers went forward in the van calling upon them to lay down their arms and join us in opposing Axis domination. Those so equipped were among the first casualties and the bitter battle went on.

It was a strange campaign in some ways. French Foreign Legion troops were fighting on both sides and at times there was difficulty in arousing enmity between them as they faced each other in battle and a redistribution had to be made to keep the kettle boiling. It was a gentleman's war, and field ambulances were always respected. On one occasion a couple of enemy planes, returning after strafing some guns in a banana grove to the rear of one of our medical posts marked with a red cross, swooped down, waved a friendly gesture and went on to strafe a unit just beyond us.

As the resistance stiffened, our casualties became heavier and the turning of the defences on the high ground beyond the Litani River was costly. We had little air support and until we captured two or three French tanks in the battle about Sidon we had none of these weapons. As the Coastal Brigade pushed on beyond the

The Syrian Campaign

Litani, the narrow coastal plain at the foot of the hills was strewn with burnt-out vehicles, blowing papers, red and blue sashes of the Legionnaires, dead men and bloated animals.

A few miles inland the advance up the valley was held at Merjayoun and the coastal advance was limited to active patrolling to conform with this check. The route of the inland advance was far more rugged than the coastal road and it was some days before we could clear the defences just north of the border on this front. The main road was well surfaced but winding and narrow, and there was a standing order that any obstruction to army vehicles had to be cleared at once. One day when I was visiting the Merjayoun sector we found our passage blocked by a deserted Arab truck, an occasional shell was bursting in the valley below and the driver, true to form, had evidently abandoned his truck, cleared out and was probably skulking somewhere behind some rocks. With the help of my driver, we took off the brakes, turned the truck towards the valley, pushed aside some boulders guarding the steep drop, and gave it a push. We watched and listened while the truck went hurtling over and over down the valley, where it disintegrated beyond repair. We had obeyed orders and achieved what both of us had secretly longed to do since we were kids.

When the advance to Jezzine on the inland route was cleared, both sectors advanced on Damour. One afternoon some Vichy French destroyers made a sortie from the north, shelling our coastal positions, and one of our batteries swung around and opened fire. We had a grandstand view of this duel, which was practically harmless to both parties, but so exasperated was one infantry officer alongside of me that he drew his pistol and emptied the magazine at the French Navy. 'I will never have a chance to do this again,' he said. As the vessels were a mile or so off shore, his gesture was satisfying but as far as I could see without any effect.

During the tough fighting about Sidon on the coast, I received a message that one of the French Legionnaire prisoners claimed to be a doctor. I went down to the compound, talked with him and was reasonably convinced of his story. As our casualties were mounting and we were rather shorthanded, I sought and gained permission for him to help in one of our medical posts, if, as he had offered, he gave his parole. For the next forty-eight hours he worked splendidly and then, when the lull came, as it always does, he had to be escorted back to the prisoners' cage. After I had thanked him and said goodbye, he asked me if I could visit a sick relative in Tyre. I was given permission to do this and drove off to the address he had given, a few miles to the rear. In a little back street I found a young girl, sick with what I took to be typhoid. There was little furniture in the house and the conditions generally were rather grim. Fortunately it was possible to improve things quite a deal and as I was leaving the father said he wanted to give me something. I pointed out that this was quite unnecessary and that his relative, the Legionnaire, had done a grand job for us. Just inside the door was a collection of various sticks and he insisted on my taking one. I pointed to a short, gnarled, rather attractive dark stick in the corner. 'Oh, that one, that's only the one I used to use on my donkey, I don't want it', and I became possessed of a little Lebanese oak stick about twenty inches long. Ever since that day this has been everywhere with me whenever I wore uniform.

This campaign was almost certainly the last in which horse cavalry will appear. We had about 300 Free French Circassian Cavalry who had crossed into Palestine under Colonel Collet, in addition to the 'Kelly Gang', which had been formed by mounting thirty-two fine Arab stallions captured from the French about Merjayoun by some of the diggers, who were delighted to find themselves astride again, and it was good to hear the jingle of harness as they moved out on patrol. To complete the cavalcade, we had Cypriot mule teams with their timorous attendants to take supplies into the more rugged of the areas.

Once Jezzine, in the mountains, had been captured, the coastal advance continued towards Damour. From Sidon, on the coast, a rugged mountain road crossed to Jezzine and a drive across to this brigade was always an occasion. The last few hundred yards descended down a steep road cut from the side of a hill. This section was fully exposed to the French and every now and then they would toss over a few shells taking pot shots at any movement though little damage was ever done. We would wait in the trees above this exposed section until a few shells had come over, then after a pause we would dash down this mad mile.

As the coastal force neared Damour, the brigade at Jezzine moved down from the hills on the French flank and when the two forces had concentrated the final battle of Damour began: the last remaining defences of Beirut. One of my dressing stations was sited in an olive grove surrounded by a low stone wall. As happened so many times during the war, an area selected by a field ambulance was equally attractive to the artillery and so it was again—the gunners moved into an area a few hundred yards in our rear and opened fire on the French positions beyond the river. I was talking to George Maitland, the C.O. of the ambulance, when the French guns opened up, searching for our battery, and the odd shell began to burst around our dressing station. This was quite legitimate, as our medical post was in a depression and the Red Cross was probably invisible to the enemy. Fortunately, we had not received any casualties up to then and George ordered his men to get under shelter till they were wanted: one of the lessons you learn in war is that, when there is nothing to do, do nothing. George looked at me and I looked at him—we nodded and both of us went to ground behind the stone wall. We were smoking and quietly chatting away about this and that when, to my astonishment, a little Arab girl in her long black dress reaching to the ground, came wandering among the trees. Every now and then she stooped to pick up empty bottles and tins and put them into a sack slung over her shoulder. She seemed quite oblivious of the shelling and was luckily unharmed, while we cravens crouched behind the sheltering wall. Again we looked at each other, nodded, and stood up. George, a D.C.M. of World War I and later a D.S.O., seemed quite nonchalant but I was rather windy as I strolled around. Fortunately the shelling soon ceased and when her sack was filled the little girl staggered off with her load. At no time did she seem aware that there was a battle going on; bottles meant far more to her.

During this final battle before the fall of Beirut, I witnessed another gentlemanly gesture from the French. Lieutenant A. R. Cutler, an artillery observation officer, who had displayed extraordinary gallantry at Merjayoun, was severely wounded at Damour. In the rugged hilly country about the battle, the unit wireless sets were often useless and Cutler decided to crawl across the river into the enemy area with his telephone and bring down fire on the machine gun posts among the rocks just above him. Late in the day, as was inevitable, he was severely wounded and lay helpless. Bearers attempting to bring him out became casualties and it was decided to wait for darkness. When night came and the bearers went out again, they couldn't find Cutler, who, attempting to crawl back with his shattered leg and probably only half conscious, had lost his way and fallen over a wall into a banana grove, where he lay all night still in enemy territory. The approach from our side was in full view and range of the enemy but at daylight it was decided to send forward a stretcher squad of prisoners with Adrian Johnson, a medical officer, holding aloft a Red Cross flag on a stick. Down the road they went and, without any interference, crossed the river and found Cutler in a very bad way. He was placed on the stretcher and the party retired, again in full view of the French, who left them alone but followed their retreat with shells bursting a hundred yards or so behind them, leaving the party in safety but demonstrating that no advance of troops would be tolerated. Fortunately we were able to get Cutler rapidly back to a surgical unit but he lost his leg, which was already gangrenous.

For his wonderful examples of inspiring gallantry, Cutler was awarded the Victoria Cross, the only Australian Artillery Officer, I believe, in either World War I or II to be so decorated. Later he was to become one of the most distinguished members of the Australian diplomatic corps and Governor of New South Wales. His tall figure, well over six feet, with his one leg and his personal charm, was always conspicuous in any gathering.

With the fall of Damour, on the coast, Denz realized his position was hopeless and at midnight on 11 July hostilities ceased. Everyone in the area was suddenly aware of a tremendous silence, at first more disturbing than the almost continuous gunfire to which we had been accustomed.

Next morning the Vichy French envoys were taken to the St Jeanne d'Arc Barracks at Acre where a convention was signed (the term 'Armistice' was not used as an agreement between two former allies). This occasion was conducted quite smoothly with two exceptions. The press were admitted to the actual signing of the drafts and an exuberant photographer became entangled in one of the flashlight flexes, blowing all the lights in the barracks, and the light from a motorcycle, together with hurricane lamps, illuminated the final scene. When all were ready to depart, it was discovered that General Catroux's beautiful gold leaf kepi had been lifted. Catroux took it in good heart and, saying that, as he knew what great soldiers they were, he forgave them.

The Vichy French were given the option of joining the Free French forces or repatriation. Practically all the officers chose their homeland but many of the other ranks came over. If there had been an Australian or British foreign legion many more would have joined us, but most of them refused to serve with the Free French. Pending their decisions the prisoners were concentrated in scattered areas under strong guard.

We entertained a number of senior Vichy French officers in our mess and these gatherings were generally pleasant except for an almost universal resentment concerning the manner in which they held the British had 'let them down' in the opening phases of the war. How powerful can propaganda prove?

The first unpleasantness was the discovery that some of our troops captured at Marjayoun had been flown to France after the signing of the convention. Their immediate return was demanded and General Denz and some of his senior officers were to be arrested as hostages pending the return of our men. When Brigadier Savage and his guards called on Denz in Tripoli, Madame Denz protested the General was too ill to leave his home. Lieutenant-Colonel Stanley Lovell, commanding the field ambulance in the sector, was sent forward to examine Denz and he gave as his opinion that Denz was suffering from sand fly fever but was fit to travel. Without further ado, off went the General under escort to Jerusalem, where the French hostages were to be held. When all the Australian troops had arrived back in Beirut from France, Denz and his fellow officers were allowed to leave for home. Thus ended an unhappy but completely successful campaign. Our cost in casualties was greater than in the desert up to that time, and with the exclusion of prisoners, greater than in Greece and Crete.

As with all campaigns in the Middle East, greater publicity was given in Australia to the Australian troops, sometimes to the exclusion of others who far outnumbered them during the operations. During the Syrian campaign, although I had a British field ambulance under my command, I was personally concerned almost exclusively with Australian troops. The success of the Syrian invasion resulted from the convergent advance of three forces—our Australian 7th Division from the south towards Beirut, a combined British, Australian and French force from the south-east on Damascus, and a British force from the west on Paymyra and Aleppo.

While the shuffling and sorting out was going on among the Vichy French, our Divisional Headquarters was quartered in the Beit Marie Hotel in the lovely little village of Brummana, set among the woods of red-stemmed pines on the foothills of the Lebanon Mountains. Below gleamed Beirut with the clear blue of the Mediterranean beyond, to the south across the deep gorge of the Nahr el Jamani. Corps Headquarters were in the village of Aley on the steeply climbing road to Damascus.

Beirut, standing on a broad promontory curving into the sea around the Bay of St George, had a magnificent setting. Immediately to the east the Lebanon Range rose to 8,000 feet and among the dark pine-clad slopes stood stone monasteries, cool summer houses and skiing resorts for the winter. Modern Beirut, with its two Universities, modern European hotels and buildings, gave no hint of its heritage from the days before the Phoenicians. On Sunday afternoons we had the privilege of honorary membership of the little racecourse. No one won or lost many piastres but it was rather fun as three of our officers had leased an Arab horse with occasional success.

After the final departure of the Vichy French, plans were developed for the defence of Syria from any Axis threat from the north through Turkey, and our Headquarters moved forward to Tripoli. Along the coastal route north of Beirut had marched the Egyptian Pharaohs, the Assyrians, the Babylonians, Alexander and his Greeks and the Romans. North of Beirut an avenue of stalwart eucalypts led the road to a narrow pass at the foot of the mountains and across the old Roman bridge over the famous Nahr el Kelb, the Dog River, where, carved into the stone cliffs above, could still be clearly traced the episodes of the conquerors over the last three thousand years. Beyond the pass the coastal plain widened around the lovely Juni Bay where the road passes through what remains of one of the oldest cities of Syria, Byblos, the gaunt Crusader castle and its walls still defying the sea, now its only threat, but the papyrus reeds, which were said to have given us the word bible, have gone. A few miles north of Byblos, the coastal plain ended as the mountains descended steeply to the shore, and the road curved through the long Ras Shagga Tunnel to emerge with a magnificent view of the coast as it sweeps on to Tripoli with occasional orchards of fig and pomegranate.

Tripoli, as its name implies, was the fusion of three ancient cities around what was once an important port, El Mina, but which now gives access to the north arm of the oil pipe line from the Iraq fields, one of the few signs of modern times among the Roman and Crusader remains throughout the area. In 1893, just off the Tripoli coast, on a bright fine afternoon, occurred a British naval disaster similar to our *Voyager* disaster in 1963. As the result of a wrong turning order during manoeuvres, H.M.S. *Camperdown* collided with the flagship H.M.S. *Victoria* and more than 300 men were drowned, including Rear-Admiral Sir George Tryon, in charge of the Squadron, who a few years earlier had commanded an Australian Navy. The English cemetery where the British sailors were buried lay just inland from El Mina.

In Tripoli the G.I. and I shared a flat above a nightclub; our balcony, hung around with loofah vines, gave a glorious view over the Mediterranean. The revelry below by night proved too much, however, for my comrade, a rather precious and sensitive soul, who retired to a quiet villa on his own.

Our Divisional task was to develop the defences of northern Syria. To this end one brigade moved forward to the Aleppo area and extended north to the Turkish border, contacting the friendly Turkish guards at the bridge over the Euphrates. Another brigade was sited in the Jebel Torbal area just north of Tripoli, with one brigade in reserve.

When leave was available many of us went over to Damascus for a day or so. From Beirut the road climbed steeply over the mountains, then down across the many tributaries of the Litani in the Great Rift Valley. Then came the stony lower levels of the Anti-Lebanons and suddenly the greenery of the Barada Valley with orchards and fields clustered around one of the oldest continually inhabited cities of the world, Damascus, an oasis on the edge of the desert. The mosques, the old buildings, and the crowded markets were an unending fascination, under great iron roofs the stalls presented the finest fabrics, silks, brocades, beautiful handwoven rugs and carpets, ornate inlaid furniture, copper and silver ware, finely fashioned weapons and all varieties of flesh and fruit. It was difficult to keep moving among the crowds of black-robed nomad Arabs from the desert, but there was no end to the interest of this strange city.

With this quiet phase of garrison duty, we were soon faced with the problem that has endangered armies over the centuries, the venereal diseases. Venereal disease has been recorded in very early medical history, but with the moral laxity of Roman times it is unlikely that syphilis could have been prevalent and missed a clinically recognizable mention. Some of the troops who had returned with Columbus were among the army of Charles VIII, King of France, when at the close of the fifteenth century he set out to conquer the Middle East. Charles met with increasing opposition and abandoned his ambitions, and his mercenary soldiers became scattered over Europe. Immediately there broke out a pandemic of syphilis—a disease recognized apparently for the first time and, according to which side you were on, called the French disease or the Neapolitan disease. But no matter who was to blame the scourge has remained with us ever since, more prominently in certain areas, among them the Middle East.

Until the recent introduction of the antibiotic drugs, these diseases and their resultant pathetic incapacities were a constant menace in all communities and before World War I were accepted as inevitable in the services (all mention of these diseases was muted in decent society). Soon after the arrival of the first A.I.F. in the Middle East the incidence of V.D. rose rapidly. Medical officers and padres were officially permitted to 'talk' to the troops but the provision of personal prophylaxis was forbidden. Only when the V.D. rate rose to the alarming figure of 3 per cent of the troops constantly incapacitated was this veto withdrawn. In the second A.I.F. all reasonable facilities were freely available and, had these been accepted and the sound advice of medical officers followed, the incidence would have been negligible, which it certainly was not in Syria. Obviously something more had to be planned.

Unofficially I consulted with our Provost-Marshal, Neville Faulkner, as to what we could do about it. Neville was an old school and Trinity comrade, an M.M. of World War I. We accepted the fact that, in spite of advice and 'blue light centres', many soldiers were prepared to chance it, and it seemed obvious to us therefore that all we could do in addition was to render the venue of their risk as safe as possible.

On the hill above the main town of Tripoli was a large, low, stone building, which the French had established as a regimental brothel. This was now vacant and here was our opportunity. 'How oft the sight of means to do ill deeds makes ill deeds done', but this was no ill deed we were about to do. It was common knowledge that such an establishment was presided over by a Madam and implemented by a various number of girls. 'How do we get hold of a Madam?' I asked Neville. 'I'll fix it,' he said, and as his duties as Provost-Marshal took him down many shady alleys and byways, within a few days he paraded six applicants for the position, all loudly protesting their experience and proficiency. We selected one, more perhaps because of her grossly crossed eyes than any professional qualifications. I asked her if she could provide the *modi operandi* and she assured me she could and would within a week.

Fortunately among my medical officers I had a highly qualified gynaecologist, Harry Fisher (also an interstate fast bowler, not that this has any bearing on his specialty), and I appointed Harry as honorary medical officer to the establishment. I explained to Madam that, when she had assembled her girls she and they must submit to a medical examination and, if clear, they would all be isolated for a week, at the end of which they would be examined again. If they were still clear, they would be engaged, but had to consent to a snap examination at any time without warning.

One of the important contributions to the V.D. problem was alcohol and we told Madam that the Provosts had free access to her 'house' and, if ever we found alcohol on the premises or any drunken soldiers, she would be put in gaol and heavily fined. All this, of course, was quite unofficial and without any authority other than that of common sense. Neville undertook to picquet the place and prevent any soldier under the influence of alcohol or without his blue light outfit from entering. Taking our cue from a flourishing chain store in Victoria, we determined the tariff as nothing over half a crown, or twenty-five piastres in the local currency, and there were to be no concessional season tickets.

Madam agreed enthusiastically to all these conditions and asked if she could hang our photos in the hall as patrons, slyly hinting that honorary membership could be arranged, but neither compliment was acceptable to us. True to her contract, at the end of the week Madam reported her establishment complete, manned or rather womanned by twelve girls. We called in Harry Fisher, Neville picqueted the building preventing any entrance or exit, and within a week all was ready for the grand première.

The news soon spread and business was brisk, but what really mattered was the dramatic fall in V.D. rate. The girls were of French and all the Middle East nationalities, and I am glad to say there were no British personnel. Some of the girls were apparently engaged to be married and were making provision for their dowry. Neville and I made unexpected visits at all hours but never saw any abuse of the rules or facilities, and Harry Fisher always reported that all was well. The girls did not seem to us physically attractive, but were always bright and cheerful and chatted away over a cup of coffee, most of them able to speak quite good English. On one of these visits we missed one of the little Cypriot girls and asked Madam where she was. 'Reading in her room, I think,' she said. We went along the corridor and knocked on her door. 'Don't come in, don't come in, I am not with my clothes.' What an odd life.

Unfortunately, Madam became involved in some trouble with the local police, who informed Neville about this, and we arranged to visit the local gaol. There we found a weeping, cross-eyed Madam on her bended knees, protesting her innocence and imploring us to get her out. Neville spoke to the official in charge, with whom we had worked in the area, and Madam, being restrained with difficulty from embracing us, was escorted back to her house.

The whole problem of V.D. in the army is very distasteful, and our actions in solving this were determined only after a deal of consideration and the acceptance of a heavy responsibility. However, when the V.D. rate dropped so dramatically and remained at a record low for the army, we realized that we had been justified.

Chapter 10 Travels through the Middle East

It was an unending joy to travel over this lovely countryside visiting the widely dispersed troops. We travelled along three routes —one road north clung to the broadening coastal plain on to Latakia, then turned inland through Idlib to Aleppo. Every mile of this coastal road was heavy with ancient history—Amrit, Tartus, the last precarious hold of the Crusaders before they escaped to Cyprus, leaving their castles to stand or fall to ruins, still features of the area, on to Binias with the lowering dark basalt Crusader fortress of Margab frowning from the hill above, and finally to Latakia. This was the old Phoenician city Ramitha, but now the capital of the Alamites and the most northerly port in Syria. Around the area were crops of cotton and the famous dark tobacco, a little of which goes a long way in any mixture. In the midst of this busy agriculture, the old Roman Arch seemed incongruous. The route from Latakia to Aleppo was not very interesting and we generally visited that northern area by travelling along the Orontes Valley.

Turning inland just north of Tripoli, the road curved across the fertile fields below Jebel Torbal, then rose through the pass between the Lebanons and the Alamite Mountains. Commanding this pass was the vast Krak de Chevaliers, the fortress of the Knights, built more than 900 years ago, which must be the strongest and most perfectly preserved of the Crusader castles. Towering above the precipitous contours, the central keep was defended by two massive stone walls, each protected by deep ditches and dominated at intervals by rounded towers, slit for the archers. The garrison quarters were within the keep, together with the Chapel, and in the centre still stood the great round stone table for the knightly concourse. Within the walls of this great stronghold was an entire Arab village. There was no appearance of ruin and one seemed almost to hear the alarms and shouts of the knights and the clattering of their arms and armour as they hurried up the worn steps to the defences in their defiance of Saladin and his Saracens. Days could be spent in exploring this wonder, but we were never able to spend more than a few hours as we pushed on to the Orontes and the city of Homs in the valley at the cross roads of the ancient routes through Syria. A few miles north we came to the green gardens of Hama with its Arabic palaces and buildings untouched by western influence and where the great wooden waterwheels creaked and groaned day and night as they raised the water from the Orontes for the irrigation.

From Hama the road skirted the malarious swamps of the river, past the little Circassian villages with their quaint beehive-like houses rising from the higher ground like yellow bubbles. Coming over the final rise the distant mosques and tall minarets of Aleppo shimmered in the sun and above all rose the great citadel, a vast warm pink mass of stone in the setting sun.

The origin of Aleppo has been lost in the mist of time but it emerged in ancient records more than 4,000 years ago. In many ways this city was to me the most fascinating in Syria, as was Acre in Palestine. The buildings were of fine stone, ornamented by beautiful wrought iron, and under the vaulted roofs and the dark recesses of the stalls in the great suk or bazaar, Marco Polo had stabled his horses centuries before. But the gem of the city was the great citadel, rising on an ancient tel, probably the Acropolis of the old city, the approach was up steep stone steps leading to stout iron studded gates guarded by two towers.

Perhaps the loveliest visit was over the mountains to an artillery camp above Baalbek in the Beka Plain. From Tripoli two roads, one on each side of the Qudisha Valley, wound steeply up the Lebanon mountain side where mulberries, vines and olives flourished among the terraced slopes once covered with the famous cedars of Lebanon. Over the centuries these had been felled, for Solomon's Temple in Jerusalem, other sacred buildings and ships, until today only a few hundred of these sombre sweeping trees remain in one dark clump 6,000 feet above the sea. Nearby was The Cedars, a large hotel in the centre of the extensive skiing runs.

The road climbs a further 2,000 feet to a saddle at the crest, where the view on a clear day over the sea below and across the Rift Valley to the Anti-Lebanon Ranges in the east was breathtaking. The road ran steeply down to Baalbek, the Lord of the Plain in the Great Rift Valley. Baalbek is as blatantly pagan as Heliopolis, the city of sun worship. The tall columns of dazzling stone, hewn into great fluted blocks, still stood around the ruined temples. The best preserved was a tribute to Bacchus, where the hedonistic carvings around the walls and on the columns clamoured for themselves.

In the clear cool of the summer's ending, these visits have remained an enduring memory, but with the sudden coming of winter the whole countryside was changed and snow fell heavily towards the end of the year; to some of the soldiers this was their first experience of snow. It was odd to see cactus hedges and banana palms growing in a snowfield. At The Cedars Hotel the only exit was from the upstairs windows and for the first time in twenty years the beaches were covered and the shallows of the sea frozen. Some of the smaller units dispersed in the mountains were isolated for days and supplies became a problem; one detachment of Bechuanalanders became of highest priority, as it was said that cannibalism had been known among them not many generations earlier. One advantage of this severe winter was the formation of a ski company, about 200 men trained as winter patrols. The headquarters of the school was at The Cedars but so heavy were the snowdrifts that no wheeled vehicle could reach the school for three weeks and supplies had to be forwarded and casualties evacuated on improvised sleds.

Driving up to Aleppo on Christmas Eve was no mean venture. In the falling snow the visibility was poor and good driver that Hatherly was, he could not avoid skidding from the slippery ice covering the ruts worn through the snow by the previous transports. Off across the snow-covered field we spun, just missing a telegraph pole and coming to a stop in a foot or so of snow facing the way we had come. 'Where do we go from here?' asked Hatherly with his cheery smile. 'I haven't any chains and I can't move the car in this mess.' 'We're heading back to Tripoli now,' I said, 'so we'll just sit in the car and try and keep warm. There is bound to be some transport soon.' After about an hour, a

French truck came chugging through the snow and we had the indignity of being towed back to the road by a coloured French legionnaire, who seemed to be delighted with the opportunity, if the broad grin splitting his face was genuine.

It was night before we eventually reached Aleppo, where I put up for the night, Christmas Eve, in a bitterly cold stone house where Lieut.-Col. Arthur Green had posted his Field Ambulance Headquarters. We tried to sleep in all our clothes, including our greatcoats, and under all the blankets we could find, but, although we heaped on the fire what we thought could be spared of the furniture, all through the bitter blizzard of that night we still felt cold. It certainly was a white Christmas with a deep felt of snow everywhere, but the Australian soldier always makes the best of his conditions. The Unit turned on a magnificent Christmas dinner and with the presence of the nurses attached to the Ambulance a grand time was had by all. Next morning the snow had ceased and when our car had been dug out, we were on our way to Tripoli, this time, thanks to our chains, without mishap.

When our Division was relieved early in January 1942 by the 9th Division, we moved south again to Palestine with our headquarters on Gaza Ridge. There were all manner of rumours as to our future (the situation in the Far East was a menace), but for some weeks we just stayed put . . . wondering. Our G.I., who had been overwrought by the racket below our flat in Tripoli, had been moved on to a less disturbing posting; his replacement was a somewhat odd fellow. Able in many fields, he had an *omnium gatherum* mind, which collected and retained a deal of haphazard and often useless information. He delighted in finding unusual words and working them into the breakfast conversation; to some of the officers this seemed evidence of rare erudition but after a time it began to pall.

To relieve the monotony of our inactivity, he decided the Divisional Headquarters would revive our study of desert night navigation by the stars and other celestial bodies. He wasn't a very good instructor and it became a rather tiresome means of spending an evening. How long this study would have continued I do not know, if one bright young officer hadn't suddenly brought the curtain down on this comedy.

One night he asked our self-appointed instructor if he knew how to determine the points of the compass with his army jack-knife. For once our G.I. had to admit uncertainty. 'Well,' said our B.Y.O., 'you take your knife out with you in a boat on the sea, or river or on to a lake, if none of these are nearby you choose a pitch dark night. You stand up, twirl the lanyard three times quickly above your head, then let it go, and at once you have one cardinal point.' Everyone was silent. At last, after a long pause, while he waited for someone to ask the obvious question, our G.I. confessed. 'Well, I'm not quite sure of it, go through the drill again.' 'You see,' said the B.Y.O., 'your knife's gone west.' That concluded the night navigation course.

Early in February Tubby Allen, our Division Commander, received a signal to assemble a small advanced Headquarters party prepared to emplane on twenty-four hours notice at a place to be designated later, en route for an undisclosed destination. I was included in this small party, the G.O.C., his P.A., his batman, the G.I., a senior member of the A. and Q. Branch, and myself. Next day we were ordered to move at first light the following morning to Tiberias on the Sea of Galilee. It was only a few hours' run through northern Palestine and there we were told that a seaplane was coming for us in about an hour. The Lake of Tiberias is shallow and on calm days glassy smooth, presenting a difficult landing for a seaplane. The small launch shot out, ruffling the surface so that the pilot could gauge his contact with the water, and before lunch time our small party had been ferried aboard. With the roar of full power, the water rushed by in a great bow wave above the windows as we rose into the air—for where?

We circled above the Jordanian Hills to the east, then over the monotonous waste of the desert into Iraq. The visibility was wonderfully clear and below we could see the occasional dark dot of a nomad camp in this dreary area. As we neared Baghdad there was an occasional flash of green in the valley of the Euphrates, where we landed for fuel on Lake Habbaniya. Off again over what is probably the only unsurveyed area in the Middle East, the Ma-dan of evil repute. In their continued isolation over the centuries, these almost unknown Arabs and their water-buffaloes have lived in their reed houses pitched upon islands of reeds among the vast marshes of the lower Tigris. Our pilot took us well down, but not too low, as these strange people shoot at anything in the sky, and it was possible to make out their villages and the high-prowed canoes, their only means of transport among the snake-like canals. It was dark when we landed on the Shat el Arab at Basra but our night was brief as we were called at 2.30 in the morning, while the air was still hot and heavy as we ferried out to our plane. Down the Persian Gulf to Bahrein, the small island, wealthy with oil concessions and pearls, and we were able to stretch our legs on the small wharf while the fuel was fed. Then across the gulf and the arid hills of Iran and Baluchistan to Karachi for a decent night's sleep till dawn. Flying over desolate areas is tiresome and the grim and rugged Sind Desert of Pakistan was no exception. Just looking at a map of northern India, it is not easy to appreciate the number or extent of lakes in that area, but twice we fuelled on ample stretches of water, at one of which the crocodiles watched us from the mud, before we came down on the Hugli near the Dalhousie Bridge in Calcutta.

Calcutta was as far as we had been routed when we left Palestine and we were to be advised there of our onward movements, but no such advice was available, and, as eastward of this area was within the daily Japanese bombing run, the pilot declined to continue any farther until a plane with a longer range was available. We put up at the Great Eastern Hotel where the G.O.C. sent off a signal seeking our destination. So tight was the security, however, that this became mutilated somewhere in the complicated decoding and it was ten days before any advice and a suitable seaplane arrived. Not that we minded very much, for the ten days passed very pleasantly. We played golf on the delightful Toligundi links, lunched off cold corned hump at the Bengal Club and lost rupees at the races. Calcutta with its remarkable contrasts held much of interest and strange smells, many fine buildings and parks and pathetic hovels, but at night one had to pick one's way carefully along the pavements to avoid treading on those wretched people who had nowhere else to sleep.

One afternoon I was having tea with Dr Maidment, an old Melburnian, in the crowded lounge of the hotel, when in came a group of four Chinese, headed by a commanding and remarkable woman. Short and slight in build, she was dressed in a tight, black cheongsam, buttoned to the neck, relieved only by a narrow cerise collar, with the same edging to the slit in her skirt to the knee. She moved forward to a reserved table as if there were no one else in that crowded room and it were her own private apartment, and the others followed behind her. I said to Maidment: 'I have never seen such an entrance.' 'Don't you know who she is?' he said. 'That is Madam Chiang Kai Shek,' and I realized then that the inconspicuous man in the rather sloppy grey suit was the General himself. I was taken over and introduced but the eyes of everyone in that room were for Madam.

At last we found our next destination was Batavia in Java, a rather tricky run. The Japanese were flying down the Bay of Bengal over Sumatra and returning over Java to Malaya, where their troops were rapidly advancing south. The Japanese being people of habit, these bombing runs conformed to a regular daily schedule and to move into the area with any reasonable safety was a matter of timing, leaving each staging post either after the regular daily performance or well before the next day's fun and games began, flying low and camouflaging the plane if possible under the tropical foliage of a river, overnight.

Our first hop was only a few hours across the many snake-like mouths of the Ganges delta to the shelter of Akyab on the coast of Burma. After a hot, sticky night with the rain rattling on the cane roof of our hut, we took off at first light down the Bay of Bengal to Port Blair in the Andaman Islands. Soon after sunrise I saw the rare sight of a complete double rainbow circle with the colours reversed in the outer ring, and a small silhouette shadow of the plane in the centre. I had read of this phenomenon but never before or since have I seen it.

Port Blair was an Indian penal settlement clustered among the lush tropical foliage of the hills around an almost land-locked harbour. After the deserts and wastes we had crossed, this was a soothing eye-bath and the shade of the vast verandahs around the bungalow where we rested until evening was delightful. When, as always in the tropics, night came suddenly, we drove down to the harbour and once again boarded our plane. The roar of the engines, the rush through the water, but no rise. Another run and the same result and we went ashore to spend the steaming night tossing in our bungalow, while the mechanics toiled on the engines. Next night we had the same experience, we could not rise from the water. Time was pressing as we had to leave in the dark, so it was decided to lighten our load and, taking a risk, some of the fuel was emptied.

With a roar we rose at last on our way to Sibolga in Sumatra, landed on a broad river and taxied the plane among the overhanging foliage along the bank. Not far inland, some villages had been bombed during the day. There was a comfortable rest house and we had a quiet, uneventful night with the flickering of fireflies in the humid heat.

Next morning on our final run into Batavia we flew low along the western coast of Sumatra and turned through the Sunda Straits with a splendid view of Krakatoa, nearly sixty years before the site of the world's greatest natural explosion. More than a cubic mile of rock was hurled into the atmosphere with a roar that was recorded 3,000 miles away, radiating shock waves that encircled the earth nearly four times and sea waves that caused flooding for hundreds of miles. What had appeared a peaked innocent island, beautifully draped with green tropical foliage, became a grim stunted black mass.

As we passed into the Java Sea, the pilot reported an unidentified plane heading rapidly towards us. Fortunately this was the routine challenge from a friend and we came down unmolested, a few hundred yards off the wharfs of Batavia where from the launch we had a climb up a rickety vertical ladder to go ashore.

A few days earlier General Wavell, commanding the area, when returning from a reconnaissance over Singapore, had stumbled from this same ladder and fractured one of his vertebral spines, not a serious, but a very painful injury and confining him to his bed. We spent the night in the Hotel Des Indes, signing chits for a variety of food and tropical fruits that I had never known before, and admiring the Dutchmen putting away their immense ricetaffels. Next morning our G.O.C., after a conference with Wavell's staff, put us in the picture: two Australian Divisions were to arrive and supplement the Dutch troops in the defence of Java. The Australian Corps Headquarters under General Lavarack had already arrived and were established at Bandung and our headquarters were to be sited in the same area among the mountains. Later that day we drove up to the Witte Witkin (White Wings) hotel, drinking in every mile of the beauty.

Gregan McMahon as Moriarty in The Adventures of Sherlock Holmes.

Grandfather.

My father.

Reading from left to right—Maj.-Gen. Allen, Gen. Wavell, Lieut.-Gen. Sir John Lavarack, Syria 1941.

Lieut.-Gen. Morshead and Gen. Douglas MacArthur.

Maj.-Gen. George Vasey.

If Singapore fell, as seemed certain, it was inevitable that the Japanese would attempt to invade Sumatra and Java, and we set out through this glorious country to prepare our appreciations. But the further the situation was studied the more certain became the conviction that seriously to attempt this defence with the limited resources to be made available could result only in a tragic sacrifice. General Lavarack determined to resist any such wastage of Australian troops, two of the only remaining battle-trained divisions in the A.I.F. (the 8th Division was already practically lost in Malaya). The first flight of our troops, a machine gun battalion, an engineer group, a pioneer battalion and a casualty clearing station, had arrived and lay anchored in the harbour. Before they could be landed, General Lavarack approached Wavell with the costly futility of the original plan, signals flashed to London and Australia, but eventually the troops were landed as a gesture and dispositions were made for them ashore. The later transports were turned back to Colombo with their troops.

It was disturbing to discover that the first flight had not been tactically loaded: the troops, their arms, equipment and stores had not been associated on the ships and when I had selected a site for the Medical Unit, I realized that they had no means of functioning. Fortunately I found a great mass of first-class medical equipment in a storehouse on the wharf, waiting shipment to Singapore. I took over the lot and told Lieut.-Col. Eadie, the C.O. of the C.C.S., to take what he wanted. I understand there were similar problems with the gunners and the engineers. We heard that a quantity of quinine was lying in the hold of a ship at Tjilaptjap in the south of the island, and I went across to collect this important but short in supply medical store, but I found it had all been dumped into the sea. All these comings and goings failed to produce any worthwhile contribution to the defence of Java, and the Japanese had already invaded Sumatra, but moving over the country opened my eyes to the loveliness of the island, the gem of the Netherland East Indies, the green necklace of the Queen of Holland. It was a quaint sight to see men and boys standing in the water of the terraced rice fields catching little fish, which were seized upon as treasures. Rubber, tea, coffee, cocoa and cinchona—the vegetable source of quinine—and a host of other productive plants grew in profusion on the hillsides among the belts of timber throwing the flash of tropical flowers and foliage into relief. Many of the roads were lined with kapok trees bearing their light green leaves on boughs rigidly horizontal from the stem, while around their feet foamed the white fluff from the bursting fallen pods.

The only interruption to the days was the occasional air raid. Our G.I., the erstwhile instructor in celestial navigation, had persuaded someone to collaborate with him in the production of a simple(?) pocket card designed to give instant discrimination between a friendly and a hostile plane. One morning I was driving down to Batavia with the G.O.C. and this remarkable man when three or four planes could be heard and then seen flying apparently directly high overhead. We stopped the car, General Allen, our driver and I dived into the roadside ditch. Not so the G.I., who stepped out, pulled his card from his pocket and with his binoculars had just identified the planes as friendly, saying, 'All's well, they're ours,' when CRUMP, CRUMP, CRUMP, down came a stick of bombs, fortunately well off the road.

We celebrated the occasion with a rice-taffel at the Hotel. It would hardly be possible for anyone except a Dutchman to go through the whole of the ritual. Twenty-two waiters with a dish in each hand, rice, many kinds of fish, slices from what seemed to be all the edible flesh and fowl, gravies, pickles, sauces, all the tropical nuts and fruits and more piles of rice. It was a splendid sight to see a Dutchman heap on to his large oval platter portions from every dish and bowl, stir them all together with a large spoon into a great pyramid of protein, fat and sugar, topping it all with gravy and cream, then to see this nauseating mass disappearing down his throat. Our servings were much more modest, as were our chits.

During the meal the G.O.C. was called to the telephone. He came back while we were enjoying the lovely coffee in the lounge and, looking round to see that no one was in earshot, whispered, 'We must leave tonight. Corps and Divisional H.Q. will embark at 2300 hours. We will be picked up here. Get busy.' We dashed back to Bandung to collect our gear, had a hasty meal, then back to the hotel to await our transport to the wharf. We tried to settle our chits, which had accumulated, but no one was interested: there was an ominous atmosphere everywhere. There suddenly came a storm, a deluge of rain, rushing with a deafening hiss, lightning tore the darkness as the thunder crashed and bellowed. The short journey down to the ship was a hazard, and the roads were covered with water, rising with the rain. By 11 o'clock our transport was packed and with four other vessels we pulled out, hoping for the dark security of the violent storm to see us safely out of range by the morning. We were lucky: when dawn came we were well clear of the Sunda Straits and into the Indian Ocean, though we heard later that three of the other ships had been sunk. In the deafening violence of that tropical storm, even the sound of gunfire and bombing was unrecognizable at any distance.

Within a few days we sailed into Colombo Harbour, crowded with transports laden with our comrades from the Middle East.

Chapter 11 New Guinea, 1942

We sailed from Colombo direct to Adelaide. Singapore had fallen, Java invaded, and the Japanese were pushing on into the string of islands in the South-West Pacific—the only remaining bastions before Australia, where the people were living under the shadow of the deepening threat. For the first time there was an awareness of possible air raids and Adelaide was practically pitch black on a moonless night, signposts were disappearing, a few air raid shelters were rising, and slit trenches were disfiguring lawns and gardens. Oddly enough, the intensity of the blackout diminished the further north we moved—later we found that Brisbane was barely brown. In Adelaide many of the soldiers were billeted in private homes to the delight of the householders—the children were entertained, the grass was cut, the hedges trimmed and the odd job cleaned up. But no one seemed to know what was to happen next and in this period of uncertainty no home leave was granted. Our northern defences were being planned and that seemed surely the direction of our next move.

After a few weeks we went on to Melbourne. Home again and I realized day by day what it meant to be away from my family and missing for all time those delightful years when one's children are growing up and growing closer, and to whom for some time at least I must have seemed somewhat of a stranger and an intruder —both they and I had grown up in the interval.

We had a few elementary exercises with landing craft in Port Phillip Bay, then were assigned to Tenterfield in the New England country of New South Wales, to concentrate the Division later in the Glass House Mountain area, north of Brisbane, before crossing to New Guinea.

Corps Headquarters under General Rowell was to move in the first flight and as Brigadier Bill Johnston, the D.D.M.S., had met with an accident, I had temporarily to take his place. Flying along the North Queensland coast was a delight, in the clear morning sunshine, the islands of the Barrier Reef were a necklace of gems, with the white beaches, ringed with a pale emerald green of their shallows over the coral as they sank into the deep blue of the Pacific Ocean. We fuelled in the grim ghost of Cooktown, then across to Moresby. As we came over the harbour I looked down on the rusting hulls of the *Macdue* and the other vessels, victims of the Japanese bombers. I had expected the lush green of the tropics but was disappointed to land on a dry, dusty strip surrounded by tall dry grass and sparse, stunted trees. This long narrow coastal plain might have been any dry area of Australia, but beyond rose the foothills of the Owen Stanley Range, a spine along the length of the island, rising to 13,000 feet. After a week, Bill Johnston flew in and I was glad to return to my Division after the rather rarefied atmosphere of Corps Headquarters. While we were in the Middle East, General Ginger Burston, the Senior Medical Officer on General Blamey's staff, had issued a questionnaire to all his senior officers in the area, seeking information as to the next posting they would select if given the choice and the opportunity arose. I had replied: 'I wish to stay with my Division, but if I have to be moved there is only one other posting I would like—that is yours, Director of the Medical Services of the A.I.F.'

Ginger replied rather nicely: 'Thank you, but as I am feeling particularly well at present, you can stay where you are.'

Only vague information concerning the situation in New Guinea had drifted down to the Australian public. A few in high places must have been in the picture, but I had little conception of what was happening and of what had gone before. Conflicting and often inaccurate press statements had been available, but it was only some days after we had landed in Moresby that I was able to appreciate details that had led up to the present situation. Few accounts are more wearisome than a dull recitation of dates, but it was essential to have some chronological sequence of events before I could prepare an appreciation for my own information and for my diary.

Just before Japan entered the war in December 1941, a militia battalion had been moved to Moresby and two additional ones had followed a few weeks later with some supporting arms. These units were composed of young men, many not yet in their twenties, ill-trained, ill-disciplined and ill-equipped for battle. Malaria and dysentery soon delayed any training and any defence preparations. The R.A.N. had posted watches along the northern coast and the R.A.A.F. possessed a small group of slow, outmoded aircraft in Moresby. How the study of military history had been neglected! The leadership, the training and, with the exception of their weapons and planes, the equipment of these unfortunate troops were inferior to those of Sir Garnet Wolseley's command in the Ashanti War nearly seventy years before, a campaign in country comparable with New Guinea in which the Ashantis employed tactics similar to those of the Japanese in the jungle and Wolseley met with tactics that later proved successful in New Guinea.

Towards the end of January 1942, an A.I.F. battalion in Rabaul was overrun by the Japanese and air raids on Moresby began. There was some damage done to the harbour, and a measure of panic and looting took place among the troops, but, what was worse than that, only three of our serviceable aircraft remained. It was nearly a month before a squadron of modern fighter aircraft arrived, after the Japanese had landed at Salamaua near Lae.

None except the Japanese seemed to be in a hurry.

Fortunately that grand A.I.F. soldier, Brigadier Selwyn Porter, with a few A.I.F. officers, arrived during April to take over the militia brigade. When Porter had recovered from the shock of surveying his command, he began forthwith to bring what efficiency was possible into his 'troppo' disgruntled troops. Slowly the morale of at least one battalion began to improve and the defences of Moresby began to develop. Towards the end of July, on a clear afternoon, the Japanese advance party landed at Gona Mission on the northern coast, unopposed until early next morning, when a solitary bomber, given the target of his life and freedom from anti-aircraft fire, dived down over the convoy and dropped all his bombs into the sea. Later in the day, when the landings were nearly completed, a flight of bombers from Moresby made a direct hit on one transport, which was run ashore to remain a rusty wreck to greet us when we eventually reached the northern coast many months later.

A few of the Mission personnel managed to escape the invaders; those who did not—men, women and children—were beheaded.

Within a day or so, some 2,000 fighting men, hundreds of Korean and native carriers, horses and bicycles had assembled round the northern beaches, and, leaving a group of base troops to prepare for the main body, pushed on to Kokoda, the spearhead of one prong of the advance on Moresby, the other to come a few weeks later from a landing at Milne Bay on the eastern tip of New Guinea.

To meet this advance, a company of what Porter considered to be the best of his bad battalions set out over the mountains. During the last few months, two battle-trained A.I.F. Divisions from the Middle East had landed and remained in Australia, but were given no training in jungle fighting. In addition, there were many thousands of trained A.I.F. reinforcements waiting to be sent overseas. However, to the request by Lieutenant-General Rowell that his A.I.F. Corps should be sent to New Guinea, there was a Nil return.

The militia Company, the first to cross the mountains on foot, had raced the Japanese to Kokoda, but were held three days farther north at the Kumussi River. Outnumbered and outmanoeuvred but fighting stoutly, this company was driven back to Kokoda and when almost surrounded retired, fought back again but was finally driven back into the mountains.

With the loss of Kokoda, it was realized that 'penny packeting' with bits and pieces against a fanatical enemy, highly trained in jungle warfare, was doomed to fail. The remainder of the original battalion was pushed forward together with another militia battalion, which proved less resolute in forward areas. At long last the A.I.F. began to stir and this was the situation as I found it when I landed in New Guinea at the end of July with Corps H.Q. but no other A.I.F. troops. Fortunately Bill Johnston soon returned to resume his position as D.D.M.S. and thankfully I returned to Tubby Allen and our 7 Divisional H.Q., which had just arrived in Moresby. Within a week only one of our battle-proven brigades, commanded by Brigadier Arnold Potts, was sent over to relieve Porter and his militia troops. All units were under strength and my one field ambulance lamentably so. The task ahead of our one brigade, of which one battalion was still at sea, was the relief of the forward militia troops and the recapture of Kokoda, twelve days stages across the mountains.

My immediate responsibility was to provide a medical service for this operation. The first consideration was the maintenance of the health of the troops in an area known to be highly malarious, where dysentery was endemic and scrub typhus areas were frequently found in the jungle clearings. Malaria and dysentery were problems we had faced in the Middle East and fortunately Brigadier Sir Neil Hamilton Fairley, a world authority on tropical diseases, had been posted to A.I.F. Headquarters. He had predicted the inevitable devastation of troops in tropical areas if adequate medical supplies were not available. A quantity of quinine had been forwarded to Brisbane but with the limited space available those responsible for loading supplies to New Guinea had considered this of low priority and there it remained for months. Later, but far too late, when nearly all the troops had been infected with malaria, some quinine was dropped to us from the air, but landed deep in the jungle and the recovery was practically nil. Fortunately we later received reasonable supplies of sulphaguanadin and when this was available in forward areas, and by the establishment of improvised but efficient latrines along the track, we were able to control the dysentery which for weeks had continued to deplete the troops, moving through the foulings in the mountains. The mortality from scrub typhus was disturbing (up to 19 per cent of those affected), as at that time we had no specific therapy for this disease. Later mite repellents were available for clothing.

But there were other problems in the New Guinea Campaign that we had not met in the Middle East, where movement by air, wheeled transport or on foot was restricted only by the operational situation. It was all very well for Napoleon to declare, 'Speed, speed, aptitude for war is aptitude for movement', but he was usually operating in fairly open country, along alternative routes. For us there was only one narrow route of advance over the densely jungle clad mountains, and this was the only route for the evacuation of our casualties. Before the war little was known of this track, which was considered impracticable for troops, but this narrow native path was to become historic as the Kokoda Trail, and to witness what was probably the last of long marches for any army. I quote from my diary:

'Imagine an area approximately one hundred miles long; crumple and fold this into a series of ridges, rising higher and higher until seven thousand feet is reached, then declining again to three thousand feet; cover this thickly with jungle, short trees and tall trees tangled with great entwining savage vines; through the oppression of this density cut a little native track two or three feet wide, up the ridges, over the spurs, around gorges, and down across swiftly flowing mountain streams. Where the track clambers up the mountain sides, cut steps, big steps, little steps, steep steps, or clear the soil from the tree roots. Every few miles bring the track through a small patch of sunlit kunai grass or an old deserted native garden, and every seven or ten miles build a group of dilapidated grass huts as staging shelter, generally set in a foul, offensive clearing. Every now and then leave beside the track dumps of discarded, putrefying food, occasional dead bodies and human foulings. In the morning flicker the sunlight through the tall trees, after midday and throughout the night, pour water over the forest, so that the steps become broken and a continual yellow stream flows downwards, and the few level areas become pools of putrid mud. In the high ridges about Myola, drip this water day and night softly over the track and through a foetid forest, grotesque with moss and glowing phosphorescent fungi and flickering fireflies.
'Such is the track which a prominent politician publicly described as being "almost impassable for motor vehicles", and such is the route to be covered for ten days from Kokoda to Ilolo.'

It was impossible to establish any hospital care forward of the Moresby area—twelve days stages in rear of the Kokoda battle. During the earlier militia operations Myola 'lake' had been discovered for the first time by white man. Apparently this lake had been known to the natives for centuries but avoided as an area of ghosts and taboo, but this kunai grass clearing in the jungle, more than a mile long, seemed a potential landing ground which would considerably reduce our supply and evacuation problems as every casualty and all supplies otherwise had to be manhandled by carriers. Signals from the forward area for this to be exploited had resulted in the use of the 'lake' only as a dropping area with a 50 per cent recovery, if we were lucky, and we had to continue to rely on ground movement along the track. Stretchers required up to ten bearers, for these and the walking casualties to cover a mile in an hour was good going, and the number of battle and sick casualties was mounting daily. With our limited means of supply and maintenance, every man to be fed in the forward area imposed an additional burden on the carriers. It was obvious under these conditions that the supply and evacuation requirements were far beyond the resources of our own troops in the area; for these purposes thousands of natives were enlisted, and 'biscuit bombers' flew, when the weather permitted, to drop from the sky, but the efficient recovery rate was never high.

So wise had been Governor Murray's policy in the early days of the Papua Administration, whereby Papua was reserved for the Papuans, that when the call went out for volunteers, carriers from villages scattered along the coast and high in the mountains came in their hundreds offering their services. It was difficult to judge their ages; some were obviously young, others as obviously old with greying hair, and there was a marked semitic appearance in many of their hairless faces. The oddities were the few albinos, with their straw coloured fuzzy hair and pink skin, contrasting with the deep chocolate colour of the others. There were many dialects and languages among them and they naturally gathered themselves into groups of those who could talk to and understand one another.

All the white women and children and non-essential men had been evacuated earlier to the mainland, but members of the Administration together with a number of white planters and miners had been formed into A.N.G.A.U.—the Australian and New Guinea Administrative Unit. These men knew and understood the natives, could speak their languages and command their loyalty and respect; an A.N.G.A.U. officer was attached to each Army unit and was responsible for the control and welfare of the carriers. This policy was responsible for the wonderful service that made our campaign possible and ultimately successful.

There was one remarkable figure continually appearing and disappearing among the natives. 'Doc' Vernon, M.C., had been a regimental officer with the Australian Light Horse during World War I and since then had dedicated his wonderful personality and medical knowledge to the care of the Papuans. He was at least seventy years old, tall and lean, and there seemed only a sheet of dark brown paper covering his bones. He was deaf from a blast on Gallipoli and his blue eyes were sunken. Vernon had refused to be evacuated early in the campaign and had walked down the mountains into Moresby hoping to enlist in the Second A.I.F., where, of course, he had been rejected. He thanked them in his husky voice and disappeared back to his natives in the mountains.

This man became a legend among the troops. He appointed himself honorary medical officer to all the carriers and as such he served magnificently throughout the campaign. He was never seen in Moresby again and one day I asked him why. 'Those blighters would keep me there,' he said. He would go forward up to the advanced troops wherever there were carriers, dash back to see that all was well with his boongs along the trail—then off forward again. He never seemed to be still or to stop, unless it was to care for one of his boys. One of my medical officers told me that one night in a forward area Doc Vernon was adjusting the dressing on one of his wounded boys in the middle of the mountains. The Japs were pressing close and the only light was a shaded hurricane lamp, held shakily by another of his boys.

'Hold that bloody light still,' he croaked.

'Taubata, they're shooting at us.'

'I can't hear them and I haven't finished yet, I told you to hold that bloody light still.' He finished his task, then, supporting the patient, shambled back to safety.

Some months later when we were nearing the northern coast, his unmistakable figure ambled along to my tent. If possible he was thinner than ever and his eyes were bloodshot. 'Got a bit of quinine, Doc?' he asked in his gruff voice. 'I've been over 104° the last couple of nights and I've run out.' This was the last time I was to see Doc Vernon. He survived the campaign, went back to his boys and died a few years later. To my very deep regret I was unable to accept the invitation to unveil a cairn now standing above Yodda River, but the memorial to Doc Vernon will remain for all time over every mile of the Kokoda Trail.

To augment the carrier supply, there were the biscuit bombers, the old D.C.3's, those wonderful planes that for more than thirty years maintained their steady service to mankind. As a general rule, if the adequate means of forward supply are available for evacuation, the casualty problem can be solved and when Myola, near the gap in the mountains, had been reported as a suitable landing ground, it was hoped that the planes would contribute to the solution of our medical problem, but this was not to be.

It was difficult for those who had not experienced attacks from the air to appreciate the necessity for dispersal in the presence of such a threat, and General Rowell had pointed this out in no uncertain terms to those responsible for the allied aircraft lined up precisely, wing to wing and tail to tail, without camouflage, on the various strips about Moresby. Air authorities agreed, but the lesson had to be learnt the hard way and early one morning our H.Q. was disturbed by a staccato series of explosions and the rising clouds of dark smoke told their tale of a bombing raid. Without warning a flight of Japanese bombers had swooped down over the mountains along the line of D.C.3's loaded with supplies for the forward troops and Flying Fortresses fuelled and loaded with bombs all standing precisely on the strip. Fifteen planes were severely damaged and five destroyed. As a consequence of this disaster, the supplies in the forward area were reduced to a precarious level and the advancing troops had to be slowed down until reserves could be established. As we had apparently no reasonable prospect of air evacuation before Kokoda was recaptured, this setback, other than the limitation of our supplies, had no effect on our medical responsibilities along the route while carriers were available. Such were the supply difficulties that every man in the forward area and along the route had to earn his keep—no hangers-on were permitted and at this stage I was not allowed to go forward. To provide the forward medical service as well as I could along the trail, I was allotted only two medical officers and thirty-two other medical ranks, but was denied hygiene duty personnel. In the battle area there was still a detachment of a militia field ambulance, two medical officers and thirteen other ranks, in support of militia troops in contact with the enemy.

Fortunately I had available among those who had served with me in the Middle East the ideal medical officer to command the situation along the route and in the forward area, Major Rupert Magarey. How magnificently Magarey, his officers and men served during that phase of the campaign is enshrined in Raymond Paul's

Retreat from Kokoda: if ever awards were richly earned it was by these men, but in the eyes of those who are not present a retirement is often considered a defeat and decorations are rare.

Magarey, pooling his slender resources, manned each staging post with two or three of his medical details and a medical officer where he decided they could be most valuable, while he himself was here, there and everywhere, seeing that all was as well as it possibly could be under those challenging conditions. That no known living casualty was abandoned during that exacting period, that in those pre-antibiotic days of the hundreds of casualties evacuated to the hospitals in Moresby after days of carriage or walking over the mountains, only four died subsequently, is a magnificent tribute to the care and devotion of Major Magarey and his men, to the care of the native bearers, and to the courage and fortitude of the casualties.

Brigadier Arnold Potts had arrived in Moresby to take over the command of the A.I.F. Brigade in the forward area and he realized at once that the Japanese had been heavily reinforced. Major-General Horii, commanding the invasion, had landed with his main body and pushed on to Kokoda. Potts was now facing thousands of fanatical, seasoned troops and, what was equally disturbing, his supplies were in a desperate state.

Each evening requisitions were signalled from the forward area, in Moresby the night was spent packing the demands in blankets, which were in short supply, for the bitter cold wet nights in the highlands. At first light, if and when the clouds permitted, off went the biscuit bombers, and with the exception of Myola the dropping grounds were small clearings in the jungle, generally overgrown, deserted native gardens. The height of the run was important: if too high the goods were scattered over a wide area of jungle and most were lost, and too low was hazardous. For the planes flying in the narrow valleys between and around the twisting ridges, between 500 and 1,000 feet was considered the ideal dropping height. A few parachutes were available later in the campaign but at that time there were none: when the pilot gave the word anyone who had happened to be available for the flight would shove out from the space usually covered by a door and hope for the best. Those below would scatter for safety, but there were casualties, a falling mortar base plate almost carving one native in two when it struck him on the shoulder. The recovery rate was low, rarely as high as 50 per cent, and every item had to be carefully inspected for damage. Sometimes the clouds did not lift for days and dropping was impossible.

Potts's signals concerning his supplies and the battle situation produced increased confusion in Moresby. Those who had not personally experienced the situation could not appreciate the discrepancies between the load sent and the supplies recovered. Even when Potts had with him his 2nd A.I.F. battalion, he was heavily outnumbered and with short supplies a fighting retirement seemed inevitable, but this was not understood in Moresby. An extraordinary order was issued to Potts to return to Divisional H.Q. and explain the situation, which was comparable with Murray fighting the Battle of Gaza from Cairo in World War I.

Rupert Magarey was obviously having on his hands all he could humanly manage and at last, rather reluctantly, I was given permission to go forward and meet him. The account of the physical endurance needed to keep going along the trail had probably been exaggerated and some of us had trained fairly solidly among the rough hills around Moresby and were reasonably fit.

So heavy were the demands of the forward troops on our limited means of supply that anyone moving forward had to be self-supporting for some days and for the first time in my life I was faced with the problem of assessing only essentials. Our jungle greens were tough, so there was no need to carry any clothing other than a change of socks, underclothes and a few hankies. A small towel, a lump of soap, razor and brush, a couple of blankets, smokes and matches in a rubber bag against mildew, hard rations (bully beef and biscuits), mess tin, pannikin and eating irons, a tough strip of hessian with folds sewn down the sides into which poles could be slipped and which, standing on four forked sticks, made an excellent bed raised above the mud, pistol and ammunition, salt tablets, hair brush and comb and a notebook—all were stowed into my pack and pouches or hung about me. In other words we carried our bedroom, wardrobe, dining room and bathroom essentials together with meals and protection. All up this load was about forty pounds, and when the webbing had absorbed perspiration, even heavier. Our excellent military boots were cleated with heavy metal studs, which, together with a stout stick which every soldier carried, made it possible to stand up and move in the mud. only the natives, with their bare, prehensile feet, could stand and move unsupported along the track and through the mountain streams. With the indispensable sweat rag around my neck, I set out early one morning with Ryan, my batman.

The first day was easy, we jeeped to where the Kokoda Trail emerged from the jungle among the rubber about Ilolo. Thereafter, for a few miles the trail rose pleasantly to the first ridge, then, what was more demanding, came the steep slope down to the little native village of Uberi, a small cluster of deserted grass huts across the Gouldie River. In the pouring rain, only our sticks and cleated boots kept us on our feet.

The huts were crowded with casualties resting overnight before their final stage to hospital and any comfort in Moresby. Under the raised floors crouched the carriers, who for ten days had borne their burdens with the tenderest of care. If night found the stretcher still on the track far from a staging post, they would find a level spot, build a shelter over their patient and make him as comfortable as possible, then fetch him water and feed him if food were available—all this before attending to their own needs and lying down to sleep four each side of the stretcher. But the walking casualties far outnumbered those who, quite unable to stagger or struggle along, had to be carried. At each staging post the dressings were adjusted, hot meals and blankets were provided and smokes if they were available, but sometimes there were graves to be dug.

It was a humbling experience to pass the nights with these men, there was hardly a grizzle or a complaint and among the other cheery souls in this village was a padre. He was a man of great bulk but little physical fitness, who was devoted to his battalion, and when his men went forward he was determined to keep up with them, but, alas, although the spirit was willing the flesh was flabby. He had managed the first day, scrambling, tumbling and probably rolling down the steep slope to Uberi, and that finished him—breathless, bruised and aching all over. Next morning he had to watch his battalion move on and I should not be surprised if he wept. He was a courageous and a gentle soul.

He couldn't face the clamber back up over the ridge which, with the aid of gravity he had descended a few days before, and, as the stage ahead was tremendously testing even for fit men, what was to be done with him? There were no mechanical devices available to hoist him over the hills ahead or back to where he could get transport to Moresby; certainly the Gouldie River coursed down to the Moresby area but rocks and cascades made the suggestion of a boat or a barrel beyond reason. It seemed as if he must be there for the duration, becoming the oldest inhabitant of the village, welcoming new arrivals, then speeding them on their way with his blessing. I found him in Uberi and there next morning I left him. 'I'll be seeing you,' he said with his laughing eyes and beaming smile and sure enough he eventually made it. A few months later I was to hear him deliver a magnificent sermon on the northern coast.

The next day began deceptively but probably was the most physically challenging of the whole advance. For a mile or so the track rose gently along the bank of the river, passing native gardens, from which all the edible fruits, bananas and paw paws, had long disappeared, then suddenly round a bend rose the steepness of Imita Ridge. To aid the first troops that had crossed, some thousands of steps had been cut along the track, but with the tramping and slithering of many cleated boots, and the incessant nightly rain, these could be discerned only as irregularities in the mud. Half way up this climb I heard a movement in the jungle near the track. We halted, I drew my pistol and Ryan slipped his safety catch. 'It's all right,' came a feeble but friendly voice, and there we found an elderly officer, lying exhausted over a fallen tree. 'I just couldn't make it,' he said sorrowfully. He had tried to keep up with his unit as it went forward but he was done and quietly slipped aside into the jungle out of sight. It was rather pathetic to hear him but he was really too old and unfit for the physical effort. After we had chatted for a while, he was persuaded to wander quietly back to Uberi and on to Moresby to face the facts of life.

'The golden stairs consisted of steps varying from 10 to 18 inches in height. The front edge of the step was a small log held by stakes. Behind the log was a puddle of mud and water. Some of the stakes had worked loose, leaving the logs slightly tilted. Anyone who stood on one of those skidded and fell with a whack in the mud, probably banging his head against a tree or being hit on the head with his own rifle. Those who had no sticks soon acquired them, not only to prevent falls, but to allow the arms to help the legs, especially with the higher steps.

'After the first half-dozen steps, it became a matter of sheer determination forcing the body to achieve the impossible. It was probably the weight more than the climb, though the climb would have been enough to tire even a lightly loaded man. On we scrambled to the crest, and these ridges were ridges—a few yards flattening out before the steep descent down the golden stairs, where originally some thousands of steps had been cut. The rear companies, where the going is always hardest, took twelve hours to complete the nine (barely four miles as the crow flies) miles. Over the first three miles the track rose 1,600 feet. It then dropped 1,200 feet before the final climb up the Imita Range—2,000 feet in the last four miles. The rear troops arrived in the dark, others going down to help them over the seemingly vertical steps of the last few hundred yards.

'Incessant rain had made the track a treacherous mass of moving mud interlaced with protruding roots that reached out hidden hands to bring the laden troops heavily to the ground. Vines trapped them. Wet boughs slapped at them. Their breath came in gulps. Their eyes filled with perspiration.'

Slipping, sliding and held upright only by our sticks, we came at last to the bottom and that noble 'Salvo' Albert Moore, who always seemed to be where he was most wanted with his tea urn. I had found it was a mistake to loosen my pack and sit down when halting; the effort of rising and harnessing my gear, made heavier with the soaking sweat, nullified the rest. I generally managed to find a tree or a stump against which I could lean back, letting it take care of my load for the time being, and thus drank my pannikins of Albert's hot sweet tea.

Off again, this time along the bed of a swiftly flowing mountain stream, slithering among the boulders for an hour or so until from the bank suddenly rose the final climb to Ioribaiwa. Before leaving the stream, we found a quiet pool where a dozen or so of the troops were bathing—we couldn't have been any wetter and, piling our gear on the bank, in we went clothes and all, refreshed for the steepness ahead.

In climbing these ridges, I found that it was almost a disaster to stop, even for a while, unless I absolutely had to. It was essential to keep my feet moving forward however slowly. If I had to stop, and at times I had to, I would look down over the way I had come and this seemed to lighten my burden and my heart and on I went. Also I found that if I kept my eyes down about my feet and did not look up to the disheartening height above, the steepness seemed less. Up and up we went with no breath left for talking, until at last through the rain I could glimpse the grass roofs on the crest.

By this time I had almost had it, but I was determined to arrive with some display of dignity and paused a few yards below the top to pull myself together. I almost made it but just as I crested the rise in front of the huts I fell flat on my face into the mud and all rank and dignity were obliterated by dirt. I rose a stinking mess, staggered the last few yards and flopped down on a log thoughtfully placed just outside the cookhouse. Ryan helped me off with my gear and brought a lovely mug of sweet tea. When years later I heard Colonel Pickering's chant to Professor Higgins after Eliza's debut at that wonderful ball, 'Tonight, old man, you did it, you did it,' my thoughts went back to that evening at Ioribaiwa Ridge, but my cleated boots, stout stick and Ryan's companionship really did it for me.

Then I had my first smoke for the day. I dangled this delight in front of my nose during each daily trudge, like the carrot and the donkey; how well Calverley knew his tobacco:

> 'Sweet when the morn is grey
> Sweet when they've cleared away
> Lunch, and at close of day
> Possibly sweetest.'

Sleep came easily at the end of the day. We were well into the mountains, where the clammy heat of the day gave way to the cold and comfort of the night. Soon after dawn next morning we were away and the day began as delightfully as a day could under those conditions; we had passed the most trying stage of the trail. Down a fairly steep slope, across a stream, then after a couple of hours on to the crest beyond for a breather. I disturbed a white cockatoo and from the ridge I watched it fly back over the valley we had crossed. In about what seemed a minute it roosted in the jungle we had left a few hours before.

After clambering through the oppressive closeness of the jungle, to come across a grassed ridge in the morning sunlight and look around for miles was like a soothing eye-bath. Later, instead of taking the ridge in its stride as usual, for once the track wound round the slope ahead and the going was reasonably good. By early afternoon we reached Naru, bright in the sunshine, before the depressing evening rain came down, but ominous with the reports of the advancing Japs.

Rumours always run riot in a battle area and the casualties were continually coming in. We heard that the enemy had pushed over the crest of the Owen Stanley Ranges through what was popularly quoted in the press as 'The Gap' and were advancing rapidly. But there was no gap or actual break in the mountain spine, which in one place rose to 13,000 feet but which for about a mile eased down to about 7,000 feet, really a long saddle.

Even when his 3rd Battalion eventually arrived, Potts was greatly outnumbered and with the supply problem unsolved retirement was inevitable. From the Japanese diaries recovered later it was obvious how costly and disappointing this stubborn fighting retirement was to the enemy.

With the Japanese pushing down from the crest, alarm and despondency broke out in Australia where it seemed that our retirement was a retreat or even a rout, and that nothing stood between the Japanese descent into Moresby but 'our defeated troops'. But it was impossible to appreciate the situation from a distance or to realize how magnificent had been the resistance of numerically inferior troops in their first encounter with a highly trained, fanatical enemy in that dreadful jungle.

Brigadier Potts and his brigade H.Q. had been heavily mortared the previous night in their huts at Menari, the stage ahead, and the retreat was on top of us. Disappointed our troops undoubtedly were, fighting till almost surrounded, breaking off, standing again until the ring almost closed, day after day, night after night, under conditions known only by experiencing them. Disappointed—yes, but downhearted—no.

I set out along the track to Menari, a fairly level strip of sticky, stinking, ankle deep mud, and in a mile or so in the darkening with the close of day, I met Arnold Potts in the pouring rain with the remnant of his H.Q. and the retiring troops. We shambled back to Naru, Potts naturally anxious and weary after his disturbed night, but full of fight and tremendously proud of his men. He was bucked to hear that a fresh A.I.F. brigade was coming forward and was reasonably cheery when we reached Naru and flopped down in a hut leaking water everywhere in the pouring rain, inwardly warmed by the inevitable mugs of hot sweet tea. While we were chatting Selwyn Porter, a good friend of Potts, who had come forward after taking back his militia troops, wandered in and explained that he was to take over the command of Potts's brigade. Arnold was to move back to Moresby again to clarify the confusion and the clouded thinking of those who had not seen fit to clear it for themselves. The day suddenly seemed to end in heavy darkness.

I moved out to leave them alone and went round to find Rupert Magarey who was everywhere directing the care and evacuation of casualties from the battle area to the stages along the track. He seemed tireless in that tiresome country and wonderfully cheerful. With the Japs pressing on, all the casualties had to be moved back as soon as possible. All through that night he somehow arranged the sorting of his sick and wounded, encouraging them and seeing that all attention possible was given, but he warned them that all walking cases had to be away before dawn, to be followed by the stretcher parties, and every casualty was fed, cared for and seen on his weary way, up to time. Doc Vernon had given the carriers a pep talk and fortunately the Japs let us get away with it.

Few slept that night at Naru and it was rather like slave driving to rouse those who had had a few hours of peace. The walkers hobbled out from the bare ground beneath the slatted boards of the hut floors, the boongs picked up their burdens and back we all went, thankful for the freedom to do so. With the exception of those who remained to man the weapon pits along the track, we reached Ioribaiwa by nightfall, where the forward troops of the fresh brigade were bivouacked. Brigadier Ken Eather commanding the new force was as always up with his advance troops to whom he was known as Phar Lap: while they struggled along, he raced.

Eather, who was new to the terrain, intended to hold the Japs from Ioribaiwa Ridge, but Porter, who had been over the ground several times, persuaded him to retire to the stronger position on Imita Ridge in the rear. In any case the fierce pressure of the enemy, in spite of their increasingly heavy casualties and desperate hunger, believing they were almost in sight of Moresby, drove our troops back to this rear position, which was rapidly developed into a strong defence. With Porter and the remnants of the 21st Brigade. which had borne the burden and the disappointment of the battles in the retirement, we passed through Eather's brigade and on down to the Moresby area. After a shower, clean clothes, and with no pack on my back, I had the feeling of being levitated from the ground as I moved around, and I now had a first-hand knowledge of the ground and condition in the forward situation.

Chapter 12 Kokoda

When those that remained of the 21st Brigade, only a few hundred men on their feet, had assembled in the Moresby area after their magnificent fighting in the mountains, a parade was called and they were addressed as men defeated 'by inferior troops in inferior numbers'; this rankled bitterly. When the news reached Australia that the fresh A.I.F. brigade was 'retreating' to Ioribaiwa and beyond, the flap became a conflagration and in Moresby stores and equipment were ordered to be prepared for evacuation or destruction and General Blamey came forward to take charge in New Guinea.

In the meantime Eather had strongly developed the defences along Imita Ridge and two field guns were dragged forward ranging on the enemy position on Ioribaiwa. For the first time the Japanese were halted and began to establish defences of logs, vines and weapon pits, but Eather's active patrols found no evidence of any further forward movement. The pressure was increased until one morning our patrols found the Japanese defences abandoned. Shelled, mortared and shot at, starved and sick, they had reached beyond their limit. This was how General Rowell had appreciated the situation would develop, but it was too late. A heresy hunt had been started, Potts was relegated to a position on the mainland and Rowell was returned to Australia. The full story of the Blamey-Rowell clash may be found in John Hetherington's *Blamey* and Raymond Paull's *Retreat from Kokoda*, an admirable account of the first phase of the New Guinea Campaign.

Lieutenant-General Herring assumed Rowell's Corps Command and 7 Div. H.Q. at last decided to move forward and carriers were assembled for their gear.

Kokoda

It seemed to me much easier and less demanding to move independently with Ryan than to march in a H.Q. Group with porters to carry the gear, and we were allowed to go on ahead. The comradeship between an officer and his batman can be very close; Ryan had been with me since Bernie had been taken away in the Middle East. He knew what I needed, when to talk and when to be silent. These were wonderful assets, and without his companionship I don't think I could have made the grade when I had gone forward earlier. We moved—you could not call it marching—one behind the other, sometimes he would pass me, sometimes I would pass him, but we started and finished together and I always had a sense of safety in his presence. Although my pack was laden as before, knowing the track as far as Naru, and the thrill of moving forward with the advancing troops, seemed to lighten the load.

The early mornings were generally calm, and crisp and bright, if the clouds had lifted, and for an hour or so the sunlight flickered through the jungle foliage. Under these conditions it was possible to enjoy what there was to enjoy in the jungle before the rain came down. There was a strange absence of animal life and our allies were surprised that the jungles harboured no lions or tigers. Certainly there were crocodiles along the coast, but in the mountains the highly prized native pig was the only animal I ever saw on the ground. Few birds could be seen, but the harsh note of the cockatoos, as they rose in flight, was not uncommon. The gravelly croak of the bird of paradise, rather than their common salmon plumage, would give warning of their presence, but once I glimpsed a momentary flash of the rare blue type. There was a quaint legend about this beautiful bird, called kummel by the natives, actually a member of the crow family.

Kummel had once a lovely voice but was so repulsively ugly that he could never find a mate, so beautiful was his voice that the other birds would neglect their nesting to listen. At last a meeting was held to solve this domestic problem and the hornbill, the wisest of birds, hit upon a plan. He suggested that if each bird would present one of his finest feathers to kummel he might find a mate and leave the other birds to their nesting. This was done and kummel threw his song to the other birds in gratitude, then flew off to see himself in his new plumage mirrored in a nearby

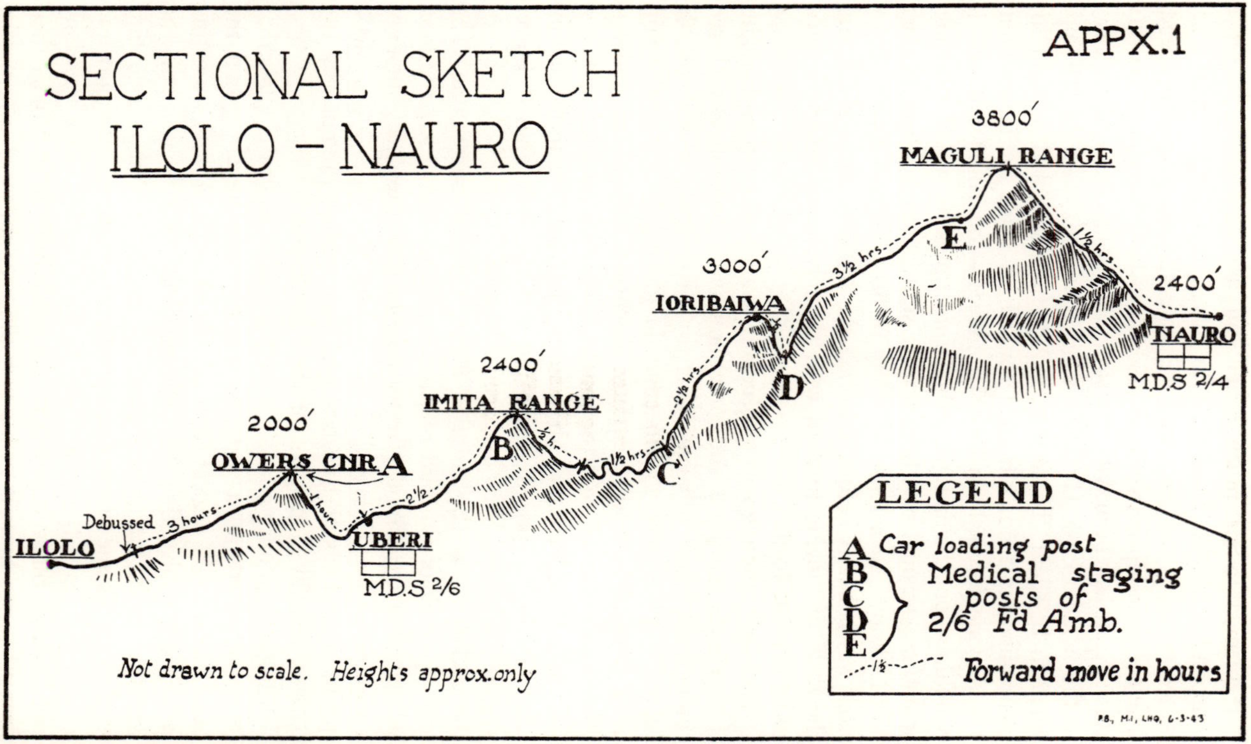
APPX.1
SECTIONAL SKETCH
ILOLO - NAURO
3800′
MAGULI RANGE
3000′
IORIBAIWA
2400′
NAURO
M.D.S 2/4
2400′
IMITA RANGE
2000′
OWERS CNR
A
B
C
D
E
ILOLO
Debussed
3 hours
1 hour
UBERI
M.D.S 2/6
2½
½ hr
1½ hrs
2½ hrs
3½ hrs
1½ hrs
LEGEND
A Car loading post
B C D E Medical staging posts of 2/6 Fd Amb.
1½ Forward move in hours
Not drawn to scale. Heights approx. only
PB., M.I, LHQ, 6-3-43

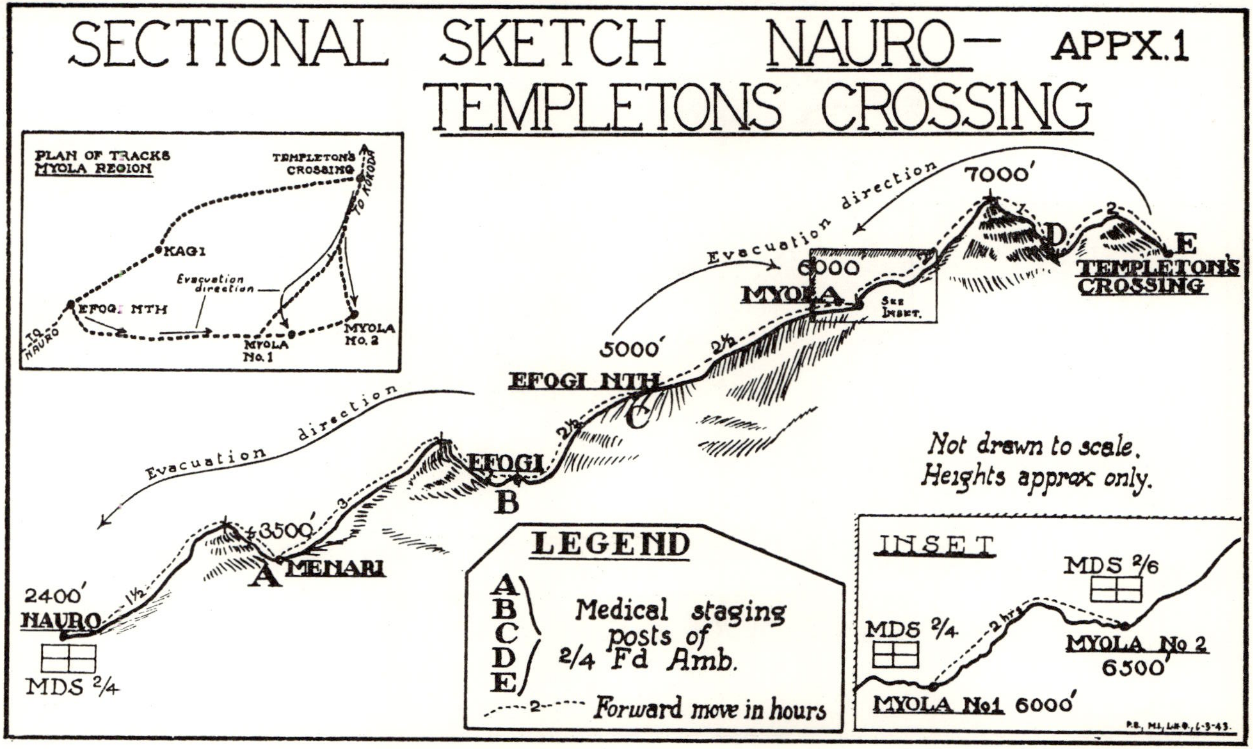
SECTIONAL SKETCH NAURO— APPX.1
TEMPLETONS CROSSING
PLAN OF TRACKS MYOLA REGION
TEMPLETON'S CROSSING
TO KOKODA
KAGI
EFOGI NTH
Evacuation direction
MYOLA No.1
MYOLA No.2
TO NAURO
7000'
Evacuation direction
6000
MYOLA
See Inset.
D
E
TEMPLETON'S CROSSING
5000'
2½
EFOGI NTH
C
2½
EFOGI
B
Evacuation direction
3
3500'
A
MENARI
2400'
1½
NAURO
MDS 2/4
Not drawn to scale.
Heights approx only.
LEGEND
A B C D E Medical staging posts of 2/4 Fd Amb.
2 Forward move in hours
INSET
MDS 2/6
MDS 2/4
2 hrs
MYOLA No 2
6500'
MYOLA No1 6000'

APPX.1

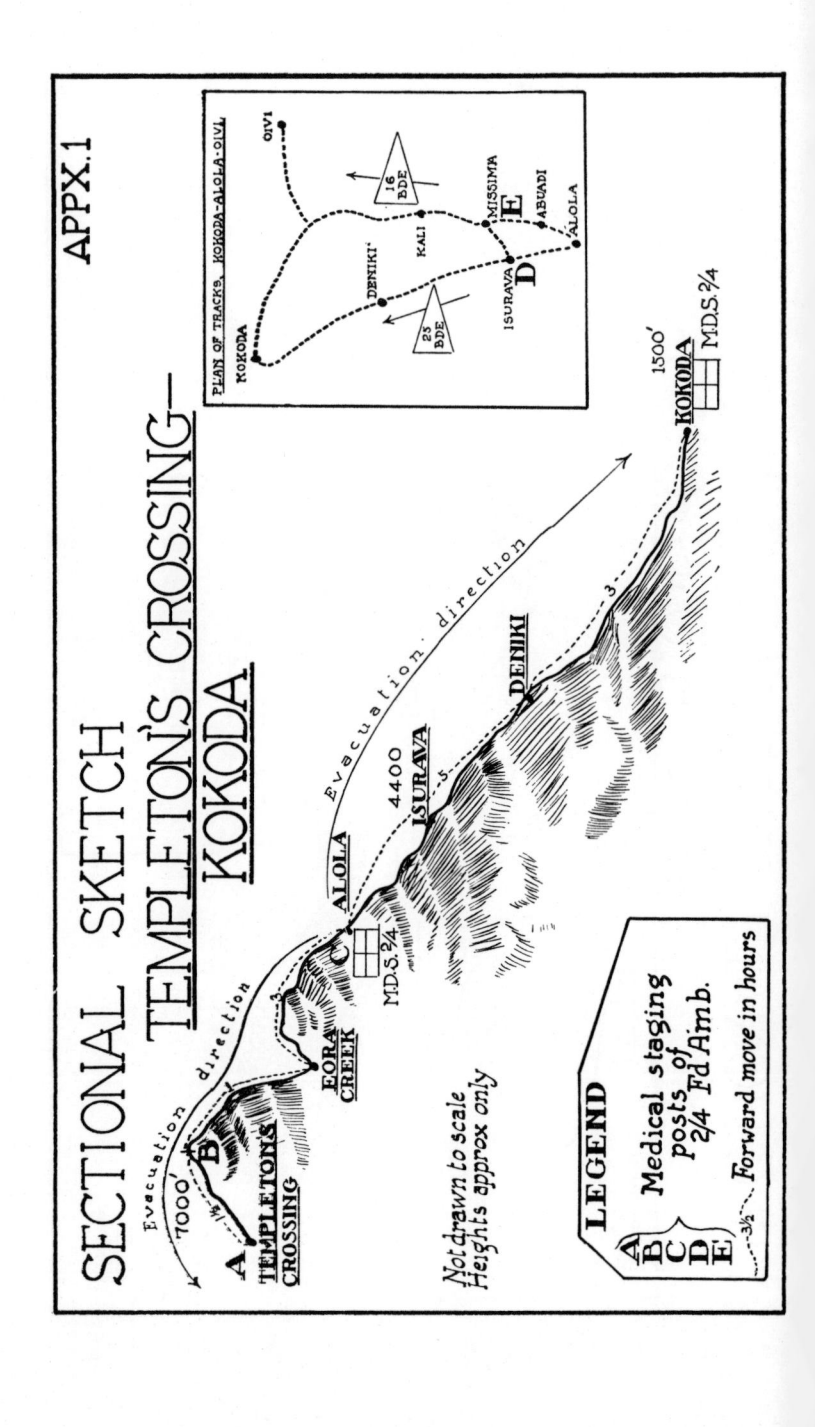

SECTIONAL SKETCH
TEMPLETON'S CROSSING — KOKODA

PLAN OF TRACKS. KOKODA-ALOLA-OIVI

- KOKODA
- OIVI
- DENIKI
- KALI
- MISSIMA — E
- ISURAVA — D
- ABUADI
- ALOLA

16 BDE
25 BDE

- A — TEMPLETON'S CROSSING — 7000'
- B
- EORA CREEK
- C — M.D.S. 2/4 — ALOLA — 4400'
- ISURAVA
- DENIKI
- KOKODA — 1500' — M.D.S. 2/4

Evacuation direction

Not drawn to scale
Heights approx only

LEGEND
- A B C D E Medical staging posts of 2/4 Fd Amb.
- ---3½--- Forward move in hours

lake. His reflection was so glorious that he cried out for joy but his voice broke and only a harsh croak came from his throat and he has croaked ever since.

In the morning sunlight over the streams fluttered green and purple and blue butterflies, some with a four or five inch span across their iridescent wings. Towards night among the native gardens there was a chattering of birds, the rhythmic flap of the hornbill's wings and the occasional swish and shuffle of the flying foxes as they glided and settled on any fruit remaining.

But the real delight of the track was the companionship of those trudging along. Sometimes we would catch up with some stragglers and move together for a while with that comradeship that arms alone can provide. More often we would be overtaken by individuals more fit or less heavily laden. I will always remember the morning when Ian Morrison of *The Times* caught up with us and we stayed together until Naru. He had the brightest blue eyes and with his quiet voice and interesting experiences he was a delightful companion. Alas, he was killed later in Korea after I had caught up with him again in that campaign.

Herbert Kienzle, our Headquarters A.N.G.A.U. officer, was another whose company was enjoyed by everyone who knew him. Kienzle, a planter at Yodda, near Kokoda, had come into the picture at the beginning of the campaign, and to Kienzle, with his wide and intimate knowledge of the natives and their dialects, together with his officers and old Doc Vernon, we owed the enlistment and the continued loyal service of the natives throughout the dangers, the disasters and the final triumph of the whole campaign.

We gauged each day's journey to arrive at the next stage in ample daylight, and setting off at dawn we reckoned on a mile in the hour with a break for a meal of bully beef and a dessert of a few dried fruits. Each day's stage generally ended at a deserted native village, nearly always at the top of a ridge as the natives felt safer away from the sound of the mountain streams, dulling the approach of any enemy.

From Ioribaiwa the Japs had retreated for miles leaving our advance unmolested until 'The Gap' was reached. As there was not the continual flow of casualties moving back to hinder our advance, other than the inevitable knee and ankle injuries and the sick, our advance was uninterrupted.

When the Japanese abandoned their defences, they abandoned discipline, and, what was more dreadful, decency and civilization. Every mile of their retreat bore evidence of their demoralization. Abandoned rusting weapons, mouldy papers, fungating rotten rice and dead, unwounded men ghastly in their emaciation, abandoned where they had finally fallen, unable to keep pace with their retreating comrades. Lying at times beside a weapon pit were the tattered moulding remains of what had been our jungle green, where many weeks before an Australian soldier had fought till he died, but generally the beetles and foul things of the jungle had left nothing but bare bones and perhaps an identity disc. The most bestial evidence of all was the remains of the mutilated bodies of two Australian soldiers: the arms had disappeared and from the thighs had been cut lumps of flesh. Later when diaries were recovered from the Japanese dead about Gorari, three independent intelligence officers translated: 'Because of the food shortage one of our Companies has been eating the flesh of the Australian soldiers. The taste is said to be good.' Confirmatory evidence of this ghoulishness came later, during the coastal battles.

From the village of Effogi, perched on a knoll, there was a steep descent, then a clamber up the ridge beyond to the gently rising ground leading to Myola. There was a small dressing station in a little clearing beside the track and there we flopped down for a breather. In a few minutes along came a man with the usual mugs of hot sweet tea, his shapeless felt hat, his bare suntanned torso above his torn, stained green trousers giving no indication of his rank. He sat down beside us and began chatting away cheerfully.

'I thought I knew all of you medical fellows along the track,' I said, 'but I can't place you.'

'No,' he said, 'I have only been up here a few days.'

'What are you? A medical orderly?'

'Not quite that,' he said.

'Well, what are you doing here?' I pressed him.

'I'm really the R.C. padre,' he said.

This was my first meeting with Padre Cunningham, one of the many splendid padres with whom I was privileged to be associated.

It was almost dark when we reached Myola. It was pouring

rain and bitterly cold and we were glad to have what shelter our Field Ambulance could provide, a leaking hut, but at least off the ground. The Japs were standing at last on the ridge a mile or so above and until they were cleared we had to stay put at Myola. So rapid had been our advance that supplies became a problem and reserves had to be established for the advance down to Kokoda, some four days ahead.

While we were delayed at Myola there came a report of a larger lake beyond and, setting out to investigate this, we climbed over an intervening ridge and came down to a much more desirable clearing some three or four miles in extent, slightly undulating and covered with coarse grass through which ran the narrow headwaters of the Iora Creek tumbling down to the Yodda River a few thousand feet below. Here surely, along the level higher ground on the farther side, was the answer to our evacuation problem and urgent signals were sent off calling for planes. Anticipating their arrival, the field ambulance was moved across and native huts and tents were erected for the mounting casualties. Landing strips were rapidly prepared and in a few days I saw one large plane land laden with supplies. When the pilot agreed to take back a few of our casualties, I felt our troubles were over. 'Sure, this is a grand little strip,' the pilot said to me. Years before World War II, Colonel Robert Fowler had lectured on the future role of Air in Casualty Evacuation and on occasions planes had been used for this purpose in the desert, but in the jungle when the only possible alternative to a ten day carry or walk was evacuation by air, requiring less than one hour's journey, no air evacuation policy was available at Myola. In spite of every urgent pleading from our forward area, other than three visits from small planes, air evacuation ceased, and we had to wait till the way was cleared to Kokoda, while the casualties crowded the dressing station or began their weary trudge over those dreadful ten days back to Moresby. Why after three years of war no ambulance planes were available, or why regular air evacuation was not undertaken from Myola, has never been satisfactorily explained.

This disappointment, added to the physical strain of the campaign, caused feelings to be rather frayed and some bitter signals were sent back. Certainly there was an almost assured air lift from the Kokoda strip four days ahead, but the Japanese, reinforced with fresh troops, were stubbornly defending in the area about the Gap in the bitter cold and the constant rain.

It was at this time I received my only seal as a soldier. The Japanese rearguard stood across and around the track as it crossed the crest above Myola, and one of our battalions was slowly winkling them from their bunkers and foxholes. One morning I went up with Major Tom Cotton, the second in command, to see how things were going with the battalion. The Japs were thirty or forty yards ahead and using a small spring mortar with an audible click, giving me time to shelter behind the stout buttress roots of a jungle tree. As a small bomb burst over to my right, a cry came from a wounded man and a bee stung me on the right leg above the knee. I looked down but there was no bee, only a small area of smouldering trouser leg, a tiny hot fragment must have brushed my leg—there was no wound, but a small burn scar about the size of a threepence has remained to tell the tale.

Every endeavour was made to outflank these strong defences, but in the rain forest of the mountains movement was painfully slow and the supply situation was precarious. The number of carriers needed to pass the supplies on to the forward troops were rapidly thinning; many of these boys had been carrying, with only short breaks, since the campaign began some months before.

It was not possible for those in Moresby to appreciate what was happening, nor why we were not sweeping through the stubborn, fanatical opposition. General MacArthur's opposite number in the U.S. Navy had achieved a notable victory in the Coral Sea Battle and the General was anxious to reinforce our troops with his own men when we reached the coast and together bring about the final dramatic re-conquest of New Guinea. One evening Tubby Allen, our Divisional Commander, showed me a signal he had just received. 'General MacArthur considers extremely light casualties indicate no serious effort yet made to destroy the enemy.' Since when did heavy casualties always indicate sound leadership? But to the bitterness of the cold and wet at Myola there were added each evening similar biting signals from Moresby. 'O.P. reports show that progress on the trail is not satisfactory, the handling of our troops is faulty.' MacArthur was becoming increasingly impatient at having to hold back his troops for the final victory. He may not have appreciated a strongly fortified Japanese position, weapon pits, bunkers roofed with stout logs, heavy and light machine guns, mortars and rifles covering every approach. Another signal: 'You should consider acting with more boldness. During the last five days you have made practically no progress.' Tubby's first reaction was to signal MacArthur: 'Come up yourself and fight the bloody battle with what I have, and see if you can do any better,' but Charles Spry, his G.I., talked him out of this. Another signal: 'In spite of your superior strength (sic) enemy appears to delay advance at will.' Tubby and I were very close those days and I realized the strain when he showed me these signals.

Finally just at dark on 27 October came the final blow: 'Consider you have had sufficient prolonged tour of duty in forward area. General Vasey will arrive by air morning 28 Oct. On arrival you will hand over command to him and return to Moresby for duty in that area.'

Tubby handed this to me but I could say nothing. 'Well, that's that,' he said, and his was the third head to roll into the basket. First went Potts, just as those under his command had fought the Japs almost to a standstill during the retreat. Rowell's just as his direction of the campaign had held and turned the Japs. Allen's within twenty-four hours of his troops fighting the Japs out of their defences and hurling them headlong down the slopes through and beyond Kokoda.

Next morning we went across to Myola II to meet our new Divisional Commander, Major-General George Vasey, who had flown in when one of the small planes was allowed to land.

I had first met George Vasey nearly forty years before, when as youngsters we had both spent our holidays at Point Lonsdale. He was at Wesley while I was at Melbourne Grammar and I don't remember seeing him again until we were in the Middle East. George's lanky legs and tall, lean body emerged from the plane, followed by his A.D.C., Bill Riggall.

Polite or profane as was suitable for the company or the occasion, beloved by all ranks under his command, including the padres, George was inspiring by his example, but was humanely hard in the fairness of his abrupt condemnation, which in some way did not engender resentment. He had the rare gift of transmitting words usually considered foul almost into terms of endearment and often greeted an old friend with, 'You dear old bastard', and when called to the phone by a senior officer he would commence the conversation with, 'Bloody old George here.' He would have succeeded in any task associated with the leadership of men and to our good fortune the men on this occasion were the soldiers of the 7th Division.

George wore his red-banded cap of a senior officer every day until the end of the campaign, and without a word he inspired those of us who were so entitled to do likewise. It never seemed to occur to him that his tall figure crowned with this incongruous colour in the jungle was dangerously conspicuous (there was still the odd Jap sniper along the track and in the trees waiting for such a target), but even if this did occur to him he ignored it, as he believed—and rightly so—in the value of this among his troops, which was all he cared about. George and Tubby spent the last night together, pooling their ideas about the tasks ahead.

Next morning, rather like a cortège, a small group of us went across with Tubby to the plane waiting at Myola II. As we walked back the silence was broken after a while. 'Poor bloody old Tubby. He really has done a grand job.' George could be very gentle and generous.

Within twenty-four hours of his departure, Tubby's planning broke the Japs' defences and instead of looking up to ridges ahead, the troops gazed down the cleft that led to Kokoda and the Promised Land beyond, which, like Moses, many were not to reach. Off went George and our Divisional H.Q. Up the steep climb to the crest, then down to Templeton's Crossing, the first stage where in the earlier battles a Colonel of that name had been killed. That night as we turned in to what remained of a native hut beside the cascading Eura Creek, I noticed that George was limping. He was not complaining—I never did hear him complain but I insisted on looking at his leg, which he profanely resented. At last when we were alone he slipped down his muddy, soaking slacks and I found his knee swollen with fluid. The day's march must have been hell for him. 'Slap some bloody bandage on it, if you like, but don't you dare say anything about this, or I'll cut your bloody throat.' This was the least intimate of George's daily threats. Each morning and night for the next few days, in the secrecy of his shelter, I had to bind his knee with a pad and bandage until the fairly level going beyond Kokoda brought him relief and he tossed 'the bloody lot' into the fire.

On and down we went, wading or crossing the streams on rocking, narrow native bridges of slats strung together with stout vines. Eura Creek, Alola, Isurava, Deniki and into the rubber plantations of the Yodda Valley. As we tramped through the welcome shade of these lovely trees, our cleated boots scored the protruding roots which wept white latex until the track became a grey, muddy pathway leading to a rise above the river and a few charred huts and poles, all that remained of Kokoda, set on a grassy knoll. Bravely some blue larkspurs and bright phlox were in flower among the reds and yellows of the tough crotons and the fragrant frangipani. There was shade from the great leaves of the bread fruit trees and the tall, slender areca palms, from which the coloured people of the East gather the betel nut, which they crush and mix with lime, wrap in a betel leaf and chew, staining their lips and teeth and spitting the red result here, there and everywhere.

On our way down the mountain, as well as the abandoned dead and debris of the Japs, we came across rusty bicycle frames on which their deluded troops had hoped to travel. We had found the first ones thousands of feet high up near the Gap, and heaven only knows how they had dragged them so far before discarding them in their desperation and disappointment. In the bed of one stream we came across the remains of what we found later was General Horii's white charger: to have ridden so far was either the height of horsemanship or the depth of cruelty.

To the carriers these rusty bicycle frames, stripped of tyres and saddles, were a delight. They vied with each other in the joy of trying to ride them with their bare feet on what remained of the pedals, until mercifully they fell into the mud rocking with laughter; they were simple, cheerful souls. Doc Vernon's entry into Kokoda was a pantomime rather than a pageant. Mounted by his boys on a tyreless bicycle with one rusty pedal remaining, this white-haired, skin-covered skeleton, with burning sunken eyes wobbled and wove his way for some distance through the rubber, surrounded by his laughing, shouting boys and held upright by their willing hands until he reached the charred remains of the village H.Q. where he fell into the mud, stood up and solemnly saluted.

At last we had an air strip and that afternoon supplies were landed, not thrown to us. We'd been on iron rations during the last few days and for the first time in weeks we had bread, which we kept back for a savoury at the end of our evening meal. Most of us, however, were violently sick during the night. It was good to meet again some of our old friends from Moresby. Bill Johnston of course was one of the first to fly in with Ned Herring and Chetty Manifold.

The Japs were stoutly defending along the track beyond Kokoda at Oivi and Gerarii and our H.Q. were held at Kokoda for some days. During this delay Bert Keinzle paraded all the available carriers in their tattered and stained ramis on the air strip, each man with a flash of bright croton leaves in his hair. It was a proud occasion, some of the boys were invested with medals and everyone was given a new rami, an army knife and wonderful words of praise from George, which Keinzle translated into the various dialects: 'Without your help we could not have crossed the Owen Stanley Ranges.'

So brutal had been the Japanese treatment of the captured natives that, when the news spread rapidly through the villages of this parade (as news does spread rapidly in some way through that country devoid of any but physical communications) more and more came in to join us, including some Koreans impressed by the Japs as porters, but who had managed to escape and subsist among the native villages.

In addition to the casualties in the battles ahead, we were now faced with the menace of malaria. We had made a survey of the mosquitoes in the mountains from Uberi to the last ridges and had not detected any anopheles, but the coastal area north of Kokoda was known to be highly infested and with a large reservoir of malarious natives. Requisitions had been signalled earlier for prophylactic facilities to be landed at Kokoda, but unfortunately these supplies were dropped by an inexperienced pilot some miles away in the jungle, and no suppressant drugs, no repellents, no nets were available as we advanced into this danger. Within a couple of weeks malaria was upon us and at each stage along the route we had to establish a small medical post for these casualties. None of my Field Ambulances had arrived in New Guinea complete in establishment and a number of officers and other ranks were still marooned at Myola II out of the picture with their hundreds of casualties. This peeling off of medical personnel from those units already under strength for malarial posts severely taxed our meagre medical resources.

In the dressing station that we had established at Myola II, anticipating air transport that did not eventuate, there still remained more than 300 casualties. As long as the enemy stood between us and any assured evacuation from Kokoda, there was no alternative for the casualties that could be moved but the weary rearward route of ten days and we just had to make the best of it.

I well know that disasters had occurred in past campaigns because of directing casualties forward with the advancing troops. (The tragedy in World War I of the Mesopotamian Campaign was the most recent: there the casualties were evacuated forward expecting to arrive at the Tigris where barges could carry them back to the base, but this did not happen and the advancing force, hindered by this policy, was surrounded by the Turks and captured.) When the air strip at Kokoda was secured and safe, although the Japs were only a few days ahead, while carriers were still available for the four days forward carry, a decision had to be made. Wolfe said war is an option of risks and I opted to evacuate stretchers and walkers forward down the mountains to Kokoda. But once the battle moved on towards the coast, no carriers were available in rear of Kokoda and Myola II was again out on a limb. It was not possible to move any hospital forward of the Moresby area until the northern coast was cleared and this did not result until nearly a year had passed since the Japanese threat to New Guinea began. At Myola as soon as possible the sick and wounded literally took up their beds and walked back those ten stages to Moresby, an odd procession, arms in plaster, legs in splints and one man with a fractured patella, the stem of a banana leaf binding each side of his leg. The last casualty walked out of Myola nine weeks after having been wounded. At Myola II the Commanding Officer, Fred Chennall, carried on magnificently during those weeks of frustration and disappointment. He was not an individual to accept without protest a situation he considered to be unreasonable and Fred did not restrict himself to military terminology in his urgent signals back to base, nor do I blame him. Fortunately till we had moved forward to stability about the coast, Fred had with him Major Doug Leslie's surgical team.

The delay when men were wounded, ten days or more from adequate surgical attention, was a very disturbing problem. To contribute to the solution, I was able to attach small surgical teams to the most forward dressing stations along the track where urgent surgery and holding for a day or so was considered safe and unimpeding to the military situation. During the early retirement these surgical stations were the first to move back and later, as the advance went forward, they leap-frogged to keep up with the troops.

In this way casualties were able to receive essential emergency attention with the least possible delay. The overall direction of the forward surgery was under Col. Charles Littlejohn, than whom no one could have been better posted to guide these younger men (all highly trained and splendid general surgeons) along the essential and sound principles of war surgery. Besides Doug Leslie I had 'Vicar' Wakefield, Bill Gayton, Tom Ackland and John Hayward available to me, and their tireless service was all that an A.D.M.S. could have wished for. There was no time or place for individual fancies and there was no question of referring to a 'fad book' as is done in many of our leading hospitals in Australia, a small routine list of essential instruments was made available and that was that. At first all instruments had to be dropped or carried in the surgeon's haversack and he got on with his job under a rotting tent fly or a leaking grass roof over a simple collapsible table standing more often than not in inches of foul mud. These were the pre-antibiotic days and scrupulous personal cleanliness had not been confounded with reliance on 'coverage of pills' and less than 4 per cent of those who received this attention died of their wounds. Later in the campaign penicillin was available and the rapid healing of gross wounds was wonderful; even in those involving deep muscle destruction, such as the horrible buttock wounds, a new era had dawned. A soldier with a severe wound in a limb was always distressed and anxious, his dread of amputation was very real, even one in the 'guts' often disturbed him less, and one in the 'backside', a wound we dreaded, was at first often a joke.

When the Japanese selected Gorari and Oivi to delay our advance beyond Kokoda, this was another example of how unpredictable they were. Two days in their rear was the wide obstruction of the unbridged Kumusi River, an ideal defence position. But no, Horii and his reinforced troops stood stubbornly about these featureless villages between us and the river. George gave them no respite and after a few days a fierce bayonet charge cleared the way. Back went Horii with his defeated remnant, not even pausing at the Kumusi but rushing to gain the perimeter of their beachhead, which Horii himself never reached: attempting to cross the swirling river on an improvised raft, he was drowned.

Kokoda had been a Government Station associated with the missions about the northern coast at Gona and Buna, and the track north fairly level going, the nearest thing to a road we had seen. Our advance troops reported that they were delayed at the Kumusi, not by the enemy, but by the 300 feet of the river rushing over and around ugly boulders in a twelve-knot current. Originally this had been bridged by a wooden span suspended from metal cables strung from stout poles on each bank, hence the native name for this place—Wirerope. By some good fortune early in the Japanese advance from the coast our bombers had destroyed this bridge, which had not been restored.

On went our Division, past Oivi and Gorarii, where the grim evidence of the battle was offensively obvious with nearly one thousand dead still unburied, to find those remarkable people, the engineers, popularly known as the gingerbeers, had cleared a dropping ground and were rigging an improvised bridge. It was a lovely stream set in the dark green of the jungle, dashing and splashing over the great boulders in the sunshine of the early morning, the fine foam spraying into myriads of glittering gems and rainbows. The bridge was soon finished and was stout enough to withstand the strong current, but sagged into the water in the middle of the span and could be crossed only on a one man front if he could hold firmly to the swaying sidelines as the river rushed against his legs.

Our H.Q. had a few days enforced rest while the troops passed slowly to the other side. One morning George and I wandered downstream for a mile or so and came to a shingly beach where lay the sprawled bodies of four Japs, drowned in their retreat and washed ashore. Around one of the bodies was a money belt crammed with sodden but still decipherable Australian pound notes crudely printed in Japan for currency in Australia. Others had pathetic water-stained photos of the families they would never see.

It was a grand sight to see (and hear!) George's gaunt, lanky frame swaying and swearing across the narrow bridge. As his legs sank into the stream the troops cheered and George risked letting go with one hand to wave his red cap—this was nearly fatal but he managed to scramble his feet back to the narrow boards and reach the other side.

Within a short distance beyond the river, the track forked: one Brigade pushed forward along the left toward Gona and we moved with the main body towards Buna. Reports came back that the Japs were standing about Soputa on the Girua River at the apex of their beachhead but the track was clear for days ahead up to that area and a landing strip was being prepared at Popindetta, a few miles in rear of our expected opposition. We pushed on, staging at deserted mission stations—Isavita, Higotura and Sangara. We reached Sangara one night during the rain and were sheltering under the leaking roof of a native hut when in came Colonel Elliot Smith from Moresby. No alcohol had been available for many weeks and when Elliot Smith produced a bottle of gin, the misery of the rain was forgotten and George's eyes lit up as he greeted the visitor with a typical Vaseyan welcome. As the gin went round, each of us was canny in his measure, and within a few minutes of having had our cautious nip things began to happen. George rose unsteadily to his feet, became rather glassy-eyed and said, as far as I could understand, 'I'm going to bed.' As he went out the whole hut and everybody inside seemed to me suddenly to be swaying and I realized that I also had had it and staggered off to my stretcher. Next morning when Ryan brought my morning tea, he asked, 'Did you feel the earthquake last night, Sir?' 'Thank goodness it was that, Ryan,' I replied. Earth tremors are common in that area and a few years later Mount Lamington, just near us that night, was to explode and inundate that little village and many of its inhabitants.

Unfortunately our advance was delayed when the clouds interrupted the supply planes for some days and some Japanse reinforcements were still being landed at the beachhead. Additional troops were soon to arrive for our final battles. An American force was flown in, and combined with our A.I.F. troops that had moved round to the area after their victory at Milne Bay, was heavily engaged on the right flank in the Buna village area against the strong Japanese bunkers among the coconut plantations. Our Division was held near Gona on the left and at the apex of the beachhead at Soputa. We were across the Kumusi by the end of November but it was two months before the coast was cleared and the last Japanese killed. The Japanese defences consisted of well sited and hidden weapon pits and heavily armed, stout bunkers of heavy logs and earth, solid enough to withstand all but direct gunfire. At last we had complete air supremacy and all hope of land reinforcements and supplies, or evacuation by sea, was denied the enemy. It came down to slowly eliminating all resistance by weapons, mosquitoes and starvation. The Japs appeared to have no shortage of ammunition, but captured diaries told of their scanty supply of food and their horrible reversion to cannibalism. In a highly malarious area, if it were possible to deny medical supplies to an enemy, it would not matter what food and ammunition he had, provided you had adequate supressive drugs and were prepared to wait for the inevitable as victory was only a matter of time. As we advanced throughout the campaign, I had found no evidence of medical service or supplies among the deserted Japanese areas.

In the Middle East, Army Malarial Control Units (A.M.C.U.) had been organized and had given splendid service in the infested areas. These units were with us when we returned to Australia, months before the New Guinea Campaign began, and signals had been sent to Moresby for this service to be made available for us. Regretfully Bill Johnston advised: 'Sufficient stores and equipment to be used are not available at present here. Urgent requisitions have been sent to mainland for these on several occasions during past few weeks and your urgent request for two M.C.U.'s with stores and equipment has also been sent off as a result of your signals.'

No one in Moresby could have done more. A little quinine had arrived early in December, a few nets and repellents a little later, but the damage had been done. Unless those dreadful conditions of the coastal swamps and jungle had been experienced, it was impossible to realize the problems of providing adequate antimalarial measures. It was difficult to ensure that all troops were taking their quinine. There was a popular belief among the soldiers that this drug was responsible for sexual impotence. Reasonable success was achieved only when George Vasey issued a characteristically worded order indicating that, however the troops thought quinine affected certain physiological functions, the effects of malaria were far more drastic and enduring in the same field.

A very few, in some extraordinary manner, seemed to be immune from malaria, but this was very rare, and by the end of December at least 75 per cent of the troops were malarious. Not that everyone who was sick went off duty: if his temperature was under 102° and the man could stand on his feet, he carried on with a rest about midday. If he was really sick and his temperature was higher, he could lie up for a few days, but if then not able to return to any duty he was evacuated from Popindetta.

With the establishment of the air strip at Popindetta and the development of Dobadura across the river as a busy airport, I moved all my personnel forward for the final battles. The only exception was Fred Chennall and his dressing station, still marooned at Myola II until the last of his casualties could be cleared, which was not until the end of December.

The weather over the mountains was still a problem and on one occasion planes would not come in for five days, during which more than 600 casualties had to be held in the dressing station on the strip. But on the next fine day more than 400 of them had been evacuated to Moresby hospitals, about one hour away, by air. Fortunately the track from the forward area to this strip was passable for jeeps converted to carry stretchers and, apart from the uncertainty of the planes, our problems were fairly simple despite the diminishing number of our medical personnel.

Buna, a village on our right flank, finally fell to the pressure of the A.I.F. and American troops and the bitter Gona battle on the left was reduced to a small beachhead perimeter. One morning George Vasey, complete with red cap, decided that his A.D.C., Bill Riggall, and I should go with him over to this area and see how the battle was going.

From Soputa the track across to that flank was a sea of mud and after a few hundred yards George, with characteristic embellishments, said, 'I am going to walk on the drier ground off this bloody track.' This sounded easy, but once you leave a jungle track, even for a few yards, you find yourself dodging trees and vines and soon you lose your sense of direction unless you keep referring to your compass and a set bearing. In a few minutes Bill and I, who had stuck close together, lost George and it was known that the odd Jap was loose in the area. We coo-eed and called but there was no answering George. 'We're for it,' said Bill. 'All we can do now is to get back to the track and push on as best we can.' Then we heard two rifle shots. 'That's that,' said Bill. 'He's gone.' In a few hundred yards we came to one of our soldiers crouching by the side of the track. 'There's a couple of Japs along there,' as he pointed in the direction we were going. 'Look out for them, they're waiting for you.' Again we moved off the track and pushed on carefully, keeping it in sight as well as we could. We soon came to two more of our soldiers, who were waiting to escort us into Jumbora, a stage on the Gona route. 'We've lost our General,' Bill said. 'He's all right—the old man's waiting at Jumbora for you and he sent us chaps back to bring you in.' Our minds, obsessed with Japs, had failed to understand the first soldier.

At Jumbora we found George again, grinning all over his face about a mug of tea. 'Well, you old bastards, what happened to you?' We explained that it was all very well for George with his long legs to stride along at miles per hour while Bill and I with our shorter ones struggled in vain to keep up with him. Long before we came to the Gona battle we could smell it, but in spite of the stench we slept soundly.

Next day we returned to Soputa, weary with trudging through the miles of mud. I flopped down on my bunk for a rest, then realized that I would have to make further medical arrangements for the Gona area. I went across to what remained of my one Field Ambulance, their huts and tents in a small clearing by the Girua River, clearly marked from the air as a medical post.

With the C.O., Arthur Hobson, and his small group of officers, we were sitting on some coconut logs and discussing our plans over a mug of tea. The sun was shining brightly that afternoon and everyone seemed as cheery as it was possible for a group of malarious men to be. Suddenly, without warning, there was a whirr of low planes, machine gun fire and bomb explosions nearby. 'Get down,' I yelled and Arthur Hobson and I lay flat on the ground as two planes with the round red blob on their Zero wings swooped down over us from a height of barely a hundred feet, machine-gunning and bombing our area. Two of the officers—Ian Macdonald and Ian Vickery—raced for the jungle a few yards away, but were caught and killed instantly; it was all over in a matter of seconds but the havoc was horrible. Fifteen men were dead and twenty-three wounded, huts set on fire with that nauseating odour of burning flesh and destroyed stores. These officers and men had given magnificent service all through the campaign, victims of a savage, inhuman attack on a clearly marked medical post.

When we had recovered our senses, we all set about putting out the fires, cleaning up the mess and digging graves. When I returned to my tent that evening, I found that two of my clerks had been killed and where I had been resting was a shambles, a metal shaving mirror, which had been hanging at the head of my bunk, was deeply furrowed and half buried in the mud. This was our darkest day.

The closing days of the Gona battle were ghastly. Finally penned into the small mission area, a clearing about a quarter of a mile along the beach and for half this distance inland to the edge of the jungle, the remnant of the Japs were bombed, shelled and mortared day and night. They had no possibility of breaking out or receiving help or supplies but they would not surrender. The last resistance came from a strongpost among the gnarled roots of a tree a few yards from the water's edge. For two hours this post fought off all attempts at capture and only when the last seven survivors had been killed was the battle over. We then understood the stench that reeked over the area and why some gas masks lay about in the mud. No attempt had been made to bury their dead; what had been men and pieces of men lay rotting over the torn ground or had been built into the defences. A few charred poles still remained of what had been a mission station and a scarred white wooden cross stood erect, a silent symbol of all this sacrifice. Down on the narrow strip of white sand sprawled the bodies of two recently dead Japanese who had obviously committed suicide. A few days later two emaciated Japanese were flushed from the jungle by a patrol. They refused to surrender and, wading into the sea, each placed a grenade on his head and pulled out the pin. We came across one Jap in the jungle, little more than a skeleton and just alive, and he was taken into one of our dressing stations. As one of our orderlies lifted him gently forward and put a mug of tea to his lips, he gathered enough strength to dash it away and bite the orderly's hand, then fell back to die in a few minutes. It was a very horrible war.

After months of travail we had reached the northern coast 'and though with great difficulty I am got hither, I do not repent me of all the trouble I have been at to arrive where I am'.

With the capture of Gona on our left and Buna on our right, the Japanese base on the beach became constricted to a mile or so about the Girua River, and there still remained the strong inland defences up to Soputa. The area still denied us was dense jungle, slime and mud and tangled sago swamps—what had been dry ground was changed overnight into a morass. Ten inches fell in the space of a few hours on one occasion. Under these conditions, men, exhausted with malaria, tropical sores and scrub itch, but inspired with the thrill of victory, were fighting a fanatical enemy, often less than fifty yards from them. One narrow track led through this area to the beach about a mile away and a fantastic situation developed. Directly facing us at Soputa were strong Japanese defences. By moving around these we had established a track block behind them, Huggins Post, beyond which lay the final Japanese defences. We had a few tanks supporting our guns and other weapons which, in more open country, would have been rapidly decisive, but with the enemy literally within every few yards of the jungle, it was a matter of exerting continual pressure, winkling out each little foxhole and bunker in turn, a slow and costly creeping process.

An Allied Unit was moved across to our command daily becoming thinner in personnel. What these new troops lacked in battle experience they made up in keenness and in theory, and one of their medical units, a 'portable hospital', came under my command. When they arrived I showed the Commanding Officer, a very charming man, a rough map of the situation. 'You are supporting that group. Move your men along the track and get established at a suitable site. I'll look you up tomorrow and see if you want anything.' Next morning I went along and found them right up with their forward troops, who were battling with enemy strongposts, less than a hundred yards away. When I asked the C.O. how his hospital fared during the night, saying that I thought he was rather far forward, he said: 'Waal, Colonel, the book says we are to get going as far forward as possible, and here we've gotten.' The frequent crack of a bullet overhead didn't seem to disturb him in the least. 'You see, Colonel, they're shootin' at us and we couldn't have any lights, but we're doin' fine.' I pointed out that if he moved his hospital farther back a few hundred yards, where he and his casualties wouldn't be shot at and where he could have lights, he would be doing even finer. He evidently did not think much of me, but he was a good soldier and reluctantly obeyed.

By a strange justice, Potts's brigade, which had fought that magnificent retirement, and the militia battalion that had made the first contact with the invading Japs had been flown in for the final victory which they had made possible months before.

Casualties and sickness had woefully thinned the ranks of my medical personnel, and in reply to many signals at last an additional Field Ambulance, which included a company of 'conscientious objectors', had been allotted to us. It is sometimes a fad among certain types of young people to declare that they would decline to bear arms. In times of war such a declaration means either cowardice, indifference, or a courageous conviction, and this group of men who were willing to serve in an unarmed medical unit were derided and sneered at by those who had fought their way through the campaign. This unit was posted to Oro Bay, a few miles along the coast to he east, where barges loaded with ammunition would come in at night to be unloaded during the darkness, and someone had ordered this Company to assist in the duty. They refused. I received an urgent signal that night telling me of the situation and in a jeep over a rough corduroy track for about a dozen miles I went across to try and sort things out—the disobedience of a lawful order in the face of the enemy is a most serious offence. I told the officer who had given the order what I thought of him, paraded the Company, told them of the seriousness of their conduct, and put them all under arrest. I discussed the situation with the C.O. and decided to move his Ambulance across to Soputa where the crisis of the battle had been reached and our casualties were mounting.

Bearers from among the 'conshies' were ordered into the battle and not one hesitated. Some were killed, others wounded, and as I watched them I did not see one man or any stretcher squad having brought out a casualty pause before returning.

Just as the men at Mons transmuted that base word contemptible into the gold of glory, so did 'conshie' become a noble word of respect and regard. This incident at Soputa was one of the most inspiring examples of moral and physical courage I have experienced.

The Commander of this Field Ambulance, Ted Palmer, was a gentle soul and a keen bird watcher. Originally he had been attached to the A.I.F. troops in Rabaul, where the first impact of the Japanese invasion fell. When what remained of our troops were driven into the jungle of New Britain, Ted held this remnant together as they moved over the mountains to the southern coast, where eventually those few who survived were picked up. Once again such leadership and devotion to duty went unrecognized.

Christmas Day came just as any other day. In the morning George Vasey called on Bill Riggall and me to go with him as a Christmas greeting to the Allied Unit holding the road block at Huggins. Our way curved round the Japs through a swamp on the flank and while the water was barely up to George's knees, which he didn't seem to mind, it went far higher on Bill and on me. We overtook a newly arrived Allied Unit moving forward to reinforce Huggins, and as I said earlier, their book knowledge was extensive. All Army hygiene text books detail 'rubbish bins, camps for the use of', emphasizing the proper fit of the lids. These unfortunate troops had known nothing but camps complete with all mod cons, including laundries to do their washing and an organized garbage clearance. To fling such troops suddenly into this type of challenging situation was beyond reason and when George found two men carrying brand new shiny galvanized iron rubbish bins, he expressed his astonishment in characteristic language. By no stretch of imagination could this foul jungle swamp be considered a standing camp. Anyway that was their business and we pushed on.

When we came to Huggins all was strangely quiet. We found the C.O., Colonel Doe, and passed our greetings down to him in his dugout on the one dry patch in his perimeter. When George commented on the quietness of things, it was explained: 'This is Christmas Day, General, and if you don't shoot at 'em they don't shoot back.'

That night at our H.Q., Christmas cheer consisted of 'gold fish', oily herrings in tomato sauce, tinned peaches and jungle juice. We had found some Jap alcohol in a captured dump and when someone produced some orange crystals, Bill and I, by trial and error, produced a palatable and a potent brew, a 'Gona Girl'. Most preferred the standard jungle juice—the milk of a green coconut, a tablespoonful of sugar and six raisins: when the raisins floated after a few days, she was right, but it was always thought advisable to stop smoking and have no naked lights at drinking time. We longed to find the person who had ever conceived of herrings and tomato sauce as a diet for debilitated soldiers in a tropical jungle. No one ever tired of bully beef: chilled in a mountain stream it made an excellent meal, mixed with powdered army biscuit or rice into a stew it was grand, and if you punctured the tin with a bayonet or a knife and flung it into the fire, you had a tasty roast. But that night we had oily gold fish, no paper hats, and the only crackers came from rifles. Anyway we all slept undisturbed to find in the morning that the rain had again flooded the place.

It was good to see Clive Disher again. He had taken over from Bill Johnston, relieved only when he became desperately sick. Clive, who always came forward to see how his medical service was going, flew over with Ned Herring commanding the A.I.F. troops and four surgical teams were moved into our forward area for the final battles.

By modern standards the facilities for surgery were appalling, urgent operations were performed under a tent fly, more or less impervious to the rain, while the surgeon moved around in the mud. Gowns and dressings were boiled in an empty petrol tin over a primus stove, one of our anaesthetists was a dentist, another was a padre, who had quickly learned to give a satisfactory 'rag and bottle' anaesthetic with an empty tomato sauce bottle filled with ether and a wick of gauze leading through the cork. I never heard a complaint about the conditions or the meagre equipment, these were accepted and made the best of with wonderful results. When air evacuation was functioning, a casualty could be brought from where he had been wounded, admitted to the care of a surgical team, taken on to the air strip and be in a base hospital in Moresby across the mountains—all within six hours. This may be compared with the debacle at Myola II where some casualties reached Moresby three months after being wounded.

Early in January the remnant of what had originally been Potts's brigade was relieved. Including Brigade H.Q. only 220 men moved out from the airstrip. Another A.I.F. Brigade—the troops who had defeated the Japs at Milne Bay and had later cleared the Buna area—was moved in under our Command. Commanding this force was George Wootton, a massive man with several square feet of prickly heat covering his naked torso. George was one of those rare people who seemed immune from malaria. He had all the patience in the world and as his troops were fighting the strong defences of Soputa, he was prepared to wait quietly until his sound planning produced results. 'They'll break,' said George, 'they'll break.' And sure enough after days and nights of winkling the way was cleared and on went the troops through the last desperate defences before the beach, and on through this stinking, devastated jungle and sago swamp. The most loathsome smell came from the rotting carcase of a dead mule on the track; from this nauseating crawling heap there pervaded a crescendo of a stench rising above the ever present foulness of the area. By the 22nd January, all resistance ceased and no Japanese remained alive. We had reconquered the whole of our Papuan territory—at a cost. Of our original Divisional troops, about 13,000 men, approximately 1,500 were killed, 2,500 wounded and 6,500 evacuated sick. When we were relieved, about 2,500 men were able to move to the air strip. Within a month all but 200 were in hospital, a situation similar to Allenby's victory in Syria in World War I.

It was a grim finale, everyone was sick and the final phase had been heavy. On the last day of January, 1942, George Vasey, Bill Riggall and I were bumped across in a jeep to the strip at Dobodura and within forty minutes landed at Moresby, which I had left five months before, on the first lap of the Kokoda handicap. None of us were feeling very fit but we decided to have dinner and a night out at the Moresby Club. It was a good meal, but after the soup we all retired to be violently sick and drove back to our quarters.

Things were rather hazy at that time but I think it was on the next morning that we flew down to Brisbane, spent the night at the Queensland Club, to find ourselves next day back in Melbourne, but I have no clear recollection of what was happening or how we arrived there.

Within a few days we were all within Heidelberg Military Hospital.

Chapter 13 Recuperation and Disease

It would be a good idea if all young doctors and nurses could suffer an illness necessitating hospital attention but from which a complete recovery is assured, better still if they could undergo an abdominal operation that completely cured the condition requiring it. I have fortunately experienced four.

When one has a sick body the mind also is sick with an uneasy, distorted and exaggerated interpretation of sensations and experiences of little moment. Our sense of value is changed and many things we take for granted assume a hitherto unknown worth and many of those achievements we sought as indispensable fade before the simple ambitions of one who is sick. The ability to sit out of bed, walk about and see things other than the four walls of a small room, however delightfully decorated with flowers, seem all that could be sought in this world. I have heard successful and strong men reduced to saying, 'If only I could go to the toilet instead of the indignity of perching precariously on a bedpan, if I could have a shower instead of being woken in the darkness of the early hours for this baby type of washing, I would ask for nothing more.' If those who serve in hospitals and make the ordinary domestic noises—slamming doors, dropping things and banging brooms against the skirting—knew by heart Florence Nightingale's notes on noise written a hundred years ago, they might not need to be sick before realizing the unconscious trauma they sometimes cause.

After a few days I began to enjoy myself and resent restraint, which meant that I was fairly fit again. It was good to wander round the wards and again meet so many comrades who could now laugh about it all, but it was better still to be home again for some leave.

With our conquest of portion of the northern coast of New Guinea, we had established forward air bases for the future and military successes impossible without air supremacy. From Wau in the mountains, another A.I.F. Brigade had fought their bitter way down to the coast at Salamaua, west of the Gona-Buna area, and the enemy had been driven into the Huon Peninsula.

For the next phase our Corps (the 7th and 9th Divisions) assembled on the Atherton Tablelands inland from Cairns, a long, broad plateau some 2,000 feet above the sea, which provided excellent jungle training. The timber of the Tablelands was of great beauty. When the original settlers opened the area, the tall trees were cut down ten or twelve feet from their bases, which were left standing in the cleared undergrowth. Some years later the beauty of these butts was realized and shipload after shipload were dragged from the ground and taken overseas for cedar and walnut veneers. One great walnut tree was said to have been sold to a piano manufacturer for more than a thousand pounds as it stood in the forest. The meanest outhouses were built of silky oak and at Youngeborough we watched beautifully figured sheets of plywood being pared from the revolving logs by a giant pencil-sharpener-like machine. Our H.Q. was at Ravenshoe near the lovely Tully Falls, and although the training was hard, as we moved through the clean forest day after day we enjoyed every minute of it.

There was much of beauty and interest about the area, the tobacco fields at Maroubra, the Barron Falls on the way down to Cairns, the fascinating crater with a dull red growth over the surface of the water far below, the charm of the two lakes, Barein and Eachem, set in the abrupt glowing green of their tropical foliage, the parasitic vines, struggling for existence in the density and the giant fig trees with their pendulous aerial roots forming impenetrable curtains. There were also the deceptive soft leaves of the gympie bush ever ready to implant their silicate barbs into a grasping hand. Fortunately alongside this menace was often a tropical lily, whose sap gave some relief from the agony of the impact, a shocking pain that lasted for days and was exacerbated by washing.

Down by the coast were the fields of sugar-cane, some in flower waving tall cream plumes like guardsmen on parade. When the cane was ripe the whole field was set on fire, the flames flashing through the dense white billowing clouds of smoke, leaving what looked like a charred stark series of sticks. These were immediately slashed down, stacked on little narrow rail trucks by the blackened cutters and milled with no apparent detriment to their sugar content.

One of our problems was the prevalence of scrub typhus in this area. This disease, which we had met in New Guinea, is spread by the bites of minute ticks, like grains of pepper, carried around by bush rodents. At that time the answer, chloromycetin, had not been available but mite repellent was supplied and all jungle clothing was impregnated. Fortunately the recovery from this disease appears to confer a subsequent immunity and with squads of those who were so protected we made mite surveys and as a result infested areas were marked on the maps and proscribed as training grounds for the troops.

It was grand to be training again with George Vasey and my old comrades of the 7th Division but it was not to last, I was moved on as D.D.M.S. of the Corps some miles away. We did, however, enjoy a grand final night at Divisional H.Q. before my divorce was made absolute.

Our Corps Commander, Lieut.-General Sir Leslie Morshead, had commanded the Australian 9th Division, which had shared in the defence of Tobruk and later contributed to the decisive victory at Alamein. Most of the Corps Staff Officers had come from his Division, and not having served at Tobruk or Alamein, I was rather outside the establishment, and the atmosphere for some time was rather different from our intimacy in the 'Silent Seventh' Divisional Headquarters. Fortunately that cheery soul, Ray Broadbent, was the A.Q. under whom the medical service was administered. Broadbent, who had served with distinction in the regular army, had resigned from his profession before the war to take over a sheep property, and although he had not served in the Middle East, had developed a broad, tolerant attitude to life generally.

I had two splendid specialist medical officers on my staff, Ted Ford and Mick Cook. Ted Ford, later professor of Public Health and Tropical Medicine in the Sydney University, was a man of essentials: hatbands, badges of rank, neat uniforms, meant nothing to him beside his dedication to the health of the troops. Another good companion was Brigadier Bob Risson, the engineer to whom any constructional problem was a delight.

Distressed by the malarial devastation of our first New Guinea campaign, Ted sought and was granted an interview with General Sir Thomas Blamey, the Army Commander. The General had allotted a quarter of an hour of his busy time, and later I had an account of this historic occasion from the A.D.C. who was present. When Ted, for once regimentally dressed, entered The Presence, he began in his quiet, slow, high voice to tell General Blamey about malaria and armies, he roamed over centuries of warfare while his silent listener, with his eye on the clock, began to rustle his papers. But time meant little to Ted, who gradually warmed to his subject as Blamey became interested, brushing aside his A.D.C., who reminded him of another appointment. After about an hour the General looked up at Ted and said: 'I think I understand you, Colonel Ford. If I don't do all these things you are advising, my troops will suffer.'

'What I've been trying to tell you, Sir, is that if you don't do these things, you won't have any bloody troops to suffer.' After that the General and Ted became fast friends.

Cooke, our hygiene officer, shared Ted's outlook and his tent. Until you knew him and had listened to his wisdom, no longer deceived by his glass eye, his quiet voice and disarming smile, you would not realize that Cooke is probably the outstanding Australian authority on leprosy and knows all there is to know about our Australian tropical diseases. The combined contribution to the health of our troops by these two truly great men was never adequately recognized, not that this mattered to them.

Soon after my arrival at Corps H.Q. I had another spell in hospital with a recurrence of malaria. At that time there was no regular army medical service, all medical and nursing personnel in hospitals and in the field being civilian volunteers. Some of them had served previously in the militia, but our Australian miltary hospitals were at least as efficient as any I had known, and Ian Wood soon had me back to my lines. One afternoon there was a scurry of motorcycles and three large army cars drew up at our

Recuperation and Disease

H.Q. From the leading car stepped an immaculate American junior officer, who held open the door for a tall, distinguished General, his cap studded with five stars but with no decorations on his beautifully laundered tropical khaki shirt. As the other cars disgorged a bevy of photographers, Leslie Morshead stepped forward, saluted and greeted General Douglas MacArthur (but this had to be repeated to the satisfaction of the camera men with their flashing bulbs).

General MacArthur dined that night in our mess and from across the table I was able to appreciate his fine, distinguished features. It was impossible to judge his age. There seemed no defined hairline to his brow as his jet black hair parted on the right side swept across his cranium in a smooth, glistening swathe: it was said that he had a large bald patch, but this was undetectable. His face reminded me of pictures I had seen of distinguished Red Indians, fine, firm, yet sensitive. He spoke little during the meal and later, while we sat around playing Chinese checkers or reading, he browsed quietly in his chair, enjoying his cigars and corn-cob pipe, speaking only occasionally in his attractive quiet voice. Next morning, before he departed, the camera boys were on the job again. It was interesting to contrast the simple, unassuming, relaxed stance of General Morshead with the carefully studied pose of the Supremo, moving his head or body this way or that as directed by the photographers to gain the correct shadows to emphasize his features. It was an interesting and revealing interlude associated with a great General who achieved overwhelming victories in his campaigns.

Plans were prepared for the next phase in New Guinea: the destruction of the Japanese in the Huon Peninsula. The 7th and 9th Divisions crossed to Moresby and our Corps H.Q. was to follow.

When we arrived the battle had been joined and Lae captured. The 7th Division, preceded by parachutists, had been flown over the mountains into the Markham Valley and fought through Nadzab and the cocoa plantations towards Lae. The 9th Division landed from barges to the east of the town but were delayed by two difficult river crossings, and the 7th Division just won this converging race into all that remained of the bombed and shot over town of Lae, the shells of a few dwellings on the Terrace and the skeletons of burnt out enemy planes on the strip.

This time facilities were available for the control of malaria. The eradication of malaria is an engineering and labour problem, while the control of the disease is a matter of personal protection, suppressant drugs and discipline, and to those who had fought only in the desert the value of malarial discipline was not at first recognized. Atebrin, an efficient suppressant except in those rare areas where a resistant strain of the parasite was endemic as we encountered later at Weewak, was issued to all units and most of the men began to take on a yellow tinge to deepen the tan of thir sunburn. Nets, veils and repellents were also issued, with strict orders as to non-exposure of the bare skin after sunset, the biting time of the anopheles. Unfortunately the villain, the female anopheles, does not buzz, nor is the bite always perceived, and troops who had not experienced the travail of the 7th Division had difficulty in realizing the importance of these additional protections even under the challenging conditions of jungle fighting, and among these the malarial rate was at first disturbing.

To hand out a supply of pills to troops does not necessarily mean that these are taken. The only satisfactory way to ensure this was to parade each platoon or small formation separately under the supervision of an officer or senior N.C.O., issue the drug to each soldier individually and watch him swallow it. This may sound rather cumbersome and unnecessary but was the only alternative to the disappearance of the 7th Division as a fighting force. The measure of a commanding officer's efficiency in the jungle may well be assessed by the malarial rate within his unit. Malarial rates are not always reliable, for the malignant tertian type of the fever can simulate many other diseases and without a simple investigation be diagnosed and treated as such. I learnt my lesson early as we escaped from Java in that crowded transport. I was called down to see a sick man in the ship's hospital. He was moaning and shocked with a rigid, tender abdomen of what seemed to me an acute abdominal condition requiring immediate surgery, but I asked Neil Fairley to see him with me. After a few minutes Neil said to me: 'We'll have a look at his blood. I think he's an M.T.' And so he proved: an operation would almost certainly have killed him, while intravenous quinine saved his life.

Recuperation and Disease

With the capture of Lae, our Divisions had diverged. The 7th pushed west along the Markham into the Ramu Valley, winkling the Japs from their defences and driving the remnants into the mountains of the Finisterre Range above. The 9th moved round the Huon Peninsula along the coast in barges for the capture of Finschhafen and the shelter of Langemak Bay.

Until these areas were secured, our Corps H.Q. remained at Dobadura living a quiet life for a few weeks, interrupted only by an occasional air raid and a day or so's visit to the Divisions. One day I was visiting one of our Field Hospitals and found two natives from a nearby village in the beds.

'Why are they here and not in the native hospital?' I asked the M.O.

'They were very ill with pneumonia and the Angau officer asked us to take them in.'

I asked him to lend me his stethoscope. Certainly I had not used the 'guessing tubes' for a year or so and what I heard when I listened to the chest was quite unfamiliar to me.

'Do you hear what I heard?' I asked the M.O.

'Oh, that's the pigs under the bed.' To a native villager his most prized possession is a pig and where he goes the pig goes—even into hospital!

After the daily work was done we were able to take our exercise or relax as we wished: some played deck-tennis, I preferred walking, and if the evenings were free we read or played simple games, a very different life from a Divisional H.Q. General Morshead's favourite pastime was 'shove ha'penny', like darts, popular in the old English pubs. Most senior Generals have their fads and foibles and those special things they particularly look for on parades or seek on inspections soon become known and anticipated. The Duke of Wellington made a fetish of asking the weight of various articles of equipment.

There was a story of the General whose well-known fancy was Fire Drill. After inspecting the lines in one barracks he returned to the Orderly Room and questioned the Adjutant about this. The officer, knowing this would come sooner or later, said: 'Yes, Sir, if you will just step outside you will find the standing orders concerning fire posted on the notice board.' The General stepped out.

'Very good,' he said. 'Now what do you do about a fire alarm?'

'Here, Sir,' he said, pointing to a large metal suspended hoop, 'is our alarm, and there is a striker alongside the post.'

'Good,' again said the General, who then departed from the recognized rules of the game by picking up the striker and hitting the alarm. This was without precedent at any of his previous inspections and exceeded the preparations of the Adjutant, who, hoping for the best, was prepared for the worst. Nothing happened. After a few minutes the General gave three hearty bangs on the alarm. Still no one seemed to move and in desperation the General, cupping his hands about his mouth, yelled at the top of his voice: 'Fire! Fire!'

For a few moments nothing stirred, then at the double appeared an orderly with a newspaper under one arm and a bundle of kindling under the other. 'Have it ready for you in a minute, Sir,' he said as he disappeared into the Orderly Room.

Leslie Morshead had no special fads but he did fancy his shove ha'penny. In fact he had his own private board and at times would disappear into his hut, it was said to have lessons from his batman, an ex regular British soldier who claimed to have been a champion at his 'local'. To facilitate the movements of the coins, one face of which was ground smooth, talc powder was sprinkled over the board. Howard Spring wrote: 'No self-respecting shove ha'penny board is polished in any other way than by allowing beer to flow over it and then rubbing it dry', but we had no beer. It was through no sycophantic attitude that we were regularly beaten by our Corps Commander: he was just too good and whenever our General went for an overnight visit to one of his Divisions, besides his essentials he always took his own board and ha'pennies. While he was away on one such visit a bright lad in the mess hit on the idea of filling the tin of Johnson's baby powder with ground up coral. However finely you grind coral, it still remains gritty and for a while we were able to hold our own, but whenever the General went for a visit after that he always took his own baby powder.

Soon after dawn next morning we flew from here up the Markham Valley in a D.C.3 loaded well above its 5,000 lb. official capacity. There were only hard metal benches along the sides of the fuselage and we could sit on the stores where we liked; those

Recuperation and Disease

in the know always chose the large sacks of bread as the most comfortable. We flew fairly low over the coffee and cocoa plantations and soon landed at Nadzab where I had a Casualty Clearing Station designed for holding about 200 patients staging between the Field Ambulances and a General Hospital. Casualties, sick and wounded, had been heavy and I found more than a thousand men being cared for in this unit. The C.O., Colonel Sam Langford, by his imagination and initiative, had in some way expanded his unit in personnel, tentage and equipment to meet this challenging emergency and provide excellent attention for all. Without complaining or seeking my help, Sam had 'managed somehow' and a very good 'somehow' it was.

Soon after dawn one morning we set out from Lae up the Markham Valley, the river slowly thinning in its upper reaches to a trickle. After an interval of what seemed only a few yards, another tiny stream began to flow westward: we were in the Ramu Valley. These valleys were softly grassed with kunai for a breadth of about a mile until the jungle closed down over the hillsides, rising on each side. Here and there along the course of the streams were small clumps of coconut palms and trees, and as we approached one of these in the Ramu Valley, the pilot called to me, 'There are some of your boys down there, let's wake them up.' The pilot came from Texas where they are said to be tough, and while certain planes are designed for diving D.C.3's are not, but this didn't deter him. 'Here we go, boys,' and swooping at an acute angle he roared his engine but just as I made sure we were for it he straightened out barely above the trees and roared with laughter. I had hardly recovered from my fright when we landed at Dumpu where 7th Div. H.Q. was sited under some trees. George Vasey was there to meet me and after his characteristic greeting he asked if I was feeling all right and I told him about our pilot. 'That bastard,' said George. 'He frightened bloody hell out of me!'

In George Vasey's advance along the Markham Valley, the Division had been held finally at Shaggy Ridge, a tall, acutely conical, commanding feature at the foothills of the Finisterres and strongly held by the Japanese in their foxholes and bunkers. Bombed, shelled and winkled from their holes the Japs had been finally cleared the day before I arrived and only a few survivors had escaped into the mountains beyond. We clambered up the slopes; George was in fine form, but I with a series of short bursts. The stench as we neared the crest was like that of the corruption at Gona. It was a physical ordeal to reach what remained of the pinnacle, without having to fight one's way yard by yard as the troops had done, and George was very proud of them.

It was like coming home to be among the warmth of them all again. I stayed with George for a few days and it was good to move around and realize what respect and real affection they all had for him.

On my return journey I spent the day at Lae. Next morning, although I had to return to Dobadura by midday, I found my wild Texan pilot and his plane no longer on the strip—and the only available aircraft was an Allied bomber not permitted to carry passengers.

'Say, General (they call all brigadiers 'General'), do you know anything about guns?' said the pilot when I approached him for a lift.

'Why?' I asked.

'Waal, you see, General, we ain't allowed to carry passengers, but I'm light of a rear gunner. If you like to crawl into that blister and call yourself a gunner, I can take you.' This seemed good enough and I crawled into the gun pit at the rear. 'They said something about a Nip raid down Dobadura way, but I don't think we'll run into trouble, here's hopin' anyway.'

This did not cheer me very much and I felt rather lonely and fearful in the isolation of my rear gun blister. The raid was over when we arrived and I crawled out, still scared but fortunately in one piece. So ended my one and only tour of duty as a rear gunner. I still don't know how to work the wretched thing!

Until an airstrip had been established at Finschhafen, we went to the 9th Division round the Huon Peninsula by a T.P. boat. There was still an occasional air raid and we would leave soon after dawn and put in at Marobe before noon, and for the remainder of the daylight lie under the jungle cover of the crocodile-infested river. Nothing could have been more delightful than to relax in the sun on the deck of one of those heavily armed fast motor craft as they rushed smoothly across the calm waters of the Huon Gulf. When darkness came we made a dash for Langemak Bay around the Cape.

Recuperation and Disease

Our first visit was tragic. Having landed safely in the dark, we drove to the Divisional H.Q. sited in the jungle above the beach. In the early hours of the morning a lone Japanese bomber, either wilfully or just getting rid of his bombs, planted a coupe of 'daisy cutters' in the area. These wretched things spray their fragments laterally and the senior gunner and another man were killed in their stretchers. It was a melancholy welcome.

Commanding the Finschhafen area was a strong Japanese position at Sattelberg on a crest above, and only with the final capture of this feature by troops and tanks, and fighting their way up through the dense bamboo over the steep slopes, was our hold on the Huon Peninsula secure. It became then only a question of hounding the remnants of the enemy as they retreated in rapidly diminishing numbers.

The establishment of an airstrip in a jungle over the slopes within a few weeks was a triumph of American engineering, and enemy craft seldom came near us. Our H.Q. moved forward from Dobadura to a gentle grass-covered slope above the old mission station at Finschhafen, but for weeks the roads among the coconut groves remained lanes of knee deep mud, passable only by track vehicle or jeeps with chains. Fortunately there was unlimited coral available and movement soon became less hazardous.

Down near the beach I was delighted to walk into the rotund padre whom I had left marooned at Uberi months before on the Kokoda trail. He was less rotund and beamed with robust health, and how or when he had arrived in this forward area I never knew, but the following Sunday at church parade he gave a sermon which, unlike many sermons, I should think few who attended have forgotten. In a clearing in the jungle, surrounded by troops relaxing at their ease, he gave us the story of Giles, a simple job gardener, who longed to have a garden of his own. Eventually, by careful saving, he was able to buy a small plot of wasteland overgrown with gorse and brambles and with heaps of discarded garbage. In his spare time Giles went to work, clearing and cultivating until one spring he had a happy garden, bright with flowers and foliage. One day the local vicar was passing as Giles was working among his plants. 'The Lord and you have made a very lovely garden, Giles, out of all that rubbish.'

'Yes,' said Giles. 'But you should have seen it when the Lord had it on his own.' No wonder he is now a bishop, God bless him.

For some time my skin had been rather a nuisance, with large red itching areas scattered here and there. I was taking atebrin regularly and this may have been one of the side effects of the drug, a type of *Lichen Planus*. Unfortunately this unpleasant sight was seen one morning under the shower by Ray Broadbent, our A.Q., and I had to fly back to Moresby for a spell in hospital. There I found George Vasey again. Rather I heard him, for the first night in hospital the most extraordinarily flow of language came from the next room; it could only be George . . . no one else had his vocabulary. I hopped out of bed and went to see, and George it was, a most comical clown-like sight. He also had some skin trouble and except for his laughing dark eyes and the split of his broad grin, his face was stark white with ointment. Another patient at that time was John McKie, the senior C. of E. padre, and many cheery games of chess we had between us. John, of course, was good at the game but George played as he fought a battle, all movement and strange words. I will never forget the night we were allowed to get up and go down to the open air picture show. George, dressed only in pyjamas, his face a white blank crowned with his inseparable red cap. made a dramatic appearance like a zombie, to the cheers and catcalls of the troops. I have forgotten what the pictures were, but all went well until the clouds burst. In a few minutes everyone was soaked and the screen fell down. As he squelched back, sopping, to the hospital the situation taxed George's vocabulary but did not exhaust it: no occasion ever achieved that!

Little snippets were taken from my skin, placed under a microscope and people learned in dermatology shook their heads to the resounding laugh of John Bellassaria, the C.O., who was so kind to us and seemed to think everything was a man-size joke.

I wasn't a bit concerned with the diagnosis of my condition; all I wanted was to get well. When a man is sick there are two things that really concern him and another that may or may not interest him. The first and most urgent: 'Am I going to get better?' If there is an assurance of this, a great load falls away and recovery is accelerated. Even if the answer is otherwise, there are few certainties as disturbing as uncertainties. Then a man wants to know how long he is going to be ill and when he will be back in circulation. If he has an answer to this, however long it may be, he becomes resigned and rested, and this also contributes to recovery. If he is inquisitive he might like to know what is wrong with him and, if this is not explained simply, his imagination tends to run riot and undo a great deal of good that has been done. Personally, if I had a satisfactory answer to questions one and two, I wouldn't mind very much what was wrong with me. Medical training emphasizes diagnosis (and rightly so, as treatment depends on this), but in the eagerness to minutely pinpoint the trouble, which is not always possible and need not delay basic essential treatment, the patient is often uneasy and bewildered by a strange conspiracy of silence. Anyway, whatever was wrong with me, I was soon on deck again and back at Finschhafen in a week or two.

For some reason our troops were chasing the disorganized Japs along the coast. We had cut them off from supplies and many took to the hills to die or to survive in the native villages. We had reason to believe that on certain nights one or two would sneak into our small isolated units, not for slaughter but for food. Certainly one night we found a couple of unarmed Japs who had crept out from the jungle to a clearing where we had a picture show, and from the back had enjoyed the entertainment, probably their only relaxation for months, until we took them.

My wretched skin became tiresome again and I had to take my shower before daylight. My tent was next to the A.Q.'s, and, carefully though I always moved, one morning I woke him. Cunningly he waited till he heard the running water, then came down, flashed his torch and there I was, blotches, scratches and all. 'Look here, Kingsley,' he said, 'this won't do.' I pleaded with him but he was adamant. 'You must go,' and go I did. This was the end.

Back in Heidelberg again, in a small room and no visitors allowed, except my family. I wonder when people will realize that, to be isolated, to brood your your disabilities, may be an added misery. TV had not arrived in Australia and I did not feel much like reading or listening to the radio, but the notice on my door, 'No Visitors', withheld many whom I would have found most restful, and above all I wanted—physical and mental rest. To the interminable, irritable restlessness of my skin, which from top to toe had now rebelled, there was added another, and fortunately my last, bout of malaria.

There seemed an idea that I needed special nourishment to regain the three odd stone that I had left in New Guinea, so I must have a good steak each day. The hospital conception of a good steak was a thin sliver of beef, tough and overdone . . . this to a member of the Beef Steak Club! I protested that if I had to have beef, could I have a tin of cold bully beef each day, but this seemed quite unknown in a military hosital and I had to wrestle with my steak. My skin wept in anguish and I was in a mess.

If ever I had to treat anyone who had the bad luck to suffer from an extensive irritable skin condition such as mine, I would slug him day and night with strong sedatives for a week or more, then he would come to life again, refreshed, instead of having lost all confidence in rest, lying awake for hours and cursing his luck.

Every week doctors get expensive literature and samples of 'the most recent and most effective sedative in all conditions', but fortunately Dr Hume Turnbull was sufficiently old fashioned to rely on a proven drug, chloral hydrate. After a time the mere presence of twenty grains in a medicine glass beside my bed was sufficient to send me to sleep and after a few weeks I was sleeping through the night with the glass still full in the morning at that dreadful hour in the dark when hospital patients are roused from their restful sleep.

Even when I was discharged from the hospital, for some time I was never without a large bottle of this mixture. The knowledge of its presence was enough, as sleep is often a matter of confidence. If you wonder if you will sleep you will generally lie awake wondering and I know of no reason why anyone should continue to sleep badly or continue in severe pain. Drug addiction is certainly a reality but beyond those who fearfully carry round tranquillizers, pep pills or pain-easing pills, how many when the need for them no longer remains continue to take drugs?

All bad things come to an end sooner or later, however, and after a few months I was allowed to roam around the wards, mingle with my comrades and have visitors. Occasionally I was even allowed home for a weekend on 'therapeutic leave' and at last the glad time came when I was to be discharged in a couple of weeks; nine months was a long time to be out of circulation.

A few days before I was due to leave hospital, George Vasey turned up. He had been in hospital in Brisbane and now claimed that he was fit again and had just been posted to command an A.I.F. Division at Weewak on the north of New Guinea. He was leaving in ten days, would I come with him? 'Just fly up with me, stay a few days or a week and let me know what you think of the medical set-up, then you can fly home. I will keep the plane for you.'

'This is grand, George,' I said. 'Just what I need to rehabilitate myself, back with you in your Division even if only for a few days,' but I told George he would have to see our D.G.M.S., General Burston. Off went George—if something had to be done, he did it. But Ginger Burston flatly refused to let me go. I pointed out that it was only for a week or ten days, kind of convalescent leave, just what I wanted, but it was no use, and with a heavy heart I had to say cheerio to George.

With Bill Riggall he flew off to Brisbane where he picked up Rupert Downes. They set off intending to stage at Cairns that night. There had been a warning of a tropical storm and the pilot was reluctant to leave Brisbane, but I can imagine the picture: George saying with all his colour, 'I can't see any bloody storm, let's get on.' George always went on till the enemy or the terrain actually stopped him. He never paused wondering if they were going to halt him, but assumed all was well until proved otherwise.

The sky and the atmosphere in Brisbane was clear, but tropical storms are treacherous and as his plane circled over the sea in its approach to Cairns, it struck the full blast, dived, and disappeared into the rising waves.

Tragic as this was, it was an end such as George Vasey would have wished. Actually I did not believe he was a fit man. His illness in Brisbane after his two campaigns in New Guinea had taken a heavy toll of him, far more than he realized or admitted, and he would have hated to go back to a Division and then have to retire because of unfitness. How fortunate were Nelson and Wolfe, suddenly in their successes passing from the sight of men as did George Vasey, a man among men. When after a few weeks I was discharged from the Army as medically unfit, the blow was softened by the knowledge that George Vasey was no longer with us and I was not leaving him.

In the C.M.F. and on active service I had been associated with the Army for more than thirty years and that life now seemed over. What was I to do with my life now?

I had little money, for my Army pay as a Brigadier on active service was less than that of Lieutenant nowadays in peacetime. My practice had disappeared: I had walked out of it in 1939, five years before. At the beginning of the war, those medical men who did not enlist were requested to ask any new patients if they had previously been under the care of any medical officer who had enlisted on service and if so to attend them until they returned, dividing the fees with the service doctor's wife or dependant. Most doctors loyally observed this and many practices were preserved. Naturally it was more difficult in a practice such as mine, which was a consultative one. The British Medical Association in Victoria had leased a building in Melbourne at 85 Spring Street as professional rooms for returned medical officers and there I slowly returned to my practice and the children's ward at the Alfred Hospital. But five years away from civilian practice with the rapidly changing face of medicine and the introduction of antibiotic drugs was a momentous challenge and while some of my old colleagues called me in consultation and the children of some of my earlier patients came along, it was an uphill battle.

Chapter 14 Post-War Appointments

The Federal Government had brought in a Commonwealth Reconstruction Training Shemes, (the C.R.T.S.). Returned men and women who had had their training or education interrupted by war service, or had indicated before enlistment their intention to undertake a course of higher education, together with those who would benefit by a refresher course in their former occupation, could receive Government aid including tuition, fees, books, equipment and certain subsistence. The Government requested the Melbourne Medical Permanent Postgraduate Committee to administer the scheme as it applied to medical men and women of the three services in Victoria and I was invited to direct this. The Committee had come into being in 1919 at the end of World War I with the purpose of providing short refresher training for returned medical officers. From this humble beginning courses of study for higher degrees had been organized, refresher courses for general practitioners and regular visits from overseas lecturers arranged.

Here was a splendid opportunity to do something for so many of my comrades who had done so much for me and it was a welcome financial help. Our office was established at the Royal Australian College of Surgeons in Spring Street and with the wonderful assistance of Miss Nancy Davidson, the secretary, off we went arranging various courses, hospital attachments and associations with specialists, whichever was indicated or desired. This brought me into close contact with many of my pre-war colleagues and with returned medical men of the three services, next to being in the Army a most happy association. Everyone was most helpful and co-operative and the returned men were glad to feel they had not been forgotten.

One of our problems concerned teachers to conduct these courses. There seems a conviction that because a doctor is appointed to a teaching hospital he can teach. For such an appointment a postgraduate degree is essential and the greater the number of such degrees the more likely is the applicant to be appointed, such is the law of multiple generalized diplomatosis. This principle does not apply only to medical education; I understand it is applied throughout the universities where no assurance of ability to impart knowledge is required. In my undergraduate days at the hospital, with only one or two exceptions, we were fortunate with our tutors. But the fact remains that the unfortunate medical students has to put up with teachers who, however profound the knowledge of their subject, have not been required to furnish any evidence of their ability to impart it, and students quite rightly soon sort out among themselves those who are worth following.

It seemed that there must be basic principles in imparting any knowledge and I approached that doyen of education, Professor George Browne, who held this chair at the Melbourne University. Like everyone else he was enthusiastically helpful and we arranged a free voluntary course on the principles of teaching for any who wished to attend. George Browne handled this, the first course of its kind in Australia, in his usual interesting and delightful manner.

On the final night I arranged a series of three short lecture demonstrations by selected teachers. In the first the audience were considered to be ancillary medical personnel such as nurses, during the second they were medical undergraduates and finally postgraduate students. The lecturers were carefully selected from a cross-section of those who were called upon to teach these three groups. The nursing lecture demonstration was just what was suitable for such an audience. For the lecture to undergraduates I selected a senior honorary with high academic qualifications, and while students had been committed to his clinic for years, his teaching ability was meagre: fortunately with no prompting or direction to do so he made a mess of his session. There was no sequence in his talk although he had prepared it. He showed slides, many of which were out of order and upside down; he mumbled, er-er-ered and, scarcely opening his mouth, spoke generally to the blackboard where, since he was something of an artist, his diagrams were good. The final lecture to postgraduates was excellent and I believe everyone concluded the course thoughtful and instructed. I am sure he did.

When the challenge of the C.R.T.S. had been met and concluded, the Committee decided that I should travel overseas with the idea of presenting to our Asian near neighbours the medical postgraduate facilities in Australia and surveying this field in the United Kingdom and in America. At midnight on 16 February 1947 I skidded from the surface of Rose Bay across Sydney Harbour.

The large Sunderland flying boat, while much slower than modern aircraft, provided a delightful, leisurely and comfortable means of travel. After the first night we came down at the end of each day and slept ashore through what was granted us of the night. Soon after our first dawn we landed at Bowen for breakfast, then across the dreary, featureless north to Darwin, gloomy in the wet season and with the harbour still studded with the stark masts of ships sunk in the Japanese air raid.

Singapore was reached just before dusk next day, where I spent the evening with the medical fraternity. During the Japanese occupation the medical school had been organized under their control. The pre-clinical years had been abolished and the entrance standards lowered with the inevitable flood of half-baked graduates and a poor standard of hospital and general medical service. The Faculty were anxious to obtain graduates from Australia to tide them over their difficult period of rehabilitation and I undertook to present this in Australia. About midnight the cool comfort of Raffles was welcome.

Rangoon was in a mess, crowded with refugees existing in improvised hovels. The gleaming gold had disappeared from the famous century old Shway Dagon Pagoda and the only colour in the drab city came from the yellow robes of the Buddhist priests.

I was conducted around the place and over the medical school by an Englishman who claimed he was the Professor of Physiology. He was an odd fellow dressed in old baggy slacks, held precariously in place by a snakeskin belt, his rumpled linen coat open between the long lapels disclosed a dark hairy chest bare of any shirt or singlet. Around his neck was a gaudy tie, unescorted by any form of collar, but emblazoned by a startling tie pin in the form of a multi-coloured beetle, altogether one of the most comical figures I have seen off the stage of a pantomime, but he was very kind. His face would break into a small smile then suddenly set into a severe scowl. He carried a stout malacca cane and as we wandered round the deserted medical school, the lecture theatres and laboratories, whenever he wished to emphasize anything he would stare through his monocle and rap me on the shins. 'You see, don't you? Don't you?' 'Yes,' I said, 'I see.' He explained that the school was empty as the students were all on strike but this apparently called for no other explanation. We dined together and I had a most illuminating and interesting evening with him, while he performed eructations with all the disarming frankness of a baby.

Rangoon, with all its war wounds, was not a tourist attraction at that time and I was glad next day to take off among the sails and paddle steamers on the broad Irrawaddy over the mountains and across the Bay of Bengal to Calcutta, then over the north of India to Karachi. Karachi means camel town and these supercilious beasts were wandering along the streets drawing their ridiculous little carts. At Karachi I broke my journey and flew down to Bombay with the excellent Indian Tata Airways.

Bombay was a keen medical centre and for the first time I found an interest concerning postgraduate medical study in Australia. I knew that sooner or later I would be challenged with the so-called White Australia policy and during my final conference with the combined medical staffs of the hospitals a dark man rose and said: 'But you won't let coloured people into Australia.'

Before I could reply a darker man stood up and said: 'I've been in Australia and everyone was kind, your Prime Minister (sic), Mr Albert Dunstan, arranged for me to have a car to travel around in.' What an Albert Memorial!

From Bombay I flew to New Delhi where I stayed with our High Commissioner, those delightful people, Sir Ivan and Lady Mackay. Sir Ivan had successfully commanded our 6th A.I.F. Division in the First Desert Campaign and through him my association with the Indian Government officials was made most pleasant. New Delhi, contiguous with the old city, is one of the created capitals, but, set in a featureless plain, lacks something of the charm of Washington and Canberra. Luytens Government buildings, however, with their red stone bases rising to a dull ochre, would grace any city as do the prophetic words around the central hall:

> 'Liberty will not descend upon a people,
> A people must raise themselves to liberty.
> It is a blessing that must be earned before it is enjoyed.'

And Queen Victoria's words:

> 'In their prosperity will be our strength,
> In their contentment will be our security.
> In their gratitude will be our best reward.'

Dr Raja, directing the Indian Government Public Medical Service, was most helpful and before I left I had to appeal to him to deliver us from an embarrassing predicament. We arose one morning to find that a wandering cow had died in the High Commissioner's drive. To the Hindu the cow is a sacred animal and must not be molested but is allowed to wander down the streets selecting what seems tasty from any of the food stalls. By midday the animal was very dead and Sir Ivan suggested that I should get in touch with Dr Raja who, as always, was understanding, and appreciating our problem suggested that if we could stick it out till dark all would be well. Next morning all was well—we asked no questions.

On the outskirts of the city lay the fascinating Red Fort, which for centuries before the Mutiny had been the seat of the Mogul Emperors. The high red tessellated walls were still pock-marked with General Wilson's assault upon the rebels. Just inside the Kashmir bastion ran the alley where John Nicholson fell, shot through the liver. Beyond was the crumbling glory of the Palace, once the setting for the fabulous Peacock Throne, the walls pitted where the precious stones had been prised from the marble. From one great gate the walls looked across to the Jumna, which over the years had receded leaving half a mile or so of glistening sand with no trace of the bridge of boats across which a little more than a hundred years before the mutineers had swarmed in to massacre the British garrison and loot the city.

Back to Karachi to pick up my onward flying boat, across the grimness of Baluchistan, Iran and Arabia, relieved only by the blue of the Persian Gulf and the occasional black dot of a nomad's tent far below. We landed at Cairo on the Nile near Gizereh Island where my old Divisional Commander, Tubby Allen, was waiting to greet me. Tubby had established some agencies in Cairo, and after tea at the Gizereh Club, in a very different atmosphere from that I had first experienced thirty-five years before and in World War II, I had a delightful evening with the family in their flat. I had seen Tubby only once since that sad day at Myola and we chuckled as we fought again our battles in Syria and New Guinea. Tubby had no bitterness about his recall: he knew, as we all did, that he had done his job. We left at midnight.

From Cairo it was a short hop to Catania in Sicily, where while the plane was fuelled I was able to buy some rice and a dozen fresh eggs. The rice disappeared somewhere but the eggs arrived safely with me in London.

The final night was spent ashore at Aix-en-Provence, then over the Alps, gleaming white in the brilliance of the sun, across the debris of the invasion coast in Brittany, with our final landing at Poole Harbour in Dorset. A quick meal at Bournemouth, then by train through the falling snow to London. The winter of 1947-48 was severe but the cold, the snow, the slush and the gloom of the early night were suddenly warmed by finding Ted Ford on the platform.

My accommodation had been arranged at London House, near Guilford Street. This residence for overseas graduates had made a remarkable contribution to advancing good inter-dominion relations. When an important post has to be filled, the United Kingdom usually has the happy faculty of providing the right person at the right time in the right place and London House was another such example, where Brigadier Pepper was the Comptroller. 'Peter' Pepper, with his splendid war service, his understanding of men and his great sense of humour, was the ideal person to ensure happiness and harmony among residents from all parts of what was still known as the British Empire. There was the delightful atmosphere of a University college, something I had not known for more than thirty years. I believe that since the war no one has contributed more than Peter Pepper and his London House to goodwill, understanding and respect among postgraduates from all the countries of the British Commonwealth.

London, so soon after the war, proudly displayed her wounds. Down every street were gaps like gums from which here and there teeth had been drawn, but there was no rubble. Where from Fleet Street I had remembered only the glimpse of St Paul's on Ludgate Hill, I now found the Cathedral standing in an open space. Where buildings had pressed upon it there were only low walls, around open basements now smiling to the sky after centuries of damp and darkness. As I looked down over the few remaining bricks, flowers and shrubs had come to life below.

My first visit was to the flat of Dr John Green with his recent bride and I placed my wedding gift on the table. When Mildred unwrapped the parcel and saw my eggs from Sicily, her eyes shone. 'Shell eggs, shell eggs,' she cried. 'Look, John, a dozen shell eggs.' We have given many wedding presents but never have I seen such joy on the face of a bride. Strict rationing had continued in Britain and egg powder in limited quantities was available, but one shell egg was a treat to be looked for each month unless one had access under the counter. Some weeks later I visited Jock Anderson in the lovely Clwyd Valley, the Eden of North Wales. Jock had been Dickie Berry's senior assistant in my Anatomy days and during the war the Australian Medical Liaison Officer in London. With his never-ending generosity Jock brought me for breakfast on my first morning one of their two shell eggs for the month and insisted on my having it. I felt horribly mean.

People grumbled of course with the usual good-natured grumble English people have and as one Cockney said to me: 'They give yer nothin' and before yer've got it they take it off of yer.' But in spite of all it was obvious from the general health of the nation that while perhaps the caviar and such things were in short supply, many people in England were better nourished during this rationing than ever before, especially the children.

London House was in the centre of the academic world as far as my mission was concerned and it was a pleasant walk across Russell Square to the London Postgraduate Federation. The Director, Sir Francis Fraser, was faced with his own problems from the pressure of many hundreds of United Kingdom medical officers, released from the services, and was finding difficulty in placing medical graduates from overseas who wandered along seeking facilities for postgraduate study. But Sir Francis was keen to help us and after discussion he agreed that if our Royal Colleges and recognized postgraduate bodies were prepared to recommend any of our graduates for such study, to the best of his ability he would place them according to their desires.

Lord Alfred Webb-Johnson, President of the Royal College of Surgeons, was most helpful. His baby, a residential hostel for students studying for their fellowship, was rising above a bombed section of the College in Lincoln's Inn Fields. Such was the repute of our students that he assured me he would reserve some of this accommodation for them when the building was opened.

This was my first contact with Webb-J with his twinkling blue eyes, his baby-smooth skin, his wonderful sense of fun and unplumbable fund of good stories. One morning he called for me at London House, to lunch at the Garrick Club. As we drove down Guilford Street in his chauffeured, sedate Rolls Royce, he turned to me: 'Do you like gulls' eggs?'

'I don't know, I have never tasted them.'

'You've a lot to learn, my lad,' he said, as he opened the glove box, took out a small newspaper packet and produced two cold, hard-boiled eggs about the size of small pullet eggs. 'Just break the shells into the paper,' he said and solemnly in the rear seat, behind his liveried chauffeur, we munched our eggs. I certainly had much to learn from Queen Mary's medical attendant.

On another occasion I found myself seated next to the amusing A. P. Herbert after whom I had the ordeal of speaking at a dinner of the Royal College of Surgeons. Around the walls hung the galaxy of past Presidents, by famous artists. For an hour over the port, Webb-J held us enthralled as he journeyed around the walls presenting his vivid and living word pictures of each portrait, the subject and the artist. It was an unforgettable night and just one of the many occasions during this and later visits when Webb-J and his lady were wonderful hosts.

For some years the Nuffield Foundation had provided scholarships for overseas graduates to study in the United Kingdom. During the war these had been suspended, but since then had been most generously distributed and many Nuffield scholars from Australia were living at London House at that time. Mr Leslie Farrer-Brown, the director, and the council were co-operative in developing this post-war field for Australians and in view of the changing circumstances, when many of the graduates were married, it was readily agreed that the amount of each scholarship should be materially increased. At the same time it was regretted that many of our medical graduates spent their time seeking further academic qualifications, which required considerable attention being directed to the United Kingdom examination technique rather than to broadening their knowledge. 'We recognize your Royal College qualifications as of the highest standard, so why not send across to us those so qualified and we will place them in association with senior men in their various specialties with whom they can work and study, unburdened by the tension and anxiety of preparing for just another academic qualification?' I explained that the dread disease of multiple generalized diplomatosis had become endemic in Australia. As a result of these views, the Foundation was no longer prepared to grant scholarships for those whose sole purpose of coming to the United Kingdom was another symptom of this disorder.

It was still very cold in London and floods had followed the heavy snowfalls but fully to appreciate the lovely gentleness of an English spring, one should be there no later than February when the etching of the bare elms is still a delicate tracery over the soft blue of the winter mist. It is as if the lights were lowered before a symphony concert. Slowly the curtain rises as does the timid spring, through a veil is seen a carpet of muted green with the slender stems of the silver birches, not treasured as in Australia but often in the neglected woods of the wastelands. Beyond as if on guard wait the darker boles of the more robust trees, the rugged oaks, the stout elms, the smooth stemmed planes and beeches, still reluctant to lose their leaves of the season that has gone. The snowdrops, the primrose, the daffodils and tulips and later the bluebells dance into song and the pale gold of the laburnum heralds the entry of the blossoms. As the bright young leaves of the trees join in the harmony, the chestnuts and the cherries fling their flowers into the crescendo of youth. In the miles of parks in the heart of London, these joys are for all, but there was much to be done before I visited other medical centres.

One interesting evening was a dinner with representatives from many countries concerned with the establishment of a World Health Organization under the United Nations. There seemed an absence of parochialism in the discussions and an honest endeavour to consider health as a global challenge.

Mr Beasley, the Australian High Commissioner, had arranged for me to call on the Prime Minister, Mr Attlee. During the Commonwealth, George Downing had purchased a plot of ground near Westminster Abbey. He was one of Cromwell's Ambassadors on the Continent and had initiated a move for Cromwell to be crowned. Ever an opportunist and sensing the direction of the wind after Cromwell's death, Downing gained the favour of Charles II by rounding up some of the regicides who had escaped to the Continent. He was granted a baronetcy and a ninety-nine years lease of his original site, which had been restored to the Crown. There he built the street of houses bearing his name.

It was a humbling experience to stand on the stone steps beneath the iron tracery holding a lamp surmounted by a crown and face the lion-headed knocker on the door of that house of history, No. 10 Downing Street. I was conducted over the brightness of the tiled hall along a narrow passage to wait in the ante-room with a magnificent grandfather clock, a round table and a row of pegs, which I presumed were for the coats and hats of cabinet ministers. In a few minutes I was ushered into the cabinet room. It was a sunny day and my first impression was of space and light within the walls of pale cream. At the far end Robert Taylor's graceful Corinthian columns led to the double doors of the room beyond, over the mantel hung Van Loo's portrait of Robert Walpole and, across the room, the windows looked out over the walled garden to the sunshine and the trees in St James's Park beyond. Down the centre of the room, beneath of row of chandeliers, stood the long cabinet table, the chairs drawn back against the walls with the exception of two, from one of which Mr Attlee rose and came forward to greet me with his gentle smile and quiet voice.

We talked for an hour or so and I was at once convinced of his keen and honest interest in our graduates coming to the United Kingdom. Gradually I had the embarrassing feeling, as he asked such simple questions, that he was a pupil seeking information from a master, but I suppressed this dreadful thought concerning the Prime Minister of Great Britain and with his sincere assurance that he would do all he could to help us I floated out and came to earth in Whitehall.

At the British Medical Association in Tavistock Square, the President, Sir Hugh Lett, was interested in establishing an Empire Medical Advisory Bureau to assist overseas medical graduates in their various needs—accommodation, study and recreation—and I was invited to attend the preliminary meetings called to this end. On the first occasion I found myself seated behind the back of a fuzzy grey-haired little man; when he turned around his deeply lined face broke into the unforgettable, wry smile of Dickie Berry. He leaned over to me: 'Do you know anything about anatomy now, Dum?'

'Not much, I'm afraid.'

'Neither do I,' he said, 'neither do I.'

In and about London there was and always will be a wealth of interest. To me it is the most human, personal and paternal of all the great cities I have known. However many times I have been there, there always remain so many new interests to be enjoyed besides those I have found but could never exhaust. Perhaps it is because my generation is closer to Great Britain than those who have been born later. 'Going home' is heard less frequently now, it is generally 'going overseas'.

Besides my commitments in London, there were ample opportunities to wander and potter among the unending delights and surprises of this great city with its kindly people. Australian travellers are often impatient and many miss the finer things and fail to appreciate the kindly hearts of a country that has been patient for centuries, patient sometimes to her own detriment. They look us over rather carefully at first, but with time no warmer hearts open than those in Great Britain, and the shirts that cover them are not really stiff and stuffy, starch is readily soluble if we are patient and behave ourselves.

Before I left London I was invited to the B.B.C. to broadcast about my mission and the important role of London House in the welfare of overseas graduates. Broadcasting in a studio is a cold, impersonal procedure, different from addressing a group of people, but everyone was kind and helpful and, with my experience with radio talks to schools in Australia, I was apparently able to avoid most of the usual gaffes of some amateurs on the air.

After my rounds in London I moved to the various medical centres throughout England, into Wales, up to Scotland. I travelled by train, in many respects the best way to appreciate the countryside. Certainly the railways generally avoid those charming little English villages in their seclusion over the centuries, reached only by the winding roads or quiet haylanes, but often the roads are sunken between high hedges beyond the ditches on each side, which seem to resent any intrusion into the privacy of the chequered fields, the gentle charm of England.

Before going to Wales I rang some friends at Llanishen, a few miles out of Cardiff, but they were in London where I eventually contacted them. Mrs England, who had been at school with my wife, said she was going back next day and suggested we meet at Paddington Station. I had not seen her for many years since we were both at school.

'How will I know you in the crowd?' I asked.

'I'll be wearing an old brown coat,' she said. 'New clothes are so hard to get, and will have my granddaughter—little Elizabeth, God bless her—with me.'

I arrived at the station well before the time and hung around the ticket office. After a while a taxi drew up, out stepped a lady in an old brown coat, holding a little girl by the hand. Years had made a change but I walked across.

'Hullo, Lil,' I greeted her as I stooped to pick up her bag.

She turned: 'I beg your pardon, sir,' she said, staring at me and, calling a porter, she swept through the gate. Men have been arrested for less but fortunately there was no policeman in sight and in a few moments my real Lil came along, anything but haughty and as delightful as ever.

It was grand to relax for a few days among old friends at Pentre Gwilym, the Englands' home, with all their charming hospitality. Nearby lived another old friend, Professor Lambert Rogers, originally a Melbourne graduate and at that time Professor of Surgery at the University of Wales in Cardiff. My mother's people were Welsh: this may be why Wales has always held a warmth for me.

At Oxford I found another link with Australia in Hugh Cairns, originally from Adelaide, and with his kindly care everyone was most generous. We dined with the students in the Great Hall of Christ College and it was just on midnight when Tom in his Tower struck the hour as the little gate was unlatched for me to return to the Mitre. It was all another world and when I dined at Lincoln I realized it was a different age. Over our port and nuts, in the privacy of the Rector's room, where we had been talking of war, after a pause one of the senior dons turned to me and said: 'That was a tragedy with those guns, but the lad got his V.C.; two in one family—father and son.' He dwelt in the past, and our conversation had focused his mind on *his* war, the Boer War more than fifty years before, with World War I and World War II since. The Boer War was my childhood war and fortunately I had read many accounts of that campaign and soon realized that he was talking of Lieutenant Roberts, who was killed at Colenso when trying to save the guns swept by the Boer fire from across the Tulega. We talked of the tragedies, the dark week of Magesfontein and Modder River and how the fighting dragged on for two years after the decisive battle of Paadeberg, of the stubbornness of De Wet and those Boer Generals, Botha and Smuts, how twelve years later we found these two generals fighting for Great Britain in World War I and how much the staunch loyalty of Jan Smuts meant to the British Empire in World War II.

I had been asked by my Postgraduate Committee to look around for a children's specialist to visit Australia on a lecturing tour the following year. I had been brought up on the tradition of Great Ormond Street Children's Hospital and the standard text books edited by members of the staff. While in London I visited this hospital in Guilford Street, a few minutes walk from London House. When I called, however, it was soon apparent that there was little interest in Australia. After Oxford I travelled north and fortunately I met the man who was to me the most inspiring children's specialist I was to find in the United Kingdom—James Spence, the charming, gentle Professor of Child Health at King's College, associated at that time with the University of Durham. Jimmy resented the idea that he had a chair at the University. 'A chair implies that I sit on my backside,' he said to me. 'Any professor worth his salt keeps moving around.' I spent many delightful days with Jimmy in the University and at his home in Brandling Park. His great pride was the babies' hospital. Little money was available for this project, so at small cost he took over a grim terrace block in a dingy and rather disreputable part of the city, knocked it about and brightened it up. I have never seen better cared for babies or more contented mothers, who lived in with their babies for some days before they were discharged, learning to care for them. It is not the number of patients, the cost or the outward appearance of a hospital, nor the elaborate interior, that marks its worthiness; it is the care of the patients and their contentment, the quality of the teaching and the advances in medical knowledge that determine the true standard of a hospital.

I was able to arrange for Jimmy to come to Australia, where I renewed a friendship I will always cherish. Among my many photographs I have a snap of Jimmy with his long legs outbent as he rode around on a child's bicycle during a delightful weekend we spent at Clive Disher's old home, Strathfieldsaye, in Gippsland. When my wife and I were in London a year or so later, Jimmy's knighthood was announced and that night we dined with his family at the ladies' annexe at the Athenaeum Club, Gladstone's old home. Before we were in London again, Jimmy had died.

On to Edinburgh, Old Reekie, where Sir Alexander Biggam, directing Medical Postgraduate Studies, was kind and helpful. Edinburgh for years had been the Mecca of many Melbourne medical postgraduates and tbere, as everywhere in Scotland, I found a warmth of interest in Australia.

Glasgow, only a few miles to the west, was a different city, commanded not by a castle but by a University rising high on the hill above Kelvin Hall below. At lunch one day with the Medical Dean, Professor Noah Morris, I tasted my first haggis and, good as it was, not until on another occasion I had wedded it to a dram of athol brose did I fully appreciate the delight of this 'Great Chieftain o' the Puddin' Race'. Granted that some parts of Glasgow are grim, within a few miles across the Clyde lie Ballater and the loveliness of Loch Lomond.

Australians generally get along very well with the Scots and during the wars there was always an early affinity between the Jocks and the Diggers. To me it is a delight to hear the broad Scot speech, difficult though it may be at times to be sure what is said. I rather like the story of the Highland Divine who, after preaching one sermon in the morning removed his dentures and gave the same discourse at night and got away with it.

Before I left Scotland I received a cable inviting me to represent the British Medical Association in Australia at the bi-centennial meeting of the American Medical Association at Atlantic City. As the date of this occasion fitted in with my itinerary in North America, I gladly accepted.

After visits to other medical centres in the United Kingdom, the time arrived for me to move across the Atlantic. The night before I left London we had a grand dinner at London House and many of those men who had been so kind and helpful came along. With all their delightful charm, some Englishmen can be ridiculously touchy and, in my innocence, certain V.I.P.'s not on speaking terms with one another had been invited. So splendidly did Peter Pepper and his staff turn it on, however, that a good time was had by all and two notable peers, who had not even nodded to each other for years, left noisily arm in arm at midnight, offering each other a lift.

Chapter 15 Through America

We took off from Heathrow in the lingering twilight of the next day to fuel at Shannon in Southern Ireland where a passenger came aboard to take the seat next to mine. As we rose I turned to him: 'Whenever I leave England I get a lump in my throat, it is all so lovely.'

'Lovely,' he snarled, 'lovely? Do you know what Cromwell did to Ireland?' And until I mercifully fell asleep I had to listen to Cromwell's cruelty nearly 300 years before, cruelty apparently surpassing that of Jeffrey's Bloody Assize and the visit of Jardine's team to Australia.

We were roused during the night at Newfoundland to squelch across in the pouring rain at Gander. A cup of coffee, a short rest, then as dawn came up we flew over the New England states and down to La Guardia airfield in New York, and the adventure of an American taxi to my hotel.

After a couple of days I went down by train to Atlantic City where after registering I had the rest of the afternoon to myself. I resisted the temptation to be wheeled in a wicker bath-chair along the Board Walk by a smiling coloured man for the price of a dollar, but wandering quietly along the pier, watching the fish nets being drawn and the people strolling along was sufficient entertainment. Next morning began the momentous bi-centenary meeting of the American Medical Association, which was to endure for a week. This was a strange and rather bewildering experience with the scale, the speed and the multiplicity of activities. I have little recollection of the scientific sessions, they came and went in a whirl, a vibrating bell would ring and like a kaleidoscope, the vast hall would be given a shake and a new pattern would appear as often as six times each half day. It seemed that speed often outpaced science. The scientific meetings were not devoid of salesmanship as frequently they would be interrupted by a lad in the buttons and pillbox hat of the page displayed in the advertisements of a well-known brand of cigarettes, who would call out: 'Paging Philip Morris. Paging Philip Morris!'

But the exhibitions were remarkably efficient. At that time university courses in Art as applied to Medical Exposition were conducted at Baltimore, Chicago and Toronto, and certainly the effectiveness of the photographic, pictorial, modelling and other visual and auditory aids as directed to medicine was a revelation to me.

There were scientific visits and the usual exhausting round of social activities at each of which a number of visitors were called upon without warning to speak. When I realized that sooner or later every visitor would have to face this ordeal, I lay awake wondering what I could contribute when my turn would come. Thinking of centenaries, a quiet bell began to tinkle: I have little memory for poetry except for what I was made to learn by heart at school and a few verses I have enjoyed since, but there floated to the surface of my indolent mind Oliver Wendell Holmes's 'One Horse Shay'. Here was the answer, an American doctor poet and a hundred years.

Sure enough, during a large social gathering one night in the ballroom, the President of the Association suddenly blew a trumpet and called for silence. 'Ladies and gentlemen, we have with us a medic from down under, from that great island continent in the South Pacific—Australia; a man who tended our brave boys in the jungles of New Guinea—we all want to hear from him, Brigadier-General NARRIS, step up here into the spotlight.' Tremendous applause and more trumpet and flashing cameras as I stepped on to the dais to give my well-prepared 'impromptu off the cuff' few words. I began what I remembered and had rehearsed:

> 'Little of all we value here
> Reaches the dawn of its hundredth year
> Without both looking and feeling queer.
> There's little on earth that retains its youth
> As far as I know but a tree and a truth.'

and concluded with a few platitudes and clichés about the tree of knowledge and the truth of medical science.

Louder trumpets but less applause as I stepped from the searching spotlight to disappear into the rear of the crowd. Thank you, Oliver, for delivering me from the lions.

On the final day they generously conferred on some of us who had come from overseas Honorary Membership of the American Medical Association and of the more exclusive Alpha Omega Alpha Society—gracious compliments to our countries. I am afraid I forgot to purchase the gold watch key symbol of the membership of the A.O.A. Society but their Medical Journal, *The Pharos*, with its interesting philosophical and historical articles comes regularly and is much enjoyed.

After the meeting at Atlantic City I took the train to Washington, a beautiful city with magnificent grey stone buildings and the wide swathe of green across the city leading to the contemplative statue of Abraham Lincoln enshrined high above a graceful sweep of the Potomac.

My first call was to the National Red Cross Headquarters. When American base hospitals had been established in Australia early in the Pacific War, our Red Cross Blood Transfusion Service had created a most favourable impression. We were told that in America blood donors were paid as much as ten to twenty dollars a pint of blood and some students paid for their courses literally in blood. Our source of blood was free and, as the Americans had been deeply impressed by the efficiency of this service, I was closely questioned as to how this was so successfull administered.

The Fulbright Bill, of particular interest to Australia, was being drafted, and I was invited to attend a session at the Capitol. The procedure in this National Parliament was new to me. There was no obvious Party division in the seating, which was arranged in a semi-circular arc facing a long dais. Bills were introduced by private members and the method of voting was intriguing. When any debate was concluded an alphabetical roll of members was called out from the dais and as his name came each member signified his verbal agreement or disagreement. This was recorded and at the conclusion of this enquiry the names were again read out in alphabetical order, together with each member's recorded decision, giving him an opportunity to reverse this if incorrect.

The final approved rolls were then taken to another room where a summation of the ayes and nays revealed the fate of the resolution. It must have taken a considerable time each year to arrive at these decisions.

To most of us in the British tradition the rectangular shape of a parliamentary chamber with a clear division of parties is taken for granted, but not only in America, in France and many other countries this is not observed. It would also seem an obvious provision in a legislative chamber that a seat should be available for every elected member. But no, in London when the House of Commons was being restored after the blitz, this question arose and an overwhelming majority, led by Winston Churchill, decided, 'that on no account would a seat be available for every member entitled to sit in the Chamber. Were this so, half the seats would be unoccupied and the essence of Parliamentary debates is intimacy. When any momentous question is before the House and members attend in their full numbers, many should stand indicating the urgent importance of the business.' And so it is at Westminster.

The picture galleries in Washington were a joy. Never before had I seen pictures so presented, giving each its full value. For some years I had been interested in that flamboyant figure, James McNeil Whistler, and in the Freer Gallery I found a fine collection of his art and the reconstruction of the famous Peacock Room that had precipitated another of Whistler's many quarrels.

I rather blotted my personal and possibly national copy book when I attended an international clinical meeting at the Bellevue Children's Hospital, during a ward round under the direction of a world famous paediatrician. A child was wheeled into a large room where we were all assembled and the history was given of a girl aged eight who had been admitted with an acute lobar pneumonia. Chest X-rays had been taken twice daily to record the progress of the disease, which clinically seemed to have subsided. However, there still appeared a faint radiological shadow at the base of the left lung and to the pundits gathered around the films this seemed very disturbing. No one examined or even looked at the little girl herself, but keenly debated whether there might be a peanut in the lung and should they 'pass the bronchoscope or start working on the sinuses.' This was all well above my ceiling so I quietly strolled over to the youngster, a bright and well looking little lass.

'And how are we today?' I asked her.

'Sure, I'm feeling fine,' she said, bouncing about the bed. 'I'd like to go out and have a ball game.'

I saw by her chart that her temperature had been normal for some days and either because I was rusty with my stethoscope or because there was nothing abnormal to hear, my examination of her chest was negative. When she told me of the large breakfast she had had, I was satisfied and wandered back to the serious fellows gathered around the films. My movement caught the eye of our mentor, who turned to me and said: 'Well now, Australia, what do you think about this problem? Where ought we to start working on her?'

I explained that personally I did not X-ray pneumonias every day and I would not have been surprised to find a faint shadow remaining in an area of so recent a lobar pneumonia. 'Anyway,' I said, 'I can't find anything wrong with the little girl now.'

'That's as may be, Doctor, but we must do something. Just look at these rays, tell us what you would do.'

'Well, as a matter of fact, I would get her out of hospital before she got sick,' I replied.

There was a dead silence. 'Oh Doctor, Doctor,' he said, shaking his head sadly and making me feel like Bateman's guardsman, who dropped his rifle on a ceremonial parade.

It was a new experience to find every policeman on point duty or in the streets heavily armed and after the scrappy post-war newspapers in London, where there was still a paper shortage, to pick up the Sunday New York Times of 278 pages was no mean effort. There was no shortage of food or drink and more brands of Scotch whisky on display than I had known existed. The towering enormity of Manhattan could be appreciated from the roof of one of the many sky-piercing colossi. I had read of Central Park in many of O. Henry's stories, but only when I stood on top of the Rockefeller Centre did I appreciate the extent of this oasis. This Centre held many delights and not the least was the remarkable tempo and precision of the seventy-odd Rockettes as their legs and arms pranced and swung in perfect simultaneous rhythm across the width of the stage. The garish flickering lights of Times Square seemed disturbing by day but with the coming of night fairyland hung in the heavens. In July the heat was oppressive, escapable I found by buying the cheapest seat in an air-conditioned picture theatre, shutting my eyes and relaxing. After the peak hour crowds in London crushing around the ticket offices and change machines of the underground, the fixed fare on the public transport in New York was a relief. At that time you just dropped your dime or appropriate coin in the slot as you entered a bus or passed through the turnstiles of the underground, and you could travel any distance, short or long.

Among the many new friends I made in New York was the delightful and interesting Chute family—Marchette, who was writing a life of Shakespeare in London, and Joy, her sister, writing stories that had been syndicated in many parts of the world and whose Mabel Williams lecture, 'When the writer comes of age', is a valuable guide and help to any author; together with their charming mother, they lived in East 63 Street. A few years later we met Marchette on her first visit to London and from her extensive researches for her biography of Shakespeare, her knowledge of Elizabethan London was illuminating.

Unlike London, it was practically impossible to get lost in New York with its numbered straight avenues along the length of Manhattan and the numbered streets across, east or west, according to their relationship to Fifth Avenue.

The touring phase of the A.M.A. Meeting was about to begin and fortunately I had put aside enough of my travellers' cheques to cover this. Those of us who had elected to visit the medical centres in the New England states and west along the lakes were asked to assemble at Grand Central Station at 8 a.m. Arriving in ample time, I found that the Station time was one hour behind the city time, so I wandered around the various station attractions. For ten cents I entered a small sentry-box affair, sat down, pressed a button, had my photograph taken, printed and presented all in less than a minute. When I looked at myself I realized that the tempo had taken its toll.

There were four Russians in our group, two men and two women. This was my first contact with the effect of the Iron Curtain: in our presence they seldom spoke to each other, never to any of us, or acknowledged each morning's greetings beyond a slight nod of the head, and not once during the various clinical meetings did they open their mouths.

There was an air of London about the older parts of Boston, across the Common where the squirrels played and strange bird-like boats sailed over the lake. Besides the excellent ward rounds, at Harvard it was interesting for me to visit the Medical School where once served the only Professor of Chemistry I know to have been hanged for murder.

I had lectured to a group of medical students on this crime, which is mentioned in one of Dickens's books. A hundred years before my visit to the University, Professor John White Webster, M.D., M.A., Ewing Professor of Chemistry and Mineralogy, of the University of Cambridge as it was then known, was heavily in debt. On Friday, 23 November 1849, he invited his main creditor to call on him at the Medical School. From that afternoon Parkman was never seen alive. This was not surprising as Webster had murdered him, dissected his body and, probably with strong caustic and fire, disposed of most of the tissues. The remaining fragments he tossed down into a pit below his privy, where within a week they were found by a janitor. The reconstruction of a recognizable body from these few remains was a forensic triumph for those days, but the identity was determined in a dramatic manner. Three years earlier Parkman had been called upon to speak at the opening of the new Medical School. He was not keen on speaking as his dentures were ill fitting and apt to fall out and for this special occasion he ordered a new set from his dentist, Dr Nathaniel Kemp. Among the sweepings from the furnace in Webster's laboratory were some teeth and a portion of a jaw; comparing these with his casts and notes Dr Kemp stated in court. 'I have as good reason to believe these are Dr Parkman's teeth as I have to believe any fact in my knowledge.' This was a hundred years ago.

In Minneapolis I learnt two things: in Australia whenever I visited a hospital ward I would go first to the senior nurse in charge and say 'Good morning' or 'Good afternoon, Sister'. On the day we visited a ward in Minneapolis the senior nurse was standing at the ward to welcome us. 'Good morning, Sister,' I said and received a stony stare. Apparently, as I was told later, I had made the equivalent of a wolfish gesture: 'Howdy, baby.'

Through America

I learnt also how to conclude a tiresome meeting. It was during the afternoon clinical session which had begun at 2 o'clock in a lecture theatre, and with no break for tea had waffled on without great enlightenment until after 5 p.m. This seemed to be unending, until a tall American in the back row stood up. 'Look here, gentlemen, this session reminds me of the time they brought those edible frogs over from France and let 'em loose out there in Lake Minnetonka. There was a close season for a coupla years and then they let us have a go at them. On the opening day I took out my net and caught a great big bull frog, which with pride I showed to my wife. "Look, honey," I said, "I've gotten a 26 lb bull frog." "Oh my," she said, "a 26 lb bull frog?" "Yes," I said, "25 lb bull and 1 lb frog."' He sat down. The meeting dissolved.

Chicago was a pool of stifling heat and it was difficult to realize that the waters of Lake Michigan freeze over in a severe winter. The quiet setting of the Mayo Clinic in Rochester was a relief, but it was a surprise to see lifelike model presentations of all the standard surgical proceedings on display in the public museum. The only memory I retain of Detroit is the soul-destroying repetitive work of the hundreds of men seated along the benches in the vast Ford Motor Works. With his mastery Chaplin had caught this atmosphere in *Modern Times*.

The two weeks of this tour by train were a whirl and it was good to be back in New York and free again before moving on to Canada. We were taken out to a model dairy-farm across the Hudson in New Jersey. Our road passed through luscious fields of alfalfa or lucerne but no cattle were in sight. Only when we arrived at the farm buildings were they visible, housed in long byres feeding from troughs. Three times a day the cows were led from their stalls, hosed down and mounted on a rotolactor, a revolving platform like a merry-go-round. The machines were clamped to their udders and when after 8 or 10 minutes they had been revolved through a complete circle, the machines were removed, the cows stepped down and were led back to their stalls: such was their complete indoor life.

In Canada I met with many friends that I had made in London over the discussions concerning the establishment of the World Health Organization. In Montreal, said to be the largest French city after Paris, it was a moving experience to visit the rooms of William Osler at the McGill Medical School and be conducted around the treasures by one who had served this great man. The guide reminded me that Dr Neil Cream, the multiple murderer in London, had graduated at Montreal in 1876. With the slopes of Mount Royal and West Mount almost in the heart of the city, fine winter sport was at the doorstep. Montreal was the great centre of the fur trade and I found the answer to the pictures in the Red Indian books of my boyhood where the fur traders were always armed with long-barrelled guns. These were not so much for range and accuracy as for barter: they exchanged their goods with the Indians, for a pile of furs standing as high as their guns. Ottawa was commanded by magnificent Gothic granite Parliament Houses, with the green softness of their copper roofs standing high above the river as the red tunics of the Mounties on guard gave another flash of colour.

Toronto was a lively medical centre, justly proud of Banting's contribution to the understanding of diabetes. The burning question of the day, however, as expressed by lengthy letters in the press, was the opposition to the proposed extension of the General Hospital, which would involve the demolition of the birthplace of Mary Pickford, 'the world's sweetheart'.

Niagara Falls, a few miles south of Toronto, have been presented in picture all over the world, but when I came from the Canadian side I had no sense of disappointment. The extent and the grace of the Falls, the mist at their feet, and with a strong wind blowing, the strange muted sound of the torrents held me. A few years later when I saw the Falls from the American side, the effect was far less impressive. I don't know how long I could have watched while Charles Blondin (or to give him his full name, Jean François Gravelot) gavotted across the Falls on a tightrope, balanced on a chair midway and drank a cup of tea before completing the passage, nearly a hundred years earlier.

Back to New York for farewells and board the train to San Francisco. While the day lingered we ran along the Hudson Valley past the grim prison of Sing Sing with the famous military college of West Point on the opposite cliffs beyond, before swinging west through the green Mohawk Valley as night came down. Lakes, pastures, woods, rivers, the high sandy wastes of Utah and

Through America

State after State flashed by as we climbed westward into the Rockies of Nevada, then winding down the Donner Pass through snowsheds, tunnels and cuttings into the greenery of the Sacramento Valley and San Francisco.

I felt more comfortable and at home in San Francisco than in any other city of the States. It was not only that I was nearer to Australia, that great eucalypts flourished in the area, or that I came across a hedge of our coastal ti-tree. Certainly cable-trams ran up and down the hills as they did in my boyhood Melbourne, and the people were so friendly and personal in this city with its lovely setting.

If only the United Nations H.Q. had been established at Angel Island in the harbour, as I understand had been offered, instead of that grim, erect glass matchbox on the east riverside of New York, I believe the deliberations would have been much more amicable and fruitful. The late afternoon mist rolling in from the Pacific Ocean, over and about the Golden Gate, was an enduring memory as I stood on the steps of the Palace of the Legion of Honour with its wealth of art, and looked out to the sun sinking down in all its glory.

It had been a most interesting mission. I had learnt a deal, made many good friends and arrived home convinced of the English speaking world's goodwill towards our graduates.

Chapter 16   D.G.M.S.

Shortly after I returned to Australia Major-General Burston, Director-General of Army Medical Services, asked me to lunch at the Club. 'Do you remember in the Middle East when I enquired of my senior officers what posting they would prefer next and you said that if you could not have my job you would like to stay with your Division?'

'Yes,' I said. 'And you replied that you were feeling particularly fit at the time and hoped to continue to do so.'

'Well, you can have my job in a couple of months when I retire, if you still want it.'

This came as a complete surprise to me; I had never for one moment thought of such a situation. When I was demobilized as medically unfit I had accepted this as the end of the Army for me.

'Bless my soul, Ginger,' I said. 'I'll have to think about it. Give me a week and I will let you know.'

'All right,' he said. 'But I would like you to take it.'

There were pros and cons and I talked it over with my wife. I had enjoyed the Army where I had made many good friends to whom I owed much, and here was a chance to pay something back. With the experience I had been granted in the various fields of the Army Medical Service, I believed I could contribute something. I did not relish the difficulties of the Army in peacetime and the pay held no attraction, about half what a Major was to get a few years later. When the compulsory contribution for the pension of a Major-General had been deducted from my pay, we would have had less than twelve pounds a week to live on, so any pension rights would have to be waived. Under the regulations I could hold the position for only five more years—and then what? Anyway, was I medically fit? But this last question was answered when I had a completely satisfactory medical examination.

I remembered how I felt as D.D.M.S. of the Corps after the grand time I had had with the 7th Division and I was not altogether happy about being a chair-borne General for a few years. As my wife said, however: 'You know you did enjoy the Army and said you would not have missed a minute of it,' so I gratefully accepted the position.

Liddell Hart, in his *Generals and Their Cure,* tells a story of Waterloo. During the French attack on Hougoumont, a brilliant young Colonel—I think his name was Le Croix—was severely wounded in the head. Napoleon, hearing of this casualty, ordered him to be taken at once to the senior surgeon, Larrey, who realizing the officer's desperate condition immediately, according to the story, removed the top of his skull, lifted out the brain and began hunting for the bullet. Suddenly the operating tent was flung back and a young A.D.C. asked if General Le Croix had received attention. 'No,' said the surgeon, 'this is a Colonel.'

'Sir, Napoleon has heard of this Colonel's gallantry and wishes to signalize this by an immediate promotion to General.'

Thereupon Le Croix grabbed the top of his skull and started to walk out.

'Hey, wait a minute,' said the surgeon, 'you've forgotten your brain.'

'That's all right,' said the patient. 'I'm a General now.'

Over many years in the Army I had advanced from unadorned sleeves or shoulder-straps as Trooper Norris to three temporary stripes and then back to bare sleeves. A few years later three pips, then a crown—another pip, then two pips above the crown and, when I was demobbed as a Brigadier, three pips. Now, on 3 May 1948, I could put up a General's badge on my cap and on my shoulders a pip surmounting crossed batons and swords, but no one told me which way these pointed. A few days after I had been regimentally dressed in my new rank and, feeling rather fine, I was waiting for my wife on the steps of the Regent Theatre in Collins Street. A lady came towards me, to my deluded pride attracted by my General's uniform—but no. 'Where do I get the five shilling seats?' she asked me and, coming down from my perch, like a polite commissionaire I led her over to the box-office and arranged for her accommodation.

The Medical Directorate of Army Headquarters occupied a fine two-storeyed bluestone building, J Block, erected about a hundred years before as a police hospital. Like all rooms and corridors in the Barracks the walls from about six feet from the floor were painted the depressing Public Works brown with a dull cream above to the lofty ceiling, and until I hung a few pictures around the room (an unheard of A.H.Q. form of decoration), the place was enough to make anyone feel depressed. Among my pictures was a fine print of Napoleon's head, 'The Last Phase', and my secretary told me that one of the cleaners had asked her, 'When did 'e work here?' Later when the painters came around on their routine maintenance, I persuaded them to jolly the whole block and before anyone could protest about something that was never done or resent this intrusion into tradition, my Directorate welcomed visitors with a cheerful shade of light duck egg green.

In the corner of my room stood an imposing safe. I had never had a safe before, so I enquired about it and asked for the key. This was a poser, but at last the Camp Commandant produced one and the heavy door swung open. Beyond a few unimportant papers and the inventory of J Block there was a small circular carton with a perforated lid and containing a white powder, 'Fast Teeth'. I was never sure to which of my predecessors this was of assistance as top and/or bottom security and for all I know it may still be there.

When I served in the ranks I felt that my C.O. at times did not know his job; when I came to command a field ambulance I realized that our troubles were higher and rested upon the A.D.M.S. of the Division. In time I became an A.D.M.S. and then it was clear that our problems could be traced to the D.D.M.S. on Corps. Ultimately this posting fell to me and at long last I realized that the source of all our frustration was the D.G.M.S. of the Service. Now I found myself the ultimate source of all the grumblings down the line and there was no one above to blame or to whom I could pass the buck.

General Burston had retired a few weeks before I had assumed my position and there was no hand-over, but I had enough experience in the basic administration of the Medical Services to appreciate most of the problems. At that time there were only two medical officers in the Australian Regular Army—the D.G.M.S. and the medical officer at the Military College, Duntroon. My staff at Army Headquarters consisted of a part-time Matron in Chief, that wonderful lady, Col. Annie Sage, an original warrant-officer promoted well above his ceiling as a Lieut.-Colonel, my Senior Staff Officer, a Major pharmacist, two junior staff officers and a few civilian clerks. Fortunately I took over a most loyal and efficient secretary, Miss Ryan, who after many years of service was able to save me from many mistakes, as my writing is bad and my spelling poor. When one retires from a senior position, the sudden loss of a secretary is catastrophic. As an establishment to direct the Medical Services of the Australian Army this situation was Gilbertian, there was no other medical officer on my staff.

At that time Army H.Q. occupied Victoria Barracks in Melbourne within Southern Command. When the D.G.M.S. was away, it was the practice for the Senior Medical Officer Southern Command to discharge his routine duties. This was unsatisfactory to me as all the D.Ds.M.S. were part-time officers with busy private practices. When I became D.G.M.S., Brigadier Harry Furnell was D.D.M.S. Southern Command and while Harry, with his long experience of the Army and his splendid war record, was perfectly fitted to have filled my full-time position, he was a busy specialist building his private practice after six years of war. As I intended to be frequently away from Army H.Q. visiting the various commands and gaining a first-hand knowledge of our medical service with the Occupational Force in Japan, I decided to correct this anomaly. Instead of writing, I went over to the Adjutant-General, who was responsible for the Medical Services, and said that I considered it essential to have a regular deputy on my establishment. I have always endeavoured to achieve a situation where I personally was dispensable. When one person or thing was essential at least two should always be available and, besides individuals, this holds for glasses, false teeth, watches, pens, pencils and diaries. The A.G., however, could not see why the old arrangement, which had worked in the past before the war, should not continue.

I understand that the Army attitude nowadays is different from what it was when I joined the regular army in 1948. At that time it required considerable adjustment at my age to settle into a life with a new environment of personal relationships after living many years among ordinary common-sense people with varying interests and a general willingness to help others. After years of good comradeship amongst all ranks of the C.M.F., I found it disturbing to experience the many discriminations between officers of different military rank and to realize the apprehension to the consequences of a career that might follow from initiative and the expression of an opinion different from that of a senior. From a world in which training was designed to maintain people alive and happy, I had moved into a world where the education of others was directed to war in which people were killed. I found it difficult to understand the reluctance of many regular officers to appear in uniform except on prescribed occasions. Other than on official occasions the community may well have been unaware that we had a Regular Army. Unlike Australia, in the United Kingdom a standing army is taken for granted, the bowler hats and neatly rolled umbrellas being recognized down Piccadilly, but it seemed to me that there was no need in Australia for this British traditional understatement. (The Duke of Cambridge once ordered a subaltern, as a punishment, to wear his uniform in London.)

The Medical Directors of the three services—Denis Pritchard and later Lionel Lockwood of the Navy, Ted Daley of the R.A.A.F. and myself—were close friends. All had had considerable peacetime and active service experience and it seemed reasonable that we should come together more or less regularly and discuss our various problems, many of which were common to the three services. There was no precedent for this but over a cup of tea and a few biscuits we met from time to time in my Directorate and came to many conclusions that were unanimously considered would be to the advancement of the armed forces. I submitted mine in writing, of course, to the Adjutant-General, explaining how these came about, and was under the delusion that my recommendations would be at least considered and discussed with me. But no. Back in writing came the direction that in future any discussion or recommendations concerning the Army Medical Service would be initiated solely by him. A later request that in the event of any medical questions being included in the deliberations of the Military Board I might be informed and given the opportunity to explain the medical implications, met with the same fate, as the A.G. in writing considered he was quite capable of appreciating any medical problems before the Military Board. It was two years before I was invited to attend an A.G.'s Conference.

To anyone who had practised a profession in a private capacity, the extraordinary attitude of the Federal Treasury towards the various Government Departments was to say the least bewildering. The Treasury is and must be the sole body responsible for the collection and distribution of public moneys as determined by Government policy. Each Government Department is required to submit a budget, the sum of the needs of its various branches for the forthcoming year. The total of these budgets may exceed the money available from the Treasury and while some Departments may have their requirements satisfied in full, others may have theirs reduced. Well and good—priorities in the overall picture must be appreciated. This allocation having been made (officially according to Government policy but, one suspects, only after Treasury's dominating decisions) that should be the end of it as far as the Treasury is concerned.

But no. Not a bit of it.

Each Department has a Treasury official watching it like Cerberus and all down the line is a litter of Cerberi, one in every branch determining how the money will be spent, whether or no these Cerberi have any knowledge or understanding of the functions of the Department or the branch over which they have this authority. The general attitude is that of inverted Micawbers, waiting for something to turn down. Perhaps promotion in the Federal Treasury depends on negatives as in some police forces it results from the number of arrests rather than from diminution of crime in an area. This tyranny of the Treasury breeds departmental uneasiness, resentment, bargaining and intrigue.

A divisional commander in the field within the overall strategic direction from his Corps Commander could commit the thousands of lives under his command to any tactical enterprise he decided, be it sound or hare-brained. But when it came to the immediate spending of money within the amount allocated to the Army for a purpose he considered necessary for the efficiency of these lives, the Treasury tentacles were around him except for a few pounds.

The Treasury officials who possibly knew nothing about a division appeared to consider him either devoid of any financial judgement or a rogue trying to get away with something.

It was the same towards anyone appointed to direct the Army Medical Services, a posting presumably made because he was judged capable of discharging the responsibilities of such an appointment. Each year my Directorate carefully prepared our budget. This was not a hit-or-miss affair nor a bargaining try-on, but was based on the best possible advice concerning what was considered necessary for the efficiency of our service. Realizing that all necessary finance might not be available, we determined a priority, prepared if necessary to defer some items.

I had been directed to prepare the stockpiling of sufficient anti-malarial drugs to protect a planned expeditionary force operating in a malarious area, assuming that for twelve months no overseas supplies would be available. With a vivid experience of the malarial decimation of our 7th Division in New Guinea, this seemed to me a task of the highest priority. I was given the order of battle of the proposed force, i.e. the number of bodies involved, and with the advice of specialists including Sir Neil Hamilton Fairley, a world authority on tropical diseases, we prepared our estimates. Paludrin had proved its worth in New Guinea but to provide for the possibility of meeting with a paludrin resistant strain of the parasite, as at Wewak, a correspondingly adequate supply of chloroquin was included. Provided the discipline was efficient, we were confident that these supplies would maintain the health of the troops as far as malaria was concerned. The costing of these drugs was checked and cross-checked and with the knowledge that every tablet and every penny had been justified by experts, I submitted my requisition.

That surely should have been simple. There was no question of the money being available—it was only a relatively small item within the total sum already allocated to the Army and there was no question as to the urgency of obtaining these supplies. But *No*—the Treasury Cerberus, who probably did not know the difference between malaria and measles, said it wasn't simple. We did not know what we were talking about and with no discussion I was notified in writing that my requisition had been reduced.

This effrontery was intolerable.

*The Golden Stairs, New Guinea, 1942.
(Courtesy: Australian War Museum.)*

The Kokoda Trail, New Guinea, 1942.
(Courtesy: Australian War Museum.)

Crossing the Kimusi River, New Guinea, 1942.
(Courtesy: Australian War Museum.)

Shaggy Ridge, New Guinea, 1942.
(Courtesy: Australian War Museum.)

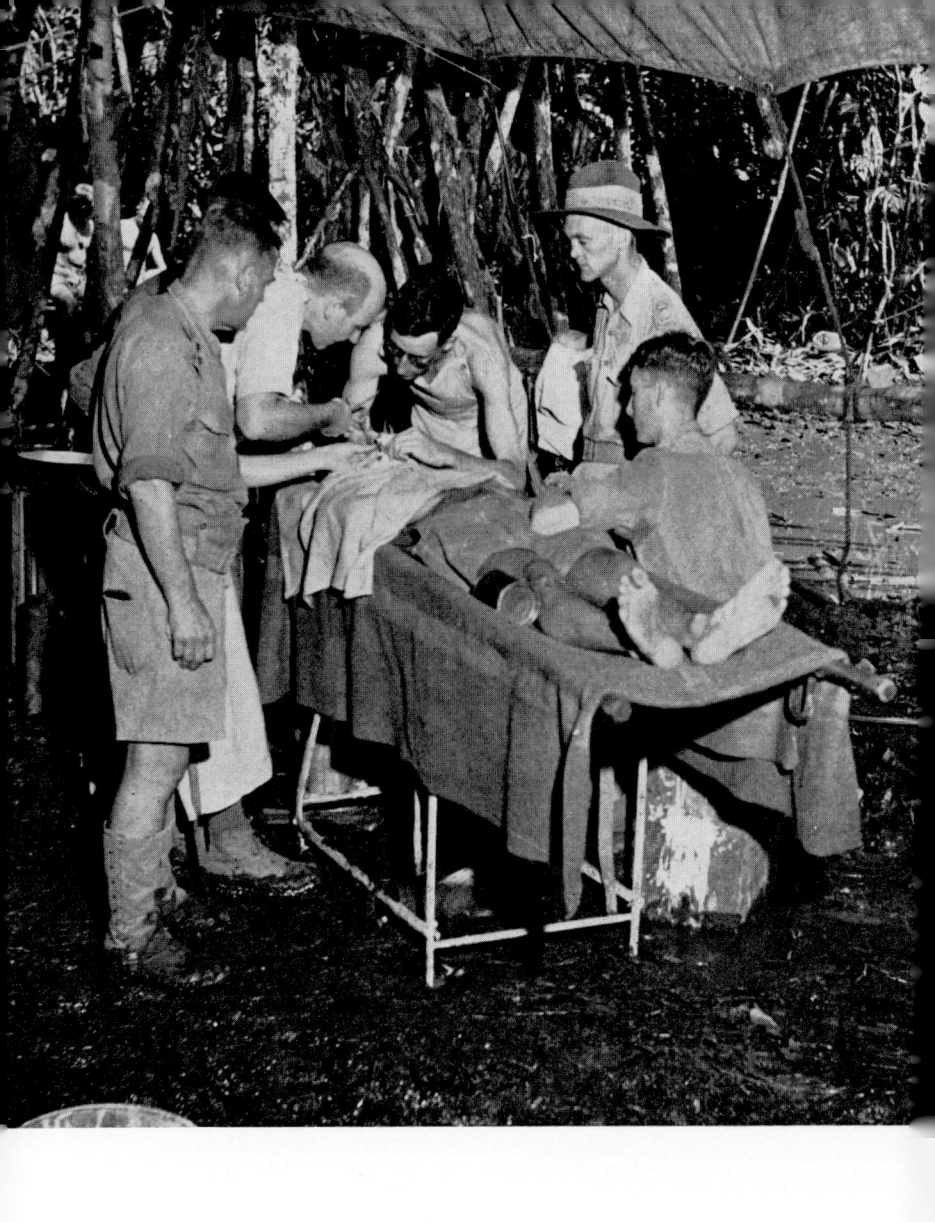

Forward operating unit at Soputa, within a quarter of a mile from Japanese for[ces]
Major Ackland operating, assisted by Captain Wakefield.
(Courtesy: Australian War Museum.)

I had been given a direction from Army Authority and the tyranny of the Treasury had frustrated me from carrying this out. I sent a memo. back to the signatory of that decision absolving my Service from the almost inevitable catastrophe resulting from this reduction and informing him that I was recording in my war diary that the full responsibility for any malarial disaster now rested on his shoulders and not upon those of the Army Medical Service.

This rang a bell as most Treasury officials, when challenged, are sensitive of accepting any positive responsibility. The total sum was received and the full supplies passed into the Depot of Medical Stores. If only others who could honestly justify their attitude rather than submit a bargaining budget would stand to their guns, such an intolerable situation might not arise.

I could not understand the quiet submission to the dictates of those dressed in a little brief authority but without any training in how to exercise it. I thought perhaps it had dated back to when an all-powerful Prime Minister had assumed the additional role of Treasurer, but when some years later I read the inner history of the battles with the Spanish Armada, 500 years before, I realized the Treasury, like the law, looks back over the centuries for precedents and principles.

In Alexander McKee's *From Merciless Defenders* there are reproduced contemporary writings at the time of the Spanish Armada. From these it can be realized that Treasury policy dates at least from the Sixteenth Century. The accepted stories and pictures of Drake placidly playing bowls on Plymouth Hoe with the Armada in sight are questionable. Drake at that time was a very angry man. The plan of the Lord High Admiral, Lord Howard of Effingham, Drake, Hawkins and the other admirals, who well knew their business, had been to sail with a favourable wind while the Armada was tied in the mouth of the Tagus. 'Stop him now and stop him for ever', but the ships' supplies were quite inadequate for battle.

Letters were sent to the Lord High Treasurer Burleigh: 'My Lord, by the advertisements that giveth the largest time for the coming out of the Spanish Forces is the month of May, being the fifteenth, then we shall have three days victuals.' 'The proportion in powder and shot for our great ordnance in Her Majesty's ships is but for one day and a half as the service may require, for the love of God and our country, let us have with some speed some great shot sent to us of all bigness and some powder with it.' 'Your good Lordship, there is here the gallantest company of Captains, Soldiers and Marines that I think was ever seen in England. It were a pity they should lack meat when they are so desirous to spend their lives in Her Majesty's Service. If it be fit to be so it passeth my reason, I think ever since there were ships of this realm it was never heard of. King Harry, Her Majesty's father, never made a proportion of supply less than six weeks.'

But the paper war was on. The Lord Treasurer replied that the requisitions had not been made out properly.

Another procedure new to me was the service method of communicating between people. Service directions even on paper are not always crystal clear: 'In reply to your enquiry the conditions governing the payment of fares to members of the C.M.F. are contained in paragraph 140 of Financial Instruction Relating to the C.M.F. The payment of such fares, however, is suspended by A.H.Q. memo. 24270 of 24 Dec 51.' And from an Admiralty Instruction dealing with storage of warheads and torpedoes in World War I:

'It is necessary for technical reasons that these warheads should be stored with the top at the bottom and the bottom at the top. In order that there may be no doubt as to which is the top and which is the bottom, for storage purposes, it will be seen that the bottom of each head has been labelled with the word "TOP".'

So what!

The reluctance to talk over and discuss matters gave way to a preference for paper and however close officers may be the memo, or memorandum, was the thing. The paper war would have been amusing had it not been so wasteful of time and material, a Parkinson's Law applied to paper, and the daily mounting bales of waste in a remote corner of the barracks was accepted without comment.

After the memo had gone to the Central Registry and possibly been redirected to what was there considered a more suitable destination, it eventually reached the address signified and was placed in the appropriate basket to receive attention in due course. However simple may have been the substance of the memo or enquiry, even if it could have been answered off the cuff, it received careful consideration, but never any acknowledgement before a reply was formulated often in a non-committal or temporizing form. It is said that the all time record reply to a memo was, 'The answer to your enquiry is Yes and No up to a point.'

Nevil Norway, who wrote under the name of Nevil Shute, had a host of readers throughout the English speaking world. Most of his books were delightful quiet romances but every now and then he would write about some idea that had been turning over in his mind, with no care as to whether such a book was popular or not. Some time before he died he told me of one of his fantasies. A paper plague was about to descend upon the world against which there was no known protection and it was inevitable that within six months all paper, all books, all records and archives would disintegrate and disappear. There still remained a short interval to decide what was worth preserving and to devise some means of doing so. Whenever I asked him how the idea was working out, Nevil with his slight stammer would say, 'I am still not sure how I would go about it.' That was the unsatisfactory state when he died. No light was thrown on this problem among the papers he left, but perhaps some ingenious author may in future adopt this theme in an imaginative writing. I tremble to think of the military panic had this Shute fantasy become a reality.

By this time I had become reasonably acclimatized to A.H.Q. and in spite of the strangeness and frustrations I began to enjoy my new life and found many grand friends in the small world which previously had been unknown to me. The Chief of General Staff, Sir Sydney Rowell, was a particularly helpful and understanding friend and it was a gross libel to hear A.H.Q. described as 'the only asylum in Australia run by the inmates'. I still retained many of my civilian associations—the Council of the B.M.A., the Medical Board, St John Ambulance Brigade, National Red Cross, the Royal Empire Society, and my clubs.

As soon as I had sorted myself out in the Directorate, it was high time I went around the various commands where the Army Medical Service was directed by part-time Senior Medical Officers in active practice. All these medical officers had distinguished war records and, in spite of the inevitable relaxation after a war, the highest standard was maintained throughout our Corps, which had been granted the title 'Royal' in recognition of a record in two World Wars.

As I had served with all my D.Ds.M.S. of the commands and had complete confidence in their reliability this considerably lightened my responsibilities. Among the first qualities of anyone with whom I am to serve I seek reliability, preferably reliability for good, but all of us have our failings, and if you know when a person is likely to fail he is far easier to cope with than if you never know when he is going off the rails.

I refuse to keep a dog and bark myself. To fill any position I have always endeavoured to select the person most suitable, explain clearly what I wanted him to do, why, when and where, then leave him alone to get on with the job. I would look him up every now and then to encourage him and to see if there was anything he wanted, but as long as he carried out my directions, I did not care how these were achieved. During the war I had realized that all along the line senior officers had more time to move around than their juniors in front of them and I felt that I had failed if any of my officers in a forward area had to come back to me for guidance.

Unfortunately some senior officers, fearful of what would happen to them if their juniors failed, keep nudging and annoying them, dispelling any confidence a junior may have in his senior's leadership.

As my absence around the Command did not seem to have impressed the Adjutant-General that a full-time deputy on my staff was essential, I determined as soon as possible to travel farther and inspect the Medical Services of the Australian component of B.C.O.F., the British Commonwealth Occupational Force in Japan, commanded at the time by that colourful Australian, Red Robbie, Lieut-General Sir Horace Robertson.

Chapter 17 Japanese Impressions

The large red brick building of our hospital on the island of Itajima had originally been a Japanese Naval College with the nearby Shrine of Admiral Togo, the hero of the Russo-Japanese war forty years before. As I looked out from my room next morning, I watched a line of small crouching figures slowly moving across the grassed circular parade ground below, I could think only of people weeding or picking mushrooms. I went down to see what was doing and found a dozen or so Japanese on their knees cutting the grass with a long type of penknife. In Japan they certainly did things the hard way! On one occasion we added an operating theatre to one of our hospitals. The floor had been laid in tiles and when the walls were erected and the doors hung, it was found that these would not close. They immediately dug up all the floor and relaid the tiles a shade lower and all was well. Tools such as saws and planes, which we push from us, are pulled towards the Japanese carpenters, and to turn on the electric light the switch is pushed up.

Every city, every village, and the countryside gave evidence of the endless industry of the people. There were no fallow fields as we know them, no empty plots of ground, no bare backyards however small; rice, barley or vegetables covered every square foot of the very limited arable ground over those stony mountainous islands. With few coastal or inland plains, only by terracing the slopes or reclaiming the land from the sea could the crops be extended, but still covered barely a fifth of the land. The day one crop was finished another was planted, all by hand as was the harvesting. This intense cultivation was possible only by constant fertilization with little available animal manure and the domestic sewage from the villages collected regularly into large wooden buckets, carried along the streets by the 'honey carts'. There was very little hard timber in Japan, even the rail sleepers being made of pinewood and these softwoods with the giant bamboo supplied most of the timber requirements.

At that time travelling by road in Japan was limited and, until the air service was established, a journey of any distance was restricted to leisurely travel by water or to the rapid and comfortable railways, within a few years to become one of the outstanding rail services in the world. One feature of the railways in Japan that intrigued me were the tunnels rather than cuttings, and if the track was duplicated two parallel tunnels were constructed. At that time tunnels under the sea, connecting the main islands, were being planned.

The surgical section of the B.C.O.F. Hospital was on the mainland at Kure. This hospital was an integrated establishment with medical officers drawn from the regular and National Service British Medical Corps and from our volunteers; the nurses came also from both sources. Under the command of Gerry Nye, an E.N.T. specialist from Melbourne, this was a very happy and efficient unit; the registrar, Leslie Lloyd, a businessman from Victoria, with his cheerfulness, without the wearisomeness of always being funny, supplied the cement that welded the personnel into one unit.

A few minutes run across the water landed me at the Kure wharf near the staggering ruins of the docks. For some years before the war Kure had been a proscribed area. It was known that great ship-building activities were being carried out, but only after the war was the magnitude of this industry realized. Here in a country with negligible coal and iron, the largest battleships in the world had been built and as we crossed the narrow strait the giant gantries and rusting, torn skeletons of the bombed buildings stood out abruptly against the soft blue-green of the hills beyond. The dock area was a revelation. To the east still stood a huge dump of metal scrap—car chassis and bodies, bicycle frames, and all manner of metal junk—crushed together in a vast heap, some hundreds of yards long and about forty feet high, then came what remained of the great smelting furnaces, the turning and rolling plants, giant lathes with one 18″ gun still in place, and finally the shipbuilding yards crammed with the debris of disintegrating naval craft, including dozens of midget submarines all yielding to the blinding heat of oxy-acetylene torches wielded day and night.

Here were built those great battleships *Yamato* and *Musashi*. Only after the war when the blueprints were found was the enormity of these ships appreciated. Each of 64,000 tons, mounting ten 18″ guns, their flanks protected by sixteen inches of hardened steel, each with a complement of 2,400 men and able, with full tanks, to steam where their 60-foot draft permitted for six months without refuelling, the largest and most powerful naval craft ever built or ever likely to be built.

Their first mission was Leyte Gulf in the Philippines, where *Musashi* was sunk. After the defeat at the Philippines, *Yamato* returned to Kure, but with the threatened invasion of Okinawa was immediately ordered back to the Pacific, just as refuelling had begun. All overseas sources of oil had been denied the Japanese by that time and with barely sufficient fuel to reach Okinawa, the ship sailed. It was a naval *Kamikaze*: before *Yamato* was half-way to the island the American Admiral Mitchener launched his air attack and in the deep waters of the Pacific lies that great mass of impotent metal and men.

I spent some days in Gerry Nye's quarters at Kure where the attention of our house-girls was excellent but the continual bowing was a strain. It seemed to me this was a gesture of respect and service rather than servility and while some of these girls were war widows, there was never any suggestion of resentment or bitterness in their smiling service.

All the domestic and general labour for the occupational forces was provided by efficient and cheerful Japanese personnel, and the attitude in the shops was equally efficient and cheerful. The Japanese are probably the most obedient people in the world, but the question was 'whom did they obey'? During the war it was the Emperor and his war lords, during the occupation it was General Douglas MacArthur.

Japan is a country of disaster, fires, earthquakes and typhoons. The cities, other than the fine modern buildings in the centre, are surrounded by shanty towns of timber. The villages were all of timber, softened in the weather to a soft, dark grey, roofed generally with dark blue tiles, and all villages hold disaster stores including large tanks of water.

After seeing all there was in the Itajima-Kure area and happy about the excellent medical arrangements for our troops, Gerry and I moved on to Tokyo, where we had a leave centre and a medical post. Our trip to Tokyo was certainly V.I.P. pageantry.

At all the main stations there were private entrances and exits for the Emperor and during the occupation these were available for our senior officers. When Gerry and I arrived at the Kure Station, the senior Japanese Railway officials were all lined up in the neck-high black uniforms with white gloves, and all bowed in unison as I stepped from my car on to the red carpet. I had been warned about all this ritual and managed to keep a straight face. With the Station Master leading the way, we were conducted to our private carriage consisting of a large observation car, bedrooms, bathroom and kitchen. When our gear had been taken aboard, Gerry told me to stand at the carriage door to take the final salute from the officials, who had now been joined by the engine-driver and the guard, both with white gloves. When I appeared the whole straight row bowed, I saluted, the engine-driver and the guard bowed again and then moved off smartly to their respective ends of the train. After a few minutes I nodded to the Station Master, he blew his whistle, they all bowed, I saluted and the train moved off as they were all still bowing. It had been a strain and I was glad to dive into my beautifully furnished bedroom and relax.

For a while the train ran smoothly along the coast of the Inland Sea, driving through tunnel after tunnel as the hills came down to the water's edge. Our carriage was air-conditioned, but as I stood at the open door the sea breezes were refreshing, although pungent with the reminder of drying fish. We then swung inland across the lush green of vegetables and paddyfields with the rice growing right up to the track. There were no fences or hedges and the grey farmhouses with little round stacks of rice straw and clumps of tall bamboo were a pleasure. Then back to the sea for a brief breath of the fish-laden air. Whenever the train stopped the same pantomime of bowing, gloved officials, salutes and whistles, was repeated. It was dark when we reached Osaka and after an excellent European dinner, cooked and served by our Japanese stewards in immaculate white, we pulled down the blinds, read for a while and then retired to bed. The bowing and whistles etc. may have continued throughout the night for all I know but, lulled with the smooth rhythm of the train, I slept until daylight.

Early next morning I had my first glimpse of Fujiyama, the loveliest natural feature I have ever seen. Most mountains are obviously masculine, rugged, abrupt and often aggressive, but the perfect, soft symmetry of Fuji, her coyness, there one minute, white crowned above the misty flurry of blue voile about her feet, then hiding shyly behind the clouds, were all so essentially timid and feminine. It was no wonder that Fuji San was worshipped. Vesuvius has the same symmetry in the beautiful setting above the Bay of Naples, but there is nothing coy or reticent anywhere near Naples.

As we neared the capital, the dreadful bombing was apparent. The twenty miles or so between Yokohama and Tokyo was still a flat, devastated waste.

Our arrival at Tokyo was one of my biggest moments. As we moved slowly into the crowded station, not only was there a reinforced band of bowers drawn up, but two lines of stout rope held back the hoi polloi from a broad red carpet. 'Heavens, Gerry,' I said, 'who on earth is arriving?' 'You are, and please keep a straight face.' I stepped to the carriage door, down went the neat row of white-gloved officials—up went my hand in salute. The senior official stepped forward, bowed again, and, somewhat surprised, took the hand I offered him, it seemed the decent thing to do. Then, led by the Station Master and flanked by his underlings, the cavalcade solemnly moved along the red carpet between the ropes and down the ramp leading to the Emperor's entrance. A large black limousine, complete with a small Australian flag and two stars, was waiting, but the mass bowing and saluting all had to be faced again before I was seated.

We drove off through what appeared to be a busy, modern city until we passed into the inevitable shanty town and finally along a narrow lane to the Thailand Embassy, which had been taken over by the G.O.C. B.C.O.F., our Lieut.-General Sir Horace Robertson. The large grey stone building was set in a typically lovely Japanese garden with iris and azaleas among the shrubs around a neat, smooth lawn, and stone lanterns beside a chuckling little stream, coursing over and around small boulders, among which grew the twisted boles and branches of miniature firs and maples beside the little hump bridge of red timber.

Sir Horace Robertson, Red Robbie, was a colourful character from his greying red hair to his highly polished shoes. He was among the first graduates to qualify at Duntroon and had served with our cavalry in World War I and commanded a brigade in the recent desert campaign. In many ways he was a gifted man but, like certain men and horses with his colouring, you never knew when they would buck. While they often achieve unpredictable heights denied to others, without warning they may plumb the depths beyond the reach of those around them. I looked on Robbie as the reincarnation of Napoleon's Marshal Ney, 'le rougeot', his colourful counterpart nearly a hundred and fifty years before him. I am confident that Robbie had no physical fear and I could see him leading the last forlorn charge at Waterloo, his horse shot under him, his uniform battle-stained and torn, but the hilt of his shattered sword still firmly in his grasp.

At the right military moment, vanity such as Robbie's could be a virtue, but divorced from such circumstance vanity could become tiresome. At no time did Robbie set a ceiling to his own military, sporting or business ability, and unfortunately he had no true sense of humour.

After I had been in Tokyo for a few days we were seated on the lawn one evening sipping our sherry. I said by way of conversation, which was not easy to initiate in Robbie's presence: 'This is a surprisingly good show of yours, Robbie.' He rose with all his dignity, of which he had plenty, glared at me, 'Surprising? Surprising? What surprises you? This is my command!' Dinner *à deux* that night was rather chilly. But like many others I was fond of Robbie and up to a point enjoyed his company, because unconsciously he was a feast of entertainment.

Robbie arranged for me to call upon five-star General Douglas MacArthur, who not only commanded all the occupational forces —he commanded Japan. What Douglas said went unquestioned. His official quarters in the Di Ichi Building in the centre of Tokyo overlooked the Plaza in front of the outer moat of the Emperor's Palace. One of his A.D.C.s told me that one morning the General was watching from his window while hundreds of

Japanese in working dress were hurrying to a gathering on the Plaza, on the far side of which was a dais with a loud speaker. He asked his A.D.C. what this was all about and told him to go down and find out. The A.D.C. returned and reported that these were a group of workers holding a stop-work meeting to consider a strike. 'But there will be no strike,' said MacArthur. 'Go down and tell them that I say so.' The A.D.C. went down again with the interpreter, who mounted the dais, interrupted the speaker, and broadcast the General's directive to the crowd. 'Immediately,' the A.D.C. told me, 'they all bowed and went back to work.'

When I was ushered into The Presence, he rose to greet me and paid generous tributes to the A.I.F. in the Islands and to the conduct of our occupational troops, 'under your grand General Sir Horace'. He was most charming and said he remembered me from our meeting on the Tableland. This delightful trait of remembering people and their names was characteristic of American officers. On the first occasion of a meeting they would always make sure of your name and repeat it, and however brief the first association, when next you met, after however long an interval, they immediately called you by your name. This is a particularly nice compliment, especially as often we do not take the trouble to be sure of the name of anyone to whom we are introduced, or soon forget it. Dr House from Los Angeles University told a story of a man who gave an address on the signs of growing old: 'The first indication was when you forget names—then you forget faces—then—then—(and after a long pause)—I forget what the next sign is!'

The General showed a keen interest in the health of his troops and asked me if I thought any more could be done to advance the medical arrangements. I said how happy I was about the medical picture and how I appreciated the help we were receiving from the American Medical Corps. 'You must come to lunch one day,' he said. 'I will arrange it with your General.' He rose from behind his huge desk in front of a striking portrait of George Washington in a battle scene, rang for his A.D.C. and saw me to the door.

Lunch a few days later was an experience. About a dozen of us had been invited and we were greeted by Mrs MacArthur. After a while the General appeared, shook hands with some of us and said: 'Gentlemen, we will go into lunch.' During the meal he spoke only to those immediately beside him and precisely at 2 o'clock he arose. We all rose. 'Good afternoon, gentlemen,' he said, and left the room. We waited. After a few minutes Mrs MacArthur appeared and as we filed out she stood at the door, shook each of us by the hand, thanked us for coming and said goodbye. We gathered our caps from the orderlies in the hall and that was that.

The Australian leave centre in Tokyo was in Ebisu, formerly Japanese Naval Quarters, where the brick barrack buildings surrounded a large circular pool in which the model submarines were tested before construction. We had established a small medical post with a dozen or so beds for emergencies and light cases, while more serious cases or those requiring surgery were admitted to the American General Hospital nearby, an elaborate and excellently conducted institution. These arrangements worked splendidly, thanks to our excellent relations with the Americans and to our medical officer, Graham Cooper, who was highly regarded by them.

About sixty miles along the coast we had another leave centre at Kuanha. This had been an exclusive Japanese country club and Gerry Nye and I passed a delightful weekend of golf. We each had two little Japanese girls in sky-blue frocks as caddies. The Japanese are a smiling race and certainly my golf was something to smile at, but it was embarrassing after each stroke to turn around and see my two little girls in blue with their hands across their faces stifling their chortles. It was the first opportunity I had had of hitting a golf ball into the Pacific Ocean and at the sixth hole I unintentionally seized it, to prolonged hand claps from my girls.

On another day we drove inland across the Tokyo Bay plain to Nikko. At the end of a long avenue of cryptomerias we came to the famous Buddhist temples with their elaborate and colourful carvings. Farther up the hill was Lake Chenzi, where in the Fall the woods coming down from the water's edge were alive with colour:

> 'Yellow and black and pale and hectic red,
> The breath of Autumn's being.'

Besides the medical centres and army establishments, there was much of interest around Tokyo. The beautifully tended war cemetery for the Allied troops was a place of quiet contemplation. The Meiji Art Gallery held a mixture of beautiful traditional Japanese art, with the delicate suggestion of foliage, of rain and wind in their landscapes, together with crude attempts at so-called modern art. The large departmental stores and shops along the Ginza displayed Mikimoto pearls, silks of all colours and texture, rich brocades, kimonos and obis, dolls that danced in traditional finery, clever mechanical toys of every description, hand-painted fans, satsuma, cloisonné and damascene ware, oil-paper umbrellas, prints and woodcuts, perfect little bamboo models of a Japanese house, small glass birds and animals (always in threes, poppa san, momma san and baby san) and a hundred and one other delights.

Treasures were to be found in tiny shops down narrow lanes, Samurai armour, gold inlaid sword hilts, bronzes, beautifully carved small ivory figures, jade, gold and silver jewellery, some embossed with a sixteen-petal chrysanthemum, the exclusive Royal Symbol of the Emperor's personal possessions and presentations. At that time all were very reasonably priced with the yen at twelve hundred to the Australian pound.

On our return to Kure, during which the bowing and the red carpet ritual all had to be accepted again, we broke our journey at Kyoto, the ancient capital during the power of the Shoguns.

Pagodas, temples and Japanese castles have only a limited attraction for me, but the beautiful gardens, with the golden carp gleaming in the lakes, were a joy. We spent most of the day watching the delicate designing and exquisite handwork in lacquer, satsuma, damascene and cloisonné but, compared with our standards, the conditions under which these people worked, men and women of all ages, were at that time appalling.

There still remained our Convalescent Depot at Miajima and after a day's rest at Kure we drove over the hills to the ferry. The road ran through Hiroshima. It had been suggested that the atomic bomb had been destined for Kure, missed the target and exploded over Hiroshima, but the city around the green mouths of the Ota River delta was the main embarkation port for Japanese troops moving overseas and the devastation was dreadfully on target. Already the city was beginning to rise again, ground zero, a thousand feet below where the bomb had actually exploded, was marked by the shell of a concrete building, crowned with the twisted steel of its domed roof. In this form the building, beside a canal, has been maintained as a memorial, a grim skeleton of that dreadful day, 6 August 1945. People were walking and working among the temporary shops and large new buildings arising around the shells of concrete chimneys, walls and bridges, all broken and scorched by the terrific blast and heat.

A few miles farther along the coast, past little fishing villages, each with its penetrating smell of drying fish, we boarded the ferry to the lovely island of Miajima with its famous red torii standing in the sea before the Buddhist Shrine. This was a perfect setting for our convalescent depot. A large hotel on the waterfront with excellent accommodation and amenities had been taken over, there were delightful walks among the wooded hills, boating and bathing, and the interesting little shops down the narrow streets of the village. The night cormorant fishing was a feature. Over the stern of the boats was a short, square platform on which the tethered birds were perched around the light from a kind of brazier. The cormorants, with metal rings at the base of their long narrow necks, dived or were tossed into the water to have their fill as far as this constriction and when they were hauled aboard, a deft squeeze ejected the catch on to the deck. The fish were small, but dried, salted raw little fish and octopuses provided a deal of the nourishment in a land of low animal protein.

I had seen all aspects of our medical service and the conditions under which our troops were living, thus completed my mission, but there was much of beauty and interest in Japan that I had not seen. This had to wait for later visits.

The Kintai Bridge over the Nishiki River was one of the most famous among the many graceful bridges in Japan. Built originally centuries ago, the bridge stood on five stout stone pillars, carrying a wooden highway about fifteen feet wide, which switch-backed up and down in steps. There was not a single metal nail in its construction. When the river had been in heavy flood, portions or all of the wooden structure were swept away, but even in the absence of such destruction, each arch was rebuilt in succession every five years. This was according to the Japanese belief that 'structures must never be allowed to fall into decay, as that would enfeeble the spirit of continuity on which the Spirit of Man depends'. Beyond the bridge the road wound along the hillside, following the course of the river below, the steep slopes clad in the harmony of pine and tall bamboo. The sun had set when we returned to Iwakuni, where the softness of the blue evening mist was coming down over the Inland Sea.

I had hoped that my absence from A.H.Q. would have impressed higher authority of the need for a full-time deputy—but no, apparently the Adjutant-General had been satisfied with what time the D.D.M.S. at Southern Command had been able to give to my responsibilities.

I knew enough of military tactics to realize that if a frontal attack failed, the pressure should be applied elsewhere. I considered this question of my deputy one of the highest priorities in the interest not only of the medical services but of the Army in general, to which I owed my loyalty. I appreciated the situation again, readjusted my forces, and put in my new attack.

A commander, having made his plan and set in motion the forces necessary to implement this, must just wait to see the outcome; being ever ready to adjust or reinforce any pressure, I waited with confidence.

Not long after my return from Japan it appeared the Prime Minister had spoken to the Minister for the Army, Mr Josiah Francis, who in turn had spoken to the military board, then it was my turn to be spoken to. I was summoned to the Minister, who said he wished me to investigate the Medical Services of the British Commonwealth abroad. I accepted this as an instruction and was asked to prepare details of this mission and submit these to the Adjutant-General. I was determined that my survey would not be a hurried military mission of a few weeks. I proposed an itinerary covering New Zealand, Canada, United Kingdom and Western Germany, extending over some months and travelling whenever possible by train. This was accepted and submitted to the movement section to prepare details, as I made private arrangements for my wife to meet me in London.

Chapter 18 World Tour

I left Sydney Harbour in a Solent flying boat just before midnight and awoke the next morning in Auckland. I travelled by the night train to Wellington, where for the first time I met my opposite number, the New Zealand D.G.M.S., 'Blim' Bull. We had often corresponded, but the days we were associated established an understanding and a regard that were to endure.

In recent years New Zealand and Australia, fostered probably by the comradeship of arms during two Worlds Wars and in B.C.O.F., have grown more closely together. Certainly the establishment of the Royal Australasian College of Surgeons has been followed by mutual appreciation and more frequent associations between medical graduates in the two countries, and throughout my visit the welcome and attention could not have been more friendly. On the afternoon of my arrival in Wellington I was entertained at a party by our Australian High Commissioner, 'Tiny' Cutler, who had won his V.C. and lost one of his legs with us in Syria.

The medical problems of National Service in New Zealand were of special interest to me, as Australia was about to introduce a similar service. New Zealand Army Medical Service had achieved what we had sought in Australia (so far without success), a common scale of medical equipment for the three Services, and they had gone further in this integration with the formation of a dental, a nursing and a physiotherapist service available to the Navy, the Army and the Air Force. There were no military or repatriation hospitals in New Zealand, as under their National Health Scheme hospital accommodation for Service personnel was provided by civilian establishments.

I drove north to Wairaki along the desert road in the middle of the North Island. We passed around Lake Taupo, teeming with trout, where I was told that a fisherman had to hide behind a tree to tie his lure. Next day we stopped for a while at Rotorua, which, in spite of its publicity, was rather a disappointment. Apart from the pungent sulphur fumes and fine dust everywhere, the sophisticated and mechanical ritual of the guide seemed to detract from what is undoubtedly one of the most interesting areas in the islands.

In Honolulu, as night came down with the suddenness of the tropics, we drove out above the Punch Bowl to a private home set in a lovely garden under the stars. The orchids, the fragrant frangipani and other tropical flowers and foliage, with the haunting, muted Hawaiian music, set a perfect scene for Somerset Maugham. The air was cool, almost chilly, and most of the ladies wore their furs; Honolulu must surely be the only city almost on the equator devoid of the somnolent clamminess of the usual tropical night. Hawaiian dishes of meat and fish and exotic fruits covered the circle of tables, altogether it was a wonderful party and only the fact that my plane left at midnight cut it short, as it was, we just made it. A signal had been sent off to the airstrip to say that I was on my way. What a way it was in that dashing staff car in the dark, right to the gangway—a rush from the car to be immediately lassoed with leis of frangipani—flashes again from the cameras—up the steps—a wave to all those people who had been so kind and generous and into my seat after a whirlwind of typical American hospitality.

I had left Auckland on the Wednesday afternoon and with the assistance of my flight eastward across the international date line—on Thursday morning we came down through the clouds as the sun rose behind the Golden Gate of San Francisco.

An hour or so on the strip for breakfast, then on along the coast with the sun gleaming on the snow over the Sierras towering beyond. Soon the clouds closed in and we might have been flying anywhere for all there was to see. When we landed at Vancouver the rain was lashing down but the warmth of my welcome at the Services Club drove away the gloom of the early night and the sharp chill of the air outside. It was a relief when I stepped into the elevator and shot up to my room high in the Vancouver

Hotel. The clouds were still lowering next day when I visited the Military Hospital and other Army establishments. This was the first time I had been in Western Canada. In the east the French influence had been apparent, in the centre I was to appreciate the more truly Canadian Canada, but in the west, especially across on the Island, I felt myself thinking rather of England.

I had arranged for my inland travelling to be by train whenever possible; in the privacy of a roomette I could relax, read and sleep in comfort and appreciate the countryside better than from the road and certainly better than from the air. Many had told me that the Canadian Pacific route through Lake Louise and Banff was a scenic wonder, but as I had to stop at military establishments along the Canadian National railway route, I travelled on that line and nothing could have been more beautiful than my days in the Canadian Rockies.

Rising soon into the snow country, we followed the Thompson River for mile after mile, round and round the gorges, the slopes timbered with sombre fir and lighter spruce, their drooping boughs heavily powdered with snow, like toy Christmas trees, while here and there gleamed the spotted white stems of the bare birches. Below the flowing stream, a thin pale green ribbon in the belts of ice, above the climbing mountains serene in the shining sun, every now and then a little log hut or small village of dark brown timber, the roofs heavy with snow. As the sun flung his final glow over the scene, the beauty was breathtaking. As night came down the train came slowly to a stop at Albreda; a snowdrift had blocked the line ahead, so there was nothing to do but have dinner, read and get off to sleep in the friendly warmth of my bed while all was quiet and there was no swaying, straining movement of the train. Easter Friday dawned and I found we had not moved. Like Good King Wenceslas, who looked out on the Feast of Stephen, when I pulled up my blind 'the snow lay round about, deep and crisp and even', feet of it everywhere. After breakfast we were off again, the track had been cleared and I had missed nothing. The sun held the mountains in a brilliant halo of light as we passed into the Fraser Valley with Mount Robson towering 13,000 feet into the clouds above. Down through Jasper Park as the snow became more sparse, with deer grazing on the tufts of turf and one indifferent brown bear showing his contempt by turning his back on the train. Soon the leaden sky and driving wind brought more whirling snow as we came into Edmonton in a blizzard.

Winnipeg, in the heart of the 'Prairies', was under heavy cloud and snow but the heated houses and other comforts defied the cold. After a day with the medical establishment, I flew with the senior Medical Officer to the Canadian-American Services establishment at Churchill near the western shores of Hudson Bay. Flying over those 800 miles of Manitoba, I realized how much of Canada was water and that human habitation was confined almost to a narrow band across the country just north of the border with America. After Wolfe's victory over Montcalm at Quebec in the middle of the eighteenth century the British Government was reluctant to annex the country from the French: the land seemed a forbidding waste of no obvious value or potential. A popular demand arose to take Guadeloupe, a rich sugar island, the largest in the Leeward Group, instead. I think it was Benjamin Franklin who persuaded the Government to hold on to Canada and now with the riches of the iron ore in Labrador, the oil in Alberta, the vast grain and timber areas, and the fishing industry, this foresight has proved justified.

At first the frozen lakes were printed in white among the dark clumps of snow-dusted timber. Slowly the woods became thinned until all was stark white except for the herds of caribou, moving like tiny ants over the vast glacier-worn area of the Laurentian Shield and for some miles the grain elevators were visible in the distance as we approached Churchill. Only for ten to twelve weeks each year is Hudson Bay open for navigation, then begins the rush of the grain from the south along the one railway to reach this port, providing the shortest route to the European markets. North of Churchill there was nothing but tundra, snow and ice and the arctic waters until in the warmer months the muskeg emerges through the snow with its mossy nourishment for the animals.

I was told that the temperatures in the Alaskan areas were below those of Churchill, but the damp and everlasting wind chill about Hudson Bay presents a more severe challenge. To meet this the establishment at Churchill had been equipped to investigate the survival of personnel, the food and clothing needs, the great problems of mechanical movement and other essentials under these conditions in war.

We landed on a smooth, narrow strip of firm snow maintained in a frozen area, ruffled by the wind into irregular heaps of ice, like a sea blasted by a turbulent gale and suddenly frozen stiff. Our quarters, flying both the Canadian and American flags, were very comfortable but rather too warm: I slept in an upstairs room with only a sheet covering me while the snow was piled high up to my window.

For this operation 'Sun Dog' many of the top scientists of the Defence Research Board were gathered under the direction of a medical man. It was an interesting and stimulating experience to be associated with these men in their various groups and activities, but the extensive 'verbalising' of nouns ('winterise', 'arcticate', arcticise') became rather wearisome. Warmly clad in our parkahs, we drove over the area in the various experimental vehicles, penguins and others with tracks and skis, sometimes making from fifteen to twenty miles an hour. Churchill village, a few miles away, was an interesting Hudson Bay trading post where the mongolian Eskimos and their dog teams from a small group of igloos nearby mingled with the Service personnel. Stefanssen had indicated the possibility of living off this inhospitable land and certain of the activities of the scientists were directed towards this. I saw no birds or animals but was told the day before we arrived a polar bear had been shot quite near our quarters.

One of the strange problems of this frozen northern area was the ferocity of the mosquitoes during the short warmer season. Fortunately these insects were culicines and not anopheles, but the number and intense irritation of their bites presented a real menace as many travellers in the area have recorded. In spite of a deal of research, what happens to these mosquitoes during the remainder of the year was, and I believe still is, a mystery. Digging through the snow into the muskeg beneath had failed to reveal eggs or larvae and none had been found on the surface. As a mosquito even with a strong wind can travel only a few miles, I wonder if the answer lies in the fur of the migrating caribou.

On the platform at Ottawa I soon met my Canadian opposite number, the colourful Brigadier Bill Coke with his smiling blue eyes and his delightful brogue harmonizing with his Canadian accent. It was a long time since I had seen such a crowded station and everyone seemed to be running to a track nearby where another train had just pulled in. I looked across and standing at the foot of the steps from their carriage were a distinguished, dignified lady in furs and a slightly shorter man whose weary, lined face emerged from beneath his neat greying fair hair above the collar of his thick tweed overcoat. A man stepped forward, bowed and took his hand, and in a moment the tired face relaxed and lit into an almost boyish smile—my mind flashed back over thirty years to an afternoon when I had glimpsed a blond young man standing up in the back of a car, smiling and waving to the cheering crowd, as the Prince of Wales drove through the streets of Melbourne.

The Château Laurier was just across from the station and it was good to walk again in the sunshine on firm, dry ground. We called on the Governor-General, Viscount Alexander of Tunis, who at once made me comfortable as we sat in two deep armchairs before a large log fire. He spoke appreciatively of the A.I.F. troops under his command in the desert and asked many sincerely interested questions about Australia, which he hoped to visit. That evening Bill Coke turned on a party at his home and for the first time I tasted the joy of duck served with wild rice. It was a grand, cheery, singing night amongst comrades.

There was much to see and learn in Ottawa among military and other establishments and I was able to see more of this lovely city than had been possible on my previous visit. British and Canadian flags were flying at that time over the impressive granite Houses of Parliament, commanding the river below, and nearby in an open area in the heart of the city was the imposing war memorial: 'They are too near to be great but our children will understand when and how our fate was changed. Nor was their agony brief or once alone imposed upon them. The wounded, the war spent, the sick received no exemption. Being cured they returned and endured and achieved our exemption. Not since her birth has our earth seen such worth loosed upon her.'

One delightful Sunday was spent in the countryside. Across the Ottawa River I was aware we were in a French area. On the Ottawa side of the bridge I was invited to 'Drink Coca Cola', on the far side to 'Buvez Coca Cola'. We drove on through the woods to the sugar bush country, an area covered with snow around the bare stems of the maples, each with a small spigot stuck into the bark, dripping the clear sap into a can below. Large cauldrons had been set up above fires and into these the cans were emptied, boiling and bubbling away, the sap soon became concentrated into the yellow-brown maple syrup. On a table nearby were shallow round pans about twelve inches in diameter, filled with soft snow, over which was poured the hot syrup, which almost at once congealed into a tacky mass of toffee while the youngsters crowded around twirling little sticks into this delight and sucking away. Only for a few weeks, while the snow is still on the ground and the sap is beginning to rise, can the syrup be gathered; once the buds appear the flavour is spoiled.

It was a pleasant run down to the Royal Canadian Military College at Kingston. One of the early settlements, Kingston had been designed as the site for the Canadian capital, but with fear of the proximity of the settlers across the narrow waterway, this plan was abandoned and a move made inland to Ottawa. The Military College was a tri-Services establishment with an entry of Navy, Army and Air Force cadets, and I was kindly invited to take the salute at a ceremonial parade. As with the Military College at West Point and other similar establishments in America, I was told that only about 50 per cent of Kingston graduates enter the armed forces, the training being designed to develop general efficiency as a preliminary to entering various professions.

Time was pressing and I entrained for my final run in Canada to Montreal, where I still had a few days to see more of the Canadian Army Medical Service, which seemed to me more seriously integrated into the Army and into the country than was the case in Australia and where ex-service medical officers carried considerable weight in the policy of this Service. Military Hospitals were established in all military areas and staffed by regular M.O.'s, a situation that did not exist at that time in Australia, where base hospital facilities for army personnel were provided by civilian-staffed repatriation hospitals. Many of the Canadian M.O.'s were of French origin but to me it was impossible to appreciate any discrimination among them and all were most kindly and unsparing in their care and attention during my visit.

It was good to be in London once again, where the flowering

cherries and pink chestnuts were blooming their welcome along the way, although it was still very cold—even as late as the end of April, it was snowing in the south of England, breaking the boughs of the trees in leaf.

St Martin's-in-the-Fields was packed for the service when a short stooped, grey-haired figure, wrapped in a heavy overcoat and leaning on the arm of a companion, slowly moved down the aisle to sit quietly in a pew just below the pulpit. After the service everyone stood as the pair walked slowly out to the portico: it was Birdie, Field Marshal Lord Birdwood. Many crowded round him as he shook hands with each of us. 'I am so glad to meet you fellows again,' he said, 'I'm sorry I can't see you.' He was blind. With his coat closely buttoned against his frail body, Birdie led us down Whitehall to the Cenotaph where, bareheaded in the falling snow, he laid his wreath, stepped back and, with a bowed head, paid a silent tribute to his Anzac comrades who had gone before.

A few weeks later Birdie died in his Grace and Favour quarters at Hampton Court.

At that time the Australian Services in London were administered from 85 Jermyn Street and I never wearied of the walk from Hyde Park corner past Green Park and along Piccadilly to turn down Duke Street with the delight of Dunhill's windows into the many interests of Jermyn Street. It was a short and pleasant walk across to the D.A.G.M.S. office in Berkeley Square, where Lieut.-General Sir Neil Cantlie and his staff kindly arranged an itinerary and transport for everything I wanted to see in the United Kingdom.

With a population more than five times that of Australia and with a standing army for more than three hundred years, the British Army policy was vastly different in detail from ours. We had practically no regular army at that time other than the Staff Corps and the Instructional Staff, and could not place any army formation in the field without delay. The Royal Army Medical Corps of Britain was a highly organized and efficient Corps, geared at all times to serve the regular army in their postings over the seven seas. In Australia the various Army Medical Services existed only in cadre form, in the event of an emergency overseas to be developed by voluntary enlistment from the militia and from the community generally, and certain of the medical establishments necessary in war did not exist at all. But however small or large an army may be, the basic essentials of the Medical Services are similar.

Within a few years of World War II a more serious appreciation was taken of our Defence Policy and a small increase was authorized in the regular army. At the time I left Australia, however, the medical component of the regular army, while highly efficient, was deficient in personnel. I had been instructed to recruit, if possible, suitable medical officers for our service. Vacancies were advertised throughout the United Kingdom and although there were about a dozen applicants, none was considered up to our standards.

While I had been gallivanting about New Zealand and Canada, my wife was travelling by sea and after I had spent a week in London arranging my itinerary, she arrived at Tilbury. The approach to most cities by the land back door is seldom attractive and the run from the docks to Liverpool St station was not very exciting, but the piling of all her luggage beside the Cockney driver of an old Austin London taxi cab, the drive around Trafalgar Square, through Admiralty Arch and along the Mall, with the tulips aglow in front of Buckingham Palace, and on to our hotel, was a thrilling welcome.

Our first weekend was spent in Wales with those delightful people, the Englands, at Llanishen. My wife and Lil England were old school friends from Merton Hall and it was she who had nearly caused my unseemly disaster at Paddington Station, when on my previous visit I had greeted with undue familiarity a strange lady by mistake. The weather was Wales at its best, and we drove across the Brecon Beacons to Tenby for the night before going on to their cottage overlooking St David's Bay with its lovely sandy beach.

During the Napoleonic wars, the French had actually landed here in 1797, but daunted by the distant sight of the tall black hats and red shawls of the Welsh women watching from the hills, whom they mistook for British Redcoats, they retreated to their ships and sailed away. Dorothy was able to drive with me to most of the Army Medical establishments, the various schools and hospitals, but on my visit alone to the high security activities at Harwell and Porton, there were her many friends in London.

Together we attended the Annual Meeting of the British Medical Association at Liverpool, staying with a charming elderly lady, Mrs Parker, in her old home set in a vast garden leading down to the Mersey. At the annual dinner of the meeting, we had the embarrassing experience of occasionally hearing, amongst the clatter of the crockery and the restlessness of the hundreds of people present, the last speaker, a Member of Parliament, who rose to his feet at twenty to one in the early morning.

From Liverpool we went to visit the Scottish Command in Edinburgh and after a few days I took my overdue leave for a trip to the Highlands. Next year I had the privilege of speaking at the St Andrew's Day dinner in Melbourne and my enduring memory of those days in the North made this easy:

'Mr President, Your Excellency and Gentlemen,
'That I have been entrusted with this toast is another example of your unpredictable generosity. Generous because no greater compliment could be paid to a guest, unpredictable because my forebears on my father's side came from the North of Ireland, Norris meaning Northish, where, I presume, they were potato stealers in the past, and the forbears on my mother's side came from the wilds of Wales where they probably followed the same occupation without any specialization. But you Scots are full of surprises, like a red-headed child, and you get away with so much. Who else but a Scots Divine could preach a sermon in the morning and in the evening take out his dentures and give the same discourse? Who else but an association of Scots could have presented me with the extraordinarily experience I had last year when, lunching with the Royal Caledonian Society, I noticed at the end of the table a very old gentleman. I remarked on him to my host the Chieftain. "Yes," he said, "he is very old. He is ninety-three and today is a great day in his life."

' "Is it his birthday?" I enquired.

' "No," he replied, "but we are going to make him an honorary life member of the Society."

'You probably know of the melancholy occasion when two Australian soldiers on leave in Scotland came to Stirling, where they were deeply impressed by that magnificent granite memorial.

"What is that?" they asked a passing Scotsman, who, removing his hat, reverently replied: "That is the Wallace Memorial."

' "Good old Edgar," replied the Diggers, "Good old Edgar."

'So much, but not enough, for your qualities.

'Your history, your glorious history of a little group of people living and loving and dying for all they held dear, than which man can do no more. Many of those great figures of your history are known to the world, but rather would I like to remember also the great common men of Scotland, the devotion of that little lawyer lad of Inverness, Roderick McKenzie, who, knowing his resemblance to Prince Charles, led Cumberland's pursuers on that false scent knowing full well that it would inevitably end in his death, as it did; but knowing also that this would give his Prince a life; and Daniel Laidlaw in that holocaust at Loos piping and inspiring the troops until he was shot down. These and many other common men of Scotland have been great. Scotland has given so much to the world that as with all great givers Scotland has great possessions.

'While England, over nine centuries, proudly pointed to her two great universities of Oxford and Cambridge, Scotland held her great St Andrew's, Aberdeen, Glasgow and Edinburgh, where by dint of sacrifice and great hardship, young men of intellect and industry came from humble homes to these great universities. Is there any other country in the world where, whether you approach the city from north, south, east or west, that city is crowned and dominated by a noble university as is Glasgow . . . if you can see it through the mist?

'Come with me down the Clyde around Dumbarton to Balloch, on by the road which winds around the quiet grace of Loch Lomond. Over the Trossacks to Oban and on through the Stevenson country of the Red Fox at Appin to those mournful hills where the lowering clouds and rolling mists seem always to weep for the tragedy of Glen Coe and the Flowers of the Forest linger in a lament. Across to the west around Loch Tay through the Pass of Killiecrankie where Dundee died in the hour of victory, on around those rugged mountains of Cairngorm, where the snow still nestles while the heather glows in its royal purple and the harebells dance, on to the quiet of Nethy Bridge, to Aberdeen and Elgin, to Lossiemouth and Nairn, over the green heath of

Cawdor and Macbeth. Pause at the field of Culloden where the heather never blooms upon those mounds that fold over the rich dead. On through Inverness, across Bonnar Bridge where the leaping salmon gleam and still farther north to the country of the Sinclairs about Wick, to the windswept John o' Groats and the most northerly point of Scotland, Dunnet Head. And on to Thurso which is Thors Harbour and you realize why that great northern area of Scotland is called Sunderland or Southland because it was the most southerly limit of the earlier Norse Empire and there among those bare hills clad only in heather and among those moors flecked with the white bog cotton, with the simple crofters' homes by the burns that tumble their troubled waters tinged Rembrandt brown with peat, you realize the rugged robustness of the Scottish men and women, and there again you are so surprising. In the midst of such dour hardship one would expect a national dish of deer horns washed down with potent acid, instead you present the soft tasty haggis blessed with a glowing dram of atholl brose.

'Come with me again south over the Spittals of Glen Shee, down to the Dee at Balmoral where those stately trees planted more than 100 years ago by the Prince Consort sweep gracefully to the ground. Down through Perthshire, where if the raspberries are in season you will taste something you have never known before, and at the end of the day come to Queen's Ferry and cross, as the sun is setting, into Edwin's Burgh, Old Reekie.

'If you have the good fortune to arrive in Edinburgh in the pink glow of an evening you will see a blush on that great Castle Rock which is equalled only by the Citadel at Aleppo.

'There are two Edinburghs. The new town with its memories of Stevenson, Simpson, Conan Doyle and his Sherlock Holmes, Scott and the great Princess Street, but across the valley is the towering glory of Castle Rock and was there ever a city so blest with such a God-given gift? Come with me to the Castle, firstly to the tiny chapel of St Margaret, which has stood for nearly 1,000 years, and quietly to that most moving war memorial built around the nascent rock as it rises from the floor, through the old castle with all those Stuart memories, through the Royal Gateway and tread softly down the Royal Mile, the most emotional mile in the world, past the heart of Midlothian and the Kirk of St Giles with the lovely little chapel of the Thistle. The thunder of John Knox still rolls from that gaunt house at the corner, the revelry of the Prince in his short-lived glory—Argyll and Montrose stripped of their power, parade to their doom—the furtive Deacon Brodie is afoot at night, the ghoulish Burke and Hare are about their grisly business, and then finally we come to the Royal residence at Holyrood, where the cries of Rizzio still echo down that dark, narrow passage where he was dragged from the Royal room to his death.

'All down the Royal Mile sound the joys and flow the tears and the blood of Scots history. In Hampton Court near London there still seem ghosts of Henry and Ann Boleyn and Wolsey, but down the Royal Mile these people of glory and tragedy seem still to be living and moving and dying in all the pageantry and tragedy of Scotland.

'Is it any wonder, gentlemen, that I cannot adequately express my pride in this privilege of inviting you to rise with me and drink this noble toast: Scotland!'

The June day of the Trooping was hot with a brilliant sun. I do not know how long the Guards had been posted round Horse Guards Parade, but when we arrived in our seats there was not a move. Just near us stood a rigid tall Guardsman, taller still with his bearskin. He never moved unless an order was given, but I watched his face grow paler and paler and the glistening beads trickle down over what could be seen of his cheeks. At times he seemed to sway and I wondered how long it would be before he went down, but he didn't. His eyes seemed closed, someone behind held his belt firmly, a stretcher was passed through the crowd and grounded unobtrusively behind him. If ever a man seemed unconscious on his feet it was he, but whenever a command rang out, his rifle, his arms and his feet spontaneously responded with precision. It was magnificent and the moving pageantry of that great occasion was unmarred. It is a hairline between pageantry and buffoonery. The British people seem alone in the preservation of the solemnity of pegeantry.

At the Royal garden party we had the honour of being presented to Their Majesties. King George VI, whose brave face bore evidence of his physical burdens, said to me, 'I do hope I can go out to Australia again. I want to go but don't think many realize what our visit to South Africa meant to me.' His Queen, with her ineffable charm and smile, talked with my wife. Someone had told her that our first grandchild was soon to be born and, holding Dorothy's hand, Her Majesty said: 'It's lovely to be a grandmother.'

One Sunday morning we walked down the crowded Petticoat Lane and came to a stall with a display of pewter, which I collect in a modest way. I noticed a small square snuff box, the mate of one I had bought some years before in Melbourne for a pound or two. 'How much?' I asked.

'Ten bob to you,' he said.

'Ten bob?' I queried, surprised at the cheapness.

'Orl right, if yer feel that way about it, yer can have it for five.'

I had it for five!

For a few weeks I was attached to the British Army of the Rhine, the occupation force in Germany. I made the crossing from Harwich to The Hook, where the breakfast of eggs and crisp Dutch bacon and good coffee was a joy. As I crossed the border the German steel rails seemed to sing as the train drove on to Badenhausen, the British Headquarters. Roddy Cameron, the Senior Medical Officer, met me at the station and everyone was most hospitable except on the first night in the mess when I was taken down for a small sum at bridge. Visiting the various training centres in the British Zone, I was driven over history. Through the Minden Gap on the Weser, where the Minden boys plucked their roses on that bright August morning two hundred years before as they marched forward in a line of British infantry . . . and broke and routed three lines of cavalry. On 1 August each year, men of those six line regiments wear roses in their caps. We travelled along the Lippe Valley through which Napoleon marched to Warsaw and on to disaster at Moscow. The countryside bore little evidence of Germany's travail during the war but the cities were grim. Hamburg was a tragedy of total war with its dreadful scars of the intensity of incendiary bombing laid bare like black jagged tooth stumps. But the great sombre statue of Bismarck still stood as, leaning on his sword, the great Chancellor stared into the West: 'Our destiny lies over the seas.'

No Memory for Pain

In 1942 Cologne was the first victim of a mass air raid when one night Bomber Harris sent over nearly 1,000 bombers. It was a desperate gamble, as practically every bomber in England was committed. The Gothic glory of Cologne Cathedral remained almost unmarred while all around, including the railway station, was a devastation of rubble.

In the Ruhr the great retaining wall of the Möhne See Dam displayed the healed scar of the breach by the dambusters and along the banks of the narrow valley below rusting chains and other debris marked the high-water mark of the thirty-three feet wall of torrential water that rushed down, inundating homes and villages and drowning thousands in its relentless destruction.

I travelled by night train to the British Sector of Berlin with all blinds drawn and armed guards at each end of the carriage as we passed down the permitted corridor. London still displayed the yawning gaps from the blitz, but all was neat and tidy; in Berlin the rubble lay around everywhere in distorted heaps of brick and stone and steel, and at night little lights twinkled where people still dwelt in this devastation.

At that time there was no Wall. As we walked down what once had been the pride of Berlin, Unter den Linden, now a grim, bare roadway, we could stare across the piles of broken stones that marked the site of Hitler's final bunker, into the Russian zone with the skeleton of the burnt-out Reichstag nearby. There seemed nothing, no wire or barrier, no sentry to prevent anyone walking across, but I was warned that while it was simple to cross into the Russian zone there would have been difficulties and delays frustrating my return. On the left side of this approach through the British Sector was a rugged, granite Russian war memorial, rapidly erected in our zone when fire ceased, and guarded ever since by two lonely Red sentries. Solemnly each day the Red guard marched in and, ignored by all, mounted their sentries and as solemnly marched back again. This went on at intervals day and night, but no one seemed to mind or pay any attention. Along this strangely quiet roadway wandered small groups of boys and girls dressed in cornflower-blue blouses, members of the Free German Youth Organization of East Berlin. They may have been titled 'free', but they seemed bewildered by the freedom in our Sector. Berlin was a depressing experience but altogether my visit to Germany with the B.A.O.R. was most valuable and interesting and the kindly attention of the R.A.M.C. officers never flagged.

One of the valuable features of training brought back to Australia was 'casualty faking' to enhance the realism of army exercises. Until that time casualties had been labelled 'G.S.W. chest', 'compound fractured femur', etc. Now with use of grease paint, putty, fragments of animal bone and glycerine dyed with carmine, we were able to simulate wounds, even to spurting 'blood' from an artery, so realistic that flies soon gathered on the wounds.

Success was later demonstrated at our School of Army Health when we staged an exercise of an atomic disaster. As the press photographers approached the 'casualties', two turned away, were violently sick and gave the afternoon away.

The night before we left England, Dorothy and I took our favourite front seats on the top of a London bus and drove down to Simpson's in the Strand for dinner. As we clambered down the steps I noticed that the conductor was whistling one of Rodolfo's arias from *Bohème*. I thanked him and asked him if he liked Puccini. 'Yes, I do,' he said, 'but *Tosca*'s my favourite.' I wonder what a Melbourne tram or bus conductor would say if anyone asked him if he liked Puccini: he would probably ask what race he was running in.

We returned to Australia in the *Port Hobart*, a fast modern cargo ship carrying twelve passengers. To be confined in a ship for four weeks or so with only ten other passengers is not without risk, but generally such travellers have wearied of the organized existence on the luxury hotel liners and certainly we were a very happy family. These ships leave London on a day and at a time predicted some months before, but when leaving Australia such are the vagaries of our wharf conditions that to travel on a mixed cargo ship may mean living out of suitcases over the uncertainty of days or even weeks.

We had a smooth run down to the Cape and there were some days of loading at Durban, where a car was made available so we were able to appreciate the city with its splendid beaches and to see something of Natal, the Valley of a Thousand Hills, Pietermaritzburg and the squalid Kaffir kraals.

One trip left a nasty taste in our mouths. We were some miles from Durban when a native dashed across the road right in front of our car and was knocked down, but our white driver did not stop until we made him. Another man in the car and I went back and found the man lying in the dirt with a fractured leg. We improvised a splint and carried him on to the verandah of a nearby store. He was obviously frightened, shocked and in pain. I went in and asked the white storekeeper for some blankets, but with one look at the native he said: 'I haven't got anything for him, leave him alone. Some of them will come along some time and pick him up.'

The brutality of this riled me and I went into the store, found some bags and in spite of the protests made the fellow as comfortable as we could. I asked the storeman to ring for an ambulance. 'Do it yourself,' he said. We found a telephone and book and after a while an ambulance arrived, but only with great difficulty was persuaded to take the man to hospital.

Later that day when we returned to the ship, my wife wanted to find out where the man was, as she would like to call and see if there was anything she could do for him, but was told this would only cause trouble and was asked to do nothing further about the man. This wretched incident has rankled.

We sailed direct to Adelaide where we landed and flew on to Melbourne after a most interesting and valuable few months.

Chapter 19 War In Korea, I

While I was abroad the Korean War had broken out and our occupational troops in Japan were involved. After my absence abroad for nearly six months, however, there were a few urgent matters on my plate before I could visit the battle zone. My report had been written on the ship in my wretched handwriting, but with Miss Ryan's ability to interpret my hieroglyphics it was ready to present to the Military Board in a few days and when the other urgencies had been cleared, I arranged to fly north.

Few in Australia seemed to realize the deep significance of the war in Korea. It was considered rather as an 'incident' and far away.

When the military forces of twenty-two nations are involved in a conflict in which it has been estimated that more than two million civilian and Service casualties resulted, is this an incident or a world war? When even in the early fifties one could leave Australia early one morning and be in the battle zone on the same day, is this far away? Miles have lost their meaning when no country is more than a day's distance from any other country.

After World War I the futility and pathetic waste of armed conflict seeped into many minds and the League of Nations came into being with all the good intentions in the world but with no ability to implement them. When in defiance of their word, Germany armed and moved into the Ruhr, Italy invaded Abyssinia and Japan raided Manchuria, there were nothing but sanctions and pious words to restrain them and World War II became inevitable. Those who had broken their word allied into a band of aggressors and defied the League.

After the tragedy of World War II the Nations again came together, each not only declared a code of decent international relationships, a determination to advance the less privileged countries and a recognition of the human rights of all people, but agreed also to contribute to the resistance of any violation of these principles.

When with no justification but brutality the Communists in Korea swept across the 28th parallel—the agreed partitioning line between the American and Soviet spheres of influence during the rehabilitation of the Republic of Korea—there suddenly arose a situation similar to the uninhibited violence that had led to World War II. But this time members of the United Nations kept their word.

During the pre-war Japanese occupation of Korea, Koreans, most of whom were peasants, had been conscripted into an Army under Japanese officers, but no Korean was allowed to rise above non-commissioned rank. When Japan entered World War II thousands of Koreans were conscripted into labour battalions, where we had come across many of them in New Guinea attempting to escape into the jungle. After the War, below the 38th parallel, a small American occupational force was supervising the implementation of the Peace Treaty designed to respect the independence and unification of the Republic of Korea. North of the parallel a Russian force was charged with the same responsibility. However, when the first election was held to establish a Korean Government, the Soviet troops in the North prohibited those Koreans under their care from voting and directed their stewardship to training a North Korean army equipped with Russian tanks and other arms and to planning war against the South.

Soon after dawn on 25 June 1950, 90,000 of the North Korean people's army, the K.P.A. as they styled themselves, swept south across the 38th parallel. So sudden had been this invasion that the feeble Republican forces of the South, the R.O.K., were overrun at the frontier and the invaders drove down the Uijambu Corridor, the historical route of all invaders in the past. Within three days the Han River was crossed and Seoul, the southern capital, occupied. With their thousands of carriers the K.P.A. troops were independent of mechanized transport.

What remained of the R.O.K. and the American occupational troops stood for the first time at Osan, thirty miles south of Seoul, but within hours their resistance was broken and the allies retreated to the Taejon area, while reinforcements of men, armour and planes began to arrive from Japan and Hong Kong, with Commonwealth and other United Nations troops from overseas. Volunteers were called from among the Australian occupational troops in Japan and from within Australia to form a 'K' force as Australia's contribution to the United Nations. Taejon fell and within six weeks of the invasion all South Korea had been overrun except a small area within the Naktong Valley where the final defences of free Korea were established, covering the port of Pusan. There around the Taegu Box the invaders were slowed, then held, during those six dreadful weeks which determined the fate of Korea and possibly the future of the United Nations.

Some day the defence of this area, the shattering of the K.P.A. and the destruction of their Air Force will be highlighted in military history.

Once the invaders were held, General MacArthur, in Supreme Command of the United Nations Force, planned and prepared his left hook. Early in September, when the defence of Pusan seemed assured, a powerful force transported in ships from six of the United Nations and escorted by British and American ships, sailed around to the west for an amphibious landing at Inchon, the port a few miles to the west of Seoul.

The approach was most difficult through the narrow Flying Fish Channel with a five knot current into an area studded with shoals and rocks in a tidal range of thirty feet. Guarding this hazardous entry was the fortified island of Wolmi-do and a twelve foot stone wall beyond which were defended hills. The whole enterprise was threatened by the sudden appearance of a typhoon in the Pacific, but true to her fickleness she swung away during those critical days. By 15 September Inchon was captured and on the following day the Eighth Army defending Taegu Box began their offensive, killing, capturing and driving north what remained of the outflanked K.P.A. Twelve days later Seoul was recaptured, the Marines driving inland from Inchon in the west and the Eighth Army advancing from the south, and Syngman Rhee's Government was re-established at the capital. During the advance the atrocities of the invaders were apparent, as thousands of bodies of executed South Koreans were found, but fewer than 30,000 of the K.P.A. escaped back across the parallel and as an army they never recovered.

Early in October the United Nations troops were on the parallel. So far the conflict had been purely a military one but at this stage world politics came into the picture. The original peace objective after World War II was 'a united, free and independent, democratic Korea'. This had been frustrated by the North Koreans under Russian influence, but as a military power North Korea had almost ceased to exist and in order to implement the unification of the peninsula it was decided to ensure stability in the whole of Korea so that the peace terms could be achieved. To this end MacArthur was authorized to drive north of the parallel provided there was no evidence of any southern advance across the Yalu by Russian or Chinese Communist forces.

At the same time unconditional surrender demands were made to the North Koreans. The answer with new proposals for the future of Korea came not from the North Koreans but from Russia and China; this in itself should have been a warning but the drive went on.

This was the situation when I arrived in Korea early in October. We flew from Australia in an old converted Lancastrian bomber, fast for those days but cramped and uncomfortable. There were few seats, no pantry or stewards but some flasks of coffee and a few sandwiches. We put down at Manila for fuel, then on to Iwakini in Japan. The rain lightened as we boarded the launch but it was dark and the loveliness of the Inland Sea was limited to the twinkling lights of the little fishing villages round the coast.

The British Commonwealth General Hospital had been concentrated at Kure and was receiving casualties from all the British Commonwealth troops in Korea: British, Australian, Canadian, New Zealand and Indian. There were bursts of activity for days, then the inevitable lull until another engagement meant more wounded.

I had brought with me on the plane a Melbourne surgeon, Bill Hughes, to join our Australian team. He was one of a number of Australian medical officers who had been too young for service in World War II but eagerly accepted the invitation to serve for a term in the Korean campaign.

The R.A.M.C. in the United Kingdom had been stretched to its limits with the various commitments of the British Army throughout the world, and only by using the young doctors in their National Service could these be met.

We had a few medical officers in K Force and only by the splendid response of these young volunteers from Australia could we meet even our limited commitments. It never ceased to surprise the seasoned regular medical officers of the other Commonwealth components that our young men could be so well trained and efficient in medicine and surgery.

I had explained to Hughes, who had been accustomed to a steady surgical practice in private and at the Royal Melbourne Hospital, that quite possibly he would have little to do for days on end and then a rush would come. As we entered the hospital at Kure that night a convoy was being admitted and Bill walked right into it: I believe he was thrilled to lose his night's sleep with the surgery before him. I had left for Korea before the inevitable lull came but he was probably too weary to resent it.

After a few days round the hospital and with B.C.O.F. Headquarters, to be put into the Korean picture Gerry and I sailed down to Iwakuni in the calm of the evening for an early morning crossing next day to Korea. Soon after dawn we flew over the mountains of Honshu (one still smoking from a recent upheaval, as happens frequently in Japan), then the deep blue of the Tsushina Straits, the graveyard of the Russian fleet nearly fifty years before. Emerging from the Baltic, this fleet nearly precipitated war with Britain when some trigger-happy gunner fired on a British fishing fleet in the North Sea, thinking they were Japanese destroyers. After sailing half way around the world, the pride of the Russian Navy entered these Straits soon after dawn on 27 May 1905. By the end of the day Rozhdesvensky, the Russian Admiral, wounded and a prisoner, was to realize that his fleet had been destroyed.

During the last few months Seoul had been fought over twice. Now one large span of the railway bridge across the Han River was dangling down, a distorted mass of steel; the station was smashed, the buildings chipped and pockmarked with gaping holes, the torn telephone and power lines twisted above the rubble in the streets, with here and there abandoned, burnt-out trams and motor cars. But the stone city gate still stood in its ancient dignity.

For the first time I saw the sadness of refugees, old and young, men, women and children, streaming south to safety. They crowded the river bank, waiting their turn to cross in the few remaining or improvised boats, all they possessed in barrows, in baskets or buckets or borne on their backs from crude wooden yokes. Their farms, ravished and fired, held nothing for them. As later we travelled north it was pitiful to see the charred ruins of the farms and the trampled paddyfields, beside many of which lay the bodies of the murdered farmers and their families.

Night came down with a merciful suddenness and with a curfew a quietness settled over this tortured old city broken only by desultory shooting, which went on through the night. In many maps Korea is marked Chosan—the country of the morning calm—and as I looked down next morning from my window in what remained of a Presbyterian mission, there was a stillness and a soft pastel mauve mist over the city and the valley beyond.

In Seoul, a hospital for Commonwealth troops had been improvised in a deserted school, one of the few reasonably intact buildings still standing, but there were few amenities. Nearly all the windows had been shattered, all power cut off (a lighting plant had been rigged, giving some illumination at night) and all water had to be drawn from a water point nearby to be carried upstairs in buckets and jerricans. The Red Cross, as usual, had done everything possible to make the place and the people cheerful and the casualties were splendidly cared for by the medical officers and nurses who had flown over from Kure. It is the people who serve in a hospital rather than the elaboration of the building and equipment that mark its worthiness.

After breakfast I called on General Edgar Hume, whom I had last seen in Honolulu and who at that time was in charge of the United States Medical Service in Korea. Together we went around the various medical establishments in the area. It had been a rather tiring day and I was glad to be bedded down at a reasonable hour, but during the night I was called to the telephone: it was Edgar Hume. He had just received a signal from the forward area that evidence had been discovered in the Northern capital indicating preparation for germ warfare, and he was flying up at daylight, and would I care to come with him?

We took off from Kimpo airfield soon after dawn and the low cloud hid the countryside, with only hill tops like islands in a quilted sea, until we came down at Pyongyang, recently the capital of the invading Northern army. After a hasty breakfast we drove by jeep to the grim red brick buildings of the University, the walls splattered by gunfire. We were led down a narrow passage smelling like the stale, soiled sawdust of the cages in the zoo. A guard opened a door into a room whose walls were lined with wire cages in which rabbits, guinea pigs and white mice were contentedly munching some stale greenstuff or darting about in their cages. It was the typical sight and smell of a laboratory animal house, which it obviously was. We were in the Medical School. Certainly there were the usual tubes and flasks, microscopes and incubators, but nothing more noxious than the animals in their smelly cages. Why anyone should have associated this set-up with germ warfare I do not know, but some people are not only trigger-happy but germ-happy and this is how rumours arise, spread, become exaggerated in the press and on the radio and are accepted as fact. Korea is such a disease soaked country that I doubt if it would be possible to introduce another germ into the place.

During the afternoon we visited the medical units in the area and the cage crowded with North Korean prisoners. The hygiene of their army must have been primitive: the men and their clothes were filthy and we watched them being deloused and dusted with D.D.T. Nearby was a large, abandoned and bombed picture theatre, now converted into a hospital for the prisoner casualties. Their wounds were foul and it was a ghastly sight to see so many wretched men writhing in the throes of tetanus as they lay on bags and palliasses crowded over the bare, sloping floor. The United Nations troops, by virtue of the standard army protection, had practically no cases of this horrible disease. I was told later that the Australian troops were the only ones that had no cases of smallpox. In this filthy, disease-trodden country, their health was outstanding: only three men died of sickness during the war.

The resistance had stiffened a few miles to the north and rifle and gunfire went on during the night. Next morning we went forward to the Australian battalion. The C.O.—Lieut.-Colonel Green—had been killed two days before, and the troops were resting in a valley. One of our young M.O.'s had gone across to help the Argylls and Sutherlands on our flank. They had been through a tough time during the night and when we called at the R.A.P. I found this young M.O. in his tent surrounded by casualties on stretchers, sitting or lying around on the ground. It was his first experience of a battle, always an ordeal, and I found him disturbingly distressed. I tried to pull him together but he looked up at me and said: 'What can I do? I have run out of penicillin.'

'Heavens above,' I answered, 'haven't you plenty of morphia, dressings, cups of tea, cigarettes and cheerful words?'

'But I've got no penicillin,' and his desperate outlook was reflected in the anxious faces of the casualties around him. We straightened things out a bit and he cheered up, but I don't think he quite believed me when I told him if an R.M.O. kept his casualties breathing, stopped their haemorrhage, closed the sucking chests, fixed the wobbling fractures, dressed their wounds, made them physically and mentally comfortable with a shot of morphia and they were cleared to a surgical team as soon as possible, nearly all would recover, even if he had no penicillin. In New Guinea I had seen miraculous introduction of penicillin into a forward area, but that a medical graduate believed nothing worth while could be done in an R.A.P. without penicillin was appalling. I don't blame him, but I do blame those who taught him.

After a few days in the northern area we flew back to Seoul where we found the hospital had been made more habitable and everyone was more cheerful. We spent a day at the convalescent depot at Inchon, as happy and healthy a site as could be found in that dreary, battered area, for at least it looked out over the sea. The Koreans in the street were understandably rather grim and silent, quite unlike the smiling chatty people of Japan, and it was interesting to see Korean women in police uniform on point duty. Japanese dressing in general was rather drab, the brilliant kimonos and obis appeared only on special occasions, but the Koreans loved bright colours. The women and little girls wore ankle length, high waisted, white skirts with full blouses of cerise or bright yellow cotton material, the babies were carried on the mother's back in a firm white swathe leaving the arms free. The old men walked along in loose, clean white pyjama-like jackets and trousers with tall black hats of stiffly woven horse hair, and long, thin bamboo-stemmed metal-bowled pipes in their mouths or carried in their hands.

Sometimes a couple of children would be seen squatting on a footpath playing 'jan-ken-pon', originally a Japanese game. It is played with a hand in one of three positions: a closed fist—'gu', a stone; an open hand—'pa' for paper; or the first two fingers thrust out from a closed hand—'chi', scissors. The formula is: rock blunts scissors, paper wraps stone, scissors cut paper. The two players would simultaneously chant: 'Jan ken pon yo, Jan ken pon', swinging the hand up and down in rhythm with the chant, until the final 'pon', when the hands were thrust out into one of the three positions chosen by each player. If one held out a closed fist—rock, and the other held out two fingers for scissors, rock would win because rock blunts scissors, if the other had held his hand out in the paper position he would have won as paper wraps rock and scissors naturally beat paper because they can cut it. If both hands are thrust out in the same position, there is no score.

It all sounds rather childish but it was good to hear the laughter of these youngsters in those sad cities as they chanted their jan ken pons and thrust out their hands. Another game that is found among children all over the world is hopscotch and we were always careful not to step on the chalk lines as we walked along.

The railway, south of Seoul through Tochon and Taegu on to Pusan, had been restored and a hospital train was running fairly regularly to army hospitals along the route. We flew down to Taegu, one of the largest apple orchard areas in the country, and spent a day around the crowded hospital before going down to Pusan. Normally a city of half a million people, Pusan had become crowded, then overcrowded and finally crammed with nearly a million refugees, living in all manner of improvised shelters. With the mounting mass of service personnel and stores from across the Straits and from overseas, at first sight the place seemed a complete shambles but in some way the U.S. Control had sorted it out fairly well and movement into and out of the area was surprisingly smooth.

I was glad to get back to Japan and the orderliness and home comforts of Kure for a few days, and report to Red Robbie that the medical arrangements for his troops in Korea and in Japan were as efficient as possible. There was a remarkable feeling of optimism, for everything in Korea seemed to be going so smoothly. Pyongyang, the northern capital, had been captured and the resistance of what remained of the K.P.A. was weakening.

During October President Truman had conferred with General MacArthur on Wake Island. When asked by the President what were the chances of Chinese or Soviet troops intervening as the United Nations troops advanced farther north, MacArthur is reported to have replied: 'Very little. Had they interfered in the first or second month it would have been decisive, but we are no longer fearful of their intervention. The Chinese have no air force and if they tried to regain Pyongyang there would be the greatest slaughter. 'Home by Christmas' had become the cry, 'the war is almost over.' If this sentence had been completed: 'the war is over the mountains', it would have been a bull's-eye.

Before I left Japan I called again on General MacArthur. He was cheerful and optimistic about his campaign in Korea. While he was saying how soon the war was to be won, he rose impressively. So perfect was the alignment of my chair and his figure that as I looked up to him Douglas MacArthur had taken the place of George Washington in the large battle picture behind him. This was the last time I was to see the General; before my next visit to Japan he had been relieved of his command.

We flew back via Hong Kong and at that time the approach to the airstrip was an adventure and permitted only in fine weather and in daylight. As we came over the harbour, crowded with shipping, we seemed to be heading for the hills, then a sharp swing to avoid the first one, a swing around another on our port beam and a gentle curve past the last one as we came down to the tarmac running out to the sea. Since then the safe approach over the water has been developed, to my comfort in later visits.

The bustling activity, the busy little boats and ferries were new to me. That night we dined at Aberdeen, so different from the Silver City by the Sea in Scotland. On this floating restaurant diners could select their fish swimming in the tank and soon have them sizzling on their plates. From our hotel on the mainland the fairy-lights twinkled on the steep hillside and seemed to mingle with the stars above. Next morning on our flight to Darwin we came down at Labuan Island off Borneo with time to visit the nearby beautifully maintained Australian War Cemetery. Just as we checked through at the airport, a group of people in immaculate white came in from a plane that had just landed. Leading them was a man with a small black furred hat like a forage cap, and dark glasses. 'Soekarno,' somebody said, and though with his dark glasses on it was not possible to appreciate his face, his mouth was grim and he certainly had a carriage of command.

It was evening as we flew over the densely wooded Celebes, and soon after dark we came down at Darwin, glad to be in Australia again.

Chapter 20 Army Medicine

At Army Headquarters there were some urgent matters on my plate. I had handed in the overseas report on my visit before I left for Korea, but I was not invited to discuss this with anyone or to comment on my seventeen recommendations. I considered two were of urgent priority and essential in the development of our Army Medical Services and in the interest of the Army: the appointment of a deputy and the establishment of a School of Army Health. I keenly awaited the fate of these as unless they were implemented I was not prepared to continue as Director-General. (One of the advantages of a University degree is that one need not abandon one's principles through fear of unemployment.) Fortunately both were accepted. The appointment of a deputy had at last been realized as a necessity and the establishment of a School of Army Health was agreed to. Now it was up to us to do something about these.

Fortunately I was able to arrange for the best man I considered available in Australia as my deputy, Bill Refshauge, a man of the finest character with a splendid academic and service record, a man who had practised private medicine and at that time was Medical Superintendent of the Royal Women's Hospital in Melbourne. In World War I gynaecologists and obstetricians filled many of the senior postings in the Army Medical Corps: General Fetherston, the D.G.M.S., and Colonel Tate Sutherland, the C.O. of my first unit, privately practised in these fields.

The establishment of the School was more difficult. We set out to find a suitable, healthy and attractive site with adequate basic accommodation in an area providing all training facilities. We

Army Medicine

found an ideal site at Sommerlea Lodge within a mile of Healesville, about an hour's run from Melbourne. The building had originally been a large guest-house, set among the foothills of the Dividing Range with heavily timbered mountains and the open country of the Yarra Valley around.

When we recommended the purchase of this building with its ninety acres, the Minister for the Army sent for me. He was dubious about the worth and the expense of such an establishment and he asked what the School would be worth to the Army.

'Sir,' I said, 'from my experience during the war and from my recent visit abroad, I can assure you that if this School is established I will provide you with at least an extra battalion of fit men in the field for every one of your Brigades and an extra Brigade for each of your Divisions.'

He seemed to accept this assurance. 'How much money will you want before you can start your School?'

'Sir, as the price asked for this property includes all the essentials we won't want any more money at present.'

'When can you start?'

'We have all our plans ready and if we take over the School next Monday we will commence our first intake during the following weekend.'

That afternoon I had the green light.

We had prepared an establishment and pencilled in a manning chart from among the best of a number of men and women already in the R.A.A.M.C. In the United Kingdom and in Canada the Army Medical Schools were commanded by medical officers, but from among our very few medical officers in the Regular Army, none was available for this position, but we did have our Wally Mac. Lieut.-Colonel MacLellan was the senior non-medical staff officer in Southern Command. We had served together for many years in peace and in World War II, where he was the quartermaster of one of my field ambulances in the Seventh Division. As he had a remarkable ability for getting things done, serving happily with others and annoying no one, he stepped right into the position of Commandant. Fortunately he was not a yes-man and was always ready to put forth his own ideas, which were generally good. He was completely reliable and it was due to him that the first intake was up to time.

Trucks piled high with dismembered old army huts began to arrive from places known only to the C.O. The loads were dumped around the School, and well-built, neatly painted stores, lecture rooms and recreation huts began to rise with no outside help or additional expense and with no intrusion on the nine-hole golf course included on the property, always referred to as the parade ground. The shrubs and gardens around the School, which had long been neglected, took on a new lease of life, tended by the students as part of their physical training, and were soon a joy.

Later came the official opening. The sun shone brightly in the crisp clean air of the hills. The Minister, the Hon. Josiah Francis, said his few well-chosen words then planted the first of a row of silver birches along the drive, to be followed by Sir Sydney Rowell, the C.G.S., Sir Samuel Burston, whom I had followed, Col. Annie Sage, the Matron-in-Chief, and the D.G.M.S. Many memorial trees have been planted since by V.I.P.'s to record their visit to the School, and others to mark great occasions such as the Coronation of Queen Elizabeth II. The School was a going concern and has gone on ever since in this lovely setting.

Above an old doorway in the Medical Directorate was an attractive iron bracket, which had held one of those old square oil-burning street lamps when the building was a police hospital many years before. I made discreet enquiries but neither the Camp Commandant nor anyone else knew anything about it or had even noticed it, and when it was removed no one seemed to miss it. Fortunately this bracket just spanned the entrance to the School and there it was placed. We now needed a lamp. The old street lamps had practically disappeared, but I remembered the standard lamps that used to light the railway stations ever so dimly. I rang Col. Max Rees, the railway M.O., with whom I had served in the Middle East. (After all, what you need to do in this world is to know to whom to turn or where to look it up.) Yes, I might find one at Newport, and at Newport Railway Yards I found the very thing, to be had for the taking. Wally Mac's truck was soon on the job and now as you enter the School the lamp in its bracket welcomes and lights you on your way, no longer burning a kerosene wick but with the cheerful glow of an electric filament.

With the introduction of National Service in Australia and the development for the first time of a Regular Field Force, our

Medical Service had to keep in step. This involved the enlistment of medical and nursing personnel in the Regular Army.

In time of war for many years to come the Royal Australian Army Medical Corps will be expanded by voluntary enlistment of medical and nursing personnel from the C.M.F. and the civilian community grafted on to a small group of regular army personnel. It had now become necessary to ensure regular medical and nursing personnel to meet the Army requirements in the field, and in the camp hospitals of the National Service training areas. A few medical officers and nurses who had served in Japan were prepared to soldier on and, with these, together with the service of private practitioners in the National Service areas, we were just able to get by, but this was only a temporary expedient. It was decided to offer short term commissions to final year medical students, with agreement that their University fees would be paid and they would be enlisted with the rank and pay of a Lieutenant, if they agreed after a year's residency in a hospital to serve in the R.A.A.M.C., commencing as Captain, for two or four years. The response was fair and soon our corps was on a more satisfactory basis and a few of these medical officers elected to serve in the regular army after their short service was completed. Some years later, two years National Service was introduced, with a deferment of a medical student till after graduation; this will ultimately solve our difficulties as it has done in the United Kingdom.

For many years our army in peacetime will be relatively small. I believe if a medical graduate served in the regular army for not more than four years and then entered competitive private practice associated with many of his colleagues, but retained his army link and gained promotion in the C.M.F., we would have a keener and more efficient Army Medical Service than one composed only of permanent medical officers with no medical life other than the security of a small regular army.

At the beginning of World Wars I and II, the C.M.F. Army Medical Service consisted only of field ambulances; the rear medical units, the C.C.S.'s the General Hospitals and Convalescent Depots had to be raised *de novo*. We proceeded to establish in peacetime militia cadres of all these units, in association with General Hospitals in the various States, and a regular Army Nursing

Service was established, commanded by that delightful lady, Colonel Jessie Bowe.

Until early in the last century enlistment into the army was in the hands of agents who received a per capita payment for their trouble and naturally were not concerned with medical standards. Later, when a soldier became entitled to a small pension, enlistment came directly under the Adjutant-General's Department and a perfunctory medical examination was laid down, directed to the presence or otherwise of obvious gross physical disabilities. How efficient this examination was can be judged by the remarkable career of Major-General James Barry.

I had read brief accounts of Barry in military journals, enough to whet my appetite for more, but only when I read Isabel Rae's study of this soldier was I able to gather the whole strange story.

About the year 1795 a baby daughter was born in London to parents shrouded in matrimonial uncertainty. Nothing is recorded of her earlier years, until at the age of fourteen she appeared in Edinburgh dressed in male clothing. 'She was very slight, barely five feet tall, with a smooth, pale face, tiny hands and reddish hair.' As James Barry she enrolled at the university as a medical student and, to save confusion, I will refer to Barry as 'he'.

Three years later Barry received his diploma as Doctor of Medicine and, unknown at the time, became the first woman medical graduate in Britain. Returning to London. Barry studied at Guys and St Thomas's, which at that time faced each other in Southwark High Street, and later received his diploma from the Royal College of Surgeons. Barry was attracted by the rising status of Army Medical Officers. These postings were either to regimental duties or to hospital responsibilities. Barry chose the latter, where his sex was less likely to be revealed.

How Barry managed to wangle through the medical examination is not known but he was posted as dresser to a series of garrison hospitals in Britain and apparently served with satisfaction. Two years later he was promoted to Assistant Surgeon and posted to the Military Hospital at Capetown. Barry had developed an aggressive, flamboyant self-assurance and when on duty he appeared in a plumed cocked hat, spurs and a dangling sword. Thanks to high heels and padded soles, he seemed to have grown a little taller, but his face was still smooth and his voice high pitched. Barry became Medical Officer to the Governor of the Cape but quarrelled with his A.D.C. and fought a pistol duel with him, fortunately with no material impact on either.

Barry was promoted Colonel, Hospital Inspector and served in the West Indies. On one occasion, when his recommendations had been frustrated by the local authorities, Barry wrote a stinging criticism of his superiors direct to the War Office. For this breach he was arrested and court-martialled, but acquitted.

Barry aged rapidly. He dyed his hair and his voice became more shrill, but before his retirement was promoted Inspector-General of Hospitals, equivalent in rank to a Major-General. In July 1865 the death is recorded of 'James Barry, a male person of at least seventy years of age, of diarrhoea'. Within a month rumours concerning Major-General Barry appeared in the London Press. An enquiry was held where the chief witness was the charwoman who had laid out Barry's body. 'The body was that of a perfect female, with marks on her body indicating that she had a child when very young.'

Only during this century has medical examination of recruits advanced in efficiency, but World War I demonstrated many costly examples of carelessness, as did World War II. During the Syrian Campaign, a man was paraded to me who had been medically classified as fit for all duties. He was a gunner and complained that he was unable to march because of his feet. When he removed his boots and socks, it was revealed that his right foot possessed only one toe, his left foot only three, frost bite in World War I having obliterated the missing members. This soldier became entitled to a pension after his discharge.

With the varied duties demanded by modern armed services, many who formerly would have been ineligible to enlist may now be fitted in somewhere. For one soldier required to withstand the rigours of front line service, many more could be posted to less demanding duties: a blind person may well possess a valuable tactile and auditory acuity beyond that of others with normal vision and hearing. Medical examination of a recruit should be directed therefore to what he or she can do, even with some medical or physical defect that is not progressive, rather than his various measurements. After all, a little man can get into and out of a tank more readily than a big man.

While the three Services each had their individual medical instruction for the examination of recruits, the three Medical Directors agreed that these could be produced in one publication, a common Medical Classification covering basic Service Medical Standards and incorporating specific requirements for special postings in each of the three Services. Together we eventually produced for the first time a Medical Instruction suitable for voluntary enlistment in the Armed Services, and for the Department of Labour and National Service, which was concerned with the call-up and medical examination of recruits for National Service. Our Medical Instruction covered a simple classification of recruits into: (1) those fitted to serve in any capacity; (2) only in certain indicated duties; and (3) those not fitted for any service. This was simple in its application by the examining medical officer. The basis of this Instruction was function, not form, with no numerical assessment (figures are horribly finite—I avoid them whenever possible).

While abroad I paid particular attention to this question in the United Kingdom, Canada and New Zealand and I was not impressed by the application of the numerical P.U.L.E.E.M.S. notation in these countries, a system which needs certain training of the examiners. Unfortunately, in our undergraduate medical training there is no place for the examination of apparently healthy people who do not complain of anything, so I included in my report a recommendation that this training should be included in the course. I understand that this has been unheeded up to date.

Soon after I was appointed D.G.M.S., I came across an example of the lingering reluctance to consider what a man can do rather than how he looked. Attached to A.H.Q. medical post was a dispensary in charge of Staff Sergeant Frank Wittman (all other qualified pharmacists in the Australian Army held a commission). Wittman was a wan, stunted, little man barely four feet tall. I had first seen this odd little figure when he coxed the Wesley crew to a series of victories years ago in the Head of the River. He often came across to my office and I was always glad to chat with this interesting little fellow, but I soon realized that he had a chip on his shoulder. Only when I heard of this man's remarkable record did I understand what was worrying him. As a qualified pharmacist he had tried to enlist at the beginning of

World War I but was rejected with scorn because of his physique. After several similar failures in other States he paid his fare to London where again he failed to enlist. The War Office turned him down again and again but he persisted and at last, probably hoping to rid themselves of this importunate person, they sent him out to Mesopotamia where I was told his service was magnificent.

Whenever I called at the dispensary, I found this quaint little figure leaning on his sticks and giving a cheerful service that satisfied everyone. One day his trouble came out. 'Sir, why am I the only pharmacist in the Australian Army with stripes on my arm? I know I am funny to look at but I did serve in World War I and have been a qualified pharmacist for more than forty years. I had my own pharmacy once and I built a long platform behind my counters so that the customers could see me when I stood up. I got this job here only because no one else would take it and all my friends ask me why I am not an officer like the other fellows.'

After another domestic battle, he got his commission.

There is more to the fitness of a service recruit than a physical medical examination and a chest X-ray. It is seldom possible to predict with accuracy anyone's reaction to an experience or an environment hitherto unencountered. Most of us are uncertain how we or anyone else will react to being under fire or in any other danger.

For various reasons, including the increasing sheltering and safety of youth between the two wars, the incidence of 'nervous breakdown'—N.Y.D.N. (not yet diagnosed nervous)—among unwounded and base troops was disturbing. In one military hospital I visited while overseas, more than half the beds were occupied by men neither ill nor physically wounded.

As D.G.M.S. it was my responsibility to confirm or reject any final Medical Board recommendation. One day I received the finding of a Medical Board that a cadet in the regular army, who had passed his final examinations at Duntroon should be discharged as medically unfit. I rang the commanding officer, who explained that although the cadet had passed all his examinations he would not be graduated as he was medically unfit. 'Wait a minute,' I said. 'I am the only one who can make this final decision; when you graduate him, as he is entitled to be, I will consider the finding of the Board.' I left it at that, but sent for the whole medical record of the man during his cadetship. His first year was medically uneventful except for the usual minor sporting injuries; the second year was similar except that his recoveries were more delayed; during the third year he had several unexplained periods in hospital; and his fourth year, in spite of his satisfactory academic record, was interrupted by similar incidents with more prolonged recoveries. Soon after he had passed his final examinations he suffered 'blackouts' but investigation failed to reveal any organic cause for these. A Medical Board was summoned before the graduation ceremony and he was declared medically unfit for further service. I was adamant that I would not confirm the finding of this Board before the seal of graduation had been placed upon this man's years of successful study. Had I determined otherwise the student would have been stigmatized as a failure and his career probably blasted. He took his rightful place with the other students at the graduation ceremony.

The man, now an officer, was given leave to his home State and as he was passing through Melbourne I arranged for him to call and see me. He looked tired and strained and from his medical record I could realize the basis of his worry. I asked him why he had entered the Army and then the explanation was clear. 'My father had served as an N.C.O. in World War I and his great ambition was for me to be a member of the Staff Corps as a commissioned officer. I wasn't keen about the Army but I'm an only son and I did not want to let him down.'

I am not a psychologist—I have difficulty even in spelling the word—but his medical history and his record were plain to anyone with even a modicum of common sense. Military service was just not his line of country. Possibly quite subconsciously he had come to realize this. As his graduation came nearer year by year his unconscious defence against this situation did not take the form of academic failure, which would have left an indelible stigma, but as with many otherwise normal but maladjusted people, was sublimated into apparent medical disabilities. When, after passing his final examinations, graduation seemed inevitable, a complete defence occurred in the form of 'blackouts'.

After discharge from the Army he was appointed to a

responsible position in an important industry and I understand has steadily advanced in a successful civilian career.

At the commencement of a nurse's training, she attends a preliminary school where those who find that after all they are not suited to continue this professional training may retire with no failure or no stigma. This principle could well be applied in other fields where a certain type of personality is essential.

The disturbingly high failure rate among first year students at our universities is not the result only of our present unsatisfactory methods of selection. The abrupt change from the academic discipline of a school to the absence of this in our universities must be at least equally responsible. Had the present policy of entry into the university been applied thirty years ago, many of our leading physicians and surgeons, being late developers, would not now be practising medicine.

Disturbed by proven misfits in the Army, the Military Board decided to establish a Psychology Corps.

Over the last few years psychology has become a blessed word in the community, almost with a halo, and, often shrouded in strange psudo-scientific jargon, is accepted at its face value. There are psychologists and psychologists, some with academic qualifications and some without, but nearly all rather arrogantly assume the monopoly of common sense—and what isn't common sense is common nonsense. Any person successful in the handling of others is a sound psychologist, even if he has never heard the word or studied the subject. It is difficult to understand how anyone not knowing the basic details, the difficulties and the challenges of military service could, with any accuracy, predict suitability for enlistment. A long list of most personal and intimate questions, most of which are looked on rather as a joke, may reveal something of a personality, but wise people who have had service experience should surely be nearer the mark.

Since its inception, the Psychology Corps has grown from strength to strength and has probably become more related to reality. But I do wish psychologists looked happy and talked about ordinary everyday subjects, and when they looked at me did not make me feel that I was being peered at through a high-powered analytical microscope. We are, however, indebted to them for unconsciously providing more jests than the Aberdonians.

Chapter 21 War In Korea, II

As the remnant of the North Korean Army retreated into the mountains just south of the Manchurian border, their government retired to the mouth of the Yalu. MacArthur announced that the war was very definitely shortly coming to an end.

To complete the control of North Korea, an amphibious landing at Wonsan on the east, meeting with little opposition, advanced north into mountainous country. By the end of November, as the snow was falling and the freezing winds swept down from Manchuria, the forward American patrols looked down on the Yalu. To the west across the mountains the Eighth Army was steadily sweeping north to within fifty miles of the border.

Suddenly all went wrong. The assembly of two hundred thousand highly trained, fanatical Chinese troops along the Yalu had been undetected. With no wheel transport, camouflaged by day and moving silently by night, they suddenly struck, each man heavily laden with ammunition and carrying six days' rations. The blow crashed down on the Americans advancing in the east and only with great difficulty and heavy losses was the remnant extricated back from Wonsan.

The right flank of the far advanced troops across the mountains was wide open and when the reinforced Chinese swung west, crushing the R.O.K. Corps and threatening their rear, the Great Bug Out began, bumper to bumper towards the Parallel, and although hampered by refugees they retired a hundred and twenty miles in eight days. But neither the freezing wind and driving snow, nor the mounting casualties delayed the Chinese advance into South Korea across the ice-laden Imjin and Han rivers. Once again the Communist flag flew over tortured Seoul.

MacArthur informed Washington that unless he was permitted to bomb the Yalu bridges and the Chinese areas north of the river, he could not hold Korea. This was refused and hasty defences were again established around the Pusan perimeter far to the south. The Government decision was passed by the traitor, Donald McLean, through Russia on to China and the Chinese then knew they could invade Korea with impunity.

The Eighth Army retreated two hundred and seventy miles until the Chinese Communist forces had run themselves into the ground far south of the 38th Parallel.

During the retreat General Walker, commanding the Eighth Army, had been killed in a jeep accident. Lieut.-General Ridgway, Deputy Chief of Staff in Washington, was hurried from the Pentagon to assume command and before the Chinese could gain their second wind, he struck back. During the remaining bitter months of winter he pushed on, constantly menaced by nightly assaults from Chinese guerillas but with the heaviest artillery and air support of the war. What remained of Seoul was regained, the rivers crossed and once again Korea, south of the Parallel, was cleared of invaders. All hopes of an advance beyond, however, were abandoned.

Reports came of Chinese equipment and reinforcements streaming south across the Yalu, presumably for a spring offensive. By early April a defence position, the Kansas Line, had been developed in depth commanding the ground across the Parallel. Again MacArthur demanded permission to bomb the Yalu area and the Chinese bases in Manchuria, and embarrassed the President by making a public announcement of his proposal.

The President immediately called his Joint Chiefs of Staff together to reconsider MacArthur's request and the consequences that might follow this showdown with Communist China. He was unanimously advised, however, that on military considerations MacArthur should be relieved of his command, and on 11 April MacArthur was informed of this decision.

Who was right? Fifty or a hundred years hence the world may know.

Ridgway immediately assumed command of the United Nations Forces and General Van Fleet became Commander of the Eighth Army in Korea.

Eight days later by the light of a full moon, and with their usual whistles, shouts and bugles, divisions of fresh Chinese troops struck at the forward area of Van Fleet's defences. The line bent but the action of the British Commonwealth troops, by their rearguard action at Kapyong, held and inflicted terrible losses. The following is an account by Ronald Batchelor, a British war correspondent of Reuters; even allowing for the journalese, the magnificence of this action can be appreciated:

'British Commonwealth troops turned back the clock 35 years to write the final and most glorious chapter in the history of this brigade along the central front this week in an action which has revived the epic phrase "They shall not pass" of the first world war.

'Three battalions—the 1st Battalion Middlesex Regiment, the 3rd Battalion Royal Australian Regiment and the Princess Patricia's Canadian Light Infantry—brought new meaning to Marshal Foch's famous words in a 48-hour battle against two Chinese divisions which swept across the 38th Parallel to break the United Nations front wide open.

'This thin red line, supported by the New Zealand artillery regiment, took the full weight of the savage Chinese lunge along a 10-mile wide divisional front held by South Korean troops who broke and fled a few hours after the Communist offensive began last Sunday night.

'It was an impossible task that was made impossibly true by the Empire troops who stood alone and hurled back wave after wave of attacking Chinese until the trenches and ridge lines where they fought a few miles north of the vital road junction town of Kapyong, astride the main Seoul-Chunchon highway, were piled high with the bodies of Communist troops.

'This Brigade, thrown in the line on the eve of being relieved by the 28th Brigade from Hong Kong, inflicted more than 4,000 casualties in those 48 hours for the loss of less than 150—nearly 30 to one—and yielded scarcely an inch of ground.

'It was a wall of guts and little else against which the Chinese flung themselves as they flooded south across the foothills and ridge lines which this Brigade had battled for nearly three weeks to seize and which had been lost in a matter of hours by the collapse of a complete South Korean division.

'The Brigade's fourth battalion—the Argyll and Sutherland Highlanders—were packed and ready to leave for Hong Kong when the Chinese offensive opened. Half their officers and N.C.O.'s were already en route and all their heavy weapons had been sent ahead. Even so, they spent the night before their departure manning the Brigade defence perimeter when it looked certain the Chinese would break through.

'With only three battalions to withstand the massed assaults of more than 10,000 Chinese, the position in the words of one Brigade staff officer was "a trifle precarious"—the most masterly understatement of this war.

'There can be no adequate description of what these Empire troops achieved, nor can or should there be any comparisons drawn between the actions of the three battalions. But it was the tough, rangy and buccaneering Australians, as the record will show, who bore the main brunt of the fanatical Chinese onslaught and who, though surrounded, for more than twelve hours stood, fought and beat back non-stop attacks against the front, flanks and rear of their positions.

'Brigade Commander, Brian A. Burke, who directed the battle without sleep and almost without food—he had to be forced to eat—declared: "Every man in this Brigade has fought magnificently. No one could have asked more from them. For the Australians I can find no words to express my admiration of what they have done."

'Driving down the narrow Kapyong river valley through which R.O.K. troops poured in confusion on Monday night, the Chinese hit the Brigade positions protecting the key pass which gave access to the main east-west highway.

'Mingling with the R.O.K. troops and the stream of ragged, bewildered refugees the Chinese were able to infiltrate into and around the Australian positions. The battle opened with the Communists firing at almost point blank range in the Australian company areas.

'The Battalion command post was quickly surrounded and cut off from the companies and the Australian commander, Lieutenant-Colonel Ian Ferguson, and his headquarters personnel fought a savage hand-to-hand battle in the moonlight to break out of the Chinese encirclement. He later rejoined his battalion, riding on the side of an American tank which broke through to bring out the wounded.

'Every company position was besieged by the Chinese who came forward in waves to the blare of bugles and shrill whistles. The Aussie infantrymen stayed firm in their trenches, mowing down hundreds with machine-guns, carbines and rifles, but still the attacks continued.

'One company forced from its positions by weight of numbers counter-attacked to regain the lost ground with a bayonet charge. One platoon led by Lieutenant Ian Montgomery of Ardrossan, South Australia, seized a small plateau, criss-crossed by a labyrinth of trenches and redoubts and heavily defended by the Chinese, killing more than seventy.

'All through Monday night the Australians swayed back and forward across their positions in close-quarter combat, shooting, bayoneting and even wrestling with the swarms of Chinese who lapped over and around them like a gigantic wave.

'Behind them the New Zealand gunners rammed shells into their 25-pounder guns as fast as they could be handled to blast Chinese concentrations and assembly points. This rain of high-explosive chopped down hundreds in their tracks and probably turned the tide.

'The Middlesex Battalion holding a position to the rear of the Australians sent forward a company to aid the isolated battalion headquarters. The Cockney troops had to carve a path through a milling mass of Chinese, packing the valley between the two features. They burst through in a phalanx, stabbing their way forward with machine-guns blazing from their hips and with cold steel. Surrounded on three sides themselves when they eventually broke through they had to march miles over the precipitous hills in order to rejoin their battalion.

'The Chinese attack slackened after dawn, but not for long. Again they poured down the hill slopes and ridges, establishing a road block behind the Australians and sealing off the only supply route.

'Without sleep, food or water the Australians battled on. Some of their wounded died for lack of a route to the aid station. The men themselves, exhausted through lack of sleep, nodded in a drunk-like doze during the infrequent lulls in the fight.

'But now there was air and artillery to help them. Jets and fighter bombers screamed overhead throughout the cloudless day to scorch and rocket the Chinese in the open. The New Zealanders, reinforced now by American batteries, continued to pound away at the massing enemy. Stripped to the waist in the hot sun, the gunners toiled throughout the day with scarcely time to quench their parched lips with mugs of steaming tea brought to the guns by their cooks.

'By mid-afternoon on Tuesday the advance party of reinforcements—the American Fifth Cavalry Regimental Combat Team—had arrived at Brigade headquarters.

'Could they reach the beleaguered Australians in time? The Australian commander, asked how long he could hold out, replied: "Another two or three hours." The American convoy slowed down on the vehicle-packed roads could not arrive in time. Colonel Ferguson was ordered to withdraw at nightfall.

'And so after eighteen hours continuous battling, the Australians, protected by American tanks, drew back about a mile into the Middlesex lines and prepared to fight it out for another night.

'The Chinese came again on Tuesday night, but this time it was the Princess Pats who withstood the shock and smashed back the surge of attackers.

'It was a repeat performance. Around, over and behind the Canadian positions the Chinese poured, but again the Empire troops stood fast.

'One Company, overrun as they described it by "hundreds and hundreds of the gooks", requested the New Zealanders to fire on to their positions. Down went the barrage on to the Canadians, who hugged their slit trenches as the 25-pounders burst among them. The Chinese, caught in the open, fell where they stood and that particular attack was broken.

'By dawn the Canadians were still holding their ground, despite heavy mortaring. But their ammunition was almost exhausted. Fresh supplies were ferried to them by helicopters which hovered over the ridge line and parachuted small arms and mortar ammunition into their defence perimeter.

'Gradually the Chinese attacks became less frequent and they began to retreat slowly into the hills. They had little time to reorganize for yesterday the American Cavalrymen with armour rolled through the British positions in an attempt to drive the Chinese from high ground.

'Tanks, artillery and mortars continued to pound at the Chinese for the rest of the day, the Americans advancing about a mile. Last night the brigade sector was virtually all quiet.

'Three Commonwealth battalions had plugged the gap. The Lion had slain the Dragon.'

Almost surrounded and with more than a thousand casualties, the brigade slowly withdrew. The action of the Gloucesters isolated on 'Gloucester Hill' above Solma-ri was described later by Van Fleet as 'the most outstanding example of unit bravery in modern warfare'. Each unit involved in this action received the Presidential Citation and every member of these units wears on his shoulder the dark blue flash of this award. This heroic rearguard action blunted the Chinese advance and permitted the Eighth Army to hold firmly north of the Han River, strike back and once again reach the parallel. With enormous losses the Chinese offences had failed and the two forces faced each other panting to regain their breath in a stalemate about the area where it had all begun just a year before.

For some time statements had been appearing in the Australian press that our casualties were being sent back to the battle area after being wounded for the second or third time, that only scanty and delayed information concerning casualties was available to the next of kin, that the rations and clothing of our troops was inadequate, that there was insufficient leave for the troops, and the usual grizzles and grouches always to be found among a few battle weary troops. Without confirmation, these were dramatically exaggerated by the press, always prepared to publish 'news', however inaccurate.

Embarrassing questions were constantly being addressed in Parliament to the Minister for the Army, a simple, sensitive soul. One afternoon while this flap was on I was summoned urgently to the Minister and after a few preliminaries he opened out: 'General, I want you to go to Korea immediately. I will give you a list of all the charges that are made in the House and I want you to investigate them all and on your return report personally to me in Canberra.'

This was an embarrassing situation, an instruction coming directly from the Minister and not through the Military Board or the Adjutant-General, who was responsible for my service. I went across to the A.G. and told him of my interview. 'Yes,' he said, 'I have just been told by the Minister. It's all very odd but there it is. I will arrange for someone from the A. Branch to go with you and I will fix your transport, you will leave early the day after tomorrow.' So that was that.

Within forty-eight hours I was in Japan again, but a blinding rain storm made us two hours late for lunch with the Australian Consul. I reported to Red Robbie, who said he had received a signal about my mission but could not make out what all the fuss was about. 'How could anything be amiss with men under my command?' he said. 'It's all bloody nonsense.'

Next day I went around the large American Hospital in Tokyo, to which, it had been reported, many of our Australian casualties were being flown direct from Korea, bypassing our own hospital at Kure. I found only two of our men there, both severely wounded, who wisely had been evacuated by the first available plane which happened to be flying from Seoul direct to Tokyo, a hop of about three hours. No better or more expeditious attention could possibly have been given to these casualties, and when I saw them they were both cheerful and well on the way to recovery.

That afternoon I visited our leave centre at Ebisu, filled to capacity with men from Korea, all apparently happy.

Next day I flew down to our hospital at Kure and as I expected all was well. I have often found that when there is an air of depression a visit to the cheery patients in a military hospital restores any sagging morale. An inspection of the convalescent depot and holding centre for reinforcements failed to reveal any substance for the complaints about men wounded many times being returned to battle. I confirmed this by personally interviewing every soldier in the convalescent depot and inspecting the records. Then across to Korea, where there certainly was a tension in the air. What remained of Seoul was tragic—less than a quarter of the normal population had survived, cowering among the ruins. Across the river troops were moving forward along the few roads in the valleys and over the hillsides mottled with the brown and purple stains of the napalm bombing.

Scattered among the ruined paddyfields there was brutal evidence of the Chinese retreat, in the bodies of the farmers who had returned to the charred remains of their homes and rice stacks. There was sporadic gunfire and the occasional rattle of machine-guns but little military activity in the forward area other than the preparation of the defences and night patrolling. Bullet-proof vests of laminated nylon, which could withstand small fragments and even dull the impact of a bullet, were available for patrols, but the more you protect a soldier the more naked and uneasy he feels when deprived of this security. I stood by one evening while a patrol was being assembled for a night raid and I heard one soldier as he fell in say: 'Sarge, someone's pinched my bloody vest, what will I do?'

Driving forward one day I stopped to speak to a small group of soldiers lounging alongside a truck with a broken axle. I offered some of them a lift in my car. 'It's all right, Sir, the unit is a couple of miles along the road, so we have sent back for another truck.' There was not a sign of any enemy, it was a cold but sunny day and the road ran along a flat valley—these were infantrymen. To anyone who had clambered over the mountains in New Guinea laden with a pack and all the bits and pieces, this seemed strange infantry training.

We had practically complete air supremacy but it was disturbing to find vehicles in a battle area moving along a dusty road in broad daylight almost nose to tail and to see the planes, devoid of any camouflage or dispersion, lined up in the open, wing to wing, along the air strip. How soon lessons are forgotten.

An Indian parachute ambulance was in support of our brigade. Our troops were enthusiastic about this unit ('they're tops') and Lieut.-Colonel Ranga-Raj, the commander of the Ambulance, could not say enough about his admiration for our men. In India this Ambulance had been commanded by Lieut.-Colonel Forster, who 'dropped' wearing his rimless monocle, and they told me that while a man was always detailed to stand by his landing, seldom or ever did the eyeglass become detached from Forster's eye and have to be retrieved. Whenever I visited this Ambulance their well-kept lines, their discipline and efficiency were most impressive and I enjoyed their cheerfulness and their brew of tea.

Helicopters were available for the evacuation of casualties from the forward area, provided the weather permitted. Fortunately there was little enemy action as these planes are sitting shots for small arms. On each side of these odd machines, looking rather like a large, wingless mosquito, was a canopied pod for the comfortable transport of a patient. One afternoon I was driving over to a group of our troops who were mining the banks of a forward river. In the distance we heard a muffled bang and as I arrived a 'chopper' was settling on the small area marked as a landing site. The medical Corporal in charge of the medical post explained that a few minutes before one of the mines had accidentally exploded and a man had been wounded. While he was applying first aid, a wireless signal had been sent to the helicopter pool a few miles in rear. Within half an hour of being wounded, the casualty was on the operating table in the nearest American M.A.S.H. (Mobile Army Surgical Hospital), and as time may be such an important factor in surgery this was a wonderful contribution. Later on my way back I called at the M.A.S.H. and found the man tucked in bed, reasonably comfortable after his surgery.

During my visit to Canada I had seen the research devoted to the development of clothing designed to withstand wet and cold. The result of this work had been applied to the clothing issued during the bitter winter campaign in Korea. The Chinese wore heavily quilted cotton uniforms as a protection. One of the winter problems in Korea resulted from the use of petrol for the heating of huts and tents, with the inevitable high incidence of burns. With no disturbance of the clothing, the affected limb or body was swathed in a large, well padded, sterile dressing firmly bandaged, the man was given a heavy sedative, a large dose of penicillin and immediately flown to the nearest base hospital. On arrival, if his condition was satisfactory, he was placed in a warm saline bath and his dressings and clothing soaked off. He was then placed in a cradled bed with a sterile sheet spread over the cradle; he could lie in a gentle warmth with his wounds exposed while transfusion and general treatment could continue. If necessary, grafting was performed as early as indicated. Of course, this hospital routine was not applicable in all cases but whenever possible was applied and the results were generally excellent.

During my residency at the Children's Hospital, more than thirty years before, and since then, I had seen a variety of dressings for burns and I had become convinced that for most burns, certainly the superficial ones, there is no dressing as good as no dressing at all or the subsided skin of a sterile, evacuated blister; certainly this procedure is the most economical in time and material.

In spite of the prophylactic facilities always available in Japan and Korea, venereal disease continued to be a problem. I privately interviewed a number of these patients and gained the impression that since the dramatic introduction of penicillin fear of V.D. was rapidly fading and that exposure to infection overseas was seldom a new experience, but rather a continuance of a practice in Australia and among more highly infected and more flaunting girls and women.

After careful enquiry and close observation, I left Korea and Japan confident that there was little substance in the sensational press reports and Parliamentary debates devoted to the care and welfare of our troops.

Our return to Australia was not uneventful. We left Iwakiui early one Sunday morning and between Japan and Manila one of our four engines conked out and another was rather sick. The pilot told us he had selected an approach to Manila to avoid the high ranges and unless there was any further engine trouble he would land us safely. 'When we leave is another matter, depending on what spares I can find in Manila: engines may have to be flown from Australia. Anyway, I hope I can get you off before Tuesday.'

'Why Tuesday?' I asked him.

'That is the day of the elections.'

This seemed to me of no significance and I was rather glad to have a day or two to look around.

We landed safely.

That evening the pilot called us all together in a private room in the Manila Hotel and locked the door. 'I told you that the general elections are on Tuesday. If we have not left by early on that morning I want you all to remain in your rooms, lock the door and do not open to anyone. If anyone knocks get under the bed, and if you can manage to have water and rations with you for a day, so much the better. This hotel is the headquarters of one of the political parties and an election in Manila is a day and a night of fun and games. Last year twenty or so were shot here.'

My ready cash was running out, but our Consul, Mr Waller, cashed a cheque for me and I felt at least financially secure for two days. We drove into the hills to see the famous bamboo organ and lunched at a delightful country club nearby.

Immediately after dinner I went up to my room overlooking the quiet and peaceful harbour, twinkling with the little lights of the slowly moving small craft. I locked my door and as I had kept fairly complete notes on each day's activities and observations during my mission I took the opportunity to draft my report before I turned in. Fortunately as long as I have my head comfortable I can sleep at any time during the day or night; one of the hardest things for most people to learn, if there is nothing to do, is to do nothing and relax. My bed in the air-conditioned room was very comfortable and after reading a few pages of a 'who dunnit' I was asleep. Some time later I was wakened in the dark by a knock on my door. I got under the bed and waited, another knock and after a pause a voice I recognized as the pilot's: 'It's me.' I was too sleepy to cavil about grammar and with my little stout stick in my shaking hand I opened the door: It *was* the pilot. 'It's all right, we will be leaving shortly after dawn, come down quietly to the front steps with your gear at 4 a.m. An armoured transport will take you all out to the airstrip.'

He was right—all went well and we arrived in Darwin later in the day, all in one piece. A few days later I read in the press that the election had been unusually quiet: only ten people had been shot in the hotel.

Three days after I arrived in Melbourne I sent my report to the Minister and within a few days he summoned me to Canberra. 'I want you to have dinner with the Prime Minister and then address a meeting of all parties on the general military situation in Korea, with particular reference to the press campaign and the complaints directed to me as Minister for the Army.' Before a map of Korea I gave a general survey of the war up to the present situation and then covered the various complaints. I did not gloss over the disabilities and discomforts inevitable during any campaign and was able to explain most of them and what was being done to reduce them. I quoted from a letter from Colonel Mackay Dick, a senior British medical officer:

'... The officers of the Middlesex Regt and of the Argyll and Sutherland Highlanders are full of praise for the 3 Bn BAR in Korea. The Englishmen said: "The Australians were easily the most outstanding troops in Korea. We knew that they were great fighters but we did not expect their great discipline and terrific spit and polish. The Chinese feared the Australian hat." What high praise indeed!

'I believe that such praise has appeared in the Australian press, but it should also appear in the Japanese news. I feel that the Australians have not received the publicity they deserve in Japan. We read all about the Highlanders and the English, but not about the Aussies. The Australian P.R.O. should be instructed to remedy that.

'... I believe that BCOF 29 Gen Hosp is the best hospital in which I have ever served, in my personal experience everyone got on extremely well. Co-operation was superb and everyone was helpful, charming and as courteous as they could possibly be. I shall never forget the great welcome given by our Australian kinsmen to us on our arrival in Kure on 27 Nov 50. You, Sir, and all your officers were present in the Mess, to greet us and lavish on us your great hospitality. It is a magnificent gesture greatly appreciated by all of us.

'Possibly we never appeared to show how much we appreciated all that the Australians did for us but that is due to our unfortunate habit of not showing our feelings when we should—however, on return to the U.K. you can rest assured that everyone we meet will know all about our gallant and hospitable kinsmen. Further, should any of you visit the old country you will be assured of a true welcome, certainly on this side of the border. . . .'

The outstanding achievements of the Australian Regular Battalion in Korea could not have been possible in a unit of low morale and continually frustrated, as asserted by the press and by private individuals. My address concluded: 'I can assure you that our troops are in good heart. In the British Commonwealth Division we have a vivid demonstration to the world of the reality of the British Commonwealth. Components from the United

Kingdom, from Canada, from New Zealand, from South Africa, from India and from Australia are fighting side by side in an atmosphere of splendid goodwill, understanding, mutual respect and admiration. Let us stop this knocking.'

Some questions were asked, most of which I was able to answer. (Questions are seldom indiscreet, it is the answers that get one into trouble.) Anyway, the press campaign petered out and later the Minister told me that he was seldom pestered with private complaints.

Chapter 22 Retirement

I was approaching the retiring age for Major-Generals but while we were well on the way, there remained phases to be completed to ensure the development of our medical service in pace with the expanding army and there was still our commitment in Korea.

There was a keenness throughout our Corps. The C.M.F. was training well in the various commands and whenever Bill Refshauge or I attended their exercises, we came away heartened and feeling confident that our Service could respond at least as ably as in the past.

There were many ex-A.I.F. medical officers on the C.M.F. active list but this would not continue for many more years. Already keen young M.O.s without service ribbons were holding field rank, which was all to the good, but it was difficult to realize that World War II was years behind us.

The C.G.S. sent for me in my final year and said he would like to extend my service for a further two years, if I were agreeable. There are phases in all activities, including commands, after which a transfusion is needed, fresh winds, new ideas, new outlooks, besides unclogging the lines of promotion. Some people enjoying their senior positions are reluctant to relinquish them and no one likes to tell them that their worth is past.

I felt, however, that the immediate post-war phase was not completed and I welcomed the privilege of seeing this through. Certainly Bill Refshauge, a tower of strength, was alongside me, but I wanted him to have a personal insight into the British Army Medical Service and be known to the British authorities before I handed over. This would now be posible and no better ambassador for our corps could be found. The happiest relationship with our opposite numbers had always existed and when arrangements were made for Bill to go abroad I knew these would be maintained.

There had recently been changes among my senior medical officers and I wanted to see the new men firmly in the saddle. The School was expanding its fields of training and rapidly becoming integrated into the whole Army pattern. Our Matron-in-Chief, Colonel Bowe, was rightly proud of her expanding Nursing Corps and the Medical Service had an increasingly happy relationship with the other arms, who were beginning to accept us as one of the family. I could not have wished for a happier command.

The war in Korea had settled down to a prolonged debate, with little relaxation for our Medical Service, and during my final visit to Japan and Korea I found them all as keen as ever. While the interminable talks were still continuing at the Teahouse at Kaesong and later at Panmunjom, the two armies faced each other across the valley of the Imjin—we could watch the northerners developing their defences as they watched ours. Only after 747 days and millions of words of bitter debate was the Korean armistice signed on 27 July 1953. I stayed with General Cassels, commanding the Commonwealth Division in the field, and although there was a truce it was uneasy, while thousands of troops were standing to their arms over the depth of their defences. The strange, sullen silence of the area was broken only when some trigger-happy soldier felt like it.

The Korean labour battalions were working and digging everywhere—new roads were appearing in the valleys and around the hills where wired areas with little red triangles marking the mine fields were expanding each day. We were driving along a winding, hilly road when we came upon a group of Koreans rocking with laughter. Stopping, we found that the huge joke was that one member of the gang had driven a pick through his foot, pinning himself to the ground. No one helped the poor fellow, who naturally had not joined in the fun: he had to tug the pick out to the still louder roars of laughter of his friends. The Koreans, said to be the most Christian of the far Asiatics, are at times most cruel.

Before I flew back to Japan, I was invited to a small gathering at General Hume's headquarters, and after a few but more than generous words I was presented with a parchment scroll, membership of the short-lived and unique 38th Parallel United Nations Medical Association. Later I presented this to the Medical Library in Melbourne but within a few months it disappeared. If there is ever a reader of these pages and by any chance he finds my scroll among his possessions by mistake, would he please return it.

After a grand farewell night in our hospital in Kure, a small party sailed through the Ondu Cut and across the Inland Sea to Iwakuni. As my plane did not leave till evening I drove to pay my farewell to the Kintai Bridge and the unforgettable loveliness of the Valley, a glory in all seasons. Many think of Japan only as it is in the cherry blossom time of early spring, but beautiful as this is, with wind and rain the blossoms fall in a few days, whereas the autumn is a lingering time of quiet loveliness.

Retirement, if ever considered, seems at first to refer to other people. I remember at a party hearing that remarkably intelligent and really funny comedian, Bob Hope, tell of an experience one night in London. He had arrived that morning and was enjoying a party. The time came to return to his hotel, but as he stepped outside he was immediately blanketed in an impenetrable fog. He could hear cars honking and for a moment could glimpse an occasional faint headlight. He stepped carefully to the edge of the footpath to hail a taxi when he saw a dim light pointing at him. He stepped to one side—the light followed and seemed to be coming nearer and nearer straight at him, until it was almost on him, when he realized the light was the glow of his cigarette.

And so retirement had come to me.

On 24 June 1955 I had my final inspection. Colonel Glyn White, the D.D.M.S., had called the parade at the Healesville School and Wallie Mac, the C.O., as usual had arranged everything perfectly. My heart was heavy as I passed along the ranks to the slow tempo of the moving melody of the band, almost a lament. There was a silence among the great trees at the foot of the mountains as I gave my farewell address to those comrades who had been splendidly loyal and of whom I was so proud. As I stepped down the clouds came over the sun—there was a chill in the air.

And so on 25 June 1955 ended after more than forty years my active association with the Army. It had been my privilege to have known people and experiences in the grand comradeship of arms, to have shared in their excitements, their tensions, and the hearty fun of good fellows, and learnt something of the true value of essentials and the fallacy of the many petty foibles of civilian life. I was fortunate in that I had served in the ranks and learnt to be led before I was called upon to lead others. To have served on active service without stripes or stars is a rare privilege for one who is later to practise medicine and ultimately become D.G.M.S. The richness of these experiences is inexplicable to those denied them.

I had lived and served with men whose life and outlook were devoted to the profession of arms. From among them I have been blessed with the friendship of many for whom I have an enduring admiration and I am in their debt for a more sound appreciation of the many challenging problems of one's daily life. I was fortunate that during my tour of duty as D.G.M.S., Lieutenant-General Sir Sydney Rowell was C.G.S. His judgement, his understanding of human beings, his rare moral courage and decision were always available to me and more than once saved me from grievous error.

The ranks of the Australian Army in war represent a cross-section of the community. With the possible exception of Egypt, where the shadow of the Battle of the Wazza in World War I still lingered, the Australian soldiers were well liked in those areas where they served and are always welcomed back, individually or in groups, and like most soldiers they are wonderful with children. The Digger leaves a nice taste in the mouth when he departs.

In time of war the Australian Army for some years to come will be recruited mainly from the C.M.F. and from the civilian community. In spite of the reputation repeated by those not in a position to judge, the Australian soldier is well disciplined and most easily led. If he is told what it is all about and treated as an intelligent human being, as he is entitled to be, and if his leaders say 'come on', not 'go on', he will do what he is asked and do it remarkably well, but you can't push him around. He is intensely proud of his reputation as he has every reason to be and the disciplined initiative of Australian soldiers is outstanding. Campaigning conditions are often grim and some troops just put up with them, as at times has to be done. While the Australian soldier will of course grumble and grouse, he will do something about it. In the desert, in the snows of Syria, in the jungle of

New Guinea and the Islands, in the incessant wet cold of the mountains, and the foul swamps of the coastal areas, the Digger somehow made himself as comfortable as possible while others just shivered or wallowed in the mud. On every possible occasion he bathed and kept himself clean and it was exceptional even in action to see an Australian soldier with more than a day's growth on his face.

In World Wars I and II the personnel of the A.I.F. came mainly from the militia and the civilian community and the Australian soldier fought not only bravely but also intelligently. There is probably a closer relationship between all ranks of Australian soldiers than in other armies.

The Australian soldier is keen to find out all he can about the place where he is stationed. Early in the Middle East, one General Hospital did not open for some months. The morale of the unit was maintained by interspersing routine training with conducted tours over this historical area. The Digger is inquisitive. It has been related that a visitor to Madame Tussaud's in London stood before a row of famous and infamous women of history. He enquired of the attendant: 'I suppose your laundry is a large item here?'

'Yes, sir, I suppose next to the wages and insurance the laundry is our biggest recurring expense.'

'I wonder if you could tell me, do all these women wear the authentic underclothes of their time?'

'Excuse me, sir, but that is known only to the staff and a few Australian soldiers!'

The Gallipoli campaign established the high prestige of the Australian soldier in battle. That a volunteer army led largely by civilian officers could achieve such repute commanded respect among their allies and their enemies. It is recorded that Lieutenant-General Sir John Monash, the most senior of these officers, was considered in 1918 for the appointment of Generalissimo of the Allied Forces in France, a command which fell to Foch.

In World War I, I served in the ranks, in World War II and in Korea as an officer. Perhaps because of these varying points of view there seemed to me a subtle change in the Australian soldier during these campaigns, while his battle tradition had been maintained. In 1939 there was not the urgent rush of recruits as in August 1914 when many young teenagers advanced their ages to enlist; rather were there many applications by old Diggers scaling down their ages to thirty-nine years (the limit for private) and hiding their ribbons.

During World War I soldiers sang on every possible occasion: 'Tipperary', 'Mademoiselle from Armentières', 'Wish me luck as you wave me goodbye', and many others. The Second World War was less melodious: 'Roll out the barrel' was the favourite and a few others were heard occasionally. In Korea singing was rare.

In World War I units generally promoted their own concert parties, some of which continued after the war. In World War II and in Korea, professional civilian parties continually travelled overseas to entertain the troops, who seemed to expect this, and certainly enjoyed them.

It had not been possible for me to contribute to an Army pension but the A.G. had persuaded the Treasury to grant a gratuity on my retirement. This was an unexpected windfall and although the total sum was less than the annual salary of my successor, it enabled me at long last to pay off our house and start for once with a clean sheet. But the sheet could not remain clean for long: we had no private income—our only investment was our house—and something had to be done about it.

Chapter 23 Civil Defence and Good Neighbour Councils

The Royal Melbourne Hospital was about to appoint a Medical Officer to a clinic for the lay staff (among the thousand or so members there was need for daily medical attention in addition to the examination before employment). As this involved only morning attendance and brought me into personal relationship with people again, I welcomed the appointment to keep the home fires burning. It needed only a few days of my new duty, however, to realize how rapidly modern civilian medical service and administration had passed me by.

Army hospitals are always commanded by an individual and directly under him are his three staff officers, medical, nursing and lay, directing their various departments but co-ordinated by the commanding officer. I found a different administration in a civilian hospital. Each of the three departments seemed an entity with little, if any, apparent co-ordinated command, without which it is difficult for departments not to think and act independently, but the only alternative to law and order is some degree of chaos and loss of efficiency. When one speaks of command in relation to a civilian enterprise, many people bristle and raise their hackles —'You're not in the army now'—but the principle of meeting military problems is basically similar to meeting the challenges of civil life.

The inefficiency of command rather than the quality of the troops commanded has led to many military disasters. In 1914 the British and French armies narrowly escaped disaster only because Von Moltke could not command or co-ordinate his armies. In 1918 the Allied line was held by five separate armies speaking five separate languages, each under the independent command of their respective Governments. Early in March the Germans attacked and burst wide the tentative contacts between these armies. Only the imminence of complete disaster forced the Allies to weld their armies under one Supreme Commander, Foch, and only then was defeat turned into victory.

The establishment of a military hospital provides one personnel for each four patients; in a civilian hospital, Parkinson's Law concerning personnel seems vindicated.

In democratic Barataria, Don Alhambra sang: 'When everybody's somebody, then no one's anybody.' With an establishment of four personnel to each patient, at times it was difficult to obtain information or decision. In a military general hospital, which as a rule is established in a series of marquees, there is a prescribed scale of equipment and no fads are permitted; there are no rigidly prescribed hours of duty, and while strict economy is observed this does not prejudice efficiency. There was always an atmosphere of intelligent discipline about a military hospital and a well-knit, happy unit spirit which recognized and appreciated authority.

I found myself sadly outmoded by the wonder of modern investigational facilities, most of which have a numerical result and are often essential. Like statistics, however, a laboratory investigation is but one facet of an overall picture and it still requires a human brain to interpret and adjust a laboratory result to a clinical finding and to the overall assessment of the patient. Figures are formal and finite but normal function is compatible with a wide range of form.

In what we had known of prescribing of medicines, I found another new world. Before the war we had three antibiotics—quinine, salvarsan and sulphanilamide. I had seen the magic of penicillin during the New Guinea Campaign. Oddly enough mouldy bread was used as a dressing for wounds more than three hundred years ago. While the availability of penicillin as a therapeutic agent was the result of Florey's brilliant research, the discovery of its bactericidal action was another example of serendipity—grasping the significance of an unforeseen or fortuitous event. Then rapidly followed a host of antibiotics efficient against an ever-widening spectrum of bacteria.

The big proprietary drug houses were proceeding to remove the art of prescribing from practising doctors and by high pressure salesmanship assuming the reponsibility of dictating modern drug therapy with its confusing nomenclature and rapidity of change with little or no implication of possible side effects.

One doctor in active practice recorded the intrusion of these salesmen into his practice during one month. He was visited by eighty importunate agents and of those who were seen each occupied an average of twenty-two and a half minutes of his time. Had they all been seen they would have taken the time equivalent to sixty consultations. During the same month two hundred and ninety-six articles, free samples and literature, were delivered personally or by post. The literature is nearly always headed 'Our recent ethical products'; one wonders what became of the non-ethical ones.

I thoroughly enjoyed my mornings in the staff clinic and it was good once again to be associated with patients. Sister Gale had trained in the old pre-war days and together we were a reasonable success in our old-fashioned way. After a few years a survey revealed that we were saving the hospital more than a thousand man-working-days a year.

As the clinic concluded about midday, the rest of the time was free. I had a number of honorary activities but these left me with ample time to accept a part-time appointment with Civil Defence.

The horror of Hiroshima and Nagasaki still hung over the world and those European countries that had recently experienced total war had maintained and developed cadres of their civil defence organizations. Within a few years murmurings arose in Australia concerning the establishment of a similar organization, but these went unheeded by the Federal Government. Taking the initiative, New South Wales formed a State Civil Defence Corps under the command of that splendid civilian soldier, Major-General Ivan Docherty. While the Federal Government still insisted that such an activity remained a State responsibility until an emergency arose, a Federal Department of Civil Defence was established under the Minister for the Interior. A Director, Brigadier Waddell, a retired regular soldier, was appointed and a school established in the charming country club on the slopes of Mount Macedon, about an hour's run north of Melbourne. The only purpose of this Federal activity was to co-ordinate any State action that might develop and to train any personnel the State might select.

Civil Defence and Good Neighbour Councils

It was at this stage that the Minister for the Interior, Sir Wilfred Kent-Hughes, a man of ideas and independence of thought, sent for me. 'Surely there should be some medical advice available to this Directorate but I see no medical adviser is included in the establishment. Would you take this on as a part-time appointment?' I asked what would be involved. 'You would be available to advise the Director on the medical aspects of the training and lecture to the students.'

'May I talk this over with the Director?' I asked. 'We served together at Army Headquarters.'

'Yes. I'll let him know that I want you to be the medical adviser on his staff.'

Next day I called on Brigadier Waddell, who seemed rather surprised that a medical adviser was necessary but kindly said that he would be delighted to have me with him. The school was commanded by that robust Air Commodore Knox-Knight with the instructional staff composed of a grand group of ex-service officers. While the school was being put in order after the vicissitudes of wartime occupation by evacuees, the staff went abroad on a brief tour covering Civil Defence developments in the United Kingdom and I prepared my lectures on atomic, biologic and chemical warfare. I knew something of these subjects and brought my knowledge up to date from the literature that was freely available. I like teaching and the salary for a part-time task was generous.

The emphasis of the School was on atomic warfare. Shortly after 08.15 hours on 16 August 1945, the listening world was aware of the most powerful man-made explosion ever known. A few minutes earlier, with a blinding flash and a searing heat, the first atomic bomb had burst about 2,000 feet above the centre of Hiroshima, the chief embarkation port for Japanese soldiers going overseas. When any world-stunning event occurs it is often assumed that this is without precedent, but two quotations are of interest: 'Only the devil could have devised this godless weapon. Mankind can never withstand the blinding flash, the searing ball. Its invention means the end of nobility.' 'Prompted by widespread fears that this new weapon of man's destruction might wipe out western civilization, the Pope today issued a Bull forbidding their use by any Christian State against another, whatsoever the provocation.' The former of these quotations dates back to the fourteenth century when the English soldiers under Edward III first used gunpowder at Cressy. The latter dates back even earlier to the twelfth century when that deadly weapon, the crossbow, was introduced into war.

The effects of an atomic bomb are those of blindness, blast, heat and radiation. While never before that August morning had mankind been submitted to such a catastrophic combination, such a simultaneous multiple of these terrible forces, all have been with us since man was on this earth. The blindness of the bomb is the result of a brilliance many times that of the sun exhausting for some hours the visual purple of our eyes or the result of a burn from the terrific heat of the explosion. Since the dawn of time the earth's surface has been submitted to the blast of the elements (when Krakatoa blew up in 1883 the blast wave went round the earth many times before its force was spent). While in the open man, except in his eardrums, can withstand the direct effects of a great blast, in a city he would be wounded by the stones, the bricks, the timber, the iron, the glass and all the missiles flung at him by the force. The hazards of heat have always been with us and basically the burn of an atomic bomb differs in no way from the burn of a bushfire or a kettle, but the effects of these forces may be complicated by the simultaneous effect of radiation.

There is nothing new in radiation. Since the beginning of time irradiating cosmic particles have descended around us from the heavens above and radioactive elements have always existed in the earth beneath. With the increasing therapeutic and diagnostic application of radioactive particles and with the application of these to watch and clock illumination, individuals are increasingly submitted to radiation. We live in a constant and inescapable but fortunately practically harmless background of radiation.

If instead of waiting for the problematical advent of an atomic bomb, we realized that we have annual national disasters and called our activity 'Disaster Planning' rather than Civil Defence, we may well contribute something of national value and have a wider community response. Burns, wounds, poisonings, drownings and electric shocks are killing each year as many of our citizens as Australian troops were killed during the whole of World War II, with the possible exception of the Japanese prisoners of war, and wounding, permanently disfiguring and disabling many more and these numbers are increasing each year. One in each thirteen deaths is due to these 'accidents'.

Every country at some time in its history has suffered national disasters. We have known our bushfires and typhoons, and had the earthquakes that rocked Adelaide a few years ago lasted another two minutes a major disaster would have resulted. By all means educate people concerning the effects of a possible atomic explosion and how these can be minimized, but let us get on urgently with the task of reducing the daily tragedies that are always with us.

In Australia we have medical personnel and services second to none in caring for a limited number of casualties, but the saving of life, the severity of wounds and the duration of disability do not depend solely on the efficiency of doctors, nurses, hospitals, police, ambulance and other services, to all of whom we leave them. To a large extent the effect of an accident may depend on those who are present at the time on the roads, by the water or in the home, but how many men or women, boys or girls, know what to do at once in these ever-present hazards?

We are great 'leavers' in Australia and we have wonderful people to whom we can leave things—if they are available. In Hiroshima, immediately after the bomb, there were no hospitals. no doctors, no nurses, no telephones, no police, no transport, no unblocked roads—just a few thousand shocked and bewildered people surrounded by vast heaps of debris.

In one of Neville Cardus's books there is a cricket story that has a bearing on the situation. The match was at Lords and Archie MacLaren's team was in the field with a fast bowler on. One particularly short ball bounced high towards the batsman's head. He put up his bat to protect himself and the ball flew high off the shoulder almost straight above the wicket. In rushed the keeper, the first slip, second slip, third slip. 'No,' shouted MacLaren from mid-on, 'leave it to Braund, leave it to Braund.' They all stepped back and the ball fell harmlessly to the ground. Braund was probably the best first slip in England but he wasn't playing that week. So our planning should be based on the assumption that Braund might not be playing, that the doctors, the nurses, the policemen and the ambulances and the telephone might not be immediately available, only the man and the woman, the boy and girl in the street, in the home or by the water. In other words, let us have at least one person in every home trained in first-aid. In Australia at present not one in a hundred is so trained in this simple subject within the capability of any normal adult, adolescent or teenage child. When I have asked education authorities why this subject is not taught in all schools, the general reply is that the curriculum is too full. When I ask them if, when they were drowning, they would prefer to have with them an honours economics scholar who knew nothing of first-aid or one who could not read or write but knew how to rescue them and start the breathing, I get the same answer.

To this end I recommended that at least a basic knowledge of first-aid should be an essential requirement of any student before entering the Civil Defence School. This was rejected. I then pointed out how essential it was for those taking the casualty rescue course to be qualified in first-aid, otherwise they would be risking their lives among burning buildings and falling rubble when rescuing casualties for whom they could not give immediate first-aid and who would possibly be dead bodies when recovered. This was not thought necessary.

I had prepared a small pocket folder with simple cartoons and explanations of what to do at once for burns, wounds, drownings, electric shocks and poisonings. The printing and household distribution of these throughout Australia would have involved only a fraction of the finance allotted to the School for publications, but this was considered to be too low a priority to warrant action. I told many of my classes this unfortunately was not available and questions were asked of the Minister in Canberra why this was so. I was politely but firmly instructed to make no further reference to this publication.

In spite of these frustrations, apparently inevitable in the Services, I very much enjoyed my weekly visits to this School and the company of the group of grand fellows on the staff. These two activities—the staff clinic at the Hospital and the Civil Defence appointment—certainly made it possible to meet my bank manager on more friendly terms and still left time for voluntary activities.

Dorothy was a Sister at the Children's Hospital.

Maj.-Gen. F. E. Hume speaks to guests at a party given in honour of the author in the Peacock Room of the Imperial Hotel, Tokyo 1949.

A few of the many hundreds of North Korean prisoners that were being sprayed with DDT dust at a prisoner of war enclosure, 1950.

A wounded marine is shown strapped in carrier attached to USMC Helicopter preparatory being flown back to a rear hospital. This was one of the first times helicopters were used for such service.

Coleg Harlech, Harlech.

School of Army Health, Healesville.

Farewell party. Author taking the march past.

I had retired from office in the Royal Empire Society, as it was then called, some years before and while I was in the Army had become associated with the establishment of an Australian postgraduate School of Nursing, and I was now able to take a more active part in its development.

Before the war, postgraduate qualifications in the various fields of the nursing profession aroused little interest in Australia. Nurses were appointed as Matrons, Ward Sisters, Theatre Sisters, or Tutors and in other responsible nursing positions, generally because they had proved to be good nurses or were popular. For some years postgraduate nursing training and qualifications had been available in London and occasionally Australian nurses had taken one or other of these courses. With the establishment in Australia of the Florence Nightingale Foundation in 1946 scholarships for this training were made available and immediately after the war a number of our ex-service nurses went to London. For some years the formation of a similar college in Australia had been discussed and in 1950 six of our senior nurses from various States crystallized these discussions by constituting the College of Nursing, Australia. This was only a beginning, the College existed only on paper but representatives from the various States agreed to bring the College to a reality. All manner of problems had to be solved and I was invited to chair these meetings in an attempt to co-ordinate the various State and individual points of view into a practical and worthwhile constructive conclusion. The State representatives assembled over a series of weekends and it was all most interesting. Finally we sorted it out and in the College of Nursing, Australia, was established at the Nurses' Memorial Centre in Melbourne and for some years I remained as Chairman. Scholarships were made available in the various States and Federal Government finance was provided under the Colombo Plan for students from nearby Asian countries. It slowly became realized in Australia that graduate nurses should be appointed to postgraduate responsibilities in their profession only if they possess recognized postgraduate qualifications.

There were other activities with which I was privileged to be associated, among which were St John Ambulance Brigade and the Good Neighbour Council.

After World War II Australia suddenly realized that while we possessed practically every raw material we wanted and the world wanted, in a country about the size of the United States eight million people could not economically develop these, nor could they defend their possessions. One of the most important postwar decisions of the Federal Government with the Labor Party in power was a courageous and energetic policy of immigration.

Europe at that time was in the turmoil of readjustment, millions of refugees were roaming over the countries seeking sanctuary and shelter in the more stable but already crowded cities. The refugee problem was a challenge to all decent countries and Australia answered this challenge by accepting a quarter of a million of these stateless people. When migrants move to another country they need shelter, food and employment. In Australia there had been a great lag in building during the war and ordinary building material was in very short supply, but with substitutes, temporary accommodation was established in industrial areas where the refugee breadwinners could be housed and fed while the dependants were accommodated generally in old army areas. Fortunately, due to the wisdom of their leaders, the trade unions in no way resented this influx of new workers and employment presented no problem.

Then came the new phase of assisted migration from the United Kingdom and the free European countries where by intergovernmental agreements adult migrants could travel to Australia for ten pounds and those under eighteen free. The response was immediate but again the problem of accommodation arose. The refugee hostels, which were rapidly emptying as self-found accommodation became available, had been designed only as temporary transit housing and it had been intended to establish better and more permanent hostels. There was a coal strike, however, with all its impact on industry, and, as National Service had been introduced, what building material was available had to be directed to the accommodation of national trainees. Either the existing hostels had to be improved or migration reduced. While many of the migrants coming under the new scheme had friends or relatives to provide accommodation on arrival, at least half of them had no such facilities. If these had been refused, Australia would not be in the happy position it is now. The hostels were improved and more amenities provided but still with the policy that other accommodation was expected to be found as soon as possible. Usually most of the European migrants had left the hostels within six months, while for various reasons those from the United Kingdom lingered longer.

Shelter, food and employment had been provided but this was not all. While a government is the only body that can move millions of migrants, no government can assure the success of this movement. It is not a question of assimilation as is so often thought, absorbing and making all alike; if every newcomer to our country became like ourselves we would gain nothing—nothing but numbers—and numbers alone never made a country great. Migration made Great Britain great in her day. Among the primitive people of those islands centuries ago came the Romans, the Saxons, the Norse and the Danes, conquering, ravishing, and while many departed, some remained. They brought arts and crafts, a fine physique, courage and a spirit of adventure, and not only weapons but words that became woven into the loom of the old English language. Later came the Norman infusion and so by slow integration grew the Englishman and his language, both end-products of immigration.

Consider a lump of cast-iron: heavy, hard, brittle and rusting. Integrate some carbon and we have steel, pliant and strong; integrate a trace of cobalt and we have stainless steel—and so with wise immigration and integration, not assimilation, we develop and advance a community.

This cannot be brought about by any government and, realizing this, our Federal Government wisely called together representatives of the various voluntary bodies whose aims and objects included assistance to newcomers. From this meeting there were formed in each of the States councils composed of these representatives and soon all became known as Good Neighbour Councils. Each had a permanent secretary and a small administrative staff financed by the Department of Immigration and an elected honorary executive under an honorary president. These voluntary bodies undertook to be good neighbours to the newcomers from their arrival, providing various services and by personal contact solving as many as possible of their personal problems, including their bewilderment and their loneliness.

A deal of publicity has been given to the number of migrants who return to their homeland and statistics have claimed that

these number about 6 per cent of those who come to Australia—a rate similar to that in Canada. But statistics need to be carefully analysed to be reliable. Migrants return to their homeland for three broad reasons:
1. they are lonely;
2. there is some temporary or permanent personal or domestic demand for the presence in their homeland;
3. having arrived here for £10, they are prepared to remain for the required two years and then return as they had originally intended.

The quoted returnee rate covers all three.

I made a survey of 25,000 British migrants who had returned home; of these nearly 19,000 had paid their own fares and come back to Australia. This fact is seldom quoted.

My association with the Good Neighbour Council in Victoria involved visits to our centres throughout the State, attendance at naturalization ceremonies, the State Conference of our branches and committees each year, and the Annual Convention at Canberra when various papers were presented and constructive recommendations forwarded to the Minister concerning the advancement of the continuing successful migration policy. It was a most interesting experience and brought me into close association with a wide range of people.

Chapter 24 Migration and Higher Education

The flow of British and European migrants has continued, although with the increasing prosperity of Europe, at a lower rate. There was no question as to the worth of this movement to Australia. The first obvious impact was the greatly increased labour force, then the widening variety of breads, cheeses, sausages and other items in the shops, and later the traditional arts and crafts and other cultures of the migrants became apparent. They brought also something that so far has been denied to Australia, national suffering and survival. Among individuals in Australia there has been great suffering, but we have been spared those years of national restrictions, fears and tragedies that Europe has faced twice in our lifetime, or the threat and the realities of invasion, conquest and suppression over the centuries. If suffering can be survived, something robust is forged that can be found in no other way.

We have gained people with these qualities but in our modern scientific and technical age there is a growing demand for more than toughness, bodies and brawn. We need also brains and trained minds, those with the know-how and the ability to pass this on to others, and there is a growing demand for tertiary education. Unfortunately our universities and centres of higher education had failed to keep step with the increasing professional, scientific, industrial and commercial demands.

Soon after World War II, however, there was an awakening to this position and the field of higher education began slowly to expand—but far too slowly. The Minister for Immigration, Mr (later Sir Alec) Downer and Sir Tasman Heyes, the splendid permanent head of his Department, were keenly concerned in this problem and my association with the Good Neighbour Council led to one of the most interesting commissions I have undertaken. Early in 1961 I was summoned to a conference in Canberra with Mr Downer and Sir Tasman and asked if I would be prepared to visit the universities and centres of higher education in Great Britain and on the Continent and there present the opportunities and implications of practising the various professions in Australia.

This was an exciting and attractive challenge, but I asked for a few days to consider it. I determined that before I gave a decision this mission would have to be acceptable to the various Vice-Chancellors and that such acceptance was to be sought by the Australian High Commissioner in London and not by some junior departmental officer. The Minister agreed with this and signalled accordingly to Australia House. I was offered a salary that would just cover what I would have to relinquish in Australia, sea travel for my wife and myself to London and return and my own travelling expenses while on duty abroad.

Anticipating a favourable reply from the United Kingdom, I set out to prepare a brochure embracing the conditions and prospects of practising the various professions in Australia, together with the financial, cultural, domestic, scholastic and recreational situations to be faced here. Leading members of the professions were most helpful, as were certain professional people who had migrated to Australia since the war. With this information, I was able to compile a fairly comprehensive booklet that answered the likely questions.

When a unanimous welcome from the universities was assured, I gratefully accepted this mission.

On 25 March 1961 we sailed on the *Fairsky*, a converted wartime aeroplane transport chartered from the Sitmar line of Italy to bring migrants to Australia and return with one-class passengers. We were most comfortable in a suite under the bridge, alongside the captain's dining saloon. Captain George Petrescu, in command of the ship (and he did command it) was a well-known and most popular captain, a little over five feet tall with massive shoulders and torso. He was a delightful character with a great fund of general geographical and nautical information and a master of English and many other languages. He hoped eventually to retire to his cattle ranch in the Argentine, which during his absence at sea was conducted by his mother. Unfortunately George was not to realize his vision as he died with his sea boots on a few years later.

Along with our four very congenial neighbours on the same deck we breakfasted alone, but at lunch and dinner the captain, his senior officers and the two Italian doctors joined with us in one jolly family over excellent food and wine. Our steward was a quaint soul, a short, thin Italian dressed in tight black trousers, a broad black cummerbund and a white shirt. Otto spoke and understood just enough English for us to get along—his one blemish was a fearfully crossed right eye with which we never quite became acquainted. His service was excellent except that he could not make a cup of tea. First thing each morning he would knock on the door, come in and say: 'Morning, Momma, morning, Sir', and put down a lukewarm pot with a few tea-leaves floating on the top. He was such a pathetic figure and so kindly and attentive that we did not like to tell him.

Nothing quite replaces the deck of a ship, and with the ship excellently commanded and at all times spotlessly clean, and with every member of the ship's company apparently happy, it was a delightful voyage.

We sailed north up the east coast of Australia, discharging the last of our migrants at Sydney and Brisbane, by which time the ship was filled with passengers for England. This route was new to us and as the weather held the passage through the Barrier Reef was fair. The ship was air-conditioned and there was no discomfort as we turned westward through the Torres Strait into the Arafura Sea. North of Cape York little islands reached out from the mainland like lingering fingers reluctant to say goodbye. The seas north of Australia were studded with islands, the visible remains of the land bridge which once bound us to Asia. Some rose stark and sheer from the sea, others with dense tropical foliage and small native fishing villages clustered along the bright ribbon fringe of sand leading down to the clear turquoise blue of the shoals over the coral. As the ship sailed close to many of these gems, the occasional outrigger canoe of the fishermen cruised in the lagoons.

Colombo had changed over the years. Before World War I there had been a sparkle about the place, the first port of call on the mailboat route from Australia, the only disturbing note being the almost universal pock-marked face of each individual. I wonder how much longer we in Australia will be spared smallpox, cholera and plague, now that those countries where these diseases are endemic are (with air travel) only a few hours away.

When we called at Colombo during the war after our escape from Java there was still an air of busyness about the place with all the naval and military activities. Since then a dampness seemed to have descended and it was pathetic to see so many weary old women with despair printed on their faces and in their movements as they worked in the streets: even the inevitable beggars seemed to have lost heart. We drove out through the Cinnamon Gardens with frangipani and hibiscus in bloom, stopping only for Dorothy to be entertained (?) by an itinerant snake charmer with his flute while the cobra rose and swayed from the basket. The zoo was a paradise of tropical flowers and shrubs with bright flashes of the blue and yellow macaws as they quizzed us from their strong cages. We had intended to lunch at Mt Lavinia but the hotel was crowded so we drove back to the Galle face. It had been said that if one waited long enough at Shepheard's in Cairo, the Galle face in Colombo or Raffles in Singapore, sooner or later one would see all the V.I.P.'s of the world. As we moved up the steps into the large half-empty dining room we realized that this once-famous hotel shared in the general air of dejection, as if an old champion were prepared to lie down without a struggle.

As we sailed past the desolate coast of Somaliland we had a warning of the welcome from Aden. Was there ever a more uninviting port? The great sombre bare rocks rising suddenly behind the ribbon of habitation along the shore where no vegetation was visible. In the days of coal Aden was of importance and before the age of air Gibraltar and Aden commanded the entrances to the Mediterranean. With the coming of oil and the mastery of the air, Aden means little beyond the showing of the flag, a small garrison centre to keep an eye on the hinterland and a duty-free port for shopping.

A car was waiting for us at Suez and as Dorothy had never been to Cairo, the few hours drive across the desert would have been of interest were it not for 'Gyppo' tummy, a vile Eastern disability that humiliates and strikes suddenly like a snake. We just made it and with the kindly care of the people at the shipping office, assisted by a stiff noggin of brandy and a large dose of enterovioform, our small party was soon more or less on its feet again. Cairo had changed since my first visit more than forty years before; in World War I Australians were apparently welcome, during World War II were tolerated, but in 1961 we were obviously resented.

During World War I Cairo was centred on the Square of Mohammed Ali, whose equestrian statue stood in the gardens, the Cairo Opera House dominated one side, across were Shepheard's and the Continental Hotel . . . this was the heart of Cairo. In 1961 the Square of Liberation by the Nile commanded the city. Gone were the old Kasa el Nil Barracks, replaced by the vast Nile Hilton Hotel overlooking the river with the heavily laden fellucas slowly moving downstream; the Cairo Museum stood at one side, Government buildings on another.

For the first time I saw the Tut-Ankh-Amen splendours of gold, turquoise and lapis lazuli, the exquisite craftsmanship of chariots and furniture encrusted with gold and precious stones. There were two floors of these treasures.

After lunch at the Hilton we drove out to the pyramids. The same old pests, the guides, the sellers of 'antikers' and blue mummy beads, of 'naringis', of coloured hard-boiled eggs, the same scraggy little donkeys and supercilious camels, but to Dorothy all was new and exciting as it had once been to me. The one joy was tea on the verandah at Mena House where during World War I I had had my appendix removed.

We had arranged to travel overland from Naples so that I could have a few days in London before commencing my first tour of the universities, which had been arranged for a little more than a week ahead. We passed through the Straits of Messina soon after dawn on our last day at sea with Stromboli smouldering in its sullenness beyond. The Mediterranean put on its loveliest blue as we sailed close to Capri with the deep shadows of the dark jagged cliffs and the grottoes giving way to the bright sunshine on the villas clinging to the high slopes above. On such a day the Bay of Naples with the gleaming white and cream of the city at the foot of the blue Vesuvius beyond was very beautiful.

As our Roman express did not leave till one p.m., we drove

out through the orchards and vegetable gardens that lined the autostrad to Pompeii. Outside the entrance of this city of the dead there was a cameo factory and it was fascinating to watch the craftsmen and women carving the flat Mediterranean shells, leaving the thin white outer coating and cutting down delicately to the pink or brown beneath, leaving all manner of intricate designs in white relief. In Pompeii the size and the preservation of the city were surprising. When the eruption occurred about 79 A.D. the sudden flood of pumice overwhelmed the city and its thousands of people. Later the excavations revealed the houses, the streets, the statuary and the encrusted bodies, many still in attitudes of centuries ago. Down the streets ran the ruts of the chariots and the carts and in certain of the houses murals preserved their original colours.

Our train ran swiftly and smoothly through the intensely cultivated irrigated country around the foothills of the Apennines and we arrived in Rome, a hundred and eighty miles, in two and a half hours. We were met by Dr Brozoli of the shipping company and his wife, who drove us to our Savoya Hotel. It was spring and as we strolled along the streets the beds of bright azaleas, the window-boxes and the hanging baskets above the doors were a constant delight.

We drove to the Colosseum and paused at the series of mosaics on the old Roman wall where in white on a black marble background was displayed the expansion of the Roman Empire. The first a small white settlement about the Tiber, then the expansion over the whole of Italy and into Greece, the third marked the movement east and southward through the Levant, Egypt and most of the northern coast of Africa and westward over Spain and France, and finally, the zenith of this vast empire, to enclose the whole of the Mediterranean and Britain.

The Colosseum beyond was an arresting sight. If anyone doubts that civilization has advanced let him stand in the arena and look up at the Emperor's royal box, the front row for the Consuls, the Senators and the citizens and the rising tiers above to seat the lower grades of Roman society. There eighty thousand people would be entertained by the slaughter of elephants, hippopotami and lions, would praise or condemn the gladiators and hiss the Christians as they were torn by the lions in this colossus of cruelty.

On one side of the Piazza Venezia stood the grim dark building where from a high balconied window Mussolini would harangue, gesticulate and clench his ugly jaws before the clamorous crowd below. But this was insignificant beside the stark white marble memorial to Victor Emmanuel, looking down on the Piazza. This extravagant mass, like the icing on a vast ostentatious wedding cake and described by someone as the greatest overstatement ever made, looked to me like an army of snowmen marching as to war.

We drove to the Spanish Steps aglow with pink and white azaleas; certainly a Spaniard designed this magnificent flight, but as they led up to a French church and the National Academy of France and the money came from France, if these lovely steps were entitled to a national name it surely should be French, but such beauty is international. The British people also are concerned as the dark brown house where Keats died stands at the foot on the right. I suppose no church in the world has been flashed on the screen or printed in pictures more than the scene from the Piazza of St Peter's in Rome, but none of these can approach the impression that lingers after standing before the obelisk, the oldest monument in the piazza in the centre of Bernini's circle of columns surmounted by his statues. Such is the perfection of each radiation of columns that, turning round 360°, each row of three columns appears only as one.

When we entered the church its vastness was not at first realized, so perfect were the proportions, but my wife and I immediately sensed a unique spiritual experience. It was worth coming half-way round the world to stand before Michelangelo's Pietà. There was no awareness of marble, the limpness of Christ's body with the complete surrender of the lifeless limbs, the unspeakable sorrow in the bowed head of the Madonna as she looked down at her dead son were unforgettable. Almost hidden on her girdle was the only signature Michelangelo ever left to posterity. Pietà and the dome of St Peter's, which Michelangelo designed and supervised till he died, spanned more than sixty years in the life of this master.

As we came down the steps we passed the Swiss Guards at the entry to the Vatican, in their slashed blue, yellow and red uniforms, holding their halberds erect. After a victorious battle in the fifteenth century, the Swiss soldiers ripped down the silk pavilions of the vanquished and patched their torn clothes. At first jeered at, this slashing with bright colours became the fashion at the time when Raphael or Michelangelo designed the Swiss uniform.

There was just time to drive to the Janiculum, the hill to the west of the Tiber, crowned by the proud statue of Garibaldi on one of the hundreds of horses in bronze or marble throughout Rome. From the hill above the Spanish Steps with its old water-clock, the view over Rome in the clear sunshine was magnificent.

It had been an unforgettable morning but we were glad to relax over a late lunch on the train as we rushed through the vineyards and fields across the Etruscan Alps and into the luscious green of the Lombardy plains. We climbed past Lake Maggiore in the moonlight, slept through the Alps and across Switzerland, to wake soon after dawn in France with the tree-lined canals and streams.

At the Gare de Lyon we crossed on to the Flèche d'Or. We had arrived in Paris during the Algerian crisis, the time-honoured barricades were being erected in the streets and all transport was crammed. At the Gare du Nord, the platform was crowded with people leaving Paris and I carefully noted the position of our carriage before I went along to the kiosk to buy a morning paper. When I returned through the jostling, gesticulating, excited and noisy crowd, our carriage was no longer where I had left it (extra carriages having been put on to cope with the refugees), and only as the train began to move did I find my anxious wife.

It was a clear sunny afternoon when we drew in to the wharf at Calais, with the English coast clearly visible across the Channel, but it was almost dusk when we landed at Dover. Even in the fading light the bluebells and primroses clinging to the cuttings, the young green of the oaks and the elms and the silver birches in the woods were a kindly welcome as the train sped on to London.

Driving across London I had my first surprise—on my previous visits I had always appreciated the smoothness of the London streets but suddenly our driver began to bob up and down at intervals. The car seemed to be riding smoothly but up and down he bobbed. At last I realized that the poor man had hiccups and needed only a little white powder.

Good Peter Pepper had arranged a flat for us at William Goodenough House in Mecklenburgh Square across Coram Park and in this comfort we did not need any rocking after we had crawled into our beds.

Chapter 25 London Revisited and British Universities

From our flat it was a pleasant half hour's stroll to the Strand and at the time I recorded this mile of history: 'Someone once said "if you would learn the history of the British people—know London", and there is no phase of history, legal, martial, cultural or commercial, that has not been touched by this great city. But could anyone really know London?'

Roman Londinium was a walled town extending for little more than two miles along the north bank of the river Amesis and inland for barely half a mile. The south-east portion of this wall still remains within the Tower of London built by the Normans centuries after the Roman occupation.

By Shakespeare's time the city had struggled for a few yards over on the southern bank and westward a mile or so to Westminster. Now Greater London sprawls over a vast area of more than five hundred square miles within which is written—if we care to read it—the story over the last two thousand years of what we now call the British people.

Let us walk for half an hour over this history. We will set off from where Mecklenburgh Street begins near Gray's Inn Road. Within a few yards—suddenly, as if snobbishly ashamed of its humble title—the Street becomes a Square, Mecklenburgh Square, facing the first practical gesture of humane social service in England. Here Captain Thomas Coram, R.N., established his Foundling Hospital more than two hundreds years ago at a time when infants in their hundreds were abandoned and exposed each year in the London streets. If Hogarth's portrait is true, Coram was a stern but kindly man and he must have possessed no end of courage and tenacity. He had the help of his great friend Handel, whose musical memories linger in the Coram Museum nearby. No trace of the hospital survives here, but in Coram Fields the happy play of children keeps alive the kindly spirit of a great man. Flanking the Fields are London House and William Goodenough House, known with kindness throughout the British Commonwealth as Residential Halls for Overseas Graduates.

A few paces along Macklenburgh Square and, such is the whimsy of London that, with no change of direction we are in Doughty Street, with its rows of stately Georgian houses side by side in all their dignity. On the wall of Number 48 on the north side is a blue plaque where Charles Dickens lived more than a hundred years ago and inside this house are treasures of his personality. Across the street at Number 14 is a brown plaque marking the house of Sydney Smith—'The Smith of Smiths'—that remarkable combination of Holy Orders and ready wit, fifty years before Dickens's time. (It might be mentioned that the underlying principle in the numbering of London streets is a carefully guarded top secret.)

Again with no warning or reason this street—less than half a mile long—suddenly changes its name for the third time to John Street. Some streets in London after travelling along under a series of aliases will turn at right angles and retain the same name; it is all rather fun but somewhat bewildering to the uninitiated. But John Street is honest about it and ends abruptly in Theobald's Road (Tibbels to the Londoner) which runs across it and led in days gone by to one of King James the First's hunting grounds at Theobald's in Hertfordshire.

Across Theobald's Road gleam the gracious trees and lawns of Gray's Inn Gardens. Here walked Francis Bacon as a student and later as Treasurer. In these gardens is a carefully guarded tree—almost grotesque in its contortions, a Catalpa tree said to have been planted by him. Here strolled Raleigh, and here Pepys quizzed the ladies of fashion. In the chambers along the South Wall, Dickens served as a clerk and gathered the legal profiles for his novels.

Turn left beyond the Gardens—down a little covered alleyway and we are in the stream of High Holborn traffic. Holebourne was an arm of the foul Fleet River, before it was converted into a sewer early in the eighteenth century. Safely across, we turn down the gentle curve of Chancery Lane. Don't let us dwell upon the lovely display of old silver in the Gallery on the right but turn through the gates, centuries old, of Lincoln's Inn. Pause for a while in the quiet of the cloisters and the stone vaulted ceiling beneath the Old Hall built in the fifth year of the reign of Henry VII where judgments were passed before the Law Courts were built. None of your modern London chimney-pots here—instead the tall graceful turning and twisting dull bricks that marked the Tudor period. Pass on by the chapel and along the path between smooth lawns bordered by masses of delphiniums and peonies nestling against the mellow walls of the Library and the Dining Hall and so through the new southern gate into the glory of Lincoln's Inn Fields with the finest of London's fine plane trees. Round and robust in their boles they are kindly in the towering spread of their shading leaves. These fields were laid out by Inigo Jones more than three hundred and fifty years ago to obliterate an area of ill repute. Here the conspirators for Mary Queen of Scots were beheaded and later Lord Russell. In the age of duelling, the Fields were a rendezvous for those who demanded satisfaction.

Along the east side austere columns lead to the Royal College of Surgeons of England—which moved here about 1835 from the Old Bailey. In this college is enshrined the history of Henry VIII and the Barbers. If we had time to cross to the other side we would soon find ourselves in Red Lion Square with William Morris and the Pre-Raphaelite Brotherhood. In the ugly domestic heaviness of the mid-Victorian age, Morris would not be denied that useful things could be beautiful; indeed there is a revival of William Morris wallpaper at present in England. Here also lived John Harrison who devised the marine chronometer more than two hundred years ago. Just beyond the Royal College, to the left down narrow Portsmouth Street, there is a picture known to half the world: 'The Old Curiosity Shop.' Overawed by surrounding modern intruders, this little gem, after more than three hundred years, looks as if at any moment it will quietly give up the struggle and slide down gently into the curving street around its feet. But we could not bear witness to such a calamity—so we press on to the right and in a moment we are in the dignity of Kingsway.

Kingsway is a newcomer to London. By boldly cutting through the dark squalid area between Holborn and the Strand and around Drury Lane, a magnificent hundred-feet thoroughfare was established and opened by King Edward VII in 1905. Kingsway ends in its twin brother Aldwych with its Saxon name. The graceful sweeping curve around an island in the Strand was constructed at the same time as Kingsway and by their combined contributions London had further ready access to the south.

Down Kingsway into Aldwych, commanded by Bush House—standing as if to take a vast salute—and we turn along the left sweep as we are bound for Australia House, set on the east end of the island. There facing us is the dignity of Wren and Gibbs—St Clement Dane—reminding us that about here centuries ago came some of the marauding people from the North Sea. The church was badly bombed in the blitz but has now been restored and serves as the Memorial Chapel of the Royal Air Force. Recently was revived the charming ceremony of 'Oranges and Lemons' that the Bells of St Clement's sang to us years ago as children.

We have been barely a mile but we have walked with hundreds of years of history, and are as yet not really within the City of London where barely five thousand people live (but half a million move in and out every weekday). The City awaits another walk: past the Law Courts and down the curve of Fleet Street, dominated by the vast dome of St Paul's high above the hill where King Lud's gate pierced the western wall of Londinium nearly two thousand years ago.

The High Commissioner was away when I arrived at London House and when I called upon his Deputy he did not seem interested in my mission, nor at any time during our tour did either make any enquiry as to its progress. This was before the coming of Sir Alec Downer as High Commissioner with his personal knowledge of English universities and his wide experience of Australia; the Immigration officials, however, were always helpful.

On my previous visits to London I had been in Australia House only to make official calls and do my banking. Now for some months I was to find myself a small cog in this strange machine—the only co-ordinating influence being the tyrannical Treasury, with the same mistrustful attitude that I had experienced in the Army.

Quite a number of the staff were from the United Kingdom with little if any personal knowledge of Australia. In certain Departments this may not have been a disadvantage but in a service to prospective migrants it certainly was. One morning I was standing near the Immigration counter and overheard a man enquiring about his prospects in Australia. Evidently he had had considerable experience in forestry throughout England and was considering trying his luck in Australia, until to my astonishment I heard the man behind the counter, who I presumed had never been there, give him little encouragement.

I went to the book counter and asked if there were any books available on Australian universities. 'Yes,' the attendant said, 'we have two: *If the Gown Fits* and a compendium on the Orr case.' The former was an account of an unhappy high official who had resigned from the Adelaide University, the latter an account of an alleged unsavoury episode in the Tasmanian University. When I enquired about films the answer was: 'Yes, we have six on Australian universities.' After one unfortunate experience I had determined not to show any film until I had seen it. Four of these films, I found, were out of date and devoted to the National University at Canberra, the remaining two were of the other universities throughout Australia as they were some years before. I did not use the films!

Another feature of Australia House that seemed strange was that within a short distance of Covent Garden Market the only floral decorations to meet those coming into the spacious ground floor were clumps of well arranged and very expensive artificial flowers.

There was available to each final year undergraduate in the United Kingdom a handbook covering details of professional opportunities and a similar production concerning the opportunities in Canada. The authorities in Australia House had been approached as to a handbook with similar information covering Australia, but, so I was informed, the suggestion was rejected. I sent for the correspondence and this was confirmed. It was surprising how little some highly placed Government officials knew about a university. One asked me to delete the term 'tertiary education' from the brochure I had prepared. 'People would not know what this meant,' he said; obviously *he* did not.

I discovered that each year some hundreds of final year graduates from the United Kingdom were flown to Canada during their final long vacation at an approximate cost of £60 return. By this experience they were able to gain a first-hand appreciation of the country and the professional opportunities. It was said that a significant number settled in Canada after graduation, but this was unknown at Australia House where unfortunately at that time no one concerned with the academic world had been posted.

Even in the early sixties many spoke of England *and* the Commonwealth and some even still referred to the Australian 'colonies'. In 1965 the Minister of Health in the British Government, addressing a gathering of young medical graduates, is reported to have deplored 'the migration of British doctors to places like the United States, Canada and New Zealand' with no reference to Australia where more than a hundred British doctors settle each year—more than migrate to all the other countries combined.

On several occasions reference was made in the press, on the radio and TV to the number of British migrants returning from Australia disgruntled and disillusioned. The fact that the majority of these 'disgruntled and disillusioned' paid their full fare and went back to settle in Australia again was never given publicity. Knowing the true facts I approached the Public Relations Department at Australia House seeking the opportunity to present the true situation through these various media, but they were unable or unwilling to obtain this for me. By other means, however, this was later arranged. In spite of our various trade delegations abroad, few of our products were known and our exported foods difficult to find. When we asked for Australian meat or butter, most of the shops expressed surprise. There was a wine shop in Frith Street near Covent Garden that stocked only Australian wines and spirits and the prices were comparable with those of many good continental wines.

To the British people generally our cricket, our servicemen and women, our tennis and our golf had determined our existence on the map more efficiently than our cultural, educational, scientific or industrial achievements. This, then, was the background from which we moved into the academic world of Great Britain.

With the exception of our visit to Northern Ireland we travelled to the universities throughout the United Kingdom by train, but whenever it was possible during the weekends, which were generally our only free time, we drove into the country with Miss Thelma Jarrett on her lecturing tours on behalf of the Good Neighbour Council. One of the problems is to get out of London and the main roads are unpleasantly crowded especially during weekends. The minor roads pass quietly through the lovely countryside and the charming little villages in the vales. Often these roads are sunken between tall hedges and little can be seen beyond the nearby trees, delights in themselves. How the rotund Gilbert Chesterton enshrined the roving English roads in his 'Flying Inn':

'Before the Roman came to Rye or out to Severn strode,
The rolling English drunkard made the rolling English road.
A reeling road, a rolling road, that rambles round the shire,
An' after him the parson ran, the sexton and the squire;
A merry road, a mazy road, such as we did tread
The night we went to Birmingham by way of Beachy Head.'

The classification of English roads seems based on width, the sealed surfaces were uniformly good extending right to the edges. Some are certainly narrow, declining to the one-way hay lanes where it is impossible to pass another vehicle or to turn until one comes to a cross lane or a gate.

There is a story told of some tourists driving quietly down the little by-ways of southern England and uncertain of their direction stopped to enquire of a hedger and ditcher the way to a village they were seeking. Like many old countrymen with a parochially confined knowledge, he couldn't help them and they turned down a little side lane hoping it would lead them in the right direction. After a few hundred yards the driver noticed in his mirror that the old man was beckoning to them. There was no room to turn so he backed slowly up the hill to find another man standing beside the non-informative hedger. 'This be brother Jarge. He don't know neither.'

With a fairly tight schedule, punctuality of arrival and departure was essential and this was ensured by the excellent British railways. The rails run on higher contours, giving a wider view of the ever-changing countryside and an awareness of passing from county to county by the subtle changes in the stone dwellings and the orderliness of the fields, the hedgerows and the haystacks.

As the universities' long vacations came during our visit, it was necessary to divide our activities and an early itinerary had been arranged agreeable to one group of universities.

Our first call was upon the Vice-Chancellors, who usually arranged a lunch or a dinner for us to meet the senior members of the staff and their ladies. A general presentation of our problem was invited and discussion followed. I explained that I fully appreciated their problems, each provincial university expanding and with four or five new ones building I did not wish to add to their burdens. As a certain number of graduates from the United Kingdom, however, travelled to other countries either for experience or to settle, we hoped that Australia would be considered. Brochures were left with each appointment officer.

It was disturbing that in so many of the universities and colleges there was little knowledge, thought and, at times, interest in Australia. After I had addressed them, many students said to me: 'Why were we not told these things in school? We have thought of Australia as a rather primitive country, far away at the other side of the world.' When I explained that miles had lost their meaning and that Australia was hours, not even days, away from England in modern times, they were thoughtful.

Some of the Vice-Chancellors and deans had visited Australia and generally they were enthusiastic about their experiences, realizing that their opposite numbers in Australia were alongside them.

Later the individual deans were interviewed in more detail and time was spent with the appointment board officers. When invited by the Staff, I addressed the students in groups or interviewed individually those who had expressed an interest in Australia. My wife accompanied me on all these visits and as many of the questions were of a domestic nature her presence was most valuable.

Our first tour covered Sheffield, Liverpool, Manchester, Keele, the University of Wales, with Colleges at Cardiff, Swansea and Aberystwyth, Nottingham and Reading. All were busy with expanding construction, but our welcome was always generous.

At Sheffield I had an odd request. The Professor of Biology asked if I could send him some live baby crocodiles from Australia. He was doing research on the evolution of the eye and believed there was some information he could find in them. I said I would certainly see what I could do but had no idea how I would go about it. The sequel is interesting. When we returned to Australia, I found that my cousin, John Wellington, an agricultural science and a veterinary science graduate, was working at the University of Queensland. I put this problem to him. A year later I heard that he had begun a regular shipment of these tiny reptiles to Sheffield.

The Dixon works have a long and honoured name for cutlery and silverware and among the dignitaries of Sheffield the 'Master Cutler' stands high, but it was strange to see the crude conditions under which the old craftsmen were working among abrasives and polishers.

We met more than a hundred Australian graduates holding high academic appointments among these universities. Some seemed rather disgruntled at their lack of advancement in Australia, others were frank in why they preferred to serve in Britain. It was not a question of salaries, which were generally higher in Australia, and anyway a dedicated academic, free of financial worry, seeks satisfaction in achievement. They resented association with universities having the high failure rate of ours, where there were many extra-departmental commitments, where research facilities were cramped, where there were fewer opportunities for close contact with colleagues of their respective faculties in other universities and where outside influences bear on university policy and activities.

I was not able to question the validity of their views but it was disturbing to find so many of this mind. Fortunately there has been an improvement in this situation, and with the expansion of our universities more of our graduates have found suitable academic opportunities.

The University College of North Staffordshire, set in the beautiful estate of Keele Hall, was the smallest of the recently established institutions and at that time had not been completed. It was interesting to find the innovation of a compulsory extra first year identical for all students. This experiment, later to be adopted by at least one of the other universities, was being critically followed in the academic world. Some viewed this with sympathy, others with condemnation, believing that the lengthening of the courses would prove a financial embarrassment to many students, the majority of whom in all the universities, including Oxford and Cambridge, were financially assisted either wholly or in part during their course. It was refreshing, however, to know that there was an innovation in a system of education which at that time still clung to the 'eleven and a half plus', a universal examination at this immature age which largely determined the future education of the youth of England.

Probably because my maternal forebears, Ffoulkes, were Welsh, I have always felt at home among the kindly people of Wales, but had not before appreciated the extent of bilingualism. We had just returned from a blow on the Mumbles with the fragrance of the gorse glowing on the cliffs and were having tea with the principal of Swansea University College. Two of his young children ran out on to the road. Their mother called to them in English but only when she repeated this in Welsh did they heed her.

Except for its lace, Nottingham is just another provincial city, but the University was a surprise, generously endowed by Boots, the Chemist. The grey granite buildings stood among noble oaks and elms on high ground sloping gently to the lake below, with a sense of space and inviting calm.

As our train drew into Reading, we passed the grim, dull brick gaol with the pathetic picture of Oscar Wilde:

> 'The vilest deeds like poison weeds
> Bloom well in prison air.
> It is only what is good in man
> That wastes and withers there.
>
> 'For he who lives more lives than one
> More deaths than one must die.'

Among the interesting features of the University of Reading were the museums, one devoted to Greek and Roman relics, the other displaying agricultural and animal husbandry, folk-lore and implements in England over the centuries.

We began our visits to the various colleges and institutions of the vast London University, dispersed over London and into the Home Counties and administered from the tall building that towers over Bloomsbury. One of the most delightful of these was the Agricultural College at Wye in Kent under the direction of the dynamic principal, Mr Skilbeck. From my quaint bedroom upstairs I looked down on a charming old flintstone church with the mossy and lichened headstones standing or leaning in the vivid green churchyard. At dinner that night the Principal pronounced grace:

> 'God be praised for all His mercies
> God preserve the Queen and the Realm
> And this our free and learned Society
> And grant us His grace all the days of our life.'

After Hall the students were gathered together and we had a couple of hours to and fro talk about Australia. It was a grand night.

Chapter 26 Europe and
European Universities

It had been arranged for us to visit Europe and as well as pursuing our academic mission to visit our various immigration centres on the Continent.

It was vacation time on the Continent and I was not able to address the students. I had forgotten most of my German and my French apparently was not 'comme il faut'. When I spoke to a gendarme in Paris, he smiled at me and said in English: 'Monsieur is American, yes?' I was able, however, to meet certain of the university authorities and the problems concerning European graduates coming to Australia seemed common to all. While graduates of European universities generally travelled for post-graduate study and experience, they moved to other European countries, the U.K. or the U.S.A.; Australia apparently was never considered and with few exceptions there seemed little knowledge or interest concerning our professional standards or achievements. Another problem was the limited reciprocal recognition of our respective graduate qualifications. The university courses in many European faculties were generally dissimilar from ours in duration and in curricula. Many of the European courses are more didactic than ours, others more practical, but there are, of course, many highly qualified scientists and engineers in Europe, Some of these, particularly European medical graduates, told me that they would have liked to migrate to Australia but were under the impression that their qualifications would not be recognized.

It was interesting to visit the immigration centres, especially in the obviously prosperous countries of Holland and Germany. When I questioned applicants in these centres as to why they still wished to travel to Australia while they were importing labour from

Spain and Italy, there was generally one answer: 'Our children. We are doing very well at present but we are not sure about the future for our children, and the letters we receive from our relatives and friends in Australia all speak of the wonderful opportunities for youth in your country.'

Discrimination among people is encountered in all countries based on caste, titles, wealth, occupation or the 'old school tie'. In Australia, a new nation, while there is the inevitable small element of snobbery and social striving, the basic discrimination among our people is based on behaviour, ability and industry. Provided one behaves oneself, accepts the educational facilities available to all and works hard, the sky is the limit and one is accepted practically everywhere with respect.

We crossed at night from Harwich to the Hook, where we found the station crowded with English boy scouts. Half of them were in wheelchairs but each chair had its healthy scout attendant giving his less fortunate comrade a few days abroad. It was good to be welcomed by Ted Waterman, the Migration Officer, who had served on Seven Division Headquarters during the war. After a few days at The Hague near our Migration Centre, we had a day in Amsterdam.

As we drove along, the barges with their gay cargoes of flowers were moving quietly along the canals to the unique flower market at Alsmeer. Through the night and the early morning the barges tied up under the vast roofs and unloaded their bundles and pots on to stands which were wheeled into the various divisions of the market. The tulips and other bulbs were over, but what with the sheafs of roses, carnations, lilies of every colour, tuberoses and pots of African violets, gloxinia and flowering cacti, the floors were fields of fragrance and colour.

At one end of this display was the auction room where behind the rostrum stood a large clockface with one hand and marked with a series of falling prices. Facing this rose semicircular tiers of seats for the bidders, each seat provided with a light switch. As soon as one lot had been presented, the clock hand was set slowly in motion from a high figure down through the lower prices. A reserve unknown to the bidders had been placed on each lot. When the clock hand began to move, a bidder's problem was to decide when to switch on his light and end the auction, at not too high a figure but before the unknown reserve was passed. This was an exciting Dutch Auction.

After our enjoyment at Alsmeer we drove on to Amsterdam with its miles of canals and hundreds of little bridges, familiar from Van Gogh's pictures. As we sailed quietly along the maze of waterways, our Vermeer prints came to life in the quaint dull red houses with their stepped Dutch roofs. Just under the ridge in front of these houses projected stout beams. So narrow were the front doors and winding stairs that any furniture for other than the ground floor had to be hoisted up outside and passed through the widely open shuttered windows.

After lunch we had some time for the Rijksmuseum—days and weeks could be spent without exhausting these treasures but even in our few hours we were able to realize the wealth and taste the feast of seventeenth century Dutch art. The Night Watch, recently refreshed and splendidly lit, held court in an alcove apart and the rollicking jollity of the Hals, the quiet charm of the Vermeers and the other great masters held us.

Our train to Denmark ran through Utrecht. (For some odd reason about the only date I remember from school is the Treaty of Utrecht, 1713, but I have forgotten who were the belligerents!) We ran across the flat fields of the lowlands relieved only by spires and windmills, then on the rising ground to the west we crossed the German border at Bentheim.

The countryside in Germany breathed prosperity with men and women toiling through the daylight in the waving wheat and among the cattle. As we passed slowly through Hamburg we saw no sign of war's tragedies: the wounds I had known a few years before had healed.

At Grossenbrode on the Baltic our train was divided into three sections, each in turn to be backed through the gaping stern of the ferry where each section, carriage by carriage, was fastened by chains to the rails. Many of the passengers remained in their seats during the crossing but we went up to the top deck for coffee and the cool wind of the twilight. It was dark when we reached Gedser in Denmark and had to go back to our carriage for the train to be reassembled and off to Copenhagen in a couple of hours.

Next morning from our hotel window we looked out over the harbour and the clean grey city with green copper roofs and twirling spires symbolizing the union of the mainland with the islands. As we drove to the Migration Centre we stopped to watch three toy soldiers in their tall bearskins, dark tunics crossed by two broad white belts and blue trousers, as, led by an N.C.O., they solemnly paraded across the cobbled square. It was the posting of the guard in the toy red and white sentry boxes at the entrance to the toy Royal Palace.

Unfortunately for us, migration from Denmark to Australia was slowing down and I received the same comments from the education authorities as I had in Holland and was later to hear in Germany.

It was difficult to drag ourselves away from the lovely pieces in the Royal Copenhagen Shop with only a few modest purchases, but our time had been fairy closely allotted. We were taken out on to the Harbour, busy with shipping but as the wind came from the fish market across the water I realized that Hamlet was on the ball: 'Something is rotten in the State of Denmark.' Just beyond a beautiful fountain we came to the exquisite bronze 'Mermaid on the Rock' rising from the sea—a memorial to Hans Andersen.

After the widespread destruction of the war there was a modern outlook concerning ecclesiastical architecture. Some of the new buildings seemed odd but the design, the clear cream stone and the soft lighting of Grünstead Church in Copenhagen were most attractive. A beautiful model of a ship with sails furled was suspended on one side of the long nave; the seafaring Danes sought Divine protection for their ships and their sailors at sea and these models were often found in the churches.

We were taken to dine at a large kursaal. At one end was a large raised stage, the tables were arranged on the floor and on a mezzanine around the sides; during dinner we were entertained by first-class turns on the stage, acrobats, jugglers, conjurers and dancers. One acrobatic turn was outstanding. A large, tall man like Hardy and a smaller, slight man like Laurel put on a series of remarkable tumbling acts. After a pause the big man stood upright facing the audience with his hands on his hips while from behind his partner, taking one extraordinary leap, landed erect on his shoulders. After terrific applause, they repeated it—this time with the little man leaping from in front—but a few seconds after he had again landed erect on the shoulders the big man seemed to subside and crumple until he lay on the ground and his partner stepped off to even greater applause. Then to the laughter of the diners the little man bent down to his prostrate partner, rolled him over and spoke to him; after a pause two attendants came over and dragged the big man off the stage by his legs. In spite of the clapping and calling there was no reappearance of the tumblers to take their bow and after a few minutes' uneasiness a man came from the wings and spoke into a microphone. Our host translated: 'They want a doctor.' But as no one came forward and our table was near some stairs leading down to the stage, it was suggested that I went down. In the wings I found a small group gathered around and the little man weeping over the dead body of his companion.

Tragedy and comedy are often face to face. It had happened before, some hundreds of people who had clapped and shouted themselves hoarse at what they thought had been a comic finale to a great act.

We took the ferry across to Malmo in Sweden. As we left the harbour we passed across the channel where Nelson had navigated in his bombardment of Copenhagen 150 years earlier and putting the telescope to his blind eye had declined to see his Admiral's signal recalling him from his dangerous position. It began to rain soon after we landed at Malmo and in the Square pigeons had settled about the large equestrian statue of Gustavus Adolphus. I wondered how that great king and general, who introduced many orderly innovations into European armies, would have reacted to pigeons perched on his horse's mane, on his hat and about his person: I was left wondering in the rain.

For once there was no one to meet us at Cologne and we had not been advised about our accommodation. After standing by our luggage for some time in the vast modern station, we spoke to a weary porter. My German is very limited and all my wife remembered was a very able recitation of the Lorelei, which in the early hours of the morning did not get us very far with the porter, who could not speak English. Eventually another aged porter came along and gave us to understand he could get us into a place quite near the station and when he picked up our luggage and started off we followed. When we reached his hotel, only two single rooms were available. We refused this isolation in an unknown hotel in a strange city. The porter said he would ring another place nearby. We were past caring as long as we could get to sleep. Yes, there was a room, he picked up our gear again and eventually we slumped into quite a good bed at four o'clock in the morning.

With the great prosperity of Germany there was practically no unemployment and with the importation of labour from southern Europe, the migration to Australia was slowing down, and there were only about half a dozen applicants in the office when I called. I was told that there were practically no applicants among the scientists and engineers in Germany, professions so essential to our national development. From the education authorities I found the same explanation as I had received in Holland.

From Cologne, after a big sweep round the city, our train ran into the beautiful valley of the Rhine, crossing the river at Bonn, now the capital of West Germany. Up and down the stream passed the busy little tugs with their long strings of low barges. In bright sunshine we ran along the foot of the terraced hills, crowned with old castles, while the vineyards marched in orderly rows down and across the slopes. At Mainz our line turned east into the valley of the Main through the fields and woods of Bavaria. War seemed remote from this peaceful area where women piled sheaves of corn against the wooden frames in the fields, pausing only to wave to the train. As day gave way to dusk timid deer came cautiously to the clearings in the sombre pines but as we came into Nuremberg the dusk deepened the grimness of the grey Spandau Prison beside the line, with its ineffaceable memories of the trial and execution of the Nazi war criminals, the one wrong note in the symphony of a lovely day.

The first grand opera I had attended was *The Meistersingers* and after dinner the floodlighting in the old city, the tall timbered houses with their glowing window-boxes and the statue of Hans Sachs were a romance come true.

Soon after leaving Nuremberg we came into the valley of the Danube. Seldom as steep as the Rhine slopes, this valley was as beautiful, with fir-clad hills and wide fields green with potatoes and turnips, jewelled here and there with blue wildflowers, occasional villages almost hidden in the deep valleys, grey or white churches and clumps of houses with steeply sloping red roofs.

We crossed into Austria at Passau where the Danube courses between rising hills with defiant, sturdy castles silhouetted against the moonlight as we ran on to Vienna.

Fortunately for the world Vienna was spared the devastation of the war. Nothing seemed new or even modern in that lovely city of squares and palaces, of columns and fountains. With the elaborate, intricate Gothic decoration carved in stone and in wood, there was a calm and gracious dignity. Although at that time Australia had no accredited representation in Austria and our diplomatic affairs were handled by the British representative, we maintained an Australian Immigration Centre in the heart of Vienna. There we met some of the Yuglosavs who were constantly trickling over the border before migrating to Australia, and generally they were fine physical specimens.

We drove out to the Schöenbrunn, the vast palace with its treasures and memories of Marie Louise, Napoleon and his only legitimate son, L'Aiglou, the King of Italy, who died there in his teens. Facing the colonnades of the palace were radiating avenues, drilled by tall firs like guardsmen at attention. The precise gardens led to the hill beyond, crowned by columns surrounding a massive marble fountain. It was all very formal with a courtly, old-world grace.

We returned through the Vienna Woods in time to take our seats in the private salon of the Hoffburg. We were in a spacious room, from a high ceiling glittered massive chandeliers, and vast historical tapestries covered the walls. The performance was *The Merry Widow*, which was first produced in this salon before the Emperor Franz-Josef, and one could well imagine that bewhiskered old gentleman in his gilded throne chuckling and nodding to the melodies. The artists were in modern evening dress and although we could not follow the language, with memories of Carrie Moore, Andrew Higginson, Florrie Young and Reginald Roberts in the Melbourne performance before World War I, it was a delightful and melodious evening and concluded with a late dinner at the Bulgarian Café nearby. Among the trees hung with fairy-lights swarthy stewards in their red and white national costume braised our chickens skewered on swords over an open fire.

On our way to the migrant centre next morning we looked in at the Spanish Riding School where the Hapsburg Greys were schooling as they had been over the past four centuries. The movements on the tan were less elaborate than those we had seen on the screen, but the complete harmony among horse, rider and music, the silent grace and precision of every revolution by these famous white horses were an enduring memory.

It was in August when we stepped from the plane in Athens and the heat hit us. Athens was one of our most active Immigration Centres, with a waiting list over the next few months. In a country such as Greece, where wealth is confined to a small minority, surrounded by a wide area of poverty, opportunities in Australia proved attractive and the rooms were crowded with applicants, many of them single girls and women for whom the dowry system determined their marital opportunities in Greece. The higher the male education and the university degree, the higher could be the dowry demanded. I spoke to one medical graduate who had no intention of practising his profession but with his university degree was good value and could expect a high dowry and marriage into one of the wealthy Greek shipowning families. Then he could, if he so wished, take any congenial position and live comfortably on father-in-law.

Beyond shipowning, there was little evidence of industry other than that pertaining to agriculture, fruits, olives, cotton and apiculture. Famous as Hymethus honey may be, I was told that bees were farmed mainly for their wax, in demand for ecclesiastical and other candles.

The heat was stifling and the air-conditioning in our hotel noisy, so we had few regrets that our itinerary allowed us only three days. Fortunately much of the glory that was Greece was centred in Athens about the Acropolis and in the archaeological museum with its rooms of treasures among which the superb Poseidon and his trident seemed supreme.

Early one morning with Admiral McNicol from Australia we drove to Delphi at first through rather dull, flat country, stopping only at the ancient temple of Daphne with its fine mosaics, but soon we were among magnificent mountains with small stone villages clinging to their steepness. In the valleys bloomed pink oleanders relieving the dull green of the olive groves. Every now and then were fields of cotton and rows of beehives with scraggy sheep, black goats and the occasional donkey blocking the roads. Even when we were close to the mountains they seemed veiled in blue in the clear, hot atmosphere. By midday we turned around the foothills of the towering blue Parnassus and looked down on Delphi and the deepening valley leading to an inlet from the Bay of Corinth.

Most old ruins soon leave me cold but the old Treasury, the stone stand of the Oracle Brazier, with the indentations for its tripod and the Greek open theatre on the hill above were most impressive. While we sat on the stone seats high at the back of the theatre we could hear our guide tearing a sheet of paper on the floor below. Did the ancients have some secret of acoustics which in spite of all our scientific advances seems to have gone astray? At lunch on a veranda overlooking the vast valley, we thought it fitting to order a wine of the country; it was not a success!

We flew to Rome where again our immigration office was crowded with enquirers; most seemed to be peasants or labourers from southern Italy, but here and there I noticed the blue eyes of the Austrian influence in the north and about Trieste. Rome in the summer is a different city from Rome in the spring that we had enjoyed a few months before. Gone was most of the gaiety of flowerbeds and window-boxes, but the enduring beauty of Rome, the buildings of rose and ochre, the noble squares, the statuary and the fountains were for all time.

As did thousands of other visitors every year, before we left Rome we paid our final visit to Bernini's dream. From down the narrow curving street we could hear the steady sigh of falling water and as we turned into the Square there was one of the most famous in the world, the Fontana di Trevi. Designed by Bernini, whose vast imagination saw in a mass of rock a noble Neptune riding on his tritons and sea horses as they plunged into the cascades gushing from the rocks, it was a century before Nicolo Salvi brought this vision into being. Silently we stood before this masterpiece, then tossing our few coins into the pool to ensure our return according to the legend, we turned away.

As we rode north along the Tiber valley towards Florence the crops and fields became more orderly and the sun was setting as we came into Florence with the city silhouetted against a burning sky. Next morning we looked down from our window to the clear summer blue of the Arne; in the early calm were two small boats below, each with a patient angler, but while we watched nothing disturbed the peace. To the right along the river the sun caught and held the softness of the lovely Ponti Vecchio.

The heat that had hit us in Athens seemed to have caught up with us again and it was blazing as we set out to walk in the city. We just wandered in syncopation, a steady movement from bar to bar, alternately beer and Coca-Cola. The Duomo commanded the glare of the Plazzo Vecchio as we sank into two shaded seats. In the centre Verrocchio's fountain, spouting dolphins held in check by bronze cupids, Cellini's Perseus in an alcove beside us and the great masculine figures fronting Giotto's Campanille. From the outside the Cathedral seemed garish with its contrasting black and white marble but inside was a vastness. The light was dim, the high windows admitting little light, the paintings around the walls were muted and the great pillars seemed to rise and disappear into the gloom. We wandered down the dark narrow streets with their leather shops, each article stamped with the Medici fleur-de-lis, through the crowded, noisy market and window-shopped on exquisite glass and china.

We crossed the Arno by the Ponti Vecchio, built on old Roman foundations. With the built-over shops we were not aware of being on a bridge but rather on a steep and narrow street until from the central arches we could look out on the river to the hills beyond, the goldsmith shops on the bridge were a feast in themselves. Beyond the bridge the galleries gave relief from the heat, with the cool of the lounges and the wealth of the pictures.

The first escape from the heat that had gripped us since Athens came when we arrived in Geneva near midnight. I spent the morning at the International Headquarters of the League of Red Cross in Geneva where the emblem of the Society was born nearly a century before. Henri Dunant, a Swiss banker, shocked by his experiences during the Battle of Solferino, brought together representatives of the European countries in an endeavour to form an institution concerned with mercy in war. Some symbol for the movement was needed and as the delegates looked out from their council room on the edge of the lake, there was the answer. From a tall pole flew the flag of Switzerland, a white cross on a red ground, and the same design with the colours reversed was adopted. Later, with the entrance of Turkey and other Mohammedan countries, the Red Crescent on a white ground was flown with the same significance, as was the Red Lion of Abyssinia. Among countries these now represent the greatest band of brotherhood the world has known. At subsequent conventions the Charter was expanded to cover disasters and needs other than those of war, but these red symbols on a white ground remain recognized and respected by more than one hundred nations.

After lunch by the lake we boarded a small steamer to Yvoir. After the sweltering heat of the south, the cool clean air was like a tonic as we sailed past the fountain in the lake shooting some hundreds of feet above, while little craft with colourful sails hurried about. From small wharves we picked up passengers until Yvoir, a delightful little village, glowing with begonias, hydrangeas and bright geraniums, brilliant against the trailing vines over the brightly painted woodwork of the old houses around the château. Along the narrow streets moved old men and women bearing on their backs bundles of firewood from the forest. Winter was a few months away but when it came the bitterness would linger.

On the day of the annual floral fête, Red Cross lunch had been arranged on the low balcony of a hotel overlooking the route of the procession, all city traffic had ceased and the streets were lined with crowds of cheering excited people. The parade was headed by a colourful band which could be heard before it was seen coming over the bridge. Then followed fantastic floats, each smothered under thousands of flowers on which reclined beautiful girls; no driver or vehicle was visible, just a series of slowly moving brilliant flowerbeds. Bands from outlying cantons were dispersed at intervals as were men and women dancing along in national dress. It was gaiety itself and when the last float and band had passed bags of confetti were handed round and everybody began smothering everybody nearby and being smothered themselves in the fun.

In the evening from a high balcony above the lake we had a perfect view of the fireworks lit from the surface of the lake below. The rockets soared into the air and burst into showers of coloured stars as little yachts sailed on to the scene then disappeared into the darkness, to be replaced by glittering coloured curtains and fountains of red, blue and golden fire until the finale of Niagara Falls. From somewhere above the lake there was a sudden broad cascade of fire, then as if a black curtain had been dropped all was dark.

Next morning after a quiet hour in the gardens by the lake, entertained by the squirrels darting and stopping among the trees, we flew off on our final hop back to England, the sun shining kindly on the snow-covered Alps.

It was towards the end of August and the universities were still on vacation. Some students, interested from our earlier university visits, had written for appointments, seeking further information. Interviewing them and writing my report on our visit to the Continent were pleasant interludes, and at last we were able to have some weekend picnics in the countryside. In Marchant Street, our nearby shopping centre, there was a typical London fish and game shop and as the grouse season had opened I hoped to have some cold birds for our lunches, but when I called at the shop the man, in his straw hat, with a blue and white apron, could not oblige. 'Sir,' he said, 'they are too dear at present, when the nobility 'ave 'ad their fill, I'll be 'aving some and will be 'appy to oblige.' Sure enough in a couple of weeks on his marble slabs exposed to the street were plump grouse at six shillings. 'Pick yer birds, sir, and I'll 'ave 'em ready in 'alf anahr.' And in half an hour there were our birds plucked, cleaned and swathed in rashers of bacon. He gave my wife minute directions in their cooking and casseroled they made a delightful cold picnic lunch.

One Sunday we lunched under an old oak in Windsor Great Park and then watched the polo where the Duke of Edinburgh was playing, the match compered by the gravelly voice of Jimmy Edwards, while the Queen watched from her pavilion. Between chukkas the onlookers were invited by Jimmy to move across the field and stamp down the divots made by the horses' hoofs.

We spent one interesting morning in the Crime Museum at Scotland Yard. Certain of the exhibits were rather gruesome, such as the photographs associated with Haigh's brutal murders, but the forgery room was a surprise. I had associated forgery with coins and bank notes but here were all manner of fakes, including train tickets, bus tickets, theatre tickets and betting tickets. Perhaps the most interesting exhibit was a ten-shilling note, every line and figure drawn by hand. Our guide explained that each note occupied three days of the forger's time and when questioned as to why he worked for three days for only ten shillings, his answer was: 'I'm not going to work for anyone but myself.'

I was invited to a luncheon on the occasion of the centenary of Moss Bros where a descendant of the founder of this world famous firm was speaking. The business had been started by one of his ancestors, a Mr Moses Moses wheeling a handcart round London collecting old clothes. Although he prospered he realized that his name might prejudice his advancement into a higher social status and with his brother the business became Moss Bros. 'Now,' said the speaker, 'there is nothing in the outer clothes that cannot be bought or hired from Moss Bros in Soho, known all over the world by those who wear clothes.' He went on to say that when the Prime Minister visited Russia during a recent winter he stepped from the plane wrapped in a thick, warm overcoat with a long Astrakan collar. He was greeted by Mr Khrushchev, who, fingering his fur collar, said: 'That is a nice piece of Moss,' which it was. Perhaps the zenith of the Moss Bros fame was reached when a request came from the Palace and was answered for some rare garment for a visiting foreign potentate.

I had spoken to several people about the possibility of inviting a group of final year undergraduates to Australia in their long vacation, as had been arranged with Canada. Mr Peter Spinogue of Rio Tinto called on me one day telling of his interest in the idea, and invited me to lunch with his directors to discuss this. Later with Mr Spinogue I called on British Heavy Industries and others who might be interested and the idea began to emerge as a practical proposition.

As the International Meeting of Red Cross in Prague was not until September there was still time to visit Oxford and Cambridge where it was important to call upon the Staff even during the vacation. These two old universities with their wealth of history and architecture were a quiet haven in the vacation and with every courtesy the officers were generous in the audiences they gave us. Probably because of the many students who had passed from Australian public schools to these universities, there seemed a more sensitive appreciation of Australia than we had experienced during some of our earlier visits. Later when the visits to Australia of final year British graduates began, the first group of 120 came almost exclusively from these Universities, although recently they have become more representative of other centres.

Early in September we crossed to Paris on our way to Czechoslovakia. It was still daylight when we reached our small hotel just off the Rue de la Paix and after an omelette and coffee on the boulevard we had an hour or two window-shopping while Paris was at its pastel best. Next morning we did our modest shopping and then strolled along to the Louvre, passing Frampton's gilded statue of Jeanne d'Arc, a bronze replica of which graced the steps of our National Gallery in Melbourne. What a setting for a gallery, in the formal flowerbeds of the Place du Carrousel leading through a stately avenue bronzed with a touch of autumn to the Champs-Elysées beyond. After wandering among the galleries we lunched on the long glass balcony overlooking the formal square then by taxi to Notre Dame to stand before that glorious Rose Window. As we came out the bright sun was throwing deep shadows and the great flying buttresses of the Cathedral stood in strong relief, I walked back to fix this moment with a colour film. As I put my camera away I felt a sense of loss and patted my pockets: my wallet with all my notes, my traveller's cheques, my passport and our railway tickets was missing from my inside coat pocket. It was 3.30 p.m. on a Saturday afternoon in Paris, our train was leaving at 9 o'clock that night and our meeting in Prague was to begin on Monday morning. It was one of those moments: 'Where did you last have it?' asked my wife, and I remembered that I had paid for our lunch at the Louvre with notes. 'What about the taxi? Do you remember his number?' No, I didn't, so back to the Louvre, no sign of my wallet and no one had heard of it: everyone was very sorry and polite but there it was. 'Where is the nearest gendarmerie?' 'Through that archway, down a narrow street to the left, then across the square at the end and through another arch leading to another narrow street, which turned into a cul-de-sac—at the end of it the gendarmerie.' These directions of course took some time to understand and note down, nevertheless, after a little more than half an hour and more enquiries, we found the place. Up a narrow stairway were three or four gendarmes lounging about a counter. By 4.30 I had explained myself and with a play of hands and a shrug of their shoulders they said they were very sorry and would see what could be done about it. We rang the Australian Consulate, but on a Saturday afternoon the Consul was out playing golf— and our train was to leave in four hours! We grabbed a taxi and went round to wait for him but some official after hearing our tale of woe told us to go back to our hotel and wait for the Consul to ring. It was 6 o'clock, train leaving in three hours, no money, no tickets, no passport!

The Consul rang and said that, while he could arrange the money, the passport would be difficult. He had rung the Czech Consulate for a visa but their Consul was not expected back before 8 p.m. and the Czechs were rather sticky. Anyway, he told me to get some passport photos at once, if I could, just in case. The train was now leaving in about an hour. As I went to the desk to ask where I could find a passport photographer on a Saturday night, the front door opened and in came a shabbily dressed man and a woman. He walked over to the desk and without a word put down a wallet. It was my wallet. I looked inside as the man moved towards the door without a word. Everything was there— my passport, my notes, my cheques and our tickets. I was just in time to stop the couple as they were passing out the door. 'Where did you find it?' I asked him. A shrug. 'Are you a taxi driver?' Another shrug, and as he turned away I pushed all my loose cash into his reluctant hand, and without a word they turned and walked away.

'How much did you give him?' asked Dorothy.

'All the francs I had in my pocket.'

'Here, give him these,' she said, handing me some notes from her bag. I hurried out to the street but there was no one in sight. Fortunately our bags were packed and we rang the Consul, apologizing for all the trouble we had given him. Then trusting our lives to the hazards of a Parisian taxi driver, whom I rashly implored to 'step on it', we hooted our way down dark, narrow streets and made the train with a few minutes to spare.

What was the explanation? Fortunately I had a card of our hotel in my wallet but when, where or by whom it was found or taken I have never discovered. When we registered at our hotel we had been required to record our next move, which was to Prague behind the iron curtain. It has been suggested that, as this information would have been passed at once to the security people in Paris, we had been followed throughout the day and in some way my wallet extracted. Nothing compromising being found, it had been returned in time for us to catch the train. Certainly the man's silence, and his reluctance to take any money were passing strange.

Next morning we travelled through the wooded valleys of Bavaria to Cheb at the Czech border and for the first time there was a delay. We were ordered out of our carriage by armed guards, who searched the carriage and rumpled among our suitcases. We were questioned about the money we had with us and when this was verified, our passports were closely inspected before we were allowed to return to our seats and told to stay there. We had to wait until the top of the train and the undercarriage were searched and after two hours the train moved off. At three o'clock in the afternoon we were at last served with lunch: a thick soup, a thin slice of pork smothered in potatoes, some fresh plums, coffee and beer.

It was dusk when we arrived at Prague. There was a strange silence about the dark station and in the streets as we were driven to the modern International Hotel where all the delegates were assembled, and for the first time there was noise as we were sorted out to our various rooms. The hotel building consisted of two large wings of four floors, with lifts and stairways, joined in the centre by a tall building of ten or twelve floors. Later we were to realize that in this modern hotel the only access to the floors on the tall central section was by two small lifts—there were no stairways—its inhabitants could be completely contained by halting the lifts. Our rooms were comfortably furnished but we had been advised not to discuss or speak on any political subject as our rooms were probably wired. In the large dining room it soon became obvious that few of the waiters were trained as they hovered about our tables listening to the conversations. We became aware of a compressive confinement and a constant caution and restraint whenever we talked.

After dinner we took a tram into the centre of the old city. There were few people about, the streets were badly lit and most of the shops were without lights. We soon wearied of this dullness and started across to a tram stop. In Czechoslovakia pedestrians do not have priority at pedestrian crossings. I had forgotten the European rule of the road and seeing all clear to my right, stepped from the footpath. How it happened I do not know, but in a moment I was flat on the ground between the front and rear wheels of a stationary car. I was surprised but not at that time aware of any pain or injury and slowly crawled out to Dorothy's relief. A small crowd had collected and an excited policeman was jabbering at the pale driver. Dorothy tried to explain that it was not the driver's fault—that he was driving slowly, but looking the wrong way I had stepped in his path. While she was speaking, the policeman was speaking, the driver was speaking and the onlookers were speaking—I was the only silent one. By some extraordinary chance I was apparently quite unhurt and the driver was allowed on his way, the policeman strolled off, the audience faded into the darkness and we caught a tram back to our hotel. As I stepped down I realized my right knee was rather stiff and when we looked at it in our bedroom it was the size of a small cantaloupe, but still there was practically no pain. Fortunately Geoffrey Newman-Morris, a senior surgeon from Melbourne, who was leading our Red Cross delegation, was in his room and I asked him about aspirating my fluctuant joint. There was a medical centre in our hotel and we went down for this treatment but unfortunately the needles were all blocked and the syringes would not work so a pad and a firm bandage had to do the trick. I had injured my knees in New Guinea during the war and was rather apprehensive that this new knock would cramp my style in the meetings starting next morning, but although the swelling and the bruising took some days to clear I had remarkably little discomfort and did not miss a session.

At first we met in small groups each day to discuss particular fields of Red Cross service, finally conclusions reached by each group were presented and discussed in three languages—English, French and Spanish—by the general assembly of delegates. There were many outstanding personalities including an Indian princess, who in perfect English brought a remarkable clarity into many of the discussions, and the contributions of Geoffrey Newman-Morris and Leon Stubbings, our General Secretary, were always received with general appreciation. The delegation from the Iron Curtain bloc were never reluctant to present their views, obviously dictated by a national and political bias rather than the international spirit of Red Cross.

The official afternoon opening ceremony was associated with a delightful string quartet in formal evening dress. Later we were all invited to a performance of Dvorak's *Jacobin* in the State Opera House. When we enquired whether this was to be a white tie, gong affair: 'Oh, no, please, your day clothes.' While many in the audience wore open shirts, slacks or shorts, the orchestra entered as they would at La Scala or any of the great opera houses, and the conductor was immaculate.

The only thing left to these poor people was some form of art. Prague has been described as the Tabernacle of the Muses. There was no competition or incentive other than fear, nor could they own their own houses or employ others (at the end of the day a Treasury official emptied the shop tills). The farmer was allowed to retain only a prescribed portion of his produce (the remainder passed to a Government pool); all the men worked as directed till sixty-five and the women till sixty with three months off during pregnancy, but their love of music could not be suppressed. Mozart dedicated his *Don Giovanni* to the citizens of Prague.

With all its shabbiness and neglected gardens, Prague was a beautiful city of spires and old buildings, and the original mediaeval city was fascinating. As we walked down the dim, curving, cobbled streets with the shop signs carved into the stone above the door, I felt at any moment d'Artagnan and his musketeers, rapiers in hand, might dash out from the dark doorways beneath the overhanging old buildings. The dull ochre of the many-spired Tyn Cathedral facing the city square was sombre and the dark interior, with its many-centuries-old organ still perfect, was depressing. Nearby was the famous astronomical clock dating from the fifteenth century. At five o'clock each afternoon carved figures of the apostles appeared two by two from each side above, bowed and withdrew. We were told that when the clockmaker had completed his masterpiece his eyes were put out so that no replica could be made.

When the Nazis seized Czechoslovakia, Hitler said he would respect stone and metal but not human lives and the old ghetto still retained its religious treasures and the tombstones still jostled one another in the old Jewish cemetery. But carved into the stone walls of the new Pinkas Synagogue were the names of more than seventy thousand Jews and the dates on which they had 'disappeared'; we were told that at least an equal number had met the same fate but had not so far been traced.

The old stone Carlova Bridge across the Ultava River led to hills, rising steeply, crowned by the Cathedral of St Vitus (founded by King Wenceslas in the tenth century), the University and the Palaces. On the crest of one hill was a tall red granite file of sculptured Soviet figures, foremost of which was a rugged Stalin staring across the river to the old city below (someone referred to these as the meat queue). This was before the fall of Uncle Joe and I have since heard that all the many statues of this man in Czechoslovakia have been broken up and used as road metal. The fourteenth century Prague University had been preceded only by Bologna and Paris. The massive Monastery on the crest, which had been the Mecca for savants over the centuries, displayed beautiful hand-illuminated manuscripts including Gregorian music, but the monks had 'disappeared' under the new régime.

In other European capitals airborne British newspapers are generally available each morning and people think and speak about world affairs, but in Prague there was a silence—conversation, the papers, books, radio and TV presented only what was permitted and the coverage was confined to Prague and Czechoslovakia. The dreadful result was that within a week we were conditioned to this constriction and I said to Dorothy: 'Do you realize that we never think or talk of anything or anybody except those around us here? Our minds have become confined to this place and, what is worse, we don't seem to miss anything.' Later when we returned to London and I saw in *The Times* that Princess Margaret and the Earl of Snowdon were receiving congratulations, I wondered what the Earl was doing in the party. During the silence behind the Iron Curtain I had heard nothing of events in London, which included the elevation of Mr Armstrong-Jones.

Before the closing ceremony, however, we were taken through the lovely countryside of what had been Bohemia and until

World War I part of the Hapsburg rule of Austria-Hungary. We visited many old castles impregnable before gunpowder on their precipitous slopes, but now converted into national museums open to the public and maintained as when owned and occupied by the nobility. The halls and reception rooms were crowded with weapons and hunting trophies—antlers, boars' tusks, wolf and bear skins and wide spreading eagle tails. The priceless tapestries, chandeliers and furniture were perfectly preserved as were the extensive gardens and lawns. At one castle which we visited in the early morning mist above a silent lake, the Archduke Ferdinand had entertained Kaiser Wilhelm before setting out for Sarajevo where he was assassinated and the flames of World War I were kindled. In another ivy-clad castle from the balcony above the courtyard we were entertained one night with music and singing to balalaikas and other strange instruments. The castle was floodlit and while owls hooted in the woods around the effect was of a vast Wagnerian setting.

We drove a few miles from Prague through a red-tiled, modern village which, phoenix-like, had arisen on the tragic site of Lidice. In the mistaken belief that this village was harbouring the Czechs who had killed the vile Nazi Heydrich, the Nazis had shot all the men, old women and boys, driven the young women and girls into slave camps, then bulldozed the village to the ground. As the victims died they shouted: 'Lidice will live again!'

On our way back we were entertained at the Pilsen brewery. No signs of war's destruction remained on the Skoda armament works nearby and the brewery built in 1842 was intact. When the beer was brewed it was passed into large wooden casks along the miles of cellars and for six months remained in the wood at a temperature a little above freezing; it was then drawn off, filtered, pasteurised and bottled. Before we left we were seated in the great hall, the tables littered with tall steins of that gentle beer and long sausages. After a rather exhausting day this was a splendid idea.

On our last morning we went into the city to shop. Our tram swung round the steeply wooded curve where Heydrich had been ambushed and around the ventilation slot in the wall of a city church were the bullet marks of the Nazis as they stormed the crypt where the Czechs had finally hidden.

There was little to buy in the shops beyond crystal, china and garnets. We saw no slovenly louts or slatternly girls or drunks and Prague seemed a city of good behaviour. The children were tidy, well nourished and happy, knowing no other way of life. But the gnarled old men and women were drab and grim, their pride battling with despair and resentment.

As we reached the station that evening it was raining for the first time since we left London, and it was pathetic to see the faces of those who had come to see us off, as they looked up to our carriage their sad eyes said so plainly: 'You can go, we must stay, always stay in Praha.'

Again the long delay at the border where we had to account for the money we had spent and hand over any Czech money remaining. It was good to be again in freedom among the fresh and tidy fields of Bavaria and until then I had not realized the relief of seeing a German flag flying over a station.

We arrived in Paris early in the morning and as our train for Calais did not leave till midday we took our lives in our hands and hired a Parisian taxi. The tooting, weaving, shouting and dodging about the city were a relief and a stimulant after the oppressiveness of Prague and we arrived at the station enlivened and in one piece.

Again we were lucky with our crossing and the softness of the white cliffs across the Channel was faint but clear from Calais. By eight o'clock we were back in our flat, welcomed by a pile of letters from home.

Chapter 27 England Again

Among the letters awaiting me was an invitation to call at the Civil Defence H.Q. in London. The officer in charge said that he had heard I was in London and knowing my position in Australia wondered if he could help me: 'What would you like to see of our set-up here?' he asked. I explained that the Minister in charge of Civil Defence in Australia had declined my request for his authority to study Civil Defence abroad and I had no official status in the United Kingdom.

'I think we have those Ministers here,' he said. 'Forget about him, you can see anything you like. How about it?' So visits were arranged to the Administrative Centre with an explanation of their plans and to a training demonstration. I asked if I could take notes and photographs. 'Certainly, anything you think worth while in Australia.'

In England Civil Defence was considered as a Fourth Arm of the Services and was grafted on to the wartime civil activities. These were far ahead of anything we were doing in Australia, where we had to initiate our post-war plans. When I returned to Australia I rang the Civil Defence Directorate at Canberra and explained that I had a deal of first-hand information and literature covering Civil Defence in England. 'It really doesn't matter,' I was told. 'We know all about it, thanks all the same.'

The London University School of Economics was just across the Strand from Australia House and there I found myself in a strange world. Years ago I thought I should know something of economics, a term constantly cropping up but to me a closed book. I went to Mr Spencer at his Hill of Content book shop and asked for something simple on this subject. That night I tackled the first page but got no further: it was a foreign language, the words and terms were new to me. I took the book back and said it was beyond me and asked for something simple. 'Well, here's the matriculation textbook, you should be able to manage that.' I took it home and managed at least four pages but again the phraseology eluded me. Back to Mr Spencer. 'I may be a dimwit, but I want a book on economics in English words of one syllable—a kindergarten book.'

'If you are really as dumb as that,' said Mr Spencer, 'here's a book Hilare Belloc wrote for his young daughter, *Economics for Helen*—surely you can manage that: she was about sixteen.' And at last I had a glimmering of what the strange words and phrases that roll off the tongues of economists really mean.

But when I visited the London School my nightmare returned —I was not in the race in that famous centre. I lunched with the staff and no one seemed interested in Australia or in the world as I knew it. I made no impact whatever (not that this mattered as I understand we already have our surfeit of economists in Australia) and after talking to some students it was a relief to pass out into the calm of London's busy traffic.

I thought I should keep my feet on the ground and walk off my luncheon, so I strolled past Covent Garden and the fascinating alleys of Soho down to the Strand. About half way along the Strand there was a small florist's shop with a few pot plants in the doorway. One of these was new to me and seemed just the thing to brighten our flat. When I asked the man its name, 'Mind your own business,' he replied. I explained that I was only asking for a name and this was the first time I had been spoken to like that in London. 'Mind your own business,' again he said and I turned to leave the shop. 'It's called "mind your own business",' he slowly repeated and we became friends: I bought it. Since then I have met two people in Australia who knew this plant with its strange name.

Now that Michaelmas term was beginning there were other universities to visit.

In Leeds there was a lively interest in Australia. For years Australian wool had made an impact on this area and the study of textiles ranked with other faculties in the University. The rain followed us on a rather dull run across to Hull, but next morning the sun was shining to welcome Lord Cohen of Liverpool, who was to open the new University Health Centre, after which we spent an interesting day with the staff and the students. Next morning in bright sunshine we crossed the Yorkshire dales and from the train we watched the pheasants leaving the woods and hedgerows for quiet corners amongst the stubble.

We felt at home among friends at Newcastle-on-Tyne, where we met many Australians. Ever since we had stayed with Jimmy Spence, the doyen of British paediatricians, we had retained a warmth for Newcastle and its lively university college cluttered with expanding buildings. Since our last visit King's College at Newcastle, incorporated in the University of Durham, now stands as a university in its own right.

Our hotel in Edinburgh, the George, was opposite Anderson's fascinating shop of Scotch textiles and other delights and each morning as we set out for the university I had almost to drag my wife from the place. The Vice-Chancellor, who had visited Australia, was fully in sympathy with our mission and once again we felt the warmth of welcome in 'Auld Reekie'.

We had the weekend to ourselves. There are always a number of Australian medical postgraduates in Edinburgh, and one from Melbourne, Alistair Cole, and his wife drove us around Arthur's Seat and down past the old church on little Loch Doddington where Walter Scott had been an Elder. We drove through Preston Pans where Prince Charles and his Scots surprised and defeated the English, then for supper to their home in the village of Guillane nestling on the south coast of the forth. Next morning we walked quietly down the Royal Mile to attend the simple service at St Gile's and after lunch crossed at Queen's Ferry into Fyfeshire and on to Stirling with its imposing granite memorial. As we drove back to Edinburgh the elms in the woods were feeling the breath of autumn with their splashes of yellow, the beeches were bronzing and the air was keen.

We took the train across the Forth Bridge in bright sunshine to Leuchars Junction where we changed into the little motor train which rattled on to St Andrews. Our hotel was across the road from the Royal and Ancient and as we looked down from our window there was a lone golfer with a long-handled wire scoop retrieving his ball from the wee 'burn'. Certain faculties at St

Andrews University were conducted at Dundee across the Tay but our call was upon the Vice-Chancellor at the Administrative Buildings at St Andrews; he was in Dundee and would not be back until the next morning. We wandered among the ruins of the vast Cathedral by the sea, like jagged teeth standing in a great lower jaw. In the streets the red gowns of the students gave a glimmer of warmth in this grey city and this was enhanced when we had our tea served by a lass with a glowing red face and a delightful smile. Before dinner we crossed the perfect turf of the home holes to the links by the sea beating on the yellow sand.

Next morning we kept our appointment with the Vice-Chancellor. He was an elderly, tired gentleman, soon to retire he told us. He was charming but seemed hardly with us and expressed no interest in our mission, asked no questions and spoke only in monosyllables, giving nothing away. We just had to leave it at that, have lunch and catch our train to Aberdeen.

We had an hour's bitterly cold wait at Leuchars Junction and it was dark when we crossed the Tay Bridge but we arrived in Aberdeen to a warm welcome in bright moonlight.

From our window next morning we looked out over the towers, the spires and the domes which dominated the city, the sun was shining after a brisk shower and the granite sparkled in this silver city by the sea.

One New Year's Day the press reported that a great drift of snow had divided Aberdeen from the rest of North Britain. This was no new circumstance. Aberdeen has always had an air of its own, a delicate air, a little aloof, proud perhaps with almost a tilt of its nose, but a warm, kindly, generous air has Aberdeen in Scotland.

We were made most welcome at the University, lunched with the staff and met many of the students. One is apt to think of Oxford and Cambridge as the only old universities in the United Kingdom, but the Scottish universities of Aberdeen, St Andrews and Glasgow were founded in the fifteenth century and Edinburgh early in the sixteenth. The most arresting feature of the old King's College was the great buttressed tower above which stood a crown surmounting a double arch of stone. Nearby were the remains of the Chapel sacked and demolished during the Reformation. The library at King's held many treasures, probably the outstanding one was the Papul Bull with the bulla, or seal, dated 10 February 1494, in excellent condition, granting the Pope's authority for the founding of the University.

After the Reformation many of the people of Aberdeen moved out from the city and settled in an area a mile or so away. New Aberdeen began to grow and at the end of the sixteenth century the Marischal College was founded, a separate entity but with a spiritual link as prayers were said in King's College Chapel of old Aberdeen, 'that a blessing might rest upon this and the neighbouring city'.

Charles the First endeavoured to eliminate this academic schism by a union which he called the Caroline University but nothing came of this. Only a little more than a hundred years ago the University of Aberdeen was established, arts and divinity remaining with King's College, and law, medicine and science passing to Marischal. Nowadays there is no geographical distinction between what were once two rival cities and is now Aberdeen as the world knows it.

We dined with the staff and the students in Crombie Hall, where the red gowns of the undergraduates gave a glow to the gathering. Many old customs survive in Scottish universities, one of the most interesting being Meal Monday, still observed twice a year. For centuries many of the students in the four universities came from humble homes and lived frugally in digs. To eke out the meagre meals provided, a weekend holiday was granted twice a year in mid-term to enable students to return to their homes and bring back bags of meal. It was not considered fitting that students should travel on a Sunday so they returned with their meal on Meal Monday.

In the days of the Stuarts, when bejewelled clothing was the fashion, pearling was an active industry in the Tay and the Dee and Scottish pearls are set in many of the Royal Crown Jewels of Scotland. Now the North Sea provides one of the great industries and before we left Aberdeen we visited the little harbour, once an important overseas port. The busy little trawlers were snuggling into their berths and discharging their slithering cargoes of codlings and herrings to the harsh squawking of the gulls above. Nearby was a scene reminiscent of the clashing of the clans—fishwives, bare to the elbow, arms and hands covered with scales, blood and innards, ankle deep in offal, were splitting the herrings.

Despite the libellous picture postcards of kilted Aberdonians, blue with cold or red with whisky, and the scandalous gibes of the inseparable association between the Aberdonian and his bawbees, we found the people of Aberdeen warm and generous and saw no one 'foo the noo'.

We ran down the east coast and crossed the waist of Scotland just below the Highlands through the quiet rolling countryside, the woods tentatively feeling the coming of winter. It was raining when we arrived in Glasgow, then we had the unique experience of three days of calm, dry sunshine. Like many other universities in the United Kingdom, Glasgow had developed a fascinating museum—the William Hunter collection. Around the walls were Whistlers, oils, water-colours and Venetian pastels, on a bench was Newcomen's original engine in which was incorporated a condenser designed by James Watt, an instrument repairer in the Science Department. Especially interesting to me were the Lister Memorials and those of Lord Kelvin.

On Sunday morning we attended service at St Enoch's, a rather austere cathedral, then caught the train to Stranraer. It was a lovely day to visit Logan, the ancestral home of the McDowalls, my wife's maternal forebears. The train ran down across the Burns country, through the golfing centres of Prestwick and Troon, then along the coast with the Isle of Arran and little Ailsa Craig rising from the sea beyond.

We lunched in Stranraer at the head of Loch Ryan, then hired a car to Logan. The original home had been established in the thirteenth century, to be replaced later by a charming soft-pink brick square-Jane tall house set in a unique garden, a show place of Scotland. One of the later McDowalls had travelled extensively and brought back all manner of strange trees and shrubs: among the old oaks and beeches grew tree-ferns, exotic shrubs with great leaves, tall rhododendrons and to our surprise a splendid grove of eucalypts, the warmth of the Gulf Stream making this possible. There were occasional red deer in the woods and the flashing colour of pheasants in the clearings which opened to the clear blue of Luce Bay. We drove to the little village of Port Logan with its white-washed cottages and tiny light-house, then back to Stranraer in time to catch our train back to Glasgow.

As I was packing that evening I noticed a small jar of Andrews Salts on the mantelpiece, evidently a gift for visitors. In spite of the many advertisements extolling its energy- and health-giving virtues, I had never taken this panacea, but it went into my case.

We travelled by night ferry to Belfast and docked at dawn. After breakfast on the boat we drove to our hotel and on to Queen's University. The Secretary had been in Australia so this made our entrée easy, and after a morning with the Vice-Chancellor and lunch with his staff, we were driven through the autumn foliage of the rough countryside to Lough Neagh, the largest lough in the United Kingdom. The fields of Ireland are certainly a vivid green but I doubt whether this is a different green from the fields of England. With the ever-present moisture in the air, Ireland is always green and the same moisture is kindly to flax and the Irish linen trade. After dinner we talked with the students, a lively and interested lot.

Next day was hectic. We visited the Health Centre, the outstanding establishment of its kind throughout the United Kingdom universities. Then interviewing with Deans, two addresses to students, press interviews at our active Migration Centre, followed by a TV interview. Then a dash to the airport twelve miles from the city and a night flight of fifty minutes to London.

Our next visit was to the West Country, Exeter and Bristol, our train from Paddington leaving at eight o'clock next morning. As I was packing I found the jar of Andrews Salts from Glasgow and decided to follow the directions and see what happened. To save time in the morning I mixed the prescribed dose in a glass of water and placed this on a shelf in our little bathroom. As soon as I woke I tossed this down and began to shave. I felt uneasy and my breathing was strange. From the bedroom my wife called, 'Are you all right?' I tried to answer but my voice was muffled in a cloud of bubbles. She came in. 'What on earth's the matter?' Again more muffles, more bubbles as I tried to explain that I had taken a dose of my Andrews Salts. 'What is the other glass doing on the shelf?' she asked. 'It's your salts, you've swallowed my hair shampoo.' Unknown to me, my wife had prepared her hair shampoo the night before with one of those sachet things and placed the glass also on the shelf. Having as I thought got rid of most of my bubbles, I could only think of that delightful ditty, 'I'm forever blowing bubbles, pretty bubbles in the air,' sung delightfully by Maud Fane in *Going Up*.

I was feeling much better until the taxi driver began to step on it. I suddenly fell from grace and had to ask him to stop while I was sick in the gutter, to his chortles of amusement at 'the gentleman's morning after'. I felt better and almost fine as we settled in our carriage and by this time I was hungry. We went along to the dining car and ordered breakfast. This began with orange juice, which did not seem to agree with the shampoo, and before I would disgrace my wife and myself, I rose and said: 'You pay the steward, I think I will go back to our carriage.' I took a few steps along the corridor, then passed out.

For what followed I must give my wife's story. She heard a fall and found me stertorous on the floor; a fellow passenger came to her help. 'Would you like me to stop the train or call the guard? The poor fellow must have made a night of it.'

'My husband is *not* drunk, he has swallowed my shampoo.' The man looked at her in wonder. They carried me to our carriage and laid me out on the seat; he offered to place his overcoat over me, but Dorothy wisely thought this too risky. I have no recollection of anything after leaving the dining car until about noon when I suddenly came good, sat up and felt quite well. I assured my wife I was all right. 'Well you don't look it,' she said, but I persuaded her to say nothing. I just had time to pull myself together when we arrived at Exeter to be greeted by the Vice-Chancellor and driven to the Univerity.

The whole episode was over as far as I was concerned and I enjoyed an excellent lunch, met the staff and addressed the students. When our train left for Bristol that night I was on top of the world.

Bristol had recovered from her dreadful war wounds and the University, which owed much to Wills tobacco, was full of activity. The Vice-Chancellor had visited Australia and was sympathetic to our mission. For the one and only time we met a lady as the Appointment Boards Officer, with a high ranking Naval Officer as her assistant, and nowhere did we find a greater interest in Australia.

On the last morning of our visit we walked to the 700 feet span of Telford Suspension Bridge over the Avon—the steep slopes of the banks were alive with autumn colour softened by a veil of early morning mist. With its curving streets and bow-windowed houses, Old Bristol, once one of the great ports of England, was full of charm.

There were still the final colleges in Wales and we moved on to the University College of North Wales at Bangor, with the Island of Anglesey across the narrow Menai Strait. Bangor was the site of one of the first churches in the United Kingdom and the museum of the College held a wealth of Welsh antiques, ecclesiastical, domestic and agricultural bygones. After dining with the staff we spent an interesting evening over supper with the students in residence. In the four Welsh centres we found a stimulating interest in Australia and I understood that each of these colleges was soon to be established as a separate university.

Although it was not on our itinerary, we had been invited to visit Colleg Harlech in North Wales. Our school song had been set to the melody of the 'Men of Harlech' and I had always wanted to visit this historic area.

The college, affiliated with the Welsh University, was set in grey, granite buildings overlooking St David's Golf Course by the Sea of Cardigan Bay. This institution as far as I know is unique. The courses are open to men and women whose education has been interrupted by employment or other circumstance and who later regret their absence of higher learning. In 1927 Mr Henry Lewis handed over the deeds of the property with twenty acres of great natural beauty and 'The College of the Second Chance' was founded for 'the enlargement of the vision of students, the development of their latent capabilities for leadership and service and the stimulation of their mental and physical growth'. The college provides the administrative, tutorial and residential facilities for eighty students and a centre for a variety of activities. The Annual Report and Handbook are bilingual, in English and Welsh. In general the students had been craftsmen, miners, metal workers, transport workers, electricians, clerks and farmers. Students came mainly from Wales but England, Scotland, the Continent and Africa had been represented. The courses cover English literature, history, economics, industrial relations, science, music, art, written and spoken English and Welsh. The students selected two major and two minor subjects. There was no desire or attempt to wean the students from their existing occupations, but rather to develop their contributions as citizens in the walks of life they had selected. When we visited the college two hundred pounds covered the year's expenses, a few scholarships were available but most students had saved for their studies. The facilities of the college included a library worthy of a University College.

The wise Warden, Mr Jeffreys Jones, and his staff each year recognized some students with university potential and after each annual course these students were encouraged to take a further year leading to a scholarship. The Welsh University had agreed to accept any of these students on the Warden's recommendation, and among those who had passed on to tertiary education no student up to that time had failed to complete his or her university course.

The entry into the college grounds was through two wrought iron gates set in an old stone wall. Above the gates was the college motto, 'Avo Penn Bid Pont'. I know no Welsh nor can I pronounce the words and this was beyond me, so I asked Mr Jeffreys Jones please to translate it. He told me that this was taken from a Welsh saga dating back beyond the Christian era.

A Welsh princess, Bronwyn, whose home was in Harlech, went across to Ireland to marry one of the Irish kings. She was treated badly in Ireland and sent back a talking bird to her brother, Bendigeidfran, calling him to her rescue. Her brother took his army across to Ireland but all the bridges over the river Shannon had been broken by the floods. Her brother was a very tall man and when he stretched himself over the river the tips of his fingers just managed to grip one side while his toes were on the other. He then told his men to place bundles of sticks over him to make a firm bridge and the army marched across his body. When he arose he spoke to his men, saying, 'Avo Penn Bid Pont': 'He who wishes to be a leader must be a bridge'.

What a splendid motto for a college that sends out each year from Harlech educated men and women, whatever their colour, nationality or occupation.

The Warden drove us into the heart of wild Wales. The autumn colouring was wonderful in the sunshine along the narrow road that wound by a happy, chuckling little stream guarded by a low, lichened stone wall. The countryside was wild with boulder-studded hills, brown with bracken, and there still remained near Cwym Bychan some of the flat stone slabs paving an old Roman road. In this rugged area moving films had been taken covering dramas such as 'The Drum', set in the hilly country of India.

We enjoyed our days at the Colleg, talking with the staff and addressing the students, who seemed sincerely interested in Australia and asked all manner of questions.

We had a morning to wander round the stout old castle, one of the chain of strongholds built by Edward I to command the routes over the country, still proudly surveying one of the finest panoramas in the United Kingdom as it faces the snows of Snowdonia. The history of the Castle is the history of the Welsh revolts, the Wars of the Roses and the Civil War. Harlech was the last Lancastrian standard to yield to York but so staunch had been the defence that the garrison were allowed to march out as free men. This was the traditional occasion commemorated in the Men of Harlech. Harlech was practically the last Royalist Castle to yield to Cromwell.

The Castle, which commands the hills around and the fields beneath, was built on precipitous slate cliffs that dropped sheer to the harbour below. Over the years time and tide, wind and rain have had their way and where the sea once washed against the slopes had now become half a mile or so of sand dunes where St David's golf course wandered over the links.

Next morning we took the little train on our way to Cardiff. In our carriage were a stenographer, an engine driver and a carpenter, students of the Colleg going home for the weekend, they all said how much they appreciated the life at Harlech.

It was a pleasant run along the coast to Dovey Junction, where we changed, then across the lovely countryside, the hills and dales of mid-Wales. What a variety of beauty and history there is in Wales, the more open, industrial area of the south, the fine coastal scenery with broad, sandy beaches, the quiet charm of our Midland route and the wild ruggedness of the north with the purple colour of the mountains.

We changed at Shrewsbury for a final run down to Cardiff. Whenever I saw a 'change here' notice on one of the big junction stations, I remembered a drawing in London *Punch*. A forlorn, bewildered little man, dressed only in his spectacles and his underclothes, standing on the platform before an open suitcase: 'They all told me to change at Crewe!'

At Llanishen autumn was breathing over the countryside, the trees were almost bare but the beeches still clung to their dark brown shiny leaves. Down in the Dingle the burning reds of the Mollis azaleas almost compensated for the absence of the riotous colour we had enjoyed earlier in the year.

Our last university was Leicester and we ran along the Severn Valley to the Midlands. After lunching with the Vice-Chancellor and his staff, I was invited to talk to the students and the Professor of Geography handed his class over to me. I had learnt practically no geography at school, the textbooks had been as dry as dust—compilations of figures and dull facts—and I had never taken a a geography class. A map of Australia was found, hung on an easel, and for a couple of hours I thoroughly enjoyed myself. All manner of questions came at me and there was no doubt either of their ignorance or of their interest in Australia. Fortunately I knew more about the place than did the students and if a tutor, rightly or wrongly, can persuade himself of this situation the rest is generally easy.

There were still some things to be done in London. With Tristan Buesst I called on the H.Q. of the National Trust in Westminster. When we explained that we had established our own National Trust in Victoria, a generous reciprocity was arranged with any of our members coming to England.

Lady Grey Turner, who had accompanied her husband, the first Visiting Surgical Professor to Australia, during 1937, had expressed a wish that some articles from the Grey Turner Collection of furniture should be presented to the Royal Australasian College of Surgeons in Melbourne. Mr Charles Osborn, a Councillor of the College, had asked me to make a selection. Lady Grey Turner entertained us at tea in her charming flat in Chelsea. It was a difficult decision but eventually my wife and I selected an old Welsh dresser, complete with old blue Delft china, and an oak refectory table. Lady Grey Turner seemed happy with our choice and said she would arrange for the pieces to be sent out to the College, which they now adorn.

So concluded our delightful and most interesting tour of the Universities in the United Kingdom, twenty-six in all, the many Colleges and Schools of the London University and the Colleg Harlech.

We had made many new friends and enjoyed many old ones. Regretfully it was time to pack and say goodbye, which we did with a party at London House, where our many friends, including Field-Marshal and Lady Slim, so kindly joined with us.

On the boat-train to Southampton we were delighted to find a student from Queen's in Belfast, who had graduated in science associated with Fishery and Wild Life. During our visit to Belfast this young man had questioned me closely about Australia and here he was on his way. Alistair Gilmour was the first professional response to our mission and now holds a position at Monash University in Victoria.

We sailed again with George Petrescu and his *Fairsky*, together with nearly twelve hundred British migrants including about four hundred children. Travelling with a cross-section of British migrants, many of whom had never been at sea before, was an interesting experience. Each day I spent a few hours writing my report to the Minister while my wife assisted the Information Officer on the deck below. I knew that every adult migrant before leaving England had been well briefed about Australia and provided with literature covering the many problems they might meet, but it was surprising how elementary were the questions at the Information Office. 'Surely you were told about that before you left England?'

'Oh yes, but I did not quite take it in.'

'Weren't you given booklets before you left?'

'I don't remember.'

'Just look in your handbag.'

'Oh, I never thought of that,' and so it went on day after day.

While crossing the Indian Ocean the captain asked me to address the migrants over the public address system on certain differing conditions they would find in Australia—among other things I stressed the fact that the Australians were some of the cleanest people in the world and as a rule showered at least once a day in running water rather than wallowing in a stagnant bath. A few days later the captain came to me and asked me to 'lay off this cleanliness: the migrants have taken it to heart and our fresh water is running low'.

The flying fish followed us across the Indian Ocean down to the Australian coast and it was good to land at the modern quayside at Fremantle. The only cloud was that I learned that a Committee had reviewed the Establishment of the Civil Defence School at Macedon and decided that there was no longer any need for the appointment of a Medical Adviser, thereby reducing my income by half.

Chapter 28 Miscellany

At that time there seemed a policy among certain Federal Departments not to discuss reports with their originators. As it had been with my report to the Minister for the Army, so it was with my recommendations to the Immigration Department. Only two of my twenty recommendations were implemented: the periodic appointment of an Australian graduate to the Immigration Branch at Australia House and the annual visit to Australia of a group of British undergraduates during their final long vacation. Certainly these are of high priority but it is unfortunate that little has been advanced to facilitate visits to Australia of appointment officers from British universities and to encourage and facilitate the immigration to Australia of European graduates trained in those fields greatly in demand for our development.

Fortunately I was able to return to my clinic at the Royal Melbourne Hospital for another year and, with a few insurance examinations and Repatriation Tribunals, all was well with ample time for other interests. Soon after the war I had resigned from the B.M.A. Council (twenty years is long enough for an individual to continue in any voluntary organization), but I retained my association with the Good Neighbour Council and the Medical Board.

The Medical Acts differ among our six States and Victoria is the only one without a compulsory year of hospital residency before legal entitlement to practise. Nearly all medical graduates in Victoria serve this year of residency but they are not legally required to do so and registration at present permits them to practise any branch of medicine on graduation.

When it was revealed that among other anomalies undergraduates at our two medical schools have no practical training in anaesthesia, I was disturbed. It seemed to me as a member of the Medical Board, a statutory body to ensure an adequately qualified medical service to the community, that these graduates were not fitted to enter medical practice as the present Medical Act permits.

For this reason, until there is a compulsory year of hospital residency for graduates in Victoria as in other States, I am not prepared to attend the Registration Meeting of the Board. Fortunately there is a move to amend this anomaly.

In 1952 I began my association with St John Ambulance Brigade. The Order of St John is the oldest order of chivalry in the British Commonwealth, dating back more than a thousand years to when the monks of Amalfi founded the St John Order of Hospitallers in Jerusalem to foster travellers to the Holy Land. I believe it is the only Order where an annual oblation is required of each member according to his or her rank. When in 1540 Henry VIII abolished the monasteries, including the Priory of the Order of St John, the Order practically disappeared in England but was revived in 1858 with Queen Victoria as the Sovereign Head. Now throughout the British Commonwealth the three Foundations are active, the maintenance of the Ophthalmic Hospital in Jerusalem, St John Ambulance Association responsible for training in first-aid and St John Ambulance Brigade, a volunteer field force to attend disaster and public occasions and apply their training gratuitously. The eight-pointed white star from the Arms of Amalfi and the black and white uniform of the Brigade continue the traditional robing of the monks serving in Jerusalem since before the Crusaders.

In the Brigade I followed Sir William Johnston as I had in various Army postings. One always followed Bill—no one could reach the qualities of one who was universally beloved by all who were privileged to know him. I have been told that Bill was recommended for a V.C. in World War I (he already held the D.S.O. and the M.C.), but no Australian medical officer had been awarded this, the highest service decoration, since Neville Howse, the first Australian V.C. in the Boer War. A direction from British High Command in World War I was interpreted by the Australian authorities as an order that the award of a V.C. should be restricted to acts of conspicuous gallantry which were material contributions to gaining a victory and that gallantry in saving life was not considered eligible.

While abroad I had been invited to preside over the Alcoholic Foundation of Victoria. This is a voluntary organization not opposed to drinking but founded to educate the community concerning alcoholism and to counsel alcoholics as to where they could receive treatment. The costly and pathetic disease of alcoholism was at last receiving world-wide attention. While the majority of adults, men and women, were social drinkers, a certain percentage variously estimated as from 4 to 7 per cent were compulsive alcoholics, to the progressive detriment of personality, home life, employment and community behaviour. Considerable research is being conducted in various countries into the cause of this.

At that time the Foundation was in a financial mess. Unfortunately the alcoholic is generally looked upon as a degraded person. A public appeal had landed us in debt and only with a number of generous guarantors were we able to carry on. We struggled through the shoals of the next few years, however, and in 1967 when we were in calmer waters I handed over to Sir Philip Phillips.

From my association with the Victorian Society for Crippled Children and Adults, I realized how often voluntary social service activities with a common basic aim failed to co-ordinate their endeavours. Enthusiasm is necessary but unwedded to wisdom tends to be wasteful. Some well-meaning persons keen to fill some community need set about forming a committee and approach prospective presidents and office-bearers. If these have not held such office before or had their names on official letterheads, they feel flattered, failing to realize that there is generally an organization with the same aim and anxious to enrol more members. When informed of this with a suggestion that the new activity should support the existing organization, many reply: 'But we would like to do it ourselves,' and so kudos frustrates service. There are at least three voluntary organizations directed to the problems of the physically handicapped.

About this time I was invited to open a picture exhibition. Since a schoolboy I had been interested in art and had gradually gathered a modest collection of Australian pictures. When my wife and I arrived at the exhibition we were disturbed by the things around the walls. I was mounted on a dais in front of a dreadful canvas, odd, jumbled-up pieces of what from one or two recognizable bits was meant to be a human figure. The whole exhibition was equally dishonest and untruthful. After a few clichés from Whistler's 'Ten O'clock' I explained to those gathered around that I had been flattered by the invitation to open the exhibition and now declared it open but, having seen the exhibits, I believed it should be closed forthwith. I stepped down and we departed. I have not been invited to any later exhibitions by this odd group. The only public repercussion was a letter in *The Age* by an art critic who asked: '. . . does the General prefer coloured slides from his camera?' Art is a means of expression, and if another medium is necessary to explain the art, surely the artist has failed. Now whenever I am asked to open an artist's exhibition, I insist on first seeing the pictures—I could not survive another experience similar to this first occasion.

If I was to comment on any exhibition I thought I should know something of the technique of painting. I had studied drawing at school under Norman MacGeorge and had passed my public exams in this subject. I had dabbled in water-colours and oils but had never had any instruction in the basic techniques of these media. I enrolled in the Adult Education course for beginners. There was one other man, most of the twenty students were middle-aged women and some quite elderly, with one young girl in tight black slacks and jumper. One of the elderly women never removed her short fur coat and turban hat.

The first instruction was to squeeze on to our palettes a blob from each tube of paint with a blob of white below each; we were then directed to mix each colour with its white mate and streak the result boldly down the sheet with no explanation of the purpose of this exercise beyond some suggestion of tone. We then discarded the sheet. A gramophone produced oriental music varying from a quiet throbbing beat to a loud roar. We were directed to make dabs and strokes of any colour we chose to the rhythm of the music. I broke down badly, my hand with the brush became fuddled in the rapidly changing tempo, blobs of paint appeared on my hands and on my clothes and finally I upset my bottle of turpentine over the sheet of the lady at the next table. She was very nice about it but as I attempted to sort out the mess she swiped two of my brushes!

When I arrived home it took some considerable time to clean myself, but fortunately I was wearing an old lovat Harris tweed sportscoat and the indelible spots of paint were not conspicuous.

The next lesson began by squeezing out our colours and then came the instruction: 'I want you to paint anger.' To a beginner this introduction to art seemed odd. Everyone had a go at it, however, and whirls and streaks of red seemed the general approach but my mind was the best whirl I could produce. And so the lessons went on. I knew what I wanted to paint but I learnt practically nothing about how to paint, the selection of media or how to choose and apply my brushes. One term saw me out, the other man having given it away after four lessons.

I tried a term at a technical college and again entered a course for beginners, hoping to catch up with the basic principles of painting. But no, each night we drew from models but never a paint nor a brush was called for. I gave it away and decided to dabble on my own, learning the hard way. I wasted a deal of time, paint and sheets of board and masonite but eventually managed to have a small seascape accepted in the medical art exhibition.

Then there was cooking. I read a recipe for a Dundee cake, gathered the ingredients, and with my wife's help followed the directions. It was too easy. If one's first endeavour in a new field succeeds, there is danger.

Gordon Oldham, who was already an advanced chef, told me he had just finished a beginner's course in plain cookery conducted by the Gas and Fuel Corporation, ten lessons from six to nine on Monday nights. 'They are mostly young brides,' he said, 'or about to become brides, so take another man with you.' Sir Clive Fitts and I enrolled and together with two other men and eight girls we began on scones. Again, they were easy, I began to feel that either this cooking was a pushover or I was rather good. Thud! The next lesson was a meat loaf but I forgot to put in my egg, and when the bell rang to say the dish was cooked I took from the oven a medley of mince, green pepper, onions and bread-crumbs devoid of any form. Perhaps it was not so easy after all or perhaps I wasn't so good. This was confirmed next lesson when I forgot to heat the oven before putting in my cake. When time was up the cake wasn't—I had failed again. Humbly and the hard way, I completed my beginners' course.

Our class had cooked by gas, but at home we had an electric stove whose gadgets were unknown to me. When I decided to treat the family to my masterpiece—scones—in my ignorance I placed these under the griller and unwittingly produced a novel but inedible dish of black discs burning with a pleasant blue flame: 'scones flambeaux'! Later, however, I mastered our oven and could present a simple edible meal of soup, crumbed cutlets, mashed potatoes and cauliflower au gratin in white sauce, with a desert of apple fritters. One day Gordon enquired if I had received my certificate yet.

'What certificate?' I asked.

'For your cooking class.'

'No,' I said, 'neither has Clive, we must have failed.'

Within a week along came a gilt-edged certificate stating to all the world that I had 'completed beginners' practical cooking class and acquired the required standard of efficiency'. Other than failure, no examiner could say less.

Flushed with success, we enrolled in the male gourmet course for the following year.

Chapter 29 Random Thoughts

When a young man rose from his seat in the tram and said: 'Sit down, dad,' I realized that I was getting on. And when, at the opening of St John Priory Headquarters in Canberra in 1968 I found I had neglected to pack my uniform trousers, I was certain.

When I was born my expectation of life was about forty. I have, however, survived to live during the reigns of six British monarchs. There are three ages of man: youth, adult age and when people greet you, as they do me, 'You are looking well.' To some old age is a burden, but the alternative is grim, and as W. S. Gilbert said: 'My experience is that old age is the happiest time in a man's life—the worst of it is there is so little of it.'

My good fortune has spanned what probably have been the most dramatic scientific advances in the world's history. In medicine some of the diseases we studied as students have practically disappeared and many of the hopeless conditions are now curable. With the conquest of the air no country is now more than twenty-four hours from any other. With the wonders of wireless we can now see events and hear sounds simultaneously with their origin and detect the presence and distance of remote objects hitherto invisible. With the disruption of the atom man has mastered a force for good or evil beyond our dreams. How far our conquest of space will lead us is unpredictable. Few of us understand these achievements, sated with wonders we take them for granted. The unique has become the commonplace—the commonplace of our day a museum piece.

Drudgery is fast diminishing but unfortunately so is effort. Our senses of smell and hearing have been dulled since man stood erect and could see his enemies. Many birds lost their ability to fly when no ground danger threatened. Our eyes have been elongated with television, our ears by radio, our hands and arms by machinery and our legs by modern transport. Have our minds been similarly elongated?

A young man said to me: 'Things must be very different now to your day.'

'Yes,' I replied, 'many things are very different from what they were in my day and generally these changes are for the good.' I suspect the preposition was lost upon him.

Language is never static, new words and expressions are continually being woven into the loom, some to wear out, others to remain. In my day boys were taught to speak and read aloud, to open their mouths and not drop their voices at the end of each sentence. There were no public address systems to aid mumblers. With the extensive use of superlatives the subtlety of simple words is being lost. When I heard John Masefield speak for almost an hour on Shakespeare's England, he did not use one superlative yet his sentences and words had light and shade. To one who listened to Melba and John McCormack in *Bohème* and enjoyed the violins of Kreisler and Mischa Elman, a deal of 'modern' music is bewildering. To one who delighted in the carefree joy of Genée and the grace of Pavlova, the modern immobility or violent contortions of the ballroom seem strange. The so-called avant garde of modern art seems to many old people a reversion to the primitive and an evasion of the hard work and sacrifices of the honest artist.

With these bewildering changes it was inevitable that individuals should differ in a sense of worth and the striving to 'keep up with the Joneses' has expanded into many fields, but it is disturbing when nations differ in values. While one-third of the people on this earth are hungry it seems unreasonable that billions of dollars should be spent on a dangerous international race to the uninhabitable moon. It seems an odd sense of values that pride should be expressed in the expenditure of half a million dollars and two years of time to produce a 1,450-page national report proving that 'flying saucers are not man-made by little green men from distant planets'.

While there have been few basic changes in clothing for men, much greater freedom has now been granted in women's garments.

The manufacturers have developed the profitable policy of using less material and charging more for the simple shifts and the mini skirts which are delightful on many young girls. These and many other novelties have been pushed on to the public by costly and often misleading advertising with a variety of gimmicks.

Compared with 'my day' there are far more attractions and distractions for youth and while the press, TV and radio highlight delinquency and violence among a small minority of young people, little attention is directed to the splendid community and social services, far ahead of 'my day', which are now given by girls and boys who far outnumber these nuisances.

Subjects that were taboo in 'my day' are now taken in their healthy stride by modern youth with no obvious catastrophe. Banks and office blocks in 'my day' bore the imprint of their designers, many to be replaced later by others more functional but often devoid of any personality.

One development from 'my day' has been the increasing urban air pollution with hydrocarbon fumes, following the increased use of oil and petrol for power. This must be a contributing factor in the incidence of lung cancer, which is less common in rural areas, where smoking is as prevalent.

Perhaps these ideas are the outlook of old age but the world continues to whizz by and while we remain here we must accept this even if we cannot keep up with it.

In spite of the general uneasiness as to the future, I am convinced that the world now is better and more kindly than in my day. The great advance as I see it lies in the development of global regard for others. With the vast advances in communications, what happens in any one country is becoming the concern of the world, and the people of the world are beginning to act benevolently to misfortune, irrespective of country, colour or creed.

Epilogue

I AM FINE, THANK YOU
By that famous writer—'ANON'

There is nothing the matter with me,
I'm as healthy as I can be;
I have arthritis in both my knees
And when I talk, I talk with a wheeze;
My pulse is weak and my blood is thin,
But I'm awfully well for the shape I'm in.

Arch supports I have for my feet,
Or I wouldn't be able to be on the street;
Sleep is denied me night after night,
But every morning I find I'm all right;
My memory is failing, my head's in a spin,
But I'm awfully well for the shape I'm in.

Old age is golden, I've heard it said,
But sometimes I wonder, as I get into bed,
With my ears in a drawer, my teeth in a cup,
My eyes on the table until I wake up,
Ere sleep comes o'er me, I say to myself,
'Is there anything else I could lay on the shelf?'

How do I know that my youth is all spent?
Well, my 'get up and go' has got up and went
But I really don't mind when I think with a grin
Of all the grand places my 'get up' has been.

I get up in the morning and dust off my wits,
Pick up the paper and read the 'Obits',
If my name is still missing, I know I'm not dead,
So I have a good breakfast and go back to bed.

The moral is this, as this tale I unfold,
That for you and me who are growing old
It's better to say, 'I'm fine,' with a grin
Than to let folks know the shape I'm in.

Index

A

Abassia military prison, F. K. N. incarcerated in, 67
Aberdeen University, F.K.N. visits, 363-4
Ackland, T., 174
Aitken, 'Pat', 32
Alcoholic Foundation of Victoria, F.K.N. presides over, 376
Alexander, Munro, 109
Alexander, Viscount, of Tunis, 119, 255
Alexandria, 65, F.K.N. disembarks at, 59
Alfred Hospital, 77, 103; F.K.N. honorary at Children's Department of, 87
Allen, Professor A. H., 47-8
Allen, Maj.-Gen. A. S., 'Tubby', 135, 140, 167-8, 169, 208
Allen, Sir Harry, 74
American Medical Association, F.K.N. attends conference of, 218-21
Anderson, 'Jock', 209
Anderson, William, 39
Andrew, Frank, 80
Armstrong, 'Bill', 53
Army Medical Corps, F.K.N. joins, 90
Army Nursing Service, 281-2
Ashton, Gerry, 88
Athenaeum Theatre, 39
Attlee, Clement, F.K.N. meets, 212-13
A27 *Southern*, transports F.K.N. to World War I, 55ff.

Austral, Florence, 84
Australia House (U.K.), F.K.N. critical of, 331-3
Australian and New Zealand Army Corps (A.N.Z.A.C.), formed at Gallipoli, 66
Australian Broadcasting Commission, F.K.N. broadcasts on, 95
Australian General Hospital (Egypt), F.K.N. operated on, at, 64ff.
Australian Imperial Forces (A.I.F.), 49; F.K.N. enlists in, 49-50; in World War I, 49-67, in World War II, 102-202 *passim*
Australian Medical Association, 94. *See also* British Medical Association

B

Baker, 'Boo', 18-19
Barrett, Sir James, 44, 98-100
Barry, Major-General James, strange case of, 282-3
Barry, Sir Redmond, 80
Batchelor, Ronald, on British Commonwealth troops in Korea, 290-4
Beard, 'Whiskers', 19
Beersheba, 113
Beirut, 126
Bellassaria, John, 198
Bellevue Children's Hospital, F.K.N. at, 221-2
Bendigo, 1, 2, 3-8 *pass.*, 9, 10
Benn, Padre 'Bowyang', 103
Bennett, Dr Annie, 81
Bennie, Peter, 81
'Bernie', Batman to F.K.N., 106-8

385

Index

Berry, 'Dickie', 44-5, 47, 85, 213
Biggan, Sir Alexander, 216
Biracchi, 31
Bird, Colonel Fred, 64, 66, 79
Birdwood, Field Marshal Lord, 257
Blackwood, 'Burr', 19-20
Blamey, General Sir Thomas, 111-12, 160, 190
Blanch, George, 'Gus', 18
Blondin, Charles, 226
Bombay, F.K.N. in, 110-11
Botha, 7
Bowe, Col. Jessie, 303; Commands Army Nursing Service, 281-2
Brain, Hugh, 98
Brett, Percy, 24
British Broadcasting Corporation (B.B.C.), 213
British Medical Association, 42, 45, 94, 237, 259; F.K.N. on Branch Council of, 93-4
Broadbent, E. 'Ted', 189
Broadbent, Ray, 198
Broadmeadows, F.K.N. stationed nearby, 51-4
Brown, 'Charlie', 20
Browne, Professor George, 204
Bruce, Lord Stanley, 33
Buckley, William, 27
Buesst, Tristan, 371
burns, treatment of, 297-8
Burrows, Gwen, 41
Burston, Maj.-Gen. Sir Samuel 'Ginger', 111, 143, 201, 280; retirement of, 282
Bush Nursing Hospitals, 44

C

Cairns, Hugh, 214-15
Cairo, 60-7 *passim*; F.K.N. stationed nearby, 59; Battle of the Wazza takes place in, 62
Cameron, R., 'Roddy', 263
Cantlie, Lieut.-Gen. Sir Neil, 257
Carney, Miss, 12
Cassels, General, commands Commonwealth Division. 303
Castles, Amy, 2
Castles, Dolly, 2
Catani, Mr, 31

Catroux, General, 125
Cavalry, Divisional Hygiene Section, F.K.N. commands, 91
Cecchi, 31
Chapman, Col. John, 111
Charles VIII, King of France, 128
Chennall, F., 173-4, 178
Cheops, pyramid of, F.K.N. climbs, 60
Chesterton, G. K., 334
Chiang Kai Shek, Madam, 136-7
Children's Hospital, 80; F.K.N. resident at, 80ff.; staff of, 81; F.K.N. Medical Superintendent at, 83; F.K.N. surgical clinical assistant at, 87
Chute, Joy, 223
Chute, Marchette, 223
Citizen's Military Forces (C.M.F.), F.K.N. commands battalion of, 101
Civil Defence Corps, establishment of, 310; F.K.N. joins, 311; description of, 311ff.; in England, 360
Clarke, Sir Rupert, 90
Clark, Heaton, 88
Coates, Sir Albert, 45, 88
Cohen, Lord, 362
Coke, Brig. W. 'Bill', 254-5
Cole, Hobill, 81; F.K.N. assistant to, 83ff.
College of Nursing, Australia, establishment of, 315
College Harlech, F.K.N. visits, 368-9
Collet, Col., 122
Colombo, 58-9
Colville, Cecil, 94
Commonwealth Reconstruction Training Schemes, F.K.N. assists, 203-5
Continuation School, 21
Cooke, 'Mick', 189-90
Cooper, Graham, 246
Coram, Thomas, 328-9
Cotton, Major Tim, 167
Cowan, Stewart, 87
Crisp, 'Reg', 103
Cumpston, Dr, 41
Cunningham, Padre, 164
Curtis, 'Tag", 18
Cutler, Sir Roden, 250; wins the V.C., 123-4

Index

D

Daley, E. 'Ted', 232
Davidson, Nancy, 203
Darling, Sir James, 19
Deakin, Alfred, 23, 33, 54, 63
Deakin, Vera, 23
Deir Suneid, F.K.N. near, 112ff.
Denz, General, 124-5
Derham, Alfred, 101
De Wet, Cronje, 7
Disher, Clive, 113, 184
Docherty, Major-Gen. Ivan, 310
Doherty, 'Mick', 31
Doctor's Dilemma, 94-5
Doe, Col., 184
Donaldson, Bertha, 81
Dorney, 'Skipper', 104
Downes, General Rupert, 87, 91, 201; D.D.M.S., 90; D.G.M.S., 102
Downer, Sir Alec, 319, 331
Dunant, Henri, 348
Dunlop, E. E. 'Weary', 111

E

Eadie, Lieut-Col., 139
Earl, 'Bill', 53
Eather, Brigadier K., 158, 160
Edward VII, H.M. King, 110
Emden, 55; sinking of, 58

F

Fairfield Hospital, F.K.N. at, 73ff.
Fairley, Brigadier Sir Neil Hamilton, 146, 192, 234
Farrer-Brown, L., 210-11
Faulkner, Neville, 43-4, 128-30
Federal Story, describes Reid, 63
Ferguson, Stewart, 81
Fielder, 'Wallie', 45
Fisher, Andrew, 49
Fisher, Harry, 129-30
Fitts, Sir Clive, 378-9
Fitzgibbon, Edmund, 24
Ford, E. 'Ted', 189-90, 208
Forrest, Rev. Fairlie, 103
Forster, Lieut.-Col., 296
Fowler, Colonel Robert, 166
Fowler, 'Jack', 39
Francis, Josiah, 280; Minister for the Army, 249
Frank, Theo, 88
Fraser, 'Andy', 109

Fraser, Sir Francis, Director of London Postgraduate Federation, 209-10
Friend, Colin, 38
Furnell, Brig. H. G. 'Harry', 231

G

Gardner, Mark, 93
Gayton, W. 'Bill', 174
Gaza, 111ff.
Geelong, 16
Gellibrand (Vic.), 16
George VI, His Majesty King, 101; F.K.N. meets, 262-3. *See also* York, H.R.H. the Duke of
Giles, 'Spuddo', 19
Gilbert, W. S., 380
Gilmour, Alistair, 372
Gloucester, H.R.H. the Duke of, 16
Good Neighbour Councils, establishment of 317-18
Graham, Jack, 20
Grand Hotel. *See* Windsor Hotel
Gravelot, Jean Francois. *See* Blondin, Charles.
Great Eastern Hotel, 136
Green, John, 209
Green, Lieut.-Col. Arthur, 134
Gregory, Dickson, 16
Gresswell, Dr, 9, 41
Grey Turner, Lady, 371
Guilfoyle, Mr, 13-14, 24
Guilfoyle, 'Willie', 13
Gutteridge, Major Eric, 90

H

Hall, 'Tommy', 36-7
Hamlet, 39-40
Hannah, Matron, 103
Harper, Robert, and Co., 21-2
Hatherly, 114, 132-3
Hayward, John, 174
Healesville, 28-30
Heidelberg Military Hospital, F.K.N. in, 186-8, 199-200
Henty, Stephen, 15
Herbert, A. P., 210
Herring, Lieut.-Gen. Sir Edmund 'Ned', 160, 172, 184
Hetherington, John, 160
Heydrich, R., 358
Heyes, Sir Tasman, 319-20

387

Index

His Majesty's Theatre, 39
Hobson, Arthur, 179-80
Holt, Bland, 38-9
Horii, General, 151, 171
Horder, Lord, 81
Hotel Des Indes, 138
Howse, Neville, 375
Hume, General Edgar, 272ff., 303-4
Hughes, W. 'Bill', 270-1
Humphries, Capt. Ronald, 117
Hurley, 'Treacle', 73

I

infant welfare, F.K.N. on, 81-2

J

John Gabriel Borkman, 39
Johnson, Adrian, 124
Johnston, Brig. Sir William 'Bill', 143, 145, 172, 177, 375
Jones, Jeffreys, 369
Jones, Keith, 109

K

Kasr el Aini Hospital (Cairo), 65
Kemp, Nathaniel, 224
Kenny, Dr, 94
Kent-Hughes, Sir Wilfred 'Billy', 21, 311
Khrushchev, N., 351
Kings Theatre, 39
Kienzle, Herbert, 163, 172
Knox, John, 56
Knox-Knight, Air Commodore, 311

L

Latham, Sir John, 37-8
Lavarack, Lieut.-Gen. Sir John, 109, 110-11, 118, 138, 139; F.K.N. appointed A.D.M.S. on the staff of, 105; sketch of, 105; 'Bernie' and, 107-8
Lawrence, 'Bob', 38
Leeper, A., 42
Leslie, Major Douglas, 174
Lett, Sir Hugh, President of B.M.A., 213
Lilydale, 1, 10, 28
Lind, Frank, 101
Lister, Joseph, 46
Littlejohn, Col. Charles, 174

Liverpool (N.S.W.) Army Camp, F.K.N. at, 104ff.
Lloyd, Leslie, 240
Lockwood, Lionel, 232
London, F.K.N. in, 69ff., 209ff., 256-7, 328ff.
London University, F.K.N. visits, 337-8
Loosli, R., 38
Lyle, 'Tommy', 37

M

MacArthur, General Douglas, 167-8, 276; in New Guinea, 191; in Japan, 241, 245-6; in Korea, 269ff.; relieved of command, 288-9
McColl, James, 1
Macdonald, Colin, 88
Macdonald, Donald, 7
Macdonald, Ian, death of, 180
MacGeorge, Norman, 377
McGill Medical School, F.K.N. visits, 226
Mackay, Alan, 81
Mackay, Sir Ivan, 206
McKee, Alexander, 235
McKie, John, 198
McKinnon, Donald, 24
McLean, Donald, 289
MacLellan, Lieut.-Col. W., 279, 304
McMahon, Gregan, 39-40
McNicoll, Admiral A. W. R., 346
Maadi, 59, 63
Magarey, Major Rupert, 150-1, 152, 158
Maidment, Dr, 136-7
Maitland, George, 123
Malaria, 120; treatment of, in New Guinea, 177-8, 234
Manifold, Sir Chester, 172
Masson, Orme, 37
Matruh, F.K.N. stationed at, 115ff.
Maryborough (Q'land), 16
Mauretania, F.K.N. Senior Medical Officer on, 109-10
Mayo Clinic, F.K.N. visits, 225
Medic, 22, 72
Medical Act of Victoria, 95
Medical Board, F.K.N. member of, 95
Melba, Dame Nellie, 24, 39-40, 92
Melbourne, 56, 57-8

Melbourne Beef Steak Club, description of, 96-100
Melbourne Church of England Girls Grammar School, 10
Melbourne Church of England Grammar School, 12, 13-14 schooling of F.K.N. at, 17-20, 32-3
Melbourne Hospital, 45, 79; F.K.N. Resident Medical Officer at, 75; history of, 76
Melbourne Medical Permanent Postgraduate Committee, F.K.N. directs, 203ff.
Melbourne Medical Society, 92-3
Melbourne Repertory Theatre, 39-40
Melbourne University. *See* University of Melbourne
Mena, 59, 65
Mervale, Gaston, 40-1
Ministering Children's League, 6
Mobile Army Surgical Hospitals, (M.A.S.H.), 297
Moore, Albert, 155
Mollison, Dr, 93-4
Monash, Gen. Sir John, 306
Moran, 'Paddy', 102
Morris, Prof. Noah, 216
Morrison, Ian, 163
Morrison, Reggie, 80
Morshead, Lieut.-Gen. Sir Leslie, 189, 191; foibles of, 193-4
Mount Buffalo, 31
Mount Juliet, 29-30
Mount Macedon, 1
Mount Munda, 29-30

N

Newman College, 34
Newman-Morris, Geoffrey, 355
Neuman-Morris, John, 94
New South Wales Lancers, 7, 49
Newton, Sir Alan, 102
Nightingale, Florence, 15
Nihil, J., 78
Norris, Dorothy, wife of F.K.N., 85-6; wins Marge Kelly Prize, 86
Norris, Maj.-Gen. Sir F. Kingsley, born at Lilydale, 1; antecedents and family of, 3; childhood of, 1-8; moves to Melbourne, 9-12; at M.G.S., 13-14, 17-20, 32-33;

adolescence of, 20-31; at Melbourne University, 34-8, 42-8; as actor, 39-41; at Trinity College, 42-4; in World War I, 49-67; in London, 68-9; return to Melbourne, 73-5;

in private practice, 76-89; marriage of, 85-7; joins Army Medical Corps, 90-2; and Melb. Medical Society, 93-4; and B.M.A. (Aust.), 94-5; and Medical Board, 95; and Melb. Beef Steak Club, 96-100; in World War II, 102-9; in the Middle East, 110-41; in New Guinea, 143-59; and the Kokoda Trail, 160-86; sickness of, 187-8; returns to New Guinea, 191-8; World War II ends, 201-2;

joins C.R.T.S., 203-5; in Asia, 205-7; in the U.K., 209-17; in U.S.A., 218-25; in Canada, 225-6; as D.G.M.S., 228-38; in Japan, 239-49; in New Zealand, 259-62; in Germany, 263-5; in South Africa, 265-6;

and Korean War, 267-77, 288-93; and Army School of Health, 278-80; and Army Medical Service, 281-2; and enlistment of troops, 282-7; investigates conditions in Korea, 294-8; in Manila, 298-9;

retires from Army, 304-5; joins Civil Defence School, 310-14; and College of Nursing, 315; and Good Neighbour Council, 315-18; visits overseas universities, 320ff.; in U.K., 328-38, 362-6, 368-71; in Europe, 339-59;

and St John Ambulance Brigade, 375-6; and art classes, 376-8; in the kitchen, 378-9
Noyes, Hal, 30, 78
Nuffield Foundation, 210-11
Nye, G., 240ff.

O

Officer, R., 103
Ogilvie, Mr, 71
Oldham, Gordon, 378-9
Oriental Hotel, 96
Ormond College, 34

Index

Orthopaedic Hospital, (Frankston), 83
Osborn, Charles, 371
Osborne, Professor W. A., 41
Osler, William, 226
Ostemeyer, Dr, 93
Oxford University, 214-15

P

Paderewski, Jan Ignace, 8
Palmer, 'Ted', Commander of Field Ambulance, 182-3
Parkman, Dr, 224
Paull, Raymond, 160
Pennington, Geoff, 88
Pepper, Peter, 208, 217, 327
Petrescu, George, 320-1, 372
Play House, The, 39
Porter, Brigadier Selwyn, 144, 158-9
Port Fairy, 15
Portland, 15
Port Said, 59
Portsea, 30-1
Potts, Brigadier Arnold, 145, 151, 152, 157-8, 160, 182
Princess Theatre, 39, 40
Pritchard, Denis, 232
Prytz, Arthur, 103
Psychology Corps, establishment of, 287
Public School Boat Race, 18
Purchas, Mr, 24

Q

Queen Mary, 109
Queens College, 34
Queensland Bushmen, 7, 49
Queen Victoria Hospital, 76
Quick, Sir John, 1

R

Raine, 'Alf', 103
Raja, Dr, 207
Ranga-Raj, Lieut-Colonel, 296
Read, Judge L., 38
Red Cross Blood Transfusion Service, 220
Rees, Col. Max, 280
Refshauge, Maj.-Gen. W. 'Bill', 278, 302-3
Reid, Sir George, addresses troops, 63

Ridgway, Lieut.-General, 289; assumes command of United Nations Forces, 289
Riggall, W. 'Bill', 168, 178, 183-4, 185-6, 201
Risson, Brig. Sir Robert, 190
Robertson, Lieut.-General Sir Horace, 238, 276, 294; description of, 244-5
Robin, P. A. 'Pat', 18
Rockefeller Centre, F.K.N. visits, 222-3
Rogers, Prof. Lambert, 214
Rommel, Field-Marshal E., 115
Romsey, 1
Roseby, D., 92
Rosencranz and Guildenstern, 39
Rothque, William, 3-5, 10, 22-3
Rowe, 'Doc', 88-9
Rowell, Lieut.-Gen. Sir Sydney, 143, 150, 160, 237, 280; appreciation of, 305
Royal Australasian College of Surgeons, 21
Royal Australian Army Medical Corps, 278ff.
Royal Canadian Military College, F.K.N. at, 256
Royal Empire Society, 237
Runic, 22, 72
Ruskin, John, 35
Russell, William, 51
Ryan, Charles, 46-7
Ryan, Miss, 267

S

Sage, Col. Annie, 231, 280
St Ives, 10
St John Ambulance Brigade, 237, 315; F.K.N.'s association with, 375-6
St Peter's Chapel, 30
St Martin's Theatre, 24
St Vincent's Hospital, 77
Savage, Brigadier, 125
Scantlebury, Vera, 81
Scholes, Dr, 73-4
Scotch College, 17, 33
scrub typhus, treatment of, 189
Second Field Ambulance, 50; F.K.N. commands, 100
Sewell, Sydney, 79

Index

Sheffield University, F.K.N. visits, 336
Shute, Nevil, 237
Silver Box, 39
Skeats, 98
Sloggett, Mr, 20
Smith, Captain Howard, 16
Smith, Col. Elliot, 176
Smith, Orme, 103
Smuts, Jan, 7
Somerset, Bowie, 103
South Yarra, 10
Soyer, Alexis, 51
Speckled Band, The, 40
Spencer, Baldwin, 35-6
Spence, James, Professor of Child Health at King's College, 215-16
'Spiller', 42-3
Spinogue, Peter, 351
Spilsbury, Dr, 93-4
Spring, Howard, 194
Springthorpe, Dr, 92-3
Spry, Brigadier Charles, 168
Stawell, Richard, 14, 79
Stephens, Harry Douglas, 81, 83
Stott, Ron, 21, 88
Stowe, Mrs, 20
Stubbings, Leon, 355-6
Suez Canal, 59, 65
Summons, Walter, 83
Sutcliffe, J. R. 'Joe', 98
Sutherland, Col. Tate, 278
Syder, 'Jack', 109
Sydney, 56; sinks *Emden*, 58
Sydney Grammar School, 33

T

Tate, Frank, 21, 88, 98
Theatre Royal, 38-9
Thomas, Sister, 82-3
Thompson, 'Boz', 20
Times, The, 41, 51
Tivoli Theatre, 39
Trilby, 40
Trinity College, 34; F.K.N. in residence at, 42-3
Tripoli, 126-7
Truman, Harry, 276
Tryon, Rear-Admiral Sir George, 127
Turnbull, Hume, 200

U

Under the Red Crescent, 46
United States Congress, 220-1
University House, 96
University of Melbourne, 9, 79; F.K.N. studies medicine at, 34-7, 44-5
University of Reading, F.K.N. visits, 337

V

Van Fleet, General, 294; Commander of Eighth Army in Korea, 289
Variety, The. See Tivoli Theatre
Vasey, Major-General George, 27, 175-6, 178-9, 183-4, 185-6, 195-6, 201; assumes command of 7th Division, 167-8; vocabulary of, 198; death of, 201-2
Vasey, Mr, father of Maj.-Gen. George Vasey, 27
venereal disease, measures of combating, in wartime, 127-30, 298
Vernon, 'Doc', 148-9, 158, 163, 171
Vickery, Ian, death of, 180
Victoria Barracks, (Melbourne), 106
Victorian Mounted Rifles, 7, 49
von Müeller, Captain, 58

W

Waddell, Brigadier, Director of Department of Civil Defence, 310
Wadhurst, 12-15. *See also* Melbourne Church of England Grammar School.
Wakefield, 'Vicar', 174
Walker, 'Foxy', 19, 35
Waller, Sir Keith, 299
Warrnambool, 15
Wavell, Lord, 118, 138, 139
Webb-Johnson, Lord Alfred, 210
Webster, Prof. John W. W., strange case of, 224
Webster, 'Reggie', 81, 83
Wells, H. G., 26
Wertheim, 'Sos', 12-13
Wesley College, 16, 17
White, Col. Glyn, 304
White, Lieut.-Col. E., 90
White, Newfort, 102-3

Index

White, Rowden, 81
White, Vera. *See* Deakin, Vera.
Wilkinson, J. F., 78-9
Williams, Stanley, 108-9
Wilson, 'Ally', 19, 35
Windsor Hotel, 96
Wittman, Frank, 284-5
Wilson, Pat, 12, 13
Wolseley, Sir Garnet, 144
Wood, Jeffreys, 81
Wood Jones, Professor F., 93, 98
Wood, 'Willie', 81

World Health Organization (W.H.O.), 211-12
Wootton, Maj.-Gen. George, 184

X
Xavier College, 17

Y
York, H.R.H. the Duke of, opens Federal Parliament, 91-2

Z
Zwar, Z., 79